The Radio Station

Sixth Edition

The Radio Station

Sixth Edition

Michael C. Keith

Focal Press is an Imprint of Elsevier Science
AMSTERDAM BOSTON HEIDEL BERG LONDON NEW YORK OXFORD
PARIS SAN DIEGO SAN FRANCISCO SINGAPORE SYDNEY TOKYO

Focal Press is an imprint of Elsevier
200 Wheeler Road, Burlington, MA 01803, USA
Linacre House, Jordan Hill, Oxford OX2 8DP, UK

∞ Recognizing the importance of preserving what has been written, Elsevier prints its books
on acid-free paper whenever possible.

Library of Congress Cataloging-in-Publication Data
Application submitted

British Library Cataloguing-in-Publication Data
A catalogue record for this book is available from the British Library.

ISBN: 0240805305

For information on all Focal Press publications
visit our website at www.focalpress.com

03 04 05 06 07 08 10 9 8 7 6 5 4 3 2 1

Printed in the United States of America

Contents

Preface

The radio industry has virtually, if not literally, metamorphosized. In fact, it has changed dramatically since the last edition of this book, and to be sure it barely resembles the description in the book's first edition. Why? Succinctly speaking—the elimination of station ownership caps. This alone has altered the landscape of the industry almost beyond recognition. For example, today one radio company can own hundreds, even thousands, of stations, whereas it could own only a handful (a few dozen) a decade ago.

Indeed, since the first publication of this book, the radio industry has witnessed seismic change. In addition to the significant regulatory revamping of the last decade, radio has undergone unprecedented technical overhauling. The advent of digital audio (high-definition radio) promises to revolutionize broadcast signal transmission and reception. Of course, with such transformations come challenges and concerns, and these will doubtlessly occupy the thoughts of broadcasters well into the foreseeable future.

When this book was first published in the mid-1980s, radio was enjoying unprecedented prosperity. The prices being paid for radio properties were soaring, and station revenues were at exceptional levels. Life was good for almost everyone in the industry, or so it seemed. Many AM station owners were not in on the opulent banquet, and a growing number were pulling the plug on their operations. Yet on the whole, the 1980s were auspicious years for the magic medium.

The tide shifted as the final decade of the 20th century began. The nation had slipped into a nasty recession, taking radio with it on its downward slide, but soon the medium's fortunes were on the upswing and broadcast properties were again attracting gargantuan sums. The catalyst of this unparalleled resurgence was the Federal Communications Commission, which eliminated station ownership caps through the groundbreaking legislation of its Telecommunications Act of 1996.

The industry has indeed experienced many ups and downs since its modest inception 80 years ago, however, and it will doubtlessly know the thrill of ascent and the angst of decline again. Radio was, is, and will continue to be a wonderfully alive and dynamic medium with a seemingly incalculable life span. It is impossible to imagine a world without David Sarnoff's radio music box, but that is not necessary—it is safe to assume that radio in some form will continue to be an integral part of our lives for a very long time to come.

The mission of this book has not changed. This edition, like the previous ones, is the result of a desire and effort to provide the student of radio with the most complete account of the medium possible, from the insider's view, if you will. It is presented from the perspective of the radio professional, drawing on the insights and observations of those who make their daily living by working in the industry.

What continues to set this particular text apart from others is that not one or two but literally hundreds of radio people have contributed to this effort to disseminate factual and relevant information about the medium in a way that captures its reality. These professionals represent the top echelons of network and corporate radio, as well as the rural daytime-only outlets spread across the country.

I have sought to create a truly practical, timely, illustrative (a picture can be worth a thousand words—stations explain and reveal themselves through visuals), and accessible book on commercial radio station operations; a book that reflects through its structure and organization the radio station's own organization. Therefore, the departments and personnel that comprise a radio station are our principal focus. I begin by examining the role of station management and then move into programming, sales, news, engineering, production, and traffic, as well as other key areas that serve as the vital ingredients of any radio outlet.

Because my strategy was to draw on the experience of countless broadcast and allied professionals, my debt of gratitude is significant. It is to these individuals who contributed most directly to its making that I also dedicate this book.

In addition, I would like to express my sincere appreciation to the many individuals and organizations that assisted me in so many important ways. Foremost among them are David Pearlman, Jay Williams, Jr., Ed Shane, Ralph Guild, Jason Insalaco, Bill Siemering, Lee Abrams, Lynn Christian, Dick Oppenheimer, Chris Sterling, Donna Halper, Bruce DuMont, Paul Fiddick, Norm Feuer, Ward Quaal, Frank Bell, Allen Myers, Ted Bolton, et al.—the list is endless. My hat is off to every individual and organization cited in this book.

Countless companies and organizations contributed to the body of this work. They include the ABC Radio Networks, Arbitron Ratings Company, Auditronics Inc., The Benchmark Company, Bolton Research, BMI, BPME, Broadcast Electronics, *Broadcasting and Cable*, Broadcast Programming, Burkhart Douglas and Associates, C-SPAN Radio, CBS, CIPB, Clear Channel Communications, Coleman Research, Communication Graphics, CFM, CRN, Denon, Direct Marketing Research, Edison Media Research, ESPN Radio, the FCC, FMR Associates, Global Radio News, Goldwave Inc., Greater Media, Halper and Associates, IGM Inc., Infinity Broadcasting, Interep Radio Store, International Demographics, Jacobs Media, Jefferson Pilot Data Systems, Katz Media Group, KD Kanopy, Library of American Broadcasting, Lund Consultants, Marketron Inc., Mediabase, Metro Traffic Network, MMR, Moose Lake Products Company, Museum of Broadcast Communications, National Association of Broadcasters, Orban, Premiere Radio Networks, Public Radio International, QuikStats, Radio Advertising Bureau, Radio Aahs, *Radio Ink*, Radiolandia, *Radio and Record's*, *RTNDA*, Radio Computer Systems, Radio SAWA, RCA, Satellite Music Network, Shane Media, Sirius Satellite, Society of Broadcast Engineers, Jim Steele, Annette Steiner, Superaudio, Talkers Magazine, Tapscan, TM Century, Westinghouse Broadcasting, Westwood One, and XM Satellite.

Since the publication of earlier editions, it is safe to assume—in an industry noted for its nomadic nature—that a significant number of contributors have moved on to positions at other stations (or in some cases left the industry). Moreover, it is equally certain that many stations have changed call letters, because that is the name of the game too. Due to the sheer volume of contributors, it would be difficult to establish the current whereabouts or status of each without employing the services of the FBI, CIA, and Secret Service. Therefore, I have frequently let stand the original addresses and call letters of contributors except when new information has become available; in those cases, changes have been made.

In any case, good evening or good afternoon, good morning or good night,
Whichever best becomes the sector of the sky
Arched over your antenna.
We wish some words with you
Concerning magic that would make a
Merlin envious
The miracle, worn ordinary now, of just such business as this
Between your ears and us, and oceantides of ether.
We mean the genii of radio
Kowtowing to Aladdins everywhere,
As flashy on the run as light, and full of services to ships at sea and planes in the air and people
in their living rooms, resembling you.

—Norman Corwin, *Seems Radio Is Here to Stay*

Foreword to the Sixth Edition

by David Pearlman

David Pearlman

Who would have bet that a $5 wager could create a $20 billion global industry that has served the world with music, news, and entertainment for over 82 years? Yet it was Dr. Frank Conrad's small stake with a fellow worker over the accuracy of his $12 wristwatch that lead to the unveiling of the world's first audio over-the-air commercial programming service. To prove his point in the gamble, the Pittsburgh-based engineer built a small receiver to hear time signals from the Naval Observatory in Arlington, Virginia. Conrad won the bet, became fascinated with his new hobby, and proceeded to build a transmitter on the second floor of his garage. For several years Conrad operated experimental broadcasts featuring favorites from his personal record collection. Only a handful of households heard him, but his employer, Westinghouse, recognized it as a business opportunity. Eight years later on November 2, 1920, KDKA aired the results of the Harding/Cox election, giving birth to the radio industry. As announcer Leo Rosenberg proclaimed the Presidential victor, the world of communications had been forever changed. The unique, unprecedented one-to-one relationship between radio station and listener had begun.

The early days of radio featured live concerts, dramas, comedies, news coverage, and re-creations of major sports events. The new "theater of the mind" allowed friends, family, or single consumers to be informed and entertained by the biggest personalities and politicians of its day. Radio created the artistic foundation for future forays in theater, film, and television. It was radio that ignited the careers of everyone from Milton Berle and Jack Benny, to Dan Rather, Dick Clark, Larry King, Bob Costas, and to Howard Stern. It is the inspirational platform from which the concepts of MTV, VH1, CMT, CNN, and others have come. It is the original culture creator and still the primary distribution source for the entire music industry.

For the past eight decades media watchers have prognosticated that every medium from movies, to TV, to CDs, to DVDs, and to the Internet would lead to the demise of radio. Every year a different poison pen predicts its death, and yet as we weave our way into the start of the 21st century the industry is at an all-time high in consumer and customer acceptance. On a weekly basis, 95.4 percent of all adult Americans tune to the radio. Both TV—including cable viewers—(95%) and newspapers (80%) have less reach than this most mobile of all medias.

When a group of Al-Qaeda terrorists attacked the United States on 9/11 it was radio that provided the base coverage for a terrified nation. When the WTC twin towers fell to the ground they brought with them the broadcast antennas of all but one New York City television station. As the chaotic Manhattan scene unfolded only one over-the-air TV station was available to the millions of panicked New Yorkers. It was All-News Radio that provided the critical link to that day's events. Citizens in New York and around the world huddled on street corners, offices, homes, and cars, glued to their radios for the latest developments.

When a pair of snipers stunned the Washington area with a series of deadly attacks, an entire region was paralyzed with fear for its safety. Three weeks into the crisis and with no arrests made, literally within minutes of a radio broadcast of a description of the suspects' car, a heroic truck driver spotted the vehicle at a rest stop and notified authorities, who subsequently arrested the suspects. The case was solved and an entire population was released back into normalcy because of a response to a radio broadcast.

When President Bush wishes to regularly communicate with the American people he does so on the radio. In a tradition started by FDR in the 1930s with his "fireside chats," presidents have long utilized the radio as a primary communications link. The Saturday Presidential Address has become a radio staple for several administrations and today is the singular consistent communiqué from the Bush White House. Although the traditional press conferences have become few and far between, President Bush never misses his Saturday date with the nation on the radio.

A radio renaissance is now upon us. With the passage of the Telecommunications Act of 1996, the ownership lids were lifted and a new world of consolidation has ensued. It has resulted in a dramatic change in the capitalization of broadcast companies and the requirements of the people who work for them. The industry has gone from an entrepreneur-based leadership to one of major publicly traded organizations. It has created a new cluster look to the local marketplace and has sent a new shockwave of requirements for the players who oversee this new world order of radio. The result is a fiscally stronger industry and greater career opportunities for the highly talented individuals in it.

Less than 10 years ago companies were limited to as little as one AM station and one FM station in a market, and 28 total stations nationwide. A corporate group president would oversee as few as eight stations in multiple markets and be a major player in the industry. Today, you can see eight stations on one floor in one market run by one GM. The group job of a decade ago is now replicated in one building. The change in ownership limits has created companies with hundreds, and in one case thousands, of stations. A meeting of local radio players would once fill a large room, but today they barely fill a large table.

With fewer owners controlling more stations, the consolidated world of radio has dictated a very different marketplace strategy. With a cluster concern rather than any single station dependence, local managers strategically approach the programming, marketing, and sales with a more group-oriented mentality. The one-stop shopping concept in revenue generation for a cluster has fundamentally changed the business of radio. In formulating formats for its stations, the cluster goals are always paramount.

Whether it is a five-station grouping in Little Rock or a six-station combination in Los Angeles, the goals of share maximization are the same. The result is a more sophisticated, strategic type of multitasking manager who needs to be a far more global thinker than ever before.

For those desiring a career in this business, the radio renaissance of the 21st century is an exciting proposition. Although there are fewer overall positions, the remaining slots are far more challenging and rewarding than ever before. For the creative, there is a larger stage to exhibit your skills. For the strategic, there is a bigger platform from which to plot your moves. For the marketer, there are more stations and options to offer your customers. For the motivator, there is a greater, more diverse universe of staff to lead. There is a rebirth of opportunity in the oldest electronic medium with more market power than ever previously imagined.

Author Michael Keith has dedicated his life to the study of radio. He is one of those rare academics who actually has spent a major portion of his career working in the trenches of the medium he so loves. The sixth edition of *The Radio Station* is the standard bearer in its field. It gives the reader a wonderful foundation on an industry that plays such an important role in all of our lives. It covers the broadcasting basics and beyond with input of the best of the best in the business. We are never far from our radios, and if you are sincerely interested in this industry, this book should not be far away from you.

David Pearlman is one of the Nation's foremost radio exectives and consultants.

State of the Fifth Estate

In the Air—Everywhere

In the first decade of the new millennium, radio continues to hold its own in the face of many new competing audio technologies and the seismic shifts in its management and operational structure due to the elimination of long-standing ownership caps and the subsequent consolidation and clustering of thousands of stations. Says station owner and communications entrepreneur Jay Williams, Jr., "The wave of consolidation rolling over radio is only one in the turbulent sea crashing through most of American business. Unleashed by the Telecommunications Act of 1996, sweeping legislation passed by Congress has affected most forms of communication causing consolidation of radio to explode."

Although overall listenership has declined (up to 12 percent between 1990 and 2000 according to one study) over the past decade due to increased competition from other audio choices, radio continues to be the most pervasive medium on earth, even more so than the Internet. There is no patch of land, no piece of ocean surface untouched by the electromagnetic signals beamed from the more than 40,000 radio stations worldwide. Nearly a third of these broadcast outlets transmit in America alone. Today, more than 13,000 stations in this country reach 99 percent of all households, and less than 1 percent has fewer than five receivers (most have at least eight). There are nearly a billion working radios in the United States.

Contemporary radio's unique personal approach resulted in a shift of the audience's application of the medium: Radio went from family or group entertainer before 1950, to individual companion after the debut of the video medium. Although television usurped radio's position as the number one home entertainment source five decades ago, radio's total reach handily exceeds that of the video tube. More people rely on radio for its multifaceted offerings than on any other medium—print or electronic. Practically every automobile (95 percent) has a radio. "There are twice as many car radios in use (approximately 140 million) as the total circulation (60 million) of all daily newspapers, and four out of five adults are reached by radio each week," contends Kenneth Costa, vice president of marketing for the Radio Advertising Bureau (RAB).

Eight out of ten adults are reached weekly by car radio. The average adult spends two hours per day listening to radio (see figure 1.2). A survey in 2002 conducted by RADAR (Radio's All Dimensional Audience Research) concluded that 95.8 percent of all persons over 12 years old tuned in to radio. As the new millennium proceeded, this computed to around 220 million Americans, and the figure continues to grow. The RADAR report also found that working women account for nearly 65 percent of radio listening by women, a statistic that reflects the times. Meanwhile, radio continued to be tremendously popular among African Americans and Hispanics, where the medium's weekly reach is about 95

FIGURE 1.1
Howard Stern was the nation's top radio personality for the under-35 crowd as the new century began. Courtesy 97.1 FM TALK.

FIGURE 1.2
Courtesy RAB.

Source: RADAR ® 71, Fall 2001 © Copyright Arbitron.

percent of that population. The number of radio receivers in use in America has risen by more than 50 percent since 1970, when 325 million sets provided listeners with a wide range of audio services. In recent years, technological innovations in receiver design alone have contributed to the ever-increasing popularity of the medium. Boxes and walk-alongs, among others, have boosted receiver sales over the $3 billion mark annu-

ally, up 30 percent since 1970. According to the *New York Times*, Americans bought nearly 60 million radios annually in the last years of the 1990s, and that trend continued into the new century. There are 25 million walk-along listeners. Radio's ability to move with its audience has never been greater. Out-of-home listeners account for over 60 percent of the average audience Monday through Friday. In addition, the RAB concluded that 7 out of 10 computer purchasers and wine and beer drinkers tune into the medium daily.

Radio appeals to everyone and is available to all. Its mobility and variety of offerings have made it the most popular medium in history. To most of us, radio is as much a part of our day as morning coffee and the ride to work or school. It is a companion that keeps us informed about world and local events; gives us sports scores; provides us with the latest weather and school closings and a host of other information, not to mention our favorite music; and asks for nothing in return. A Katz Radio Group study concluded that "only radio adapts to the lifestyle of its audience." The report dispelled the belief that radio listening drops during the summer, as does TV viewing, proving that radio is indeed a friend for all seasons.

It is difficult to imagine a world without such an accommodating and amusing cohort, one that not only has enriched our lives by providing us with a nonstop source of entertainment, but has also kept us abreast of happenings during times of national and global crisis. To most Americans, radio is an integral part of daily life.

A Household Utility

Although radio seems to have been around for centuries, it is a relatively recent invention. Many people alive today lived in a world without radio—hard to imagine, yet true. The world owes a debt of gratitude to several "wireless" technologists who contributed to the development of the medium. A friendly

Radio's Weekly Reach

Read: *Radio reaches 95.8% of persons 12 and older each week.*

Persons	
• 12+	95.8%
Teens	
• 12-17	99.2%
Men	
• 18+	96.6%
• 18-34	98.3%
• 25-54	98.0%
• 35-64	97.5%
• 65+	89.3%
Women	
• 18+	94.3%
• 18-34	95.8%
• 25-54	96.5%
• 35-64	96.4%
• 65+	86.2%

Source: RADAR ⁽ᴿ⁾ 71, Fall 2001, ⁽ᶜ⁾ Copyright Arbitron
(Monday-Sunday, 24 hours, based on weekly cume)

debate continues to be waged today as to just who should rightfully be honored with the title "father of radio." There are numerous candidates, some who date as far back as the 19th century. For example, there is physicist James Clerk Maxwell, who theorized the existence of electromagnetic waves, which later in the century were used to carry radio signals. Then there is German scientist Heinrich Hertz, who validated Maxwell's theory by proving that electromagnetic waves do indeed exist.

The first choice of many to be anointed grand patriarch of radio is Guglielmo Marconi, who is credited with devising a method of transmitting sound without the help of wires—thus the name wireless telegraphy. A host of other inventors and innovators can, with some justification, be considered for the title. Nikola Tesla experimented with various forms of wireless transmission, and although he has been largely neglected by historians, today there are Tesla Societies that maintain he is responsible for the invention of wireless transmission and modern radio. Lee De Forest, Ambrose Fleming, Reginald Fessenden, and David Sarnoff are a few others whose names have been associated with the hallowed designation. (A further discussion of radio's preeminent technologists can be found in Chapter 10.) However, of the aforementioned, perhaps the pioneer with the most substantial claim is Sarnoff. A true visionary, Sarnoff reportedly conceived of the ultimate application of Marconi's device in a now-famous memorandum. In what became known as the "radio music box" memo, Sarnoff supposedly suggested that radio receivers be mass-produced for public consumption and that music, news, and information be broadcast to the households that owned the appliance. According to legend, at first his proposal was all but snubbed. Sarnoff's persistence eventually paid off, and in 1919 sets were available for general purchase. Within a very few years, radio's popularity would exceed even Sarnoff's estimations. Recently some scholars have argued that Sarnoff's memo may have been written several years later, if at all, as a means of securing his status in the history of the radio medium. The latest consensus gives Sarnoff credit for proposing radio as we know it.

FIGURE 1.3
Radio announcing was a new and glamorous profession. Courtesy WBZ-AM.

Daily In-Car Radio Audience

*The audience flow chart below shows the percentage of Arbitron diary mentions
by quarter-hour, Monday-Friday, 5 a.m. to midnight.*

Distribution of Total Mentions

Source: PD PROFILE ® 718,700 Diarykeeper Study June 2002 © 2002, Research Director, Inc. Original data by Arbitron, Inc.

A Toll On Radio

Though not yet a household word in 1922, radio was surfacing as a medium to be reckoned with. Hundreds of thousands of Americans were purchasing crude, battery-operated crystal sets of the day and tuning the two frequencies (750 and 833 kc) set aside by the Department of Commerce for reception of radio broadcasts (a third frequency was soon added). The majority of stations in the early 1920s were owned by receiver manufacturers and department stores that sold the apparatus. Newspapers and colleges owned nearly as many. Radio was not yet a commercial enterprise. Those stations not owned by parent companies often depended on public donations and grants. These outlets found it no small task to continue operating. Interestingly, it was not one of these financially pinched stations that conceived of a way to generate income, but rather AT&T-owned WEAF in New York.

According to most broadcast historians, the first paid announcement ever broadcast lasted 10 minutes and was bought by Hawthorne Court, a Queens-based real estate company. (Radio scholar Donna Halper contends that Boston's WGI actually aired a commercial before WEAF.) Within a matter of weeks other businesses also paid modest "tolls" to air messages over WEAF. Despite AT&T's attempts to monopolize the pay-for-broadcast concept, a year later in 1923 many stations were actively seeking sponsors to underwrite their expenses as well as to generate profits. Thus, the age of commercial radio was launched. It is impossible to imagine what American broadcasting would be like today had it remained a purely noncommercial medium as it has in many countries.

Birth of the Networks

The same year that Pittsburgh station KDKA began offering a schedule of daily broadcasts, experimental network operations using telephone lines were inaugurated. As early as 1922, stations were forming chains, thereby enabling programs to be broadcast simultaneously to several different areas. Sports events were among the first programs to be broadcast in network fashion. Stations WJZ (later WABC) in New York and WGY in Schenectady linked for the airing of the 1922 World Series, and early in 1923 WEAF in New York and WNAC in Boston transmitted a football game emanating from Chicago. Later the same year, President Coolidge's message to Congress was aired over six stations. Chain broadcasting, a term used to describe the earliest networking efforts, was off and running.

The first major broadcast network was established in 1926 by the Radio Corporation of America (RCA) and was named the National Broadcasting Company (NBC). The network consisted of two dozen stations—several of which it had acquired from AT&T, which was encouraged by the government to divest itself of its broadcast holdings. Among the outlets RCA purchased was WEAF, which became its flagship station. Rather than form one exclusive radio combine, RCA chose to operate separate Red and Blue networks. The former comprised the bulk of NBC's stations, whereas the Blue network remained relatively small, with fewer than half a dozen outlets. Under the NBC banner, both networks would grow, the Blue network remaining the more modest of the two.

Less than two years after NBC began operation, the Columbia Broadcasting System (CBS, initially Columbia Phonograph Broadcasting System) began its network service with 16 stations. William S. Paley, who had served as advertising manager of his family's cigar company (Congress Cigar), formed the network in 1928 and would remain its chief executive into the 1980s.

A third network emerged in 1934. The Mutual Broadcasting System went into business with affiliates in only four cities—New York, Chicago, Detroit, and Cincinnati. Unlike NBC and CBS, Mutual did not own any stations; its primary function was that of program supplier. In 1941, Mutual led its competitors with 160 affiliates. The network left the air in April 1999 following a long series of financial difficulties.

Although NBC initially benefited from the government's fear of a potential monop-

FIGURE 1.5
David Sarnoff, the
man who helped put
radio into the home.
Courtesy RCA.

oly of communication services by AT&T, it
also was forced to divest itself of a part of its
holdings because of similar apprehensions.
When the Federal Communications Commission (FCC) implemented more strin-
gent chain broadcasting rules in the early
1940s, which prohibited one organization
from operating two separate and distinct
networks, RCA sold its Blue network, retaining the more lucrative Red network.

The FCC authorized the sale of the Blue
network to Edward J. Noble in 1943. Noble,
who had amassed a fortune as owner of the
Lifesaver Candy Company, established the
American Broadcasting Company (ABC)
in 1945. In the years to come, ABC would
eventually become the largest and most
successful of all the radio networks.

By the end of World War II, the networks
accounted for 90 percent of the radio audience and were the greatest source of individual station revenue. Today most of the
major networks are under the auspices of
megacorporations. In 1995, Disney purchased Cap Cities/ABC and Westinghouse
bought CBS. A few years earlier, GE
reclaimed NBC.

Conflict in the Air

The five years that followed radio's inception saw phenomenal growth. Millions of
receivers adorned living rooms throughout
the country, and more than 70 stations were

FIGURE 1.6
Radio fans circa 1921.
Courtesy
Westinghouse Electric.

transmitting signals. A lack of sufficient regulations and an inadequate broadcast band contributed to a situation that bordered on catastrophic for the fledgling medium. Radio reception suffered greatly as the result of too many stations broadcasting, almost at will, on the same frequencies. Interference was widespread. Frustration increased among both the listening public and the broadcasters, who feared the strangulation of their industry.

Concerned about the situation, participants of the National Radio Conferences (1922–1925) appealed to the secretary of commerce to impose limitations on station operating hours and power. The bedlam continued, however, because the head of the Commerce Department lacked the necessary power to implement effective changes. However, in 1926, President Coolidge urged Congress to address the issue. This resulted in the Radio Act of 1927 and the formation of the Federal Radio Commission (FRC). The five-member commission was given authority to issue station licenses, allocate frequency bands to various services, assign frequencies to individual stations, and dictate station power and hours of operation.

Within months of its inception, the FRC established the Standard Broadcast band (500–1500 kc) and pulled the plug on 150 of the existing 732 radio outlets. In less than a year, the medium that had been on the threshold of ruin was thriving. The listening public responded to the clearer reception and the increasing schedule of entertainment programming by purchasing millions of receivers. More people were tuned to their radio music boxes than ever before.

Radio Prospers During the Depression

The most popular radio show in history, *Amos "n" Andy*, made its debut on NBC in

A BULLETIN OF NEWS AND NOTES ON THE ADVANCEMENT OF FREQUENCY MODULATION . . . . . ISSUED ONLY FOR MEMBERS OF **FM** BROADCASTERS, INC., AT 52 VANDERBILT AVENUE IN NEW YORK CITY . . . . .

Number 77   October 11, 1941

THIS IS FM TODAY....

Two weeks ago, with justifiable curiosity, FMBI sent questionnaires to all FM licensees, including both those on the air and those with stations under construction. The returns were rather good, although hardly epochal. After twelve days, about 50% of all FM licensees have been heard from.

Of the 17 stations actually on the air, however, the percentage was excellent. Only one is still missing, and FMBI knows its case history anyway. A break-down of information supplied by these on-the-air stations gives us useful, even encouraging, data.

EQUIPMENT:

Six are using REL transmitters; three, General Electric; two, Western Electric; two, RCA; while four built up their own on a composite basis. REL has installed two 50-kilowatt and two 10-kilowatt units, plus a three and a one-kilowatt installation. G-E's score includes two threes and a one-kilowatt; W.E., a 10 and a one. The composite equipment counts a 10-, 20- and 50-kilowatt station.

The combined operating power of commercial FM transmitters now on the air is 115,000 watts. Complete installations, when finished,

1929, the same year the stock market took its traumatic plunge. The show attempted to lessen the despair brought on by the ensuing Depression by addressing it with lighthearted humor. As the Depression deepened, the stars of *Amos "n" Andy*, Freeman Gosden and Charles Correll, sought to assist in the president's recovery plan by helping to restore confidence in the nation's banking system through a series of recurring references and skits. When the *Amos "n" Andy* show aired, most of the country stopped what it was doing and tuned in. Theater owners complained that

FIGURE 1.7
An early FM newsletter promoting the young medium.

on the evening the show was broadcast, ticket sales decreased dramatically.

As businesses failed, radio flourished. The abundance of escapist fare that the medium offered, along with the important fact that it was provided free to the listener, enhanced radio's hold on the public.

Not one to overlook an opportunity to give his program for economic recuperation a further boost, President Franklin D. Roosevelt launched a series of broadcasts on March 12, 1933, which became known as the "fireside chats." Although the president had never received formal broadcast training, he was completely at home in front of the microphone. The audience perceived a man of sincerity, intelligence, and determination. His sensitive and astute use of the medium went a long way toward helping in the effort to restore the economy.

In the same year that Roosevelt took to the airwaves to reach the American people, he set the wheels in motion to create an independent government agency whose sole function would be to regulate all electronic forms of communication, including both broadcast and wire. To that end, the Communications Act of 1934 resulted in the establishment of the Federal Communications Commission (FCC).

As the Depression's grip on the nation weakened in the late 1930s, another crisis of awesome proportions loomed—World War II. Once again radio would prove an invaluable tool for the national good. Just as the medium completed its second decade of existence, it found itself enlisting in the battle against global tyranny. By 1939, as the great firestorm was nearing American shores, 1,465 stations were authorized to broadcast.

Radio During World War II

Before either FM or television had a chance to get off the ground, the FCC saw fit to impose a wartime freeze on the construction of new broadcast outlets. All materials and manpower were directed at defeating the enemy. Meanwhile, existing AM stations prospered and enjoyed increased stature. Americans turned to their receivers for the latest information on the war's progress. Radio took the concerned listener to the battlefronts with dramatic and timely reports from war correspondents, such as Edward R. Murrow and Eric Sevareid, in Europe and the South Pacific. The immediacy of the news and the gripping reality of the sounds of battle brought the war into stateside homes. This was the war that touched all Americans. Nearly everyone had a relative or knew someone involved in the effort to preserve the American way of life. Broadcast news emerged as a major programming factor during the war and would play a central role in every subsequent conflict.

Programs that centered on concerns related to the war were plentiful. Under the auspices of the Defense Communications Board, radio set out to do its part to quash aggression and tyranny. No program of the day failed to address issues confronting the country. In fact, many programs were expressly propagandistic in their attempts to shape and influence listeners' attitudes in favor of the Allied position.

Programs with war themes were popular with sponsors who wanted to project a patriotic image, and most did. Popular commentator Walter Winchell, who was sponsored by Jergen's Lotion, closed his

FIGURE 1.8
In the 1930s, radio offered an impressive schedule of programs for children.

programs with a statement that illustrates the prevailing sentiment of the period: "With lotions of love, I remain your New York correspondent Walter Winchell, who thinks every American has at least one thing to be thankful for on Tuesday next. Thankful that we still salute a flag and not a shirt."

Although no new radio stations were constructed between 1941 and 1945, the industry saw profits double and the listening audience swell. By war's end, 95 percent of homes had at least one radio.

Television Appears

The freeze that prevented the full development and marketing of television was lifted within months of the war's end. Few radio broadcasters anticipated the dilemma that awaited them. In 1946 it was business as usual for the medium, which enjoyed newfound prestige as the consequence of its valuable service during the war. Two years later, however, television was the new celebrity on the block, and radio was about to experience a significant decline in popularity.

Although still an infant in 1950, television succeeded in gaining the distinction of being the number one entertainment medium. Not only did radio's audience begin to migrate to the TV screen, but many of the medium's entertainers and sponsors jumped ship as well. Profits began to decline, and the radio networks lost their prominence.

In 1952, as television's popularity continued to eclipse radio's, 3,000 stations of the faltering medium were authorized to operate. Several media observers of the day predicted that television's effect would be too devastating for the older medium to overcome. Many radio station owners around the country sold their facilities. Some reinvested their money in television, and others left the field of broadcasting entirely.

Recalling this bleak period in radio's history in a 1958 magazine article in *Wisdom*, David Sarnoff wrote: "In the

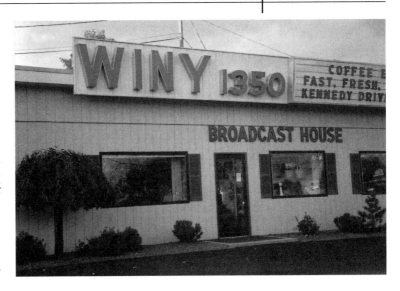

FIGURE 1.9
Many small market AM stations are still profit centers.

Spring of 1949, the cry went up that "radio is doomed." Some of the prophets of doom predicted that within three years sound broadcasting over national networks would be wiped out, with television taking its place.

"I did not join that gloomy forecast in '49, nor do I now. Years have passed, and radio broadcasting is still with us and rendering nationwide service. It plays too vital a role in the life of this nation to be canceled out by another medium. I have witnessed too many cycles of advance and adaptation to believe that a service so intimately integrated with American life can become extinct.

"We would be closing our eyes to reality, however, if we failed to recognize that radio has been undergoing fundamental changes. To make the most of its great potentials, it must now be operated and used in ways which take cognizance of the fact that it is no longer the only broadcast medium. A process of adjustment is necessary, and it is taking place."

A New Direction

A technological breakthrough by Bell Laboratory scientists in 1948 resulted in the creation of the transistor. This innovation provided radio manufacturers the chance to produce miniature portable receivers. The new transistors, as they were popularly called, enhanced radio's mobility. Yet the medium continued to flounder throughout the early 1950s as it attempted to formulate a strategy that would offset the effects of television. Many radio programmers felt that the only way to hold onto their dwindling audience was to offer the same material, almost program for program, aired by television. Ironically, television had appropriated its programming approach from radio, which no longer found the system viable.

By 1955, radio revenues reached an unimpressive $90 million, and it was apparent to all that the medium had to devise another way to attract a more formidable following. Prerecorded music became a mainstay for many stations that had dropped their network affiliations in the face of decreased program schedules. Gradually, music became the primary product of radio stations, and the disc jockey (deejay, jock) their new star.

Radio Rocks and Roars

The mid-1950s saw the birth of the unique cultural phenomenon known as rock "n" roll, a term invented by deejay Alan Freed to describe a new form of music derived from rhythm and blues. The new sound took hold of the nation's youth and helped return radio to a position of prominence.

In 1955, Bill Haley's recording of *Rock Around the Clock* struck pay dirt and sold over a million copies, thus ushering in a new era in contemporary music. The following year Elvis Presley tunes dominated the hit charts. Dozens of stations around the country began to focus their playlists on the newest music innovation. The Top 40 radio format, which was conceived by Todd Storz (while at his favorite watering hole in Omaha) and developed by a slew of programming innovators about the time rock

made its debut, began to top the ratings charts. In its original form, Top 40 appealed to a much larger cross section of the listening public because of the diversity of its offerings. At first artists such as Perry Como, Les Paul and Mary Ford, and Doris Day were more common than the rockers. Then the growing penchant of young listeners for the doo-wop sound figured greatly in the narrowing of the Top 40 playlist to mostly rock "n" roll records. Before long the Top 40 station was synonymous with rock and teens.

A few years passed before stations employing the format generated the kind of profits their ratings seemed to warrant. Many advertisers initially resisted spending money on stations that attracted primarily kids. By 1960, however, rock stations could no longer be denied since they led their competitors in most cities. Rock and radio formed the perfect union.

FM's Ascent

Rock eventually triggered the wider acceptance of FM, whose creator, Edwin H. Armstrong, set out to produce a static-free alternative to the AM band. In 1938 he accomplished his objective, and two years later the FCC authorized FM broadcasting. However, World War II and RCA (which had a greater interest in the development of television) thwarted the implementation of Armstrong's innovation. Construction on FM stations did not begin until 1946. Yet FM's launch was less than dazzling. Television was on the minds of most Americans, and the prevailing attitude was that a new radio band was hardly necessary.

More than 600 FM outlets were on the air in 1950, but by the end of the decade the number had shrunk by 100. Throughout the 1950s and early 1960s, FM stations directed their programming to special-interest groups. Classical and soft music were offered by many stations. This conservative, if somewhat highbrow, programming helped foster an elitist image. FM became associated with the intellectual or, as it was sometimes referred to, the "egghead" community. Some FM stations purposely expanded on their snob appeal image in an attempt to set themselves apart from popular, mass appeal radio. This, however, did little to fill their coffers.

FM remained the poor second cousin to AM throughout the 1960s, a decade that did, however, prove transitional for FM. Many FM licenses were held by AM station operators who sensed that someday the new medium might take off. An equal number of FM licensees used the unprofitable medium for tax write-off purposes. Although many AM broadcasters possessed FM frequencies, they often did little when it came to programming them. Most chose to simulcast their AM broadcasts. It was more cost effective during a period when FM drew less than 10 percent of the listening audience.

In 1961 the FCC authorized stereo broadcasting on FM. This would prove to be a benchmark in the evolution of the medium. Gradually more and more recording companies were pressing stereo disks. The classical music buff was initially considered the best prospect for the new product. Since fidelity was of prime concern to the classical music devotee, FM stations that could afford to go stereo did so. The "easy listening" stations soon followed suit.

Another benchmark in the development of FM occurred in 1965 when the FCC passed legislation requiring that FM broadcasters in cities whose populations exceeded 100,000 break simulcast with their AM counterparts for at least 50 percent of their broadcast day. The commission felt that simply duplicating an AM signal did not constitute efficient use of an FM frequency. The FCC also thought that the move would help foster growth in the medium, which eventually proved to be the case.

The first format to attract sizable audiences to FM was Beautiful Music, a creation of program innovator Gordon McLendon. The execution of the format made it particularly adaptable to automation systems, to which many AM/FM combo operations resorted when the word came down from Washington that simulcast days were over. Automation kept staff size and production expenses to a minimum. Many stations assigned FM operation to their engineers, who kept the system fed with reels of music tapes and cartridges containing commercial material. Initially, the idea was to keep the FM as a form of garnishment for the more lucrative AM operation. In other words, at combo stations the FM was thrown in as a perk to attract advertisers—two stations for the price of one. To the surprise of more than a few station managers, the FM side began to attract impressive numbers. The more-music, less-talk (meaning fewer commercials) stereo operations made money. By the late 1960s, FM claimed a quarter of the radio listening audience, a 120 percent increase in less than five years.

Contributing to this unprecedented rise in popularity was the experimental progressive format, which sought to provide listeners with an alternative to the frenetic, highly commercial AM sound. Rather than focus on the best-selling songs of the moment, as was the tendency on AM, these stations were more interested in giving airtime to album cuts that normally never touched the felt of studio turntables. The progressive or album rock format (also called underground and freeform), conceived by Larry Miller and Tom ("Big Daddy") Donahue, slowly chipped away at Top 40's ratings numbers and eventually earned itself part of the radio audience.

The first major market station to choose a daring path away from the tried and true chart hit format was WOR-FM in New York. On July 30, 1966, the station broke from its AM side and embarked on a new age in contemporary music programming. Other stations around the country, foremost among them KMPX in San Francisco, did not take long in following its lead.

The FM transformation was to break into full stride in the early and mid 1970s. Stereo component systems were a hot consumer item and the preferred way to listen to music, including rock. However, the notion of Top 40 on FM was still alien to most. FM listeners had long regarded their medium as the alternative to the pulp and punch presentation typical of the Standard Broadcast band. The idea of contemporary hit stations on FM offended the sensibilities of a portion of the listening public. Nonetheless, Top 40 began to make its debut on FM and for many license holders it marked the first time they enjoyed sizable profits. By the end of the decade, FM's profits would triple, as would its share of the audience. After three decades of living in the shadow of AM, FM achieved parity in 1979 when it equaled AM's listenership. The following year it moved ahead. In the late 1980s, studies demonstrated that FM attracted as much as 85 percent of the radio audience.

With nearly as many AM stations (4,784) as FM stations (5,720), and only a quarter of the audience, the older medium was faced with a unique challenge that could determine its very survival. In an attempt to retain a share of the audience, many AM stations dropped music in favor of news and talk. WABC-AM's shift from music radio to talk radio in 1982 clearly illustrated the metamorphosis that AM was undergoing. WABC had long been the nation's foremost leader in the pop/rock music format.

In a further effort to avert the FM sweep, hundreds of AM stations went stereo in the latter part of the last century. AM broadcasters hoped this would give them the competitive edge they urgently needed. It was hoped that music would return to the AM side, bringing along with it some unique format approaches. A number of radio consultants believed that the real programming innovations in the years ahead would occur at AM stations. "Necessity is the mother of invention," said Dick Ellis, programming consultant and former radio format specialist for Peters Productions in San Diego,

California. "Expect some very exciting and interesting things to happen on AM," predicted Ellis over a decade ago. In some respects, his vision was on target, but the full realization of his prediction did not come to pass.

AM Stereo

Hoping to help AM radio out of its doldrums, in the early 1980s the FCC authorized stereocasting on the senior band. However, the commission failed to declare a technical standard, leaving that task to the marketplace. This resulted in a very sluggish conversion to the two-channel system, and by the 1990s only a few hundred AM outlets offered stereo broadcasting. Those that did were typically the more prosperous metro market stations that ultimately featured talk and information formats.

Eventually, the FCC declared Motorola the industry standard-bearer, but by the mid-1990s the hope that stereo would provide a cure for AM's deepening malaise had dimmed considerably. By this time, many AM outlets, which may have benefited by having a stereo signal, were in a weaker financial state and unable to convert or were less than enthusiastic about any potential payback. Many were just holding on in the hope that the impending conversion of radio to digital would help level the playing field for AM.

Noncommercial Radio

More than 1,500 stations operate without direct advertiser support. Noncommercial stations, as they are called, date back to the medium's heyday, and were primarily run by colleges and universities. The first "noncoms" broadcast on the AM band but moved to the FM side in 1938. After World War II the FCC reconstituted the FM band

and reserved the first 20 channels (88 to 92 MHz) for noncommercial facilities. Initially this gave rise to low-power (10-watt) stations known as Class D's. The lower cost of such operations was a prime motivator for schools that wanted to become involved with broadcasting.

In 1967 the Corporation for Public Broadcasting (CPB) was established as the result of the Public Broadcasting Act. Within three years National Public Radio (NPR) was formed. Today over 400 stations are members of NPR, which provides programming. Many NPR affiliates are licensed to colleges and universities, and a substantial number are owned by nonprofit organizations.

Member stations are the primary source of funding for NPR. They contribute 60 percent of its operating budget. Affiliates in turn are supported by listeners, community businesses, and grants from the CPB. Program underwriting (the equivalent of sponsorships) is a primary way that public stations meet their operating budgets. These on-air announcements run approximately 15 seconds and include sponsor name and information but no direct selling or hype. They are purchased by sponsors much the same way that spots are sold on commercial stations—from a rate card based on ratings. (Public radio station web sites usually provide more detail on this subject.)

The Corporation for Public Broadcasting claims that 22.2 million listeners tune into public radio stations on a weekly basis. NPR claims that over 13 million Americans tune into their member stations. Their literature states "NPR's news and performance programming attracts an audience distinguished by its level of education, professionalism, and community involvement." (Programs such as *All Things Considered* and *Morning Edition* have become the industry's premier news and information features, achieving both popular and critical acclaim.) Research shows NPR listeners are consumers of information from many sources and are more likely than average

FIGURE 1.10
NPR News reaches millions of listeners daily and is regarded by many as the medium's foremost news service. Courtesy National Public Radio and Corey Flintoff. Photo credit: Shannon Henry.

Americans to buy books. They are motivated citizens involved in public activities, such as voting and fund-raising. They address public meetings, write letters to editors, and lead business and civic groups.

Public Radio International (formerly American Public Radio) debuted in 1983 and operated much like NPR. It provided

FIGURE 1.11
A Public Radio International promotional piece. Courtesy PRI.

William Siemering | On Public Radio

FIGURE 1.12
William Siemering.

Although the distance between commercial and public radio has narrowed in recent years they remain notably different. Since the largest single source of income for public radio stations is listener contributions, the programming is listener-driven and the program directors read the Arbitron ratings just as their commercial colleagues do. However, their programming must be significantly different in content and quality from commercial programs to elicit free-will contributions. (In many European countries, public service broadcasting is supported by a tax on receivers, not voluntary contributions.) Commercial stations, though often involved in community service, have one goal: Make a profit. Public stations have a mission to serve unmet cultural, information, and community needs.

The most listened-to programs on public radio are news and information programs: *Morning Edition*, *All Things Considered*, and *Fresh Air*. These are characterized by both the thoroughness of their coverage and breadth of subjects. They regard news of the arts/ popular culture to be as important to understanding the world as news of politicians. No commercial network comes close to replicating these programs. Local stations frequently sponsor town meetings on important public affairs issues or sponsor concerts in the community to strengthen their local links. Local stations may broadcast jazz, Triple A (Adult Alternative Album), blue grass, acoustic, classical music, or an array of talk programs. Some stations are directed to specific audiences such as Hispanic or Indian.

Public radio listeners tend to be educated, and tend to include decision makers and influentials in their communities, so their influence is great. Eight out of ten newspaper editors rely on it as an important source of information as do network television producers and anchors. *Publishers Weekly* said public radio is the single most important medium for the book business.

In addition to support from listeners, public radio also receives corporate and business underwriting, and grants from foundations and the Corporation for Public Broadcasting, which was created in 1967 to distribute federal funds and protect stations against political pressure on programming. Managing a public radio station is, therefore, more complex because its funding is so diverse. At the same time it must protect the independence of the programming from funder influence.

Recently, some politicians have questioned continued federal funding for public broadcasting and various alternative systems of this support are being explored.

listeners with additional noncommercial options, airing popular programs like Garrison Keillor's *A Prairie Home Companion* and many others.

Noncommercial stations can be divided into at least three categories: public, college (noncommercial educational), and community. A fourth category, noncommercial religious stations, has emerged during the last couple of decades.

Many public radio stations, especially those affiliated with NPR, choose to air classical music around the clock; others opt to set aside only a portion of their broadcast day for classical programming. According to the Intercollegiate Broadcasting System (IBS), more than 800 schools and colleges hold noncommercial licenses. The majority of these stations operate at lower power, some with as little as 10 watts. Since the late 1970s, a large percentage of college stations have upgraded from Class D and now radiate hundreds of watts or more. Most college stations serve as training grounds for future broadcasters while providing alternative programming for their listeners.

Community noncoms are usually licensed to civic groups, foundations, school boards, and religious associations. Although the majority of these stations broadcast at low power, they manage to satisfy the programming desires of thousands of listeners.

In some instances, noncoms pose a ratings threat to commercial stations. However, this threat is usually in the area of classical music and news programming. Consequently, commercial and noncommercial radio stations manage a fairly peaceful and congenial coexistence. (See "Suggested Further Reading" for additional information on noncommercial radio.)

Proliferation and Frag-out

Specialization, or *narrowcasting* (also known as demassification) as it came to be called, salvaged the medium in the early 1950s. Before that time, radio bore little resemblance to its sound during the age of television. It was the video medium that copied radio's approach to programming during its golden age. "Sightradio," as television was sometimes ironically called, drew from the older electronic medium its programming schematic and left radio hovering on the edge of the abyss. Gradually radio station managers realized they could not combat the dire effects of television by programming in a like manner. To survive they had to change. To attract listeners they had to offer a different type of service. The majority of stations went to spinning records and presenting short newscasts. Sports and weather forecasts became an industry staple.

Initially, most outlets aired broad-appeal music. Specialized forms, such as jazz, rhythm and blues, and country, were left off most playlists, except in certain regions of the country. Eventually these all-things-to-all-people stations were challenged by what is considered to be the first popular attempt at format specialization. As legend now has it, radio programmer Todd Storz and his assistant Bill Steward of KOWH-AM in Omaha, Nebraska, decided to limit their station's playlist to only those records that currently enjoyed high sales. The idea for the scheme struck them at a local tavern as they observed people spending money to play mostly the same few songs on the jukebox. Their programming concept became known as "Top 40." Within months of executing their new format, KOWH topped the ratings. Word of their success spread, inspiring other stations around the nation to take the pop-record approach. They too found success.

By the early 1960s other formats had evolved, including Beautiful Music, which was introduced over San Francisco station KABL, and All-News, which first aired over XETRA located in Tijuana, Mexico. Both formats were the progeny of Gordon McLendon and were successfully copied across the country.

The diversity of musical styles that evolved in the mid-1960s, with the help of such disparate performers as the Beatles and Glen Campbell, gave rise to myriad format variations. While some stations focused on 1950s rock "n" roll ("blasts from the past," "oldies but goodies"), others stuck to current hits, and still others chose to play more obscure rock album cuts. The 1960s saw the advent of the radio formats of soft rock and acid and psychedelic hard rock. Meanwhile, country, whose popularity had been confined mostly to areas of the south and midwest, experienced a sudden growth in its acceptance through the crossover appeal of artists such as Johnny Hartford, Bobbie Gentry, Bobby Goldsboro, Johnny Cash, and, in particular, Glen Campbell, whose sophisticated country-flavor songs topped both the Top 40 and country charts.

As types of music continued to become more diffused in the 1970s, a host of new formats came into use. The listening audience became more and more fragmented. *Frag-out*, a term coined by radio consultant Kent Burkhart, posed an ever-increasing challenge to program directors whose job it was to attract a large enough piece of the radio audience to keep their stations profitable.

The late 1970s and early 1980s saw the rise and decline of the disco format, which eventually evolved into urban contemporary, and a wave of interest in synthesizer-based electropop. Formats such as soft rock faded from the scene only to be replaced by a narrower form of Top 40 called contemporary hit. New formats continue to surface with almost predictable regularity. Among the most recent batch are All-Comedy, Children's Radio, All-Sports, Eclectic-Oriented Rock, All-Weather, Churban, New Age, All-Motivation, All-Business, and All-Beatles.

Although specialization saved the industry from an untimely end over three decades ago, the proliferation in the number of radio stations (which nearly quadrupled since 1950) competing for the same audience has brought about the age of hyperspecialization. Today there are more than 100 format variations in the radio marketplace, compared to a handful when radio stations first acknowledged the necessity of programming to a preselected segment of the audience as the only means to remain in business. (For a more detailed discussion on radio formats, see Chapter 3.)

Profits in the Air

Although radio has been unable to regain the share of the national advertising dollar it attracted before the arrival of television, it does earn far more today than it did during its so-called heyday. About 7 percent of all money spent on advertising goes to radio. This computes to billions of dollars.

Despite the enormous gains since WEAF introduced the concept of broadcast advertising, radio cannot be regarded as a get-rich-quick scheme. Many stations walk a thin line between profit and loss. Although some major market radio stations demand

and receive more than $1,000 for a one-minute commercial, an equal number sell time for the proverbial "dollar a holler."

Though the medium's earnings have maintained a progressive growth pattern, it also has experienced periods of recession. These financial slumps or dry periods have almost all occurred since 1950. Initially television's effect on radio's revenues was devastating. The medium began to recoup its losses when it shifted from its reliance on the networks and national advertisers to local businesses. Today 70 percent of radio's revenues come from local spot sales as compared to half that figure in 1948.

By targeting specific audience demographics, the industry remained solvent. In the 1980s, a typical radio station earned $50,000 annually in profits. As the medium regained its footing after the staggering blow administered it by television, it experienced both peaks and valleys financially. In 1961, for example, the FCC reported that more radio stations recorded losses than in any previous period since it began keeping records of such things. Two years later, however, the industry happily recorded its greatest profits ever. In 1963 the medium's revenues exceeded $636 million. In the next few years earnings would be up 60 percent, surpassing the 1.5 billion mark, and would leap another 150 percent between 1970 and 1980. FM profits have tripled since 1970 and have significantly contributed to the overall industry figures.

The AM daytimer segment of the industry has found it the most difficult to stay in the black. These radio stations are required by the FCC to cease broadcasting around sunset so as not to interfere with other AM stations. Of the 2,000 daytimers in operation, nearly a third reported losses at one time or another in the 1980s.

Concerning the challenges of programming an AM daytimer, station manager Dan Collier observes, "You don't have the money for staff. You don't have the budget for talented people. You don't have the resources for new equipment or to even maintain the equipment you have, which is typically in disrepair. These stations are a very tough sell to advertisers, so they lapse into decline and many eventually go silent. It doesn't have to be that way, but good management of this type of station is almost as scarce as advertising dollars."

The unique problem facing daytime-only broadcasters has been further aggravated by FM's dramatic surge in popularity. The nature of their license gives daytimers subordinate status to full-time AM operations, which have found competing no easy trick, especially in the light of FM's success. Because of the lowly status of the daytimer in a marketplace that has become increasingly thick with rivals, it is extremely difficult for these stations to prosper, although some do very well. Many daytimers have opted for specialized forms of programming to attract advertisers. For example, religious and ethnic formats have proven successful.

Over the years, a number of proposals to enhance the status of AM stations have been considered by the FCC. One such proposal suggested that the interference problem could be reduced if certain stations shift frequencies to the extended portion (1605 to 1705 kHz) of the AM band. FCC Docket 87-267, issued in the latter part of 1991, cited the preceding as a primary step in the improvement of the AM situation. It inspired many skeptics who regard it as nothing more than a bandage. Other elements of the plan include tax incentives for AM broadcasters who pull the plug on their ailing operations and multiple AM station ownership in the same market.

As a consequence of the formidable obstacles facing the AM daytime operation, many have been put up for sale, and asking prices have been alarmingly low.

However, many full-time metro market AMs have sold for multimillions, for the simple reason that they continue to appear in the top of their respective ratings surveys. Meanwhile, the price for FM stations has skyrocketed since 1970.

Acid Rock	Jazz
Adult Contemporary	Lite
Album-Oriented Rock	MAC
Arena Rock	Mellow Rock
Beautiful Music	Middle-of-the-Road
Big Band	Mix
Black	Modern Rock
Bluegrass	Motown
Bubble Gum	News
Children's	News/Talk
Classical	New Wave
Classic Hits	Nostalgia
Classic Rock	Oldies
Contemporary Country	Pop
Contemporary Hits	Progressive
Country and Western	Punk Rock
Chicken Rock	Religious
Dance	Rhythm and Blues
Disco	Soft Rock
Easy Listening	Southern Rock
Eclectic	Standards
English Rock	Talk
Ethnic	Top 40
Folk Rock	Urban Contemporary
Free Form	Urban Country

FIGURE 1.13
Some popular radio program formats from 1960 to the present. New formats are constantly evolving.

In general, individual station profits have not kept pace with industry-wide profits due to the rapid growth in the number of outlets over the past two decades. To say the least, competition is keen and in many markets downright fierce. It is common for 30 or more radio stations to vie for the same advertising dollars in large cities, and the introduction of other media in recent years, such as cable, satellite, and Web radio, intensifies the skirmish over sponsors.

FIGURE 1.14
Radio receiver ownership expands and spreads.

U.S. Ownership of Radio Receivers: 1925–1975

Year	Percent of Households Owning Radio	Average Receiver Cost	Percent of Households With FM Sets	Percent of Cars with Radio	Total Produced (Thousands)
1925	10	$83	—	—	2,000
1935	67	55	—	9	6,026
1945	88	40	N/a	23	500
1955	96	20	N/a	60	14,190
1965	99	N/a	48% [1966]	79	41,726
1975	99	N/a	93	95	34,515

(Source: Sterling and Kittross (2002), pp. 862–863, citing various industry sources, chiefly Electronic Industries Association. Final column from Sterling (1984), pp. 212–213.)

Economics and Survival

Following the general financial euphoria and binge-buying of the 1980s, the early 1990s experienced a considerable economic downturn, which had a jarring impact on the radio industry. Had the medium become a "top-down" industry, to use the vernacular of the day? (See figure 1.15)

Many people consider 1991 to have been one of the worst years ever. "As a result of the proliferation of stations, the excessively high prices paid for them during the deregulatory buying and selling binge of the late 1980s, and the recession, more than half of the stations in the country ran in the red," observed Rick Sklar of Sklar Communications. (Mr. Sklar passed away shortly after this interview.)

Producer Ty Ford agreed with Sklar, adding, "The price fallout of the late 1980s and early 1990s was due in great part to the collapse of the property-value spiral that was started by deregulation and the negative effect that investors had on the broadcasting business. This resulted in depressed or reduced salaries and an inability to make equipment updates due to the need to pay off highly leveraged station loans."

According to leading radio consultant Kent Burkhart, "The recession in the first third of the 1990s crippled financing of radio properties. The banks were under highly leveraged transaction (HLTs) rules regarding radio loans; thus the value of stations dropped by one-third to one-half. The recession created advertising havoc too. Instead of five-deep buys, we were looking for one through three deep. Emotional sales pitches were rejected. Stations streamlined costs due to the economic slump. Airshifts were expanded and promotion budgets slashed. The top ten to fifteen markets did reasonably well in the revenue column, but those markets outside of the top majors went searching for new ad dollars, which were difficult to find." The total value of radio station sales declined 65 percent in a six-month period between 1990 and 1991, and radio revenues dropped 4 percent during the same period, according to statistics in *Broadcasting* magazine (September 9, 1991). All of this took place during a time when operating expenses rose. These were troubling figures when compared to the salad days of 1988 when $5.8 billion was paid for 955 radio stations.

Cash flow problems were the order of the day, and this resulted (as Ty Ford pointed out) in significant budgetary cuts. This was made very evident by a report in the December 1991 issue of *Broadcast Engineering* magazine that stated, "All radio budgets

FIGURE 1.15
In the early 1990s stories like this revealed the downside of one of radio's most turbulent years. Courtesy *Broadcasting.*

FCC SAYS RADIO IS IN 'PROFOUND FINANCIAL DISTRESS'

"**S**mall [radio] stations—the bulk of the industry—are in profound financial distress."

That's the first line and bottom line of an internal FCC report on the state of the radio business distributed to Chairman Alfred Sikes and other commissioners last week.

"Radio today is a world of large haves and little have-nots," the report says. "Industry revenue and profits are overwhelmingly concentrated in the small number of large radio stations, while most small stations struggle to remain solvent."

One indicator of the "distress": by the FCC's count, 287 radio stations have gone dark, 53% in just the last 12 months.

Not surprisingly, the findings undergird pending proposals to relax the radio ownership rules, which prohibit a company from owning more than one AM or FM in a market and from owning more than 12 AM's and 12 FM's. (A minority-controlled company may own up to 14 stations of each type.) The FCC may vote on the ownership proposal in March or April.

"The potential economies from consolidation would materially improve industry profitability," the report says. "If a conservative 10% of general and administrative costs could be eliminated, for example, the savings would raise industry profitability by 30%," the report continues. "Alternatively, these savings could immediately boost flat per-station programing outlays by 5% and still raise industry profits by 15%," the report says.

The top-50 large-market stations, just one-half of 1% of the some 10,000 stations now on the air, account for 11% of industry revenue and 50% of industry profit in 1990, the report says. Yet stations with less than $1 million in annual revenues—75% of all stations—on average, lost money in 1990, it says. —**RW** show a decrease." The survey showed that budgets for equipment purchases were being delayed and that "planned spending for most areas is somewhat below last year's."

To counter the sharp reversal of fortunes, many broadcasters formed local marketing (also called *management*) agreements (LMAs), whereby one radio station leases time and/or facilities from another area station. The buzzword in the early 1990s became LMAs.

LMAs allowed radio stations to enter into economically advantageous, joint operating ventures, stated the editors of *Radio World*. They believe that LMAs should remain the province of the local marketplace and not be regulated by the federal government. The publication asserted that LMAs provide broadcasters a means of functioning during tough economic times and in a ferociously competitive marketplace.

Those who opposed LMAs feared that diversity would be lost as stations combined resources (signals, staffs, and facilities). A few years later, the relaxation of the duopoly rules would raise similar concerns. Proponents argued that this was highly improbable given the vast number of frequencies that light up the dial. In other words, there is safety in numbers, and the public will continue to be served. However, radio station general manager Pat McNally presciently observed, "In the long run LMAs and consolidation may cause a loss of available jobs in our business and help to continue the erosion of creative salesmanship and conceptual selling. Radio station sales staffs will become like small rep firms."

In the 1990s, Century 21 Programming's Dave Scott observed that LMAs had inspired some interesting arrangements. "Some of the novel partnerships include a suburban station north of Atlanta that bought a suburban station south of Atlanta and created one studio to feed them both. A similar situation occurred in San Francisco/San Jose, and I believe they're on the same frequency (or maybe a notch apart). Around Los Angeles, someone got two or three stations on the same frequency. Necessity is the mother of invention, they say."

Although many industry people were guardedly hopeful about the future of radio, many saw change as inevitable. "Major adjustments are being made as the consequence of the recent mini-crash. In the future, we will depend on fewer nonrevenue producers at stations. We'll see less people per facility. The belt will be tightened for good," notes Bill Campbell, former vice president and general manager of WSNE-FM in Providence, Rhode Island.

Rick Sklar accurately predicted that satellite-supplied stations would have a role in this. "To save money and stay in business, large numbers of stations are going satellite and others are turning to suppliers of twenty-four-hour formats for their programming because of the economic environment." (See Chapter 11 for more on syndicated programming.)

Fred Jacobs, president of Jacob's Media, assessed the state of the Fifth Estate: "In the first third of the 1990s, everything seemed to be converging, and radio's future was up in the air. Many operators were in debt and were feeling the pressures of a long economic recession. Similarly, the FCC was not providing regulatory focus. There was no consensus about the legality of LMAs, multiple station ownership in the same market, and so on. Format fragmentation had made for a more competitive environment in most cities, including medium markets. The available revenue pie was now being split among more players. Like cable television, radio has become very niche-oriented. To make matters even more uncertain, Digital Audio Broadcasting (DAB) was and remains a murky issue. It's coming, but we don't really have a fix on when and in what form. Will it create even more outlets? If so, where will existing broadcasters end up and what will be the value of their properties? Will there be enough advertising revenue to go around?"

Despite the medium's shaky start in the 1990s, publisher Eric Rhoads possessed a positive outlook. "I believe that radio is poised for a strong future over the next ten years. Cable is floundering in its local sales efforts, and TV is having huge problems. Nationally the networks are still high-priced and have reduced viewing. In the end, radio is the only stable medium. It is targeted and cost effective. This fact will keep the industry alive for a long time. Radio will survive and thrive."

RAB's senior vice president emeritus of radio, Lynn Christian, believed that the economic ills of radio had been overstated. "To paraphrase Mark Twain, 'Reports of radio's death have been grossly exaggerated.' At a recent RAB Management gathering, the mood was pretty upbeat. In fact, a number of broadcasters said their profits were up. I think the recession of the early 1990s has been less injurious to the medium than it has been to other industries. Radio's going to be fine."

Consolidations, Downsizings, and Clusters

As the medium entered the middle of the decade, it was doing more than just fine. The headlines in the industry trade publications revealed exactly how well the medium had recovered: "Radio Draws Advertisers as Economy Strengthens" (*Broadcasting*, May 1994), "Recovery" (*Radio Ink*, December 1993), "Radio Revenues Hit One Billion in May" (*Radio World*, August 1994), "National Spot Revenue up 38 percent" (*Broadcasting*, May 1995).

The primary cause of this dramatic upsurge was the relaxation of FCC rules, foremost among them station ownership caps and duopoly. With the advent of the Telecommunications Act of 1996, individual companies could own several stations in the same market (up to eight in large markets and no limits on national totals), and this spurred active trading and mergers

of broadcast properties. (See figure 1.16) The idea was to reduce competition and thus overhead. The consolidation and downsizing prompted by LMAs would pick up steam with the elimination of the duopoly rule, which prevented dual station ownership in the same market. Says Greater Media's David Pearlman, "The Telecommunications Act of 1996 is the biggest piece of legislation in radio history. It has changed everything."

Observes Lynn Christian, "Consolidation—market by market—is the word best describing what was happening in commercial radio in the 1990s. The legal authority to own and operate several radio stations in almost every market has rapidly changed radio's landscape. Radio station operators have become more like local cable operators, offering a variety of formats on the FM and AM dials."

One alarming effect of consolidation and subsequent downsizing for aspiring broadcasters is the reduction of available jobs. "Individual station staffs get small as companies grow in station holdings. A direct result of duopoly softening and the increase in ownership limits is fewer jobs, more generalization, and less specialization. Jacks and Jills of all trades will be valuable. Group presidents will be taking jobs as station managers, especially in clusters or multiple station operations," observes Ed Shane, president of Shane Media.

Another concern inspired by consolidation is the potential loss of programming diversity. Says Christian, "While cost savings and profits are central to the concept behind downsizing and multiple ownership, the creative forces in radio are taking a hit. In point of fact, in the past few years no exciting new programming ideas have been developed."

On this topic, Jay Williams, Jr., observes, "Many argue that consolidation is bad, charging that radio programming has become less innovative and diverse, that local radio news is in decline, and the lack of competition within each local market has

FIGURE 1.16
Telecommunications
Act of 1996 as
outlined on the FCC's
web site.

 Federal
Communications
Commission

FCC Home | Search | Updates | E-Filing | Initiatives | For Consumers | Find People

Telecommunications Act of 1996

 FCC > 1996 Telecom Act

site map

Search:

[ ] Go

Help | Advanced

Act Text

FCC Materials

Implementation Proceedings

Other Resources

Telecommunications Act of 1996

The Telecommunications Act of 1996 is the first major overhaul of telecommunications law in almost 62 years. The goal of this new law is to let anyone enter any communications business -- to let any communications business compete in any market against any other.

The Telecommunications Act of 1996 has the potential to change the way we work, live and learn. It will affect telephone service -- local and long distance, cable programming and other video services, broadcast services and services provided to schools.

The Federal Communications Commission has a tremendous role to play in creating fair rules for this new era of competition. At this Internet site, we will provide information about the FCC's role in implementing this new law, how you can get involved and how these changes might impact you.

This page will include information listing the proceedings the FCC will complete to open up local phone markets, increase competition in long distance and other steps. You will find copies of news releases summarizing action, announcements of meetings where these items will be discussed, and charts describing the work ahead of us and where (within the FCC) and when it will be completed. **Please note:** some of the links on this page lead to resources outside the FCC. The presence of these links should not be taken as an endorsement by the FCC of these sites or their content.

For more information about the referenced documents, contact the person listed on the document.

Please let us know what topics most interest you or where you have questions about this new law. We will soon begin to post a series of Questions & Answers with Commission officials designed to answer your questions.

Text of the Act

The FCC maintains ASCII Text and Adobe Acrobat versions *(128 pages)* of the Telecommunications Act of 1996, as well as WordPerfect and Adobe Acrobat versions *(335 pages)* of the completely updated Communications Act of 1934, as amended by the 1996 Act. The official citation for the new Act is: Telecommunications Act of 1996, Pub. LA. No. 104-104, 110 Stat. 56 (1996). The official printed slip law is available from the Government Printing Office.

Materials from the FCC

- Revised schedule of proceedings to implement the Act. This implementation schedule is an outline of statutory requirements pursuant to the Telecommunications Act of 1996 and is a guide to the actions taken by the FCC to implement the Act. The schedule is divided into five sections. The first section identifies the specific issues and the bureau handling those issues. The second section contains the statutory language and page references to S. Rept. 230, 104th Cong. 2nd Sess. (1996). The third section identifies the FCC proceeding to implement the statutory requirement including the bureau docket number and the FCC number of the documents released related to the proceeding. The fourth and fifth sections contain information regarding the timetable and status of the proceeding. (Revised January 13, 1997)

- The Report on FCC Implementation of Telecommunications Act of 1996 is a cumulative report of all actions taken since February 8, 1996, by the FCC to implement the Act. This report has two sections: (1) Commission Actions and (2) Facilitating Public Information.

- Transcript of Proceedings from the FCC Telemedical Advisory Committee meeting on September 17, 1996 [Text Version | WordPerfect Version].

- Transcript of Proceedings from the FCC Telemedical Advisory Committee meeting on July 11, 1996 [Text Version | WordPerfect Version].

- Chairman Hundt's Statement and related Report on the FCC Implementation of the Telecommunications Act presented to the Subcommittee on Telecommunications and Finance, Committee on Commerce of the U.S. House of Representatives on July 18, 1996.

- Transcript of Proceedings from the FCC Telemedical Advisory Committee meeting on June 12,

FIGURE 1.16
continued

1996 [Text Version I WordPerfect Version].

- Telecommunications and Health Care Advisory Committee Members Announced (Released 6-5-96)

- Nominations Accepted for the Telecommunications and Health Care Advisory Committee to Assist Implementation of the Telecommunications Act. (Released 4-25-96)

- Chairman Hundt Announces Appointment of Solomon Trujillo as Interim Chairman of the Telecommunications Development Fund

- Telecommunications Development Fund Request for Board of Directors Nominations

- Suggestions solicited for improving FCC services and procedures

- Improving Commission Processes, Notice of Inquiry, (PP Docket No. 96-17) [Text Version I Wordperfect Version]

- Statements by FCC Chairman Hundt and Commissioners Quello, Barrett, Ness, and Chong praising passage of the Act. (February 8, 1996)

- 21 FCC Proposals to "Reinvent" the Agency, Adopted By the Act. (February 8, 1996)

FCC Proceedings to Implement the Act

Cable Services Bureau

- Order in the Matter of Implementation of Section 703(e) of the Telecommunications Act of 1996, Amendment of the Commission's Rules and Policies Governing Pole Attachments (CS Docket No. 97-151, FCC 98-20) (February 6, 1998). [Text Version I Wordperfect Version]

- Notice of Proposed Rule Making in the Matter of Implementation of Section 703(e) of the Telecommunications Act of 1996, Amendment of the Commission's Rules and Policies Governing Pole Attachments (CS Docket No. 97-151, FCC 97-234) (August 12, 1997) [Text Version I WordPerfect Version]

- Notice of Proposed Rule Making in the Matter of Amendment of Rules and Policies Governing Pole Attachments (CS Docket No. 97-98, FCC 97-94) (March 14, 1997) [Text Version I WordPerfect Version]

- In the Matter of Implementation of Section 305 of the Telecommunications Act of 1996 NPRM on Closed Captioning and Video Description of Video Programming, Video Programming Accessibility (MM Docket No. 95-176) (January 17, 1997)(*Comment Date: February 28, 1997, Reply Comment Date: March 24, 1997)* [News Releases I Text Version I Wordperfect Version]

- Order in matter of Implementation of Section 703 of the Telecommunications Act of 1996, Amendments and Additions to the Commissions Rules Governing Pole Attachments (CS Docket No. 96-166) (August 6, 1996) [News Releases I Text Version I Wordperfect Version]

- Report & Order, Memorandum & Opinion & Order, and Further Notice of Proposed Rulemaking in the matter of Preemption of Local Zoning Regulation of Satellite Earth Stations; Implementation of Section 207 of the Telecommunications Act of 1996, restrictions on Over-the Air Reception Devices: Television Broadcast Service & Multichannel Multipoint Distribution Service (IB Docket 95-59, CS Docket No. 96-83) (August 6, 1996) [Text Version I Wordperfect Version]

- First Order on Reconsideration in the matter of Implementation of Section 302 of the Telecommunications Act of 1996, Open Video Systems (CS Docket No. 96-46) (July 23, 1996) [Text Version I Wordperfect Version]

- Report & Order on Implementation of Section 301(j) of the Telecommunications Act of 1996, Aggregation of Equipment Costs By Cable Operators (CS Docket No. 96-57) (June 7, 1996) [Text Version I Wordperfect Version]

- Order on Implementation of Section 302 of the Telecommunications Act of 1996, Open Video Systems (CS Docket No. 96-46) (June 7, 1996) [Text Version I Wordperfect Version]

- Second Report & Order on Implementation of Section 302 of the Telecommunications Act of 1996, Open Video Systems (CS Docket No. 96-46) (June 3, 1996) [Text Version I Wordperfect Version]

FIGURE 1.16
continued

- Order on Implementation of Section 301(d) of the Telecommunications Act of 1996, Definition of Markets for purposes of the Cable Television Mandatory Television Broadcast Signal Carriage Rules (CS Docket No. 95-178) (May 24, 1996)
  [Text Version I Wordperfect Version]

- Notice of Proposed Rulemaking on Implementation of Sections 207 of the Telecommunications Act of 1996, Restrictions on Over-the-Air Reception Devices: Television Broadcast And MultiChannel Multipoint distribution Service.
  (CS Docket No. 96-83) (April 4, 1996)
  [Text Version I Wordperfect Version]

- Order on Implementation of Sections 202(f), 202(i) and 301(i) of the Telecommunications Act of 1996, Cable Television Antitrafficking, Network Television, and MMDS/SMATV Cross ownership Rules (CS Docket No. 96-56)
  [Text Version I Wordperfect Version]

- Commission will not enforce or implement section 505 of the Telecommunications Act of 1996 "Scrambling of Sexually Explicit Adult Video Service Programming" as result of court order.
  [Public Notice]

- Notice of Proposed Rulemaking to Implement Section 302 of the Telecommunications Act of 1996 Open Video Systems, Telephone Company-Cable Television Cross Ownership Rules
  [Text Version I Wordperfect Version]

- Implementation of Section 505 of the Telecommunications Act of 1996, Scrambling of Explicit Adult Video Service Programming (CS Docket No. 96-40)
  [Text Version I Wordperfect Version]

- Extension of the comment period for the Notice of Inquiry on closed captioning and video description, so that parties have an opportunity to comment on the Telecom Act provisions affecting these issues. (February 27, 1996)
  [Text Version I WordPerfect Version]

- Order extending time for cable operators to file their annual equipment forms, because Telecom Act permits cable operators to aggregate equipment costs, and requires the FCC to modify its rules and forms within 120 days of enactment. (February 27, 1996)
  [text version I WordPerfect Version]

FIGURE 1.17
AM/FM share of listening. Courtesy of National Database.

driven up rates for advertisers. Others counter that radio 'research' combined with the demand for higher ratings had already eliminated programming innovation. Proponents for consolidation point to the stations previously competing in the same format head-to-head that are now co-owned allowing one of the stations to carve out a new format. They suggest that television and 24-hour cable news competition, plus the rising costs of radio news programming, had already precipitated the decline of radio news well before consolidation, and that new technologies, such as the continuous news updates on the Internet, have only accelerated the pace. And they point to the increasing variety of other media and promotional options open to advertisers as the reasons that radio rates will always remain competitive. It might be better if consolidation were viewed as being neither good nor bad but as a reaction to the changing realities of business."

Williams gives a brief overview of a major West Coast cluster inspired by the consolidation approach: "Clear Channel's greater San Diego cluster consists of 13 stations. They also oversee two additional suburban stations in Temecula, California about 50 miles away. The Temecula stations simulcast two of the San Diego stations but add local content. The two suburban stations have a local sales manager and local sales staff. In addition to the stations, they also operate Clear Channel Traffic (similar to, but competitors of, Shadow and Metro traffic) and the Padres sports network as separate business entities out of this facility."

Despite the many concerns, business improved after the mid-1990s. The dollar volume of station transactions (number of stations changing hands) approved by the FCC soared. In the new millennium, the radio business is robust, to say the least. Annual revenues have reached $19 billion and are climbing. A handful of radio corporations, many owning hundreds of stations, recorded yearly earnings in the billion-dollar range.

Buying and Selling

Today brokerage firms handle the sale of many radio stations. "It's difficult to overlook the importance of Wall Street and the financial community in the future of radio," notes Ed Shane. Bill Campbell, co-owner

FIGURE 1.18
The price for stations continues to climb. Courtesy Radio Ink.

Money And Finance

RADIO INK DEAL TRACKER

PROPERTY	BUYER	SELLER	PRICE	BROKER
WEVD-AM New York	ABC Radio Inc.	Forward Broadcasting	$78 M	Media Venture Partners
Brill Media stations	Regent Communications	Brill Media	$62 M	
Sabre Communications stations	Backyard Broadcasting	Sabre Communications	$42 M	Patrick Communications
WKSM-FM, WNCV-FM, WYZB-FM, WZNS-FM, WFTW-AM	Cumulus Media	East Mississippi Broadcasters	$30 M	
KKRG-FM Albuquerque, KIOT-FM Los Lunas, KOSZ-FM Rio Rancho, KKSS-FM & KRQS-FM Santa Fe	Hispanic Broadcasting	Simmons Media Group	$22 M	Star Media Group
KURS-AM San Diego	Hi-Favor Broadcasting	Pacific Spanish Network	$8.5 M	
WZBR-FM Kinston, WHRT-FM Morehead City, WNBR-FM Oriental, WCBZ-FM Williamston, NC	Archway Broadcasting	Eastern Carolina Broadcast	$6.5 M	Snowden Assoc.
KJON-AM Carrollton, TX	Family Worship Center	Monroe-Stephens Broadcasting	$4.2 M	MGMT Services/ The Connell Co.
WKCL-FM Pekin, IL	AAA Entertainment	Kelly Communications	$4 M	Media Services Group
WKCD-FM Pawcatuck, CT	John Fuller	AAA Entertainment	$3.75 M	Media Services Group
KFIG-AM Fresno	Radio Central LLC	Big Dawg Broadcasting	$2 M	
KSLK-FM Visalia	Nelson Gomez	New Visalia Broadcasting	$1.2 M	
WBYA-FM Islesboro, ME	Mariner Broadcasting LP	Gopher Hill Communications	$1.15 M	

SOURCE: BIA MEDIA ACCESS PRO

of Blue River Communications, says the future is now. "Wall Street is where much of the buying and selling of radio outlets occurs nowadays. Things have changed to where stations are sold through lawyers and brokerage houses more than they are from broadcaster to broadcaster. Those are pretty much bygone days, and that is kind of sad. It became the 'three-piece-suiters' game in the 1990s. There is little direct negotiating, no bargaining between owners over a drink at the corner pub. Stations are commodities to be bought and sold by people who sometimes have little appreciation or understanding of what radio is really all about. Of course, the economic inertia of the first part of this decade inspired more direct negotiations (strategic alliances) between owners, and I think that is good. I'm also detecting a move to drive the MBAs out of our business.

Broadcasters who gain general experience beyond just management are the future."

For their services, brokers receive an average commission of 7 to 8 percent on sales, and in some cases they earn additional incentives based on the size of the transaction. In recent years brokers have been very successful in negotiating large profits for their clients (see figure 1.18).

Brokerage firms promote the sale of stations through ads in industry trade magazines, direct mailings, and appearances at broadcast conferences. Interested buyers are provided with all the pertinent data concerning a station's geographical location, physical holdings, operating parameters, programming, and income history, as well as economic, competitive, and demographic information about the area within reach of the station's signal.

Another recent approach to the buying and selling of radio properties is the auction method, although this means of selling a station is perceived by some as a kind of last-resort effort at getting rid of profitless stations, most of which are AM. (See figure 1.18) Due to the upsurge in radio's fortunes, this approach has declined.

The average price of an AM station in the late 1980s was $450,000, with some selling for as little as a few thousand dollars and others for as much as several million. In 1986 New York station WMCA-AM sold for $11 million, and in 1992, WFAN-AM received a bid of $70 million, proving that AM stations can still command enormous sums.

The average price for FM stations is higher than it is for AM. In the early 1990s the average price for an FM station exceeded several million, and in 2002 was in the tens, if not hundreds, of millions.

Many AM broadcasters look for full-time status, improved reception, and stereo to increase the value of their properties in the coming years. Likewise many await the conversion to digital audio broadcasting to level the playing field with FM.

Digital Revolution

Digital Audio Broadcasting (DAB) makes analog amplitude modulation (AM) and

FIGURE 1.19
Mega mergers have changed the communication industry landscape. Courtesy Viacom.

frequency modulation (FM) outmoded systems. With the great popularity of home and portable digital music equipment (CD, DAT, and mini-disks), broadcasters are forced to convert their signals to remain competitive. Thus, DAB looms large in the future of radio. The days of analog signal propagation are numbered. (For an explanation of both digital and analog signaling, see Chapters 9 and 10.)

In the mid-1980s, compact disc players were introduced to the consumer market. Today, CD players rank as the top consumer item for home music reproduction. Turntables have gone by the board, and the analog tape cassette market is all but gone. Digital is here to stay, at least until something better comes along.

At first DAB was perceived as a threat by broadcasters. The National Association of Broadcasters (NAB) looked at the new sound technology adversarially. In an interview in the July 23, 1990, issue of *RadioWeek*, John Abel, NAB's executive vice president of operations, stated, "DAB is a threat and anyone who plans to stay in business for a while needs to pay careful attention."

As time went on, DAB was regarded as a *fait accompli*, something that was simply going to happen. Soon broadcasters assumed a more proactive posture regarding the technology, and then the concern shifted to where to put the new medium and how to protect existing broadcast operations.

Early on, NAB proposed locating DAB in the L-band portion of the electromagnetic spectrum. It also argued for in-band placement. Eventually the FCC saw fit to recommend that DAB be allocated room in the S-band, and it took its proposal to the World Administrative Radio Conference (WARC) held in Spain in February 1992. This spectrum designation is expected to help in-band terrestrial development. In-band, on-channel (IBOC) digital signaling, developed by iBiquity Digital Corporation, would permit broadcasters to remain on their existing frequencies. This is something

they favor, as satellite DAB signal transmission is regarded as a significant threat to the local nature of U.S. broadcasting. On the other hand, many countries are fully supportive of a satellite DAB system because they do not have the number of stations the United States possesses and thus lack the coverage and financial investment.

As of this writing, some DAB issues continued to be debated by the National Radio Systems Committee (NRSC), and this will likely be the case in the months, if not years, ahead. However, it appears a relative certainty that DAB will be available to the U.S. public in the not-too-distant future. Of course, this will require a whole new direction in home/car/walk-along receiver design. Simply put, DAB renders existing radios obsolete. This is cause for some anxiety among broadcasters who wonder how quickly the buying public will convert. However, considerable confidence exists, since consumers' huge appetite for new and improved sound shows no sign of abating.

Considered another plus of digital radio is its capacity to do other things. For example, iBiquity has developed a technology that allows those stations broadcasting digitally to transmit data to portable digital services, including cell phones. This is attractive to the station operator's bottom line.

America is a nation of audiophiles, demanding high-quality sound. Analog broadcasting cannot compete with the interference-free reception and greater frequency dynamics of digital signals. Digital signaling heralds a new age in radio broadcasting. Jeff Tellis, former president of the Intercollegiate Broadcasting System (IBS), explains why. "The reason for the great interest in DAB is its considerable number of advantages." Among them are:

- Significantly improved coverage using significantly less power
- Dramatic improvement in the quality of the signal; compare CD to vinyl

- More precise coverage control using multiple transmitters similar to cellular phone technology
- No adjacent channel reception problems
- On-channel booster capabilities eliminating the need to use separate frequencies to extend the same signal
- Easy transmission of auxiliary services, including format information, traffic, weather, text, and selective messaging services
- Sharing of transmitting facilities — common transmitter and antenna

Telecommunications professor Ernest Hakanen expands on the cost advantages of digital broadcasting. "DAB also promises to be economically efficient. Since there is no interstation interference between DAB signals and because of the appeal of the spectrum efficiency provided by the interleaved environment, all of the channel operators in an area could utilize the same transmitter. The transmission facilities could be operated by a consortium for the construction, operation, and maintenance of the common transmission plant. Antenna height for DAB systems is also lower than current FM standards. Electrical power conservation and savings are a huge advantage of DAB."

Picking up on Hakanen's point about consolidating broadcast operations, Lynn Christian says, "The consortium (radio station malls or clusters) approach to maintaining and operating a station is commonplace because of economic reasons, and DAB is very conducive to a collaborative relationship among broadcasters."

Prior to the WARC meeting in 1992, NAB's DAB Task Force proposed a set of standards to ensure that the technology would operate effectively. The specifications included:

- CD-quality sound
- Enhanced coverage area
- Accommodation of existing AM and FM frequencies
- Immunity to multipath interference

- Immunity to stoplight fades
- No interference to existing AM and FM broadcasters
- DAB system interference immunity
- Minimization of transmission costs
- Receiver complexity
- Additional data capacity
- Reception area threshold

After nearly a century of analog signal transmission, radio is about to venture into the digital domain, which will keep it relevant to the demands of a technologically sophisticated listening marketplace as it embarks on its next 100 years. In his opening remarks at the 2002 NAB Radio Show, the association's president, Eddie Fritts, heralded high definition radio as the wave of the medium's future, saying "Transitioning to digital will give radio even better opportunities to serve [its] listeners."

Satellite and Cable Radio

Radio broadcasters retain a wary eye on the evolving digital audio services being made available by satellite companies (see figure 1.20). It is the threat of increased competition that inspires contempt for the new and evolving audio options. Although broadcasters have long employed satellite programming and network services to enhance their over-the-air terrestrial signals, the idea of a direct-to-consumer alternative is not greeted with enthusiasm, especially since these are already available in digital sound, something broadcasters are still anticipating. For several years, the FCC debated the question of satellite radio. In the waning years of the 1990s, the feds gave licenses to companies, such as CD Radio and XM Satellite Radio, to launch their services. Meanwhile the NAB vociferously argued against its introduction into the local marketplace. Despite all the brouhaha, XM Satellite (xmradio.com) launched its service in September 2001 and a year later claimed nearly a quarter of a million subscribers. Less than a year after XM Satellite rolled out its audio service, Sirius Satellite Radio debuted. It quickly became clear to terrestrial broadcasters that there was a new kid in town, one who would further accelerate the splintering of the radio listening audience.

Over the air broadcasters contend that their local orientation betters the services of the satellite audio companies, which are nationally based programmers. Says Infinity Broadcasting's senior vice president, David Pearlman, "Broadcast radio is locally rooted and the satellite companies can't fulfill that need at the present time. This will be our saving grace and aid our ability to withstand this frontal attack. With our selling of local news, traffic, weather, events, personalities, and services, the product differentiation will work in our current industry's favor."

Satellite radio is fee driven and offers a wide array of program options. A monthly cost of $9.95 is charged for the coast-to-coast signals (continuously in broadcast range), but subscribers also have to invest several hundreds of dollars for receiver equipment. Both satellite companies have signed contracts with car manufacturers to install their digital receivers, and each predicts the acquisition of an impressive segment of the drivetime listening audience in the not too distant future.

To compound the competition for the listening audience, cable companies provide in-home music services for most of their subscribers. For example ATT Broadband cable users receive more than 50 channels of music that are often quite niche specific. These commercial-free channels of diverse nonstop music are very attractive to subscribers and frequently result in the loss of another portion of traditional radio's listening audience.

Internet Radio

Over the last few years, many listeners accessed their favorite radio station via their computers. However, with the specter of costly copyright royalty fees imposed on stations streaming music, their numbers dwindled and the future of Internet radio was cast in doubt. At this writing, a proposed royalty rate compromise bill, known as the Small Webcaster Settlement Act (H.R. 5469), was passed by Congress. It is designed to mitigate the burden, so the future for the medium looks brighter. Rates established by the Digital Millennium Copyright Act of 1998 have forced many radio broadcasters — both commercial and noncommercial — to programming are the likeliest to remain in the webcasting business. Those that don't stream audio will maintain a web site for promotional purposes and will expand on the interactivity capabilities of cyberspace. Comments Jay Williams, Jr., "In the initial surge of the dot.com boom, radio stations rushed to create a web site that included station, music, and local event information as well as billboard ads. After the Internet bloom faded from the vine and many stations stopped streaming audio, many radio station web sites languished. Recently, however, web sites are becoming more vital. Many national advertisers are asking for a Web presence, allowing station listeners to win prizes, interact with information, online promotions and a link to their own web sites. Radio stations are beginning to use their own sites to promote local advertisers, promotions, events, and to create e-mail clubs to build loyalty."

Despite the formidable issues confronting webcasters, the RAB determined that over 4,000 stations were streaming their content as of April 2002, and Arbitron/Edison Media Research calculated that online radio listening actually grew from 14 percent in 1999 to 23 percent in 2001. Meanwhile MeasureCast reported that Internet radio listening was continuing to grow a year later, so the practice was far from moribund. *Radio Ink* magazine cited Jazz FM and Virgin Radio in London, L-Love Radio in Sacramento, ESPN Radio in Connecticut, and WQXR/FM Radio in New York as the top five simulcast streamers during the summer of 2002.

Indeed, today stations continue to view the Internet as a viable supplement to their on-air signals, especially for promotion and audience research purposes. Interactive radio is a growing reality, as is the opportunity for everyone with the right computer and software to be a broadcaster or cybercaster. With an Internet encoder, the home user can transmit to an international audience. This prospect prompts a collective sigh from station managers,

reconsider their plans to webcast. According to radio industry publisher Eric Rhoads, "With the current fees, the economics do not make sense for anyone intent on building a business from this. Unless Congress steps in and makes a change, the RIAA fees are unreasonable and will kill the music side of online radio."

Most broadcasters still feel that it is important to retain a Web presence, but it may not include music streaming (see figure 1.21). Stations broadcasting news, sports, talk, and other nonmusic forms of who are losing track of the new forms of competition.

Notes longtime broadcaster Lynn Christian, "The major concern regarding the future of radio is centered on new competition from satellite, cable, and online sources. Those companies which are planning to partner with these new media choices, and develop data services, will undoubtedly be the big winners in the 21st century. Broadcast radio, as I have known it during the past 40 years, will not be the same in the next few years. But what American business is the same now? These are revolutionary times in radio and in the world."

Professors Jeff Harman and Bruce Klopfenstein have attempted to determine (in a special Delphi Forecast Study for the NAB) the future of new and evolving technologies in the radio industry. Among other things, their research concluded that by the year 2000 most radio stations were engaged in some form of wide-area datacasting, computer paging, digital transmission (DARS), smart receivers (RDS), high-speed data broadcasting, digital production, and Internet services.

Cognizant of the many obstacles and challenges that exist in the age of the Internet, most radio broadcasters forecast a long-term relation between the two mediums, one that will benefit both. As radio heads warp speed into this "future world," it is obvious that aspiring broadcasters will have to know their way around a computer, because the audio studio will exist within the digital and cyber domains.

LPFM (Low Power FM)

A micro radio movement surfaced in the 1990s and raised the ire of both broadcast regulators and the industry. The debate positioned the NAB against what it labeled radio "pirates." After lengthy reflection, FCC Chairman William Kennard proposed rule-making designed to legitimize these unauthorized, tiny wattage outlets. The argument used to justify support of LPFMs cited the erosion of programming diversity in commercial radio as the consequence of widespread consolidation and mergers. According to Kennard this new species of broadcaster would give voice to those alienated or disenfranchised by mainstream corporate radio. The FCC's proposal sought to create two types of new licenses on the FM band. Power would span 10 (LP10) to 100 (LP100) watts with service areas restricted to three to nine miles. Among many stipulations, the FCC requires that LPFM licensees be nonprofit organizations. This rule helped placate commercial broadcasters' concerns that the new category of stations would represent yet another competitive threat. The LPFM rules further require that this "sub" or "secondary" category of radio stations not interfere with the signals of regular full power outlets.

The greatest threat to the existence of microstations is the looming conversion of regular radio outlets to IBOC digital. This will all but squeeze out any chance for the continued survival of the community-centric medium.

Executive director of Allston-Brighton Free Radio, Stephen Provizer, gives this view of his medium. "As an open platform for all voices, we have two goals: to disseminate programming that would otherwise be unavailable and to empower our participants which, to the greatest extent possible, encompasses the entire community. The first goal becomes increasingly important as the range of consumer choice becomes narrower due to ongoing corporization and an obsession with demography-driven advertising. The second goal, participation, is driven by our belief that direct participation is the key to empowerment. If an individual in our media-drenched culture is going to be able to exercise critical judgment toward mainstream media, he or she must have the process demystified and clarified. Perhaps if media literacy education was more available in lower school this would not be necessary,

FIGURE 1.22
The Apple iPod represents yet another competitive threat to broadcast radio. At this writing, the youth listening market was enthusiastically embracing the new audio alternative causing further anxiety among already besieged radio station programmers and managers.

but such is not now and has never been the case."

Radio and Government Regulations

Almost from the start it was recognized that radio could be a unique instrument for the public good. This point was never made more apparent than in 1912, when, according to legend (which was recently challenged by scholars who contend that others were involved), a young wireless operator named David Sarnoff picked up the distress signal from the sinking *Titanic* and relayed the message to ships in the vicinity, which then came to the rescue of those still alive. The survivors were the beneficiaries of the first attempt at regulating the new medium. The Wireless Ship Act of 1910 required that ships carrying 50 or more passengers have wireless equipment on board. The effective use of the medium from an experimental station in New York City's Wanamaker Building helped save 700 lives.

Radio's first practical application was as a means of communicating from ship to ship and from ship to shore. During the first decade of this century, Marconi's wireless invention was seen primarily as a way of linking the ships at sea with the rest of the world. Until that time, when ships left port they were beyond any conventional mode of

communications. The wireless was a boon to the maritime services, including the Navy, which equipped each of its warships with the new device.

Coming on the heels of the *Titanic* disaster, the Radio Act of 1912 sought to expand the general control of radio on the domestic level. The Secretary of Commerce and Labor was appointed to head the implementation and monitoring of the new legislation. The primary function of the act was to license wireless stations and operators. The new regulations empowered the Department of Commerce and Labor to impose fines and revoke the licenses of those who operated outside the parameters set down by the communications law.

Growth of radio on the national level was curtailed by World War I, when the government saw fit to take over the medium for military purposes. However, as the war raged on, the same young wireless operator, David Sarnoff, who supposedly had been instrumental in saving the lives of passengers on the ill-fated *Titanic*, was hard at work on a scheme to drastically modify the scope of the medium, thus converting it from an experimental and maritime communications apparatus to an appliance designed for use by the general public. Less than five years after the war's end, receivers were being bought by the millions, and radio as we know it today was born.

As explained earlier, the lack of regulations dealing with interference nearly resulted in the premature end of radio. By 1926 hundreds of stations clogged the airways, bringing pandemonium to the dial. The Radio Act of 1912 simply did not anticipate radio's new application. It was the Radio Act of 1927 that first approached radio as a mass medium. The Federal Regulatory Commission's five commissioners quickly implemented a series of actions that restored the fledgling medium's health.

The Communications Act of 1934 charged a seven-member commission with the responsibility of ensuring the efficient use of the airways, which the government views as a limited resource that belongs to the public and is leased to broadcasters. Over the years the FCC has concentrated its efforts on maximizing the usefulness of radio for the public's benefit. Consequently, broadcasters have been required to devote a portion of their airtime to programs that address important community and national issues. In addition, broadcasters have had to promise to serve as a constant and reliable source of information, while retaining certain limits on the amount of commercial material scheduled.

The FCC has steadfastly sought to keep the medium free of political bias and special-interest groups. In 1949 the commission implemented regulations making it necessary for stations that present a viewpoint to provide an equal amount of airtime to contrasting or opposing viewpoints. The Fairness Doctrine obliged broadcasters "to afford reasonable opportunity for the discussion of conflicting views of public importance." Later it also stipulated that stations notify persons when attacks were made on them over the air.

Although broadcasters generally acknowledge the unique nature of their business, many have felt that the government's involvement has exceeded reasonable limits in a society based on a free enterprise system. Since it is their money, time, and energy they are investing, broadcasters feel they should be afforded greater opportunity to determine their own programming.

In the late 1970s, a strong movement headed by Congressman Lionel Van Deerlin sought to reduce the FCC's role in broadcasting, in order to allow the marketplace to dictate how the industry conducted itself. Van Deerlin actually proposed that the Broadcast Branch of the commission be abolished and a new organization with much less authority created. His bill was defeated, but out of his and others' efforts came a new attitude concerning the government's hold on the electronic media. President Reagan's antibureaucracy, free-enterprise philosophy gave impetus to the deregulation move already under way when he assumed office. The FCC, headed by Chairman Mark

Fowler, expanded on the deregulation proposal that had been in-itiated by his predecessor, Charles Ferris. The deregulation decision eliminated the requirement that radio stations devote a portion of their airtime (8 percent for AM and 6 percent for FM) to nonentertainment programming of a public affairs nature. In addition, stations no longer had to undergo the lengthy process of ascertainment of community needs as a condition of license renewal, and guidelines pertaining to the amount of time devoted to commercial announcements were eliminated. The rule requiring stations to maintain detailed program logs was also abolished. A simplified postcard license renewal form was adopted, and license terms were extended from three to seven years. In a further step the commission raised the ceiling on the number of broadcast outlets a company or individual could own from 7 AM, 7 FM, and 7 television stations to 12 each. As of March 1992, the FCC saw fit to raise the caps on ownership again, this time to 30 AM and 30 FM. Later in the year, these were reduced to 18 AM and 18 FM. Three years later, with a Republican Congress in place, a new telecommunications bill proposed to eliminate ownership caps completely. The bill also sought to relax the cross-ownership rule, which kept a single entity from possessing a radio, TV, and newspaper company in the same market. Meanwhile, radio license terms were to be raised to 10 years.

On August 4, 1987, the FCC voted to eliminate the 38-year-old Fairness Doctrine, declaring it unconstitutional and no longer applicable to broadcasters. A month before, President Reagan had vetoed legislation that would have made the policy law.

The extensive updating of FCC rules and policy was based on the belief that the marketplace should serve as the primary regulator. Opponents of the reform feared that with their newfound freedom, radio stations would quickly turn their backs on community concerns and concentrate their full efforts on fattening their pocketbooks.

Those who support the position that broadcasters should first serve the needs of

FIGURE 1.23
Some useful web sites. Courtesy michaelckeith.com.

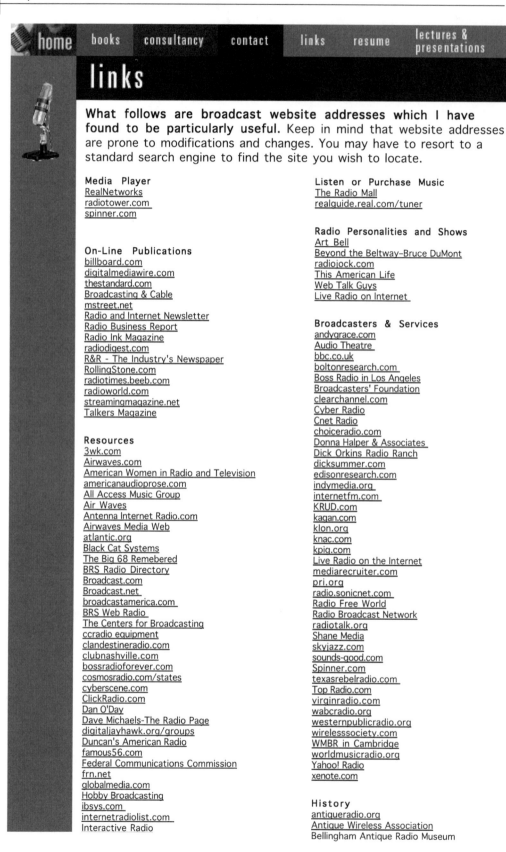

home books consultancy contact links resume lectures & presentations

links

What follows are broadcast website addresses which I have found to be particularly useful. Keep in mind that website addresses are prone to modifications and changes. You may have to resort to a standard search engine to find the site you wish to locate.

Media Player
RealNetworks
radiotower.com
spinner.com

On-Line Publications
billboard.com
digitalmediawire.com
thestandard.com
Broadcasting & Cable
mstreet.net
Radio and Internet Newsletter
Radio Business Report
Radio Ink Magazine
radiodigest.com
R&R - The Industry's Newspaper
RollingStone.com
radiotimes.beeb.com
radioworld.com
streamingmagazine.net
Talkers Magazine

Resources
3wk.com
Airwaves.com
American Women in Radio and Television
americanaudioprose.com
All Access Music Group
Air Waves
Antenna Internet Radio.com
Airwaves Media Web
atlantic.org
Black Cat Systems
The Big 68 Remebered
BRS Radio Directory
Broadcast.com
Broadcast.net
broadcastamerica.com
BRS Web Radio
The Centers for Broadcasting
ccradio equipment
clandestineradio.com
clubnashville.com
bossradioforever.com
cosmosradio.com/states
cyberscene.com
ClickRadio.com
Dan O'Day
Dave Michaels-The Radio Page
digitaljayhawk.org/groups
Duncan's American Radio
famous56.com
Federal Communications Commission
frn.net
globalmedia.com
Hobby Broadcasting
ibsys.com
internetradiolist.com
Interactive Radio

Listen or Purchase Music
The Radio Mall
realguide.real.com/tuner

Radio Personalities and Shows
Art Bell
Beyond the Beltway–Bruce DuMont
radiojock.com
This American Life
Web Talk Guys
Live Radio on Internet

Broadcasters & Services
andygrace.com
Audio Theatre
bbc.co.uk
boltonresearch.com
Boss Radio in Los Angeles
Broadcasters' Foundation
clearchannel.com
Cyber Radio
Cnet Radio
choiceradio.com
Donna Halper & Associates
Dick Orkins Radio Ranch
dicksummer.com
edisonresearch.com
indymedia.org
internetfm.com
KRUD.com
kagan.com
klon.org
knac.com
kpig.com
Live Radio on the Internet
mediarecruiter.com
pri.org
radio.sonicnet.com
Radio Free World
Radio Broadcast Network
radiotalk.org
Shane Media
skyjazz.com
sounds-good.com
Spinner.com
texasrebelradio.com
Top Radio.com
virginradio.com
wabcradio.org
westernpublicradio.org
wirelesssociety.com
WMBR in Cambridge
worldmusicradio.org
Yahoo! Radio
xenote.com

History
antiqueradio.org
Antique Wireless Association
Bellingham Antique Radio Museum

FIGURE 1.23
continued

intervox.com
kagan.com
katzinteractive.com
kenradio.com
listen.com
listen.to/playtime
live365.com
Los Angeles Radio People
measurecast.com
MIT list of Radio Stations on the Internet
msn.com
National Public Radio
National Radio Club
Native Media Resource Center
offshore-radio.de
Old Time Radio
rab.org
radioage.com
radioboston.com
radiocentral.com
radiojump.com
radioinkhelpwanted.com
radioguy.com
radioguide.com
Radio Classics
Radio Drama
Radio 411
Radio Info
radiomania.com
radio.oneworld.net
radiorow.com
radiosurfer.com
radioparadise.com
Radio-Television News Directors Assoc.
radiowave.com
RCA Electronics
reelradio.com
shoutcast.com
Sonicbox.com
surfernetwork.com
This American Life
TvRadio World
transom.org
Uncle Rick's Reel Top 40
virginradio.com
virginradio.co.uk
warpradio.com
wgnspike.com
wolfradio.com
worldcasters.com

bham.net/ahrs
charlesherrold.org
hhscott.com
Radio History - U.S. Marconi Museum
The Hammond Museum of Radio
Library of American Broadcasting.com
The Museum of Television & Radio
Media History Project
mztv.com
Museum of Broadcast Communications
newseum.org
Pavek Museum of Broadcasting
perham.org
radioera.com
radiohistory.org
radiostory.org
wirelesssociety.com

society are concerned that deregulation (unregulation) has further reduced the medium's "good-citizen" role. "Radio, especially the commercial sector, has long since fallen down on its 'interest, convenience, and necessity' obligation born of the Radio Act of 1927, while a small segment of the industry does exert an effort to address the considerable problems facing society today, the overwhelming majority continue to be fixated on the financial bottom line. There needs to be more of a balance," observes Robert Hilliard, former FCC Chief of Public and Educational Broadcasting. Proponents of deregulation applauded the FCC's actions, contending that the listening audience would indeed play a vital role in determining the programming of radio stations, since the medium had to meet the needs of the public in order to prosper.

Although the government continues to closely scrutinize the actions of the radio industry to ensure that it operates in an efficient and effective manner, it is no longer perceived as the fearsome, omnipresent Big Brother it once was. Today broadcasters more fully enjoy the fruits of a laissez-faire system of economy. (See figure 1.25)

In the spring of 1996, the Telecommunications bill (made a Telecommunications

Jay Williams, Jr.

The Future of Radio

FIGURE 1.24
Jay Williams, Jr.

Winds carrying technological advances, changing regulations, new competitors, and shifting consumer patterns have begun to sweep across the radio landscape. The foundations of this 80-year-old industry are beginning to shift. Radio is in the eye of a hurricane of change.

Telecommunications: Digital technology has already revolutionized every aspect of our lives by propelling systems and devices only dreamed of a few years ago. Once meaningless letter and alphanumeric combinations like MP3, DVD, CD, PS2, and GPS have become necessities. Digital technology will churn out new devices that will be more powerful even as they diminish in size. Once a monopoly, telephone companies must now fight against cable, satellite, wireless, and Internet providers to supply consumers with entertainment, information, and communications

options. Even as Wi-Fi networks become prevalent, newer ultra-wideband (UWB) technology looms on the horizon. Once unique, radio's advantage of portability will be challenged when the consumer can listen to a myriad of choices on a wireless headset.

In light of these new delivery systems, communications, computer, and content providers will employ acquisitions, mergers, and alliances to capture more of the consumers' time, money, and involvement. Despite the problems of the AOL Time Warner merger, program and content providers will align themselves with existing and emerging delivery systems in ever-evolving combinations. The money and resources required to compete worldwide will encourage more consolidation.

Consolidation and Technology in Radio: Digital technology has helped facilitate radio ownership consolidation permitted under the relaxed regulations of the Telecom Act of 1996. Unattended operations, digital workstations, ISDN lines, and centralized billing and traffic systems have streamlined radio operations. Voice-tracking and recording hour-long music programs in minutes, from the studio or anywhere in the country, has improved productivity and flexibility. Rush Limbaugh and Howard Stern proved that superior national talent can grab big ratings locally, so group operators are likely to unite their best people to create exciting new regional stations for each format. Technology will allow these stations to be live and sound local, as better talent improves quality and reduces costs. Locally

programmed stations operated by dedicated broadcasters will still thrive, although their numbers will decline. The golden age of local radio is over.

American broadcasters now race across borders to vie against British and European counterparts to buy and merge with established media and synergistic businesses that can enable them to enrich content, reduce overhead, reach more people, and deliver multimedia presentations to advertisers. Media giants are attempting to build global platforms from existing resources while they last.

Regulation: With the vast and growing array of media choices from around the world now available, the justification for U.S. government ownership and content regulation has evaporated. Yet in our free society, free speech on the radio is still threatened by regulation. Technology is often constrained or diverted by legislation, sometimes sabotaged by politics and special interests. Although issues from competing interests must be resolved, new technology will create a greater choice and diversity of ownership than could ever be mandated by regulation.

Radio's New Competition: These are exciting, competitive times for radio. Satellite radio providers XM and Sirius offer almost 100 channels each, but initial consumer demand was weak and both are heavily in debt. Many traditional radio broadcasters do not view satellite radio as a threat and say, "Why would anyone pay for radio when it's free?" They are wrong. TV is free. Water is free. People gladly pay for both. Satellite radio strikes at the Achilles heel of terrestrial radio: it's tired. Too much talk, too many commercials, lack of compelling content, limited music variety, and mediocre audio have contributed to radio's fatigue. In-band digital, the audio solution promised by terrestrial broadcasters, will be too great a technical compromise to ward off complaints. As satellite radio becomes standard equipment on more new cars, it will begin to draw more listeners. And when a standout personality is introduced, satellites will rip away 20 percent of radio's highest quality listeners within five years.

Even more exciting is the promise of Internet radio. Before the Recording Industry Association of America's (RIAA) lawyers quashed music streaming with usurious "performance fees" and draconian reporting requirements, more than 3,000 sites were streaming online. Formats that ranged from jukebox channels to streaming audio from local radio stations had combined to offer a wealth of choice. By mid 2000, 4 percent of Americans were already listening regularly, and 20 percent occasionally, to web radio. Then the music stopped. As increasingly powerful wireless access becomes essential to life, and sophisticated software profiles listener preferences to create customized "personal radio stations," Internet radio is set to explode. RIAA lawyers, though, are set to slow the pace of real ownership diversity.

Technology and the Consumer:
The VCR was the innovative technology that upended broadcast media; it forever changed how it is used. The VCR created "my time" out of "real time." Consumers, not broadcasters or moviemakers, were given the power to determine when they would watch TV. "Personalization technology," at the heart of digital services such as TiVo and Replay TV, continues to ease and enhance consumer control of media utilizing software that monitors usage to offer compatible program suggestions. "My time" is time that matters.

My Time and personalization technologies will make broadcasting to an audience obsolete. Terrestrial broadcasters must learn more one-on-one marketing tactics and become more interactive just to survive. The listener needs the opportunity to talk back to the station and be acknowledged. Radio stations will realize the need to reach out to core listeners and begin an interactive dialog. Stations will develop more incentive, benefit, and reward programs to increase listener loyalty. In addition, radio must do battle with the music oligopoly over fees to stream on the Web. Streaming is essential to protect terrestrial radio's interactive digital future; the music industry must compromise or risk damaging an important ally in the music business.

People over age 50 account for 50 percent of the discretionary spending, yet only 10 percent of all advertising is directed toward them. This realization will spur intelligent new formats and increased revenue for radio. The innovators creating these adult formats will be syndicators, satellite, or "national radio." Advertiser demands for results and improvements in customer targeting and response technology will force ad agencies to give up the big-idea concept of advertising, embrace one-on-one marketing, or be fired.

Although the skies are threatening, radio's core strengths remain. Radio serves as a companion and friend, a listener and entertainer. And in this world of increasing choice and complexity, radio also serves as an editor, saving the consumer time and energy by selecting the most interesting, entertaining, and popular sources of music and information. Radio will be there to let people relax, listen, interact, and be entertained, in more ways than ever before.

Act) mentioned earlier became a reality and ownership caps were all but eliminated. The act opened up the floodgates for those radio groups wanting to vastly expand their portfolios. For example, by 2002 Clear Channel Radio had acquired nearly 1,400 stations.

Jobs and Equality in Radio

Today the radio industry employs tens of thousands, but with all the downsizing and consolidation, this figure is eroding and likely will continue to do so in the coming years. Says WBZ/WODS general manager, Ted Jordan, "Consolidation is causing a lack of a career path because so many middle and upper management positions have been eliminated." Since 1972, 75,000 individuals have found full-time employment in radio. Today, opportunities for women and minorities are greater than ever. Until fairly recently, radio has been a male-dominated profession. In 1975 men in the industry outnumbered women nearly four to one. But

Fine Guide

Violation	Fine
Construction/operation without authorization	$10,000
Failure to comply with prescribed lighting/marking	$10,000
Violation of public file rules	$10,000
Violation of political rules (reasonable access, lowest unit charge, equal opportunity, discrimination)	$9,000
Unauthorized substantial transfer of control	$8,000
Violation of children's television commercialization or programing requirements	$8,000
Emergency Alert System equipment not installed or operational	$8,000
Alien ownership violation	$8,000
Failure to permit inspection	$7,000
Transmission of indecent/obscene materials	$7,000
Interference	$7,000
Importation/marketing of unauthorized equipment	$7,000
Exceeding of authorized antenna height	$5,000
Fraud by wire, radio or television	$5,000
Use of unauthorized equipment	$5,000
Exceeding power limits	$4,000
Failure to respond to FCC communications	$4,000
Violation of sponsorship ID requirements	$4,000
Unauthorized emissions	$4,000
Using unauthorized frequency	$4,000
Failure to engage in required frequency coordination	$4,000
Construction/operation at unauthorized location	$4,000
Violation of requirements pertaining to broadcasting of lotteries or contests	$4,000
Violation of transmitter control/metering requirements	$3,000
Failure to file required forms or information	$3,000
Failure to make required measurements or conduct required monitoring	$2,000
Failure to provide station ID	$1,000
Unauthorized pro forma transfer of control	$1,000
Failure to maintain required records	$1,000
Failure to implement rate reduction or refund order	$7,500
Violation of cable program access rules	$7,500
Violation of cable leased-access rules	$7,500
Violation of cable crossownership rules	$7,500
Violation of cable broadcast carriage rules	$7,500
Violation of pole attachment rules	$7,500
Failure to maintain directional pattern within prescribed parameters	$7,000
Violation of main studio rule	$7,000
Violation of broadcast hoax rule	$7,000
AM tower fencing	$7,000
Broadcasting telephone conversations without authorization	$4,000
Violation of enhanced underwriting requirements	$2,000

FIGURE 1.25
FCC Fine Guide.
Courtesy *Broadcasting and Cable.*

insistence on equal opportunity employment within the broadcast industry makes prospects good for all who are interested in broadcasting careers.

Still there is room for improvement in the participation levels of different ethnic groups in the radio industry. Says NAB's vice president for human resources, Dwight Ellis, "Current employment trends reported by the FCC reveal very little growth between 1980 and 1999 in Native American broadcast employment, for example. Other groups have experienced slow growth too. The NAB is committed to assisting the growth of employment and station ownership for minorities in the industry. The NAB has been a vanguard for minority progress in broadcasting. Nevertheless, more must be done."

A common misconception is that a radio station consists primarily of deejays with few other job options available. Wrong! Nothing could be further from the truth. Granted, disc jockeys comprise part of a station's staff, but many other employees are necessary to keep the station on the air.

An average-size station in a medium market used to employ between 18 and 26 people, but today due to consolidation a fraction of that number may be used where several stations form a cluster or radio mall, and on-air personnel may comprise most of that figure. Stations are usually broken down into three major areas: sales, programming, and engineering. Each area, in particular the first two, requires a variety of people for positions that demand a wide range of skills. Subsequent chapters in this book will bear this out.

Proper training and education are necessary to secure a job at most stations, although many will train people to fill the less demanding positions. Over a thousand schools and colleges offer courses in radio broadcasting, and most award certificates or degrees. As in most other fields today, the more credentials a job candidate possesses, the better he or she looks to a prospective employer.

that has changed. Now women are being hired more than ever before, and not just for office positions. Women have made significant inroads into programming, sales, and management positions, and there is no reason to think that this trend will not continue. Says Ed Shane, "Females have made exceptional inroads, especially in sales." It will take a while, however, before an appropriate proportion of women and minorities are working in the medium. The FCC's

FIGURE 1.26
FCC organizational chart.

Perhaps no other profession weighs practical, hands-on experience as heavily as radio does. This is especially true in the on-air area. On the programming side, it is the individual's sound that wins the job, not the degree. However, it is the formal training and education that usually contribute most directly to the quality of the sound that the program director is looking for when hiring. In reality, only a small percentage of radio announcers have college degrees (the number is growing), but statistics have shown that those who do stand a better chance of moving into managerial positions.

Many station managers look for the college-educated person, particularly for the areas of news and sales. Before 1965 the percentage of radio personnel with college training was relatively low. But the figure increased as more and more colleges added broadcasting curricula. Thousands of communications degrees are conferred annually, thus providing the radio industry a pool of highly educated job candidates. Today, college training is a plus when searching for employment in radio. The job application or resume that lists practical experience in addition to formal training is most appealing. The majority of colleges with radio curricula have college stations. These small outlets provide the aspiring broadcaster with a golden opportunity to gain some much-needed on-air experience. Some of the nation's foremost broadcasters began their careers at college radio stations. Many of these same schools have internship programs that provide the student with the chance to get important on-the-job training at professional stations. Again, experience is experience, and it does count to the prospective employer. Small commercial stations often are willing to hire broadcast students to

How FCC Rules Are Made

I. Initiation of Action

Suggestions for changes to the FCC Rules and Regulations can come from sources outside of the Commission either by formal petition, legislation, court decision or informal suggestion. In addition, a Bureau/Office within the FCC can initiate a Rulemaking proceeding on its own.

II. Bureau/Office Evaluation

When a petition for Rulemaking is received, it is sent to the appropriate Bureau(s)/Office(s) for evaluation. If a Bureau/Office decides a particular petition is meritorious, it can request that the Dockets department assign a Rulemaking number to the petition.

A similar request is made when a Bureau/Office decides to initiate a Rulemaking procedure on its own. A weekly notice is issued listing all accepted petitions for Rulemaking. The public has 30 days to submit comments. The Bureau/Office then has the option of generating an agenda item requesting one of four actions by the Commission. If a Notice of Inquiry (NOI) or Notice of Proposed Rulemaking (NPRM) is issued, a docket is instituted and a docket number is assigned.

III. Possible Commission Actions

Major changes to the Rules are presented to the public as either an NOI or NPRM. The Commission will issue an NOI when it is simply asking for information on a broad subject or trying to generate ideas on a given topic. An NPRM is issued when there is a specific change to the Rules being proposed.

If an NOI is issued, it must be followed by ei-ther an NPRM or a Memorandum Opinion and Order (MO&O) concluding the inquiry.

IV. Comments and Replies Evaluated

When an NOI or NPRM has been issued, the public is given the opportunity to comment initially, and then respond to the comments that are made. When the Commission does not receive sufficient comments to make a decision, a further NOI or NPRM may be issued.

It may be determined that an oral argument before the Commission is needed to provide an opportunity for the public to testify before the Commission, as well as for the Bureau(s)/Office(s) to present diverse opinions concerning the proposed Rule change.

V. Report and Order Issued

A Report and Order is issued by the Commission stating the new or amended Rule, or stating that the Rules will not be changed. The proceeding may be terminated in whole or in part.

The Commission may issue additional Report and Orders in the docket.

VI. Reconsideration Given

Petitions for reconsideration may be filed by the public within 30 days. They are reviewed by the appropriate Bureau(s)/Office(s) and/or by the Commission.

VII. Modification Possible

As a result of its review of a petition for reconsideration, the Commission may issue an MO&O modifying its initial decision or denying the petition for reconsideration.

Provided by FCC

FIGURE 1.27
Courtesy of Radio World.

FIGURE 1.28
Native-owned stations provide radio jobs for American Indians. Courtesy KTNN.

fill part-time and vacation slots. This constitutes professional experience and is an invaluable addition to the resume.

Entry-level positions in radio seldom pay well. In fact, many small market stations pay near minimum wage. However, the experience gained at these small-budget operations more than makes up for the small salaries. The first year or two in radio constitutes the dues-paying period, a time in which a person learns the ropes. The small radio station provides inexperienced people with the chance to become involved in all facets of the business. Rarely does a new employee perform only one function. For example, a person hired as a deejay will often prepare and deliver newscasts, write and produce commercials, and may even sell airtime.

To succeed in a business as unique as radio, a person must possess many qualities, not the least of which are determination, skill, and the ability to accept and benefit from constructive criticism. A career in radio is like no other, and the rewards, both personal and financial, can be exceptional. "It's a great business," says Lynn Christian, former senior vice president of the Radio Advertising Bureau. "No two days are alike. After forty-some years in radio, I still recommend it over other career opportunities."

CHAPTER HIGHLIGHTS

1. The average adult spends two hours per day listening to radio. Radio is the most available source of entertainment, companionship, and information.

2. Guglielmo Marconi is generally considered the father of radio, although David Sarnoff and Lee Deforest are likely contenders.

3. As early as 1922, the Department of Commerce set aside two frequencies for radio broadcasts. WEAF in New York and WGI in Boston aired the first commercials.

4. Today, most radio networks have been subsumed by major corporations (Disney, GE, Westinghouse, Westwood One).

5. Station networks, first called chain broadcasting, operated as early as 1922. Radio Corporation of America (RCA) formed the first major network in 1926, the National Broadcasting Company (NBC). Columbia Broadcasting System (CBS) was formed in 1928, and Mutual Broadcasting System (MBS) followed in 1934. American

Broadcasting Company (ABC), formed in 1945, became the largest and most successful radio network.

6. Early station proliferation led to overlapping signals. Signal quality decreased, as did listenership. The Radio Act of 1927 formed the Federal Radio Commission (FRC), a five-member board authorized to issue station licenses, allocate frequency bands, assign frequencies to individual stations, and dictate station power and hours of operation. The FRC established the Standard Broadcast band (500 to 1500 kc).

7. Radio prospered during the Depression by providing cost-free entertainment and escape from the harsh financial realities. *Amos 'n' Andy*, which made its debut in 1929, was the most popular radio show in history. President Franklin D. Roosevelt's fireside chats began on March 12, 1933. The Communications Act of 1934 established the seven-member Federal Communications Commission (FCC).

8. World War II led the FCC to freeze construction of new broadcast outlets; therefore, existing AM outlets prospered.

9. Two years after the war's end, television usurped the entertainment leadership.

10. The Bell Lab scientists' invention of the transistor in 1948 helped save radio by providing portability. Music became radio's mainstay.

11. The Top 40 radio format, conceived about the same time as the emergence of rock music, became the most popular format with younger audiences.

12. Edwin H. Armstrong developed the static-free FM band in 1938. The FCC authorized stereo FM broadcasting in 1961, and in 1965 it separated FM from AM simulcasts in cities with populations in excess of 100,000. Beautiful Music was the first popular format on FM, which relied heavily on automation. The progressive format focused on album cuts rather than Top 40. By the mid-1980s FM possessed 70 percent of the listening audience.

13. Today FM commands 80 percent of the audience although some AM stations top their market ratings.

14. The Corporation for Public Broadcasting was established in 1967. Three years later National Public Radio began providing funding and programming to member stations. More than 800 schools and colleges hold noncommercial radio licenses.

Words from Larry King

"I started my career in May 1957. I did news and sports. In 1960 I began a talk show in Miami and have been hosting talk ever since. Back then I also did sports for the Miami Dolphins. Sports is a big love of mine. I've never regarded what I do as a 'challenge,' per se. It is a love affair. My desire is to inform and entertain the listener. That gets me going. For those young people out there who want to pursue a career in radio, I'd say never give up. Always be yourself. Don't try to be Larry King. The only secret is there is no secret. Your talent will come out if you are good. As far as the future of radio is concerned, it is hard to predict. Talk is always in good shape. The public tends to grow as part of radio. There will always be a need for what the medium offers. Bottom line: the opportunities will be there for those good enough to take advantage of them."

FIGURE 1.29
CNN's Larry King Live is simulcast by over 350 radio stations. Courtesy Larry King.

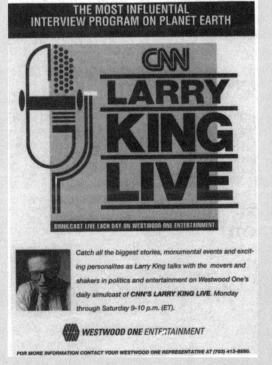

THE MOST INFLUENTIAL INTERVIEW PROGRAM ON PLANET EARTH

SIMULCAST LIVE EACH DAY ON WESTWOOD ONE ENTERTAINMENT

Catch all the biggest stories, monumental events and exciting personalites as Larry King talks with the movers and shakers in politics and entertainment on Westwood One's daily simulcast of *CNN'S LARRY KING LIVE*. Monday through Saturday 9-10 p.m. (ET).

WESTWOOD ONE ENTERTAINMENT

FOR MORE INFORMATION CONTACT YOUR WESTWOOD ONE REPRESENTATIVE AT (703) 413-8550.

15. Narrowcasting is specialized programming. Frag-out refers to the fragmentation of audience because of numerous formats.

16. Highly leveraged transactions (HLTs) created economic problems for many stations. Local marketing agreements (LMAs) allowed broadcasters to form contracts with one another for mutually beneficial purposes.

17. Consolidation, downsizing, and mergers have been prompted by the FCC's relaxation of the duopoly and ownership rules.

18. Seventy percent of radio's revenues come from local spot sales.

19. Brokerage firms handle the sale of most radio stations. Brokers receive a commission of between 7 and 8 percent on sales.

20. Digital audio broadcasting (DAB) is set to replace the conventional analog system of signal transmission and reception.

21. Satellite and cable radio services are providing listeners with options besides traditional terrestrial signal reception.

22. Internet radio has become debilitated by music copyright fees and its future is in doubt, although station web sites provide broadcasters a way to promote their outlets and interface with their audience.

23. Micro- or low-power FM stations constitute a new category of noncommercial radio outlets, but the likely conversion to IBOC digital by regular broadcast outlets may mean the end to the community-oriented medium.

24. In 1949 the FCC formulated the Fairness Doctrine, which obligated broadcasters to present opposing points of view. In 1987 the FCC declared the doctrine unconstitutional and eliminated it.

25. The Republicans wrote a new telecommunications bill designed to lift significant sanctions from broadcasters. The Telecommunications Act of 1996 all but eliminated radio station ownership ceilings.

26. The radio industry employs fewer people today due to consolidations and the subsequent downsizings. Women and minorities have made significant gains in recent years. A combination of practical experience and formal training is the best preparation for a career in broadcasting.

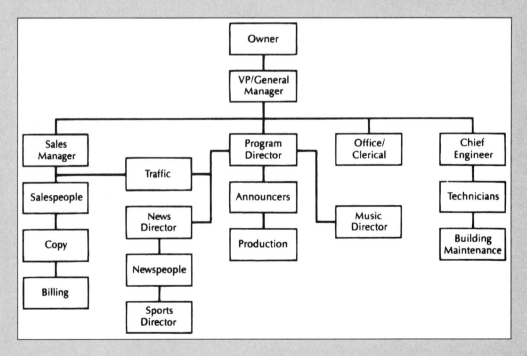

FIGURE 1.30
Organizational flowchart for a nonclustered medium market radio station. Consolidation has resulted in many new and revised positions.

Bruce DuMont

On the Museum of Broadcast Communications

FIGURE 1.31
The Museum of Broadcast
Communications at the Chicago
Cultural Center is located on
Michigan Avenue at Washington
Street.

The Museum of Broadcast Communications is one of only two broadcast
museums in America. It is a museum
of popular culture and contemporary
American history that preserves and
presents historic moments from radio
and television. It contains a collection
of 75,000 radio and television programs and commercials depicting the
historic moments of the past 50
years.

Public programs are presented frequently, featuring many of radio and
television's major personalities, as
well as those who work behind the
scenes. The significant moments of
world history in the past 50 years
have been captured by microphones
and cameras, and the museum's
archives represent an opportunity for
students, scholars, and the general
public to tap into that history.

The archives are fully computerized
and are accessible to the general
public seven days a week. The
Museum of Broadcast Communications contains America's only Radio
Hall of Fame, which includes 85 of
the major personalities and leaders of
the medium. Working radio and television studios provide visitors with an
opportunity to experience the thrill of
being "on-the-air."

FIGURE 1.32
(A) The look of radio
at its inception. (B)
The look of radio
today. Courtesy
Broadcast Electronics
and Westinghouse.

A

FIGURE 1.32
Continued

B

FIGURE 1.33
Radio Sawa is
designed to promote
the long-range
interests of the U.S.
in the Arab world.

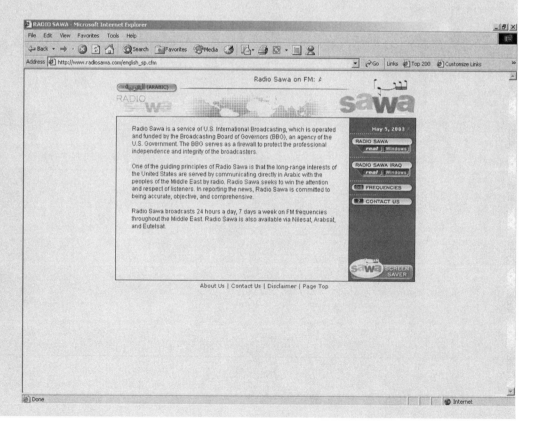

SUGGESTED FURTHER READING

Aitkin, Hugh G.J. *Syntony and Spark.* New York: John Wiley and Sons, 1976.

American Women in Radio and Television. *Making Waves: The 50 Greatest Women in Radio and Television.* Chicago: Andrews McMeel Publishing, 2001.

Archer, G.L. *History of Radio to 1926.* New York: Arno Press, 1971.

Aronoff, Craig E., ed. *Business and the Media.* Santa Monica, Calif.: Goodyear Publishing Company, 1979.

Baker, W.J. *A History of the Marconi Company.* New York: St. Martin's Press, 1971.

Barlow, William. *Voice Over: The Making of Black Radio.* Philadelphia: Temple University Press, 1999.

Barnouw, Erik. *A Tower of Babel: A History of Broadcasting in the United States to 1933,* vol. 1. New York: Oxford University Press, 1966.

—. *The Golden Web: A History of Broadcasting in the United States 1933 to 1953,* vol. 2. New York: Oxford University Press, 1968.

—. *The Image Empire: A History of Broadcasting in the United States from 1953,* vol. 3. New York: Oxford University Press, 1970.

—. *Media Marathon: A Twentieth-Century Memoir.* Durham, N.C.: Duke University Press, 1996.

—. *The Sponsor: Notes on a Modern Potentate.* New York: Oxford University Press, 1978.

Bergreen, Laurence. *Look Now, Pay Later: The Rise of Network Broadcasting.* Garden City, N.Y.: Doubleday, 1980.

Bittner, John R. *Broadcasting and Telecommunications,* 2nd ed. Englewood Cliffs, N.J.: Prentice Hall, 1985.

—. *Professional Broadcasting: A Brief Introduction.* Englewood Cliffs, N.J.: Prentice Hall, 1981.

Blake, Reed H., and Haroldsen, E.O. *A Taxonomy of Concepts in Communications.* New York: Hastings House, 1975.

Brant, Billy G. *College Radio Handbook.* Blue Ridge Summit, Pa.: Tab Books, 1981.

Broadcasting Yearbook. Washington, D.C.: Broadcasting Publishing, 1935 to date, annual.

Browne, Bartz, and Coddington (consultants). *Radio Today—And Tomorrow.* Washington, D.C.: National Association of Broadcasters, 1982.

Buono, Thomas J., and Leibowitz, Matthew L. *Radio Acquisition Handbook.* Miami, Fla.: Broadcasting and the Law, 1988.

Campbell, Robert. *The Golden Years of Broadcasting.* New York: Charles Scribner's Sons, 1976.

Cantril, Hadley. *The Invasion from Mars.* New York: Harper & Row, 1966.

Chapple, Steve, and Garofalo, R. *Rock 'n' Roll Is Here to Pay.* Chicago: Nelson-Hall, 1977.

Cox Looks at FM Radio. Atlanta: Cox Broadcasting Corporation, 1976.

Delong, Thomas A. *The Mighty Music Box.* Los Angeles: Amber Crest Books, 1980.

Ditingo, Vincent M. *The Remaking of Radio.* Boston: Focal Press, 1995.

Douglas, Susan J. *Inventing American Broadcasting, 1899–1922.* Baltimore: Johns Hopkins University Press, 1987.

—. *Listening In.* NY: Times Books, 1999.

Dreher, Carl. *Sarnoff: An American Success.* New York: Quadrangle, 1977.

Dunning, John. *Tune in Yesterday.* Englewood Cliffs, N.J.: Prentice Hall, 1976.

Edmonds, I.G. *Broadcasting for Beginners.* New York: Holt, Rinehart, and Winston, 1980.

Erickson, Don. *Armstrong's Fight for FM Broadcasting.* Birmingham: University of Alabama, 1974.

Fang, Irving E. *Those Radio Commentators.* Ames: Iowa State University Press, 1977.

Fornatale, Peter, and Mills, J.E. *Radio in the Television Age.* New York: Overlook Press, 1980.

Foster, Eugene S. *Understanding Broadcasting.* Reading, Mass.: Addison-Wesley, 1978.

Fowler, Gene and Crawford, Bill. *Border Radio.* Austin: University of Texas Press, 2002.

Geller, Vallerie. *The Powerful Radio Workbook.* Washington, D.C.: M Street Corp., 2000.

Grant, August E., ed. *Communication Technology Update.* Boston: Focal Press, 1995.

Hall, Claud, and Hall, Barbara. *This Business of Radio Programming.* New York: Hastings House, 1978.

Halper, Donna. *Invisible Stars.* Armonk, N.Y.: M.E. Sharpe, 2001.

Hasling, John. *Fundamentals of Radio Broadcasting.* New York: McGraw-Hill, 1980.

Head, Sydney W., and Sterling, C.H. *Broadcasting in America: A Survey of Television, Radio, and the New Technologies,* 7th ed. Boston: Houghton Mifflin, 1993.

Hilliard, Robert L. *The Federal Communications Commission: A Primer.* Boston: Focal Press, 1991.

—, ed. *Radio Broadcasting: An Introduction to the Sound Medium,* 3rd ed. New York: Longman, 1985.

—. *Global Broadcasting Systems.* Boston: Focal Press, 1996.

—. *Waves of Rancor: Tuning the Radical Right.* Boston: Focal Press, 1999.

—, and Keith, Michael C. *The Broadcast Century: A Biography of American Broadcasting.* Boston: Focal Press, 1992.

Hilmes, Michele. *Radio Voices: American Broadcasting, 1922–1952.* Minneapolis: University of Minnesota Press, 1997.

Horten, Gerd. *Radio Goes to War.* Berkeley: University of California Press, 2002.

Hunn, Peter. *Starting and Operating Your Own FM Radio Station.* Blue Ridge Summit, Pa.: Tab Books, 1988.

Inglis, Andrew F. *Behind the Tube.* Boston: Focal Press, 1990.

Keirstead, Phillip O., and Keirstead, S. K. *The World of Telecommunication.* Stoneham, Mass.: Focal Press, 1990.

Keith, Michael C. *Signals in the Air: Native Broadcasting in America.* Westport, Conn.: Praeger Publishing, 1995.

—. *Voices in the Purple Haze: Underground Radio and the Sixties.* Westport, Conn.: Praeger Publishing, 1997.

—. *Talking Radio: An Oral History of Radio in the Television Age.* Armonk, N.Y.: M. E. Sharpe, 2000.

—. *Sounds in the Dark: All Night Radio in American Life.* Ames, Iowa: Iowa State Press, 2001.

Ladd, Jim. *Radio Waves.* New York: St. Martin's Press, 1991.

Lazarsfeld, Paul F., and Kendall, P.L. *Radio Listening in America.* Englewood Cliffs, N.J.: Prentice Hall, 1948.

Leinwall, Stanley. *From Spark to Satellite.* New York: Charles Scribner's Sons, 1979.

Levinson, Richard. *Stay Tuned.* New York: St. Martin's Press, 1982.

Lewis, Peter, ed. *Radio Drama.* New York: Longman, 1981.

Lewis, Tom. *Empire of the Air: The Men Who Made Radio.* New York: HarperCollins Publishers, 1991.

Lichty, Lawrence W., and Topping, M.C. *American Broadcasting: A Source Book on the History of Radio and Television.* New York: Hastings House, 1976.

Looker, Thomas. *The Sound and the Story.* Boston: Houghton Mifflin, 1995.

MacDonald, J. Fred. *Don't Touch That Dial: Radio Programming in American Life, 1920–1960.* Chicago: Nelson Hall, 1979.

Matelski, Marilyn. *Vatican Radio.* Westport, Conn.: Praeger Publishing, 1995.

McLuhan, Marshall. *Understanding Media: The Extensions of Man.* New York: McGraw-Hill, 1964.

Morrow, Bruce. *Cousin Brucie.* New York: Morrow, 1987.

Nachman, Gerald, O'Donnell, Lewis B., et al. *Radio Station Operations: Management and Employee Perspectives.* Belmont, Calif.: Wadsworth Publishing, 1989.

Naughton, John. *A Brief History of the Future: From Radio Days to Internet Years in a Lifetime.* Woodstock, NY: Overlook Press, 2000.

Orlik, Peter B. *Electronic Media Criticism.* Boston: Focal Press, 1994.

Paley, William S. *As It Happened: A Memoir.* Garden City, N.Y.: Doubleday, 1979.

Pease, Edward C., and Dennis, Everette E. *Radio: The Forgotten Medium.* New Brunswick, N.J.: Transaction Press, 1995.

Pierce, John R. *Signals.* San Francisco: W. H. Freeman, 1981.

Pusateri, C. Joseph. *Enterprise in Radio.* Washington, D.C.: University Press of America, 1980.

Radio Facts. New York: Radio Advertising Bureau, 1988.

Rhoads, B. Eric. *Blast from the Past.* West Palm Beach, Fla.: Streamline Press, 1996.

Routt, Ed. *The Business of Radio Broadcasting.* Blue Ridge Summit, Pa.: Tab Books, 1972.

Sarnoff, David. *The World of Television.* Agoura Hills, Calif.: Wisdom, 1958.

Schiffer, Michael B. *The Portable Radio in American Life.* Tucson: University of Arizona Press, 1991.

Seidle, Ronald J. *Air Time.* Boston: Holbrook Press, 1977.

Settle, Irving. *A Pictorial History of Radio.* New York: Grosset and Dunlap, 1967.

Shapiro, Mitchell E. *Radio Network Prime Time Programming, 1927–1967.* Jefferson, N.C.: McFarland, 2002.

Sipemann, Charles A. *Radio's Second Chance*. Boston: Little, Brown, 1946.

Sklar, Rick. *Rocking America: How the All-Hit Radio Stations Took Over*. New York: St. Martin's Press, 1984.

Smith, F. Leslie. *Perspectives on Radio and Television: An Introduction to Broadcasting in the United States*. New York: Harper & Row, 1979.

Soley, Larry. *Free Radio*. Denver: Westview Press, 1999.

Sterling, Christopher H., ed. *Encyclopedia of Radio*. New York: Fitzroy Dearborn, 2003.

Utterback, Ann S. *Broadcasters Survival Guide*. San Francisco: Bonus Books, 1997.

Vowell, Sarah. *Radio On: A Listener's Diary*. New York: St. Martin's Press, 1997.

Wertheim, Arthur F. *Radio Comedy*. New York: Oxford University Press, 1979.

Whetmore, Edward J. *The Magic Medium: An Introduction to Radio in America*. Belmont, Calif.: Wadsworth Publishing, 1981.

—. *MediaAmerica*, 4th ed. Belmont, Calif.: Wadsworth Publishing, 1989.

Woolley, Lynn. *The Last Great Days of Radio*. Dallas: Republic of Texas Press, 1995.

Yoder, Andrew. *Pirate Radio Stations*. New York: McGraw-Hill, 2001.

Station
Management
2

Nature of the Business

Today radio management means something different than it did just a decade ago. In most markets, especially in larger ones, things have gone from managing a single outlet to overseeing the operations of a half dozen, often clustered in the same building. More than ever, the medium's unique character requires that the manager deal with a broad mix of people, from on-air personalities to secretaries, and from sales personnel to technicians. Few other businesses can claim such an amalgam of employees. Even the station manager of the smallest outlet with as few as six or eight employees must direct individuals with very diverse backgrounds and goals. For example, radio station WXXX in a small Maine community may employ three to four full-time air people, who likely were brought in from other areas of the country. The deejays have come to WXXX to begin their broadcasting careers with plans to gain some necessary experience and move on to larger markets. Within a matter of a few months the station will probably be looking for replacements.

Frequent turnover of on-air personnel at small stations is a fact of life. As a consequence, members of the air staff often are regarded as transients or passers-through by not only the community but also the other members of the station's staff. Less likely to come and go are a station's administrative and technical staff. Usually they are not looking toward the bright lights of the bigger markets, since the town in which the station is located is often home to them. A small station's sales department may experience some turnover but usually not to the degree that the programming department does. Salespeople also are likely to have been recruited from the ranks of the local citizenry, whereas air personalities more typically come from outside the community.

Running a station in a small market presents its own unique challenges (and it should be noted that half of the nation's radio outlets are located in communities with fewer than 25,000 residents). Stations in larger markets, however, typically are faced with stiffer competition and fates that often are tied directly to ratings. In contrast to station WXXX in the small Maine community, where the closest other station is 50 miles away and therefore no competitive threat, an outlet located in a metropolitan area may share the airwaves with 30 or more other broadcasters. Competition is intense, and radio stations in large urban areas usually succeed or fail based on their showing in the latest listener surveys. The metro market station manager must pay close attention to what surrounding broadcasters are doing, while striving to maintain the best product possible in order to retain a competitive edge and prosper.

Meanwhile, the government's perception of the radio station's responsibility to its consumers also sets it apart from other industries. Since its inception, radio's business has been Washington's business, too. Station managers, unlike the heads of most other enterprises, have had to conform to the dictates of a federal agency especially conceived for the purpose of overseeing their activities. Failing to satisfy the FCC's expectations can result in stiff penalties such as fines and even the loss of an operating license; as a result, radio station managers have been obliged to keep up with a fairly prodigious volume of rules and regulations.

The 1980s and 1990s deregulation actions designed to unburden the broadcaster of what had been regarded by many as unreasonable government intervention have made the life of the station manager somewhat less complicated. Nevertheless, the government continues to play an impor-

tant role in American radio, and managers who value their license wisely invest energy and effort in fulfilling federal conditions. After all, a radio station without a frequency is just a building with a lot of expensive equipment.

The listener's perception of the radio business, even in this day and age when nearly every community with a small business district has a radio station, is often unrealistic. The portrayal by film and television of the radio station as a hotbed of zany characters and bizarre antics has helped foster a misconception. This is not to suggest that radio stations are the most conventional places to work. Because it is the station's function to provide entertainment to its listeners, it must employ creative people, and where these people are gathered, be it a small town or a large city, the atmosphere is sure to be charged. "The volatility of the air staff's emotions and the oscillating nature of radio itself actually distinguishes our business from others," observes Kentucky station manager J.G. Salter.

Faced with an audience whose needs and tastes sometimes change overnight, today's radio station has become adept at shifting gears as conditions warrant. What is currently popular in music, fashion, and leisure-time activities will be nudged aside tomorrow by something new. This, says broadcast manager Randy Lane, forces radio stations to stay one step ahead of all trends and fads. "Being on the leading edge of American culture makes it necessary to undergo more changes and updates than is usually the case in other businesses. Not adjusting to what is currently in vogue can put a station at a distinct disadvantage. You have to stay in touch with what is happening in your own community as well as the trends and cultural movements occurring in other parts of the country."

The complex internal and external factors that derive from the unusual nature of the radio business make managing today's station a formidable challenge. Perhaps no other business demands as much from its

FIGURE 2.1
Newspaper listing of radio stations in a major market. Large cities such as New York, Chicago, Los Angeles, and Philadelphia often have more than 60 stations.

Station	AM	FM	Station	AM	FM
WABC	770		WLIR		92.7
WADB		95.9	WLIX	540	
WADO	1280		WLTW		106.7
WALK	1370	97.5	WMCA	570	
WAPP		103.5	WMCX		88.1
WAWZ	1380	99.1	WMGQ		98.3
WBAB		102.3	WMJY		107.1
WBAI		99.5	WMTR	1250	
WBAU		90.3	WNBC	660	
WBGO		88.3	WNCN		104.3
WBJB		90.5	WNEW	1130	102.7
WBLI		106.1	WNJR	1430	
WBLS		107.5	WNNJ	1360	
WBRW	1170		WNYC	830	93.9
WCBS	880	101.1	WNYE		91.5
WCTC	1450		WNYG	1440	
WCTO		94.3	WNYM	1330	
WCWP		88.1	WNYU		89.1
WDHA		105.5	WOBM	1170	92.7
WERA	1590		WOR	710	
WEVD		97.9	WPAT	930	93.1
WFAS	1230	103.9	WPIX		101.9
WFDU		89.1	WPLJ		95.5
WFME		94.7	WPOW	1330	
WFMU		91.1	WPRB		103.3
WFUV		90.7	WPST		97.5
WGBB	1240		WPUT	1510	
WGLI	1290		WQXR	1560	96.3
WGRC	1300		WRAN	1510	
WGSM	740		WRCN	1570	103.9
WHBI		105.9	WRFM		105.1
WHLI	1100		WRHU		88.7
WHN	1050		WRKL	910	
WHPC		90.3	WRKS		98.7
WHTG	1410	106.3	WRTN		93.5
WHTZ		100.3	WRVH		105.5
WHUD		100.7	WSBH		95.3
WHWH	1350		WSIA		88.9
WICC	600		WSKQ	620.0	
WINS	1010		WSOU		89.5
WIXL		103.7	WSUS		102.3
WJDM	1530		WTHE	1520	
WJLK	1310	94.3	WUSB		90.1
WKCR		89.9	WVIP	1310	106.3
WKDM	1380		WVOX	1460	
WKJY		98.3	WVRM		89.3
WKMB	1070		WWDJ	970	
WKRB		90.9	WWRL	1600	
WKTU		92.3	WXMC	1310	
WKWZ		88.5	WYNY		97.1
WKXW		101.5	WYRS		98.7
WLIB	1190		WZFM		107.1
WLIM	1580				

managers. Conversely, few other businesses provide an individual with as much to feel good about. It takes a special kind of person to run a radio station.

The Manager as Chief Collaborator

There are many schools of thought concerning the approach to managing a radio station. For example, there are the standard X, Y, and Z models or theories of management (which admittedly oversimplify the subject but give the neophyte a basic working model). The first theory embraces the idea that the general manager is the captain of the vessel, the primary authority, with solemn, if not absolute, control of the decision-making process. The second theory casts the manager in the role of collaborator or senior advisor. The third theory forms a hybrid of the preceding two; the manager is both coach and team player, or chief collaborator. Of the three models, broadcast managers tend to favor the third approach.

Lynn Christian, who has served as general manager of several radio stations, preferred working for a manager who used the hybrid model rather than the purely authoritarian model. "Before I entered upper management, I found that I performed best when my boss sought my opinion and delegated responsibility to me. I believe in department head meetings and the full disclosure of projects within the top organization of the station. If you give someone the title, you should be prepared to give that person some authority, too. I respect the integrity of my people, and if I lose it, I replace them quickly. In other words, 'You respect me, and I'll respect you,' is the way I have always managed."

Randy Bongarten, radio network chief, concurs with Christian and adds, "Management styles have to be adaptive to individual situations so as to provide what is needed at the time. In general, the collaborator or team leader approach gets the job done. Of course, I don't think there is any one school of management that is right one hundred percent of the time."

Jim Arcara, another radio network head, also is an advocate of the hybrid management style. "It's a reflection of what is more natural to me as well as my company. Employees are capable of making key decisions, and they should be given the opportunity to do so. An effective manager also delegates responsibility."

General manager Pat McNally finds the collaborative approach suitable to his goals and temperament. "My management style is more collaborative. I believe in hiring qualified professional people, defining what I expect, and allowing them to do their job with input, support, and constructive criticism from me. My door is always open for suggestions, and I am a good listener. I consider this business something special, and I expect an extra special effort."

This also holds true for general manager Steven Woodbury. "I hire the best people as department heads and then work collaboratively with these experts. Department heads are encouraged to run their areas as if they had major ownership in the company. That instills a sense of team spirit too. Their energy level and decision-making efforts reflect this."

The manager/collaborator approach has gained in popularity in the past two decades. Radio functions well in a team-like atmosphere. Since practically every job in the radio station is designed to support and enhance the air product, establishing a connectedness among what is usually a small band of employees tends to yield the best results, contends station manager Jane Duncklee. "I strongly believe that employees must feel that they are a valid part of what is happening and that their input has a direct bearing on those decisions which affect them and the operation as a whole. I try to hire the best people possible and then let them do their jobs with a minimum of interference and a maximum of support."

Marlin R. Taylor, founder of Bonneville Broadcasting System and former manager of several major market radio outlets, including WRFM, New York, and WBCN, Boston, believes that the manager using the collaborative system of management gets the most out of employees. "When a staff member feels that his or her efforts and contributions make a difference and are appreciated, that person will remain motivated. This kind of employee works harder and delivers more. Most people, if they enjoy the job they have and like the organization they work for, are desirous of improving their level of performance and contributing to the health and well-being of the station. I really think that many station managers should devote even more time and energy to people development."

Station general manager Paul Aaron believes that managers must first assert their authority; that is, make it clear to all that they are in charge, before the transition to collaborator can take place. "It's a sort of process or evolution. Actually, when you come right down to it, any effective management approach includes a bit of both the authoritarian and collaborative concepts. The situation at the station will have a direct impact on the management style I personally deem most appropriate. As the saying goes, 'different situations call for different measures.' When assuming the reins at a new station, sometimes it is necessary to take a more dictatorial approach until the organization is where you feel it should be. Often a lot of cleanup and adjustments are necessary

FIGURE 2.2
Keeping the station solvent is the manager's primary task. Companies like this one help the manager do this. Courtesy CFM.

CASH FLOW MANAGEMENT - THE "KEY" TO SUCCESS IN RADIO

You know how it goes: Advertising sales made ... a commercial runs ... you bill the client or agency ... and finally, 60 to 90 days later, you receive payment for your services.

It's the nature of the business.

But delayed revenue can keep radio stations painfully short of cash. That restricts sales staff and puts a stranglehold on growth.

CAN YOU AFFORD TO LEAVE YOUR STATION ON HOLD?

FACTORING CLEARS THE WAY

Cash Flow Management has the answer. We specialize in operating capital for the radio industry. We will purchase your accounts receivable and monitor collections.

Factoring relieves cash flow problems on the spot, making cash available to drive sales.

Having **Dollars** available for operating capital is the key to success in the radio industry.

The **Bottom Line**. More profit potential.

EXPERIENCED FINANCIAL SERVICE

Cash Flow Management operates as an extension of your accounting department. You decide what level of your receivables you want to sell. You pay a nominal fee. We take it from there.

Operating in your name, we:
• Provide accounts receivable ledgering
• Review credit on all current and prospective customers
• Monitor invoices
• Submit bi-monthly aging reports

Our long experience in commercial finance can really pay off for you. Already we have established good working relationships in the industry. This means a professional for your team.

THE END OF RESTRICTED CASH FLOW

Why wait three to four months for your much needed revenues? With **Cash Flow Management** there's no debt, no more valuable time spent on hold, and you have immediate cash to apply to your company's growth.

Let us free your capital from the accounts receivable bottleneck today. We offer our services nationwide. For more details, use the reply card or call toll free 1-800-553-5679.

CASH FLOW MANAGEMENT
Reduce The Receivables Cycle

RADIO STATION → SALES → RUN ADVERTISEMENT → BILL AD AGENCY → BILL CLIENT → CLIENT PAYS AGENCY → AGENCY PAYS RADIO STATION

$ | $ CASH FLOW MANAGEMENT

Yes, my working capital has been on hold long enough! Tell me how **Cash Flow Management** can end the bottleneck and get my money moving again.

Name _____

Position _____

Company _____

Address _____

City _____ State ____ Zip _____

Phone _____ Ext. _____

Fax _____

REPLY CARD

TVandRadioJobs.com

VP/GENERAL MANAGER SOUGHT

Categories:	**Radio** **Television**
Ad Number:	**3166**
Date Posted:	**08/05/2003**
Contact:	Christy Norris Fair Bluff, NC
Telephone:	
E-Mail:	gmopening@wzfb.com
Web Site:	http://www.wzfb.com

Description

Music Radio 1480 WZFB is looking for a street savvy VP/General Manager who will lead our station to new heights in the Columbus, Robeson, Dillon and Marion Counties of North & South Carolina. We are a 24 hour Classic Hits station with a strong local following. Winning candidate must put sales first and be motivated by money. This is a great opportunity for a Sales Manager or high producing AE who is looking for that first big break into management. Salary is determined by results- you don't produce, you don't get paid: you do produce, you get paid handsomely. Only true producers need apply. Opening is limited to those within driving distance of the station; or, those who are willing to move themselves at their own expense.

Are you up to the challenge? Prove yourself by sending an email, with a resume attachment.

All inquiries will be held in strict confidence. Females & minorities are encouraged to apply. Solomon Radio Partners, Inc. is an equal opportunity employer.

before there can be a greater degree of equanimity. Ultimately, however, there should be equanimity."

Surveys have shown that most broadcast executives view the chief collaborator or hybrid management approach as compatible with their needs. "It has pretty much become the standard *modus operandi* in this industry. A radio manager must direct as well as invite input. To me it makes sense, in a business in which people are the product, to create an atmosphere that encourages self-expression, as well as personal and professional growth. After all, we are in the communications business. Everyone's voice should at least be heard," contends Lynn Christian.

FIGURE 2.3
Courtesy
TVandRadioJobs.com.

What Makes a Manager?

As in any other profession, the road to the top is seldom a short and easy one. It takes years to get there, and dues must be paid along the way. To begin, without a genuine affection for the business and a strong desire to succeed, it is unlikely that the position can ever be attained. Furthermore, without the proper training and experience, the top job will remain elusive. So then what goes into becoming a radio station manager? First, a good foundation is necessary. Formal education is a good place to start. Hundreds of institutions of higher learning across the country offer programs in broadcast operations. The college degree has achieved greater importance in radio over the last decade or two and, as in most other industries today, it has become a standard credential for those vying for management slots. Anyone entering broadcasting in the 2000s with aspirations to operate a radio station should acquire as much formal training as possible. Station managers with master's degrees are not uncommon. However, a bachelor's degree in communications gives the prospective station manager a good foundation from which to launch a career.

In a business that stresses the value of practical experience, seldom, if ever, does an individual land a management job directly out of college. In fact, most station managers have been in the business at least 15 years. "Once you get the theory nailed down you have to apply it. Experience is the best teacher. I've spent thirty years working in a variety of areas in the medium. In radio, in particular, hands-on experience is what matters," says station general manager Richard Bremkamp, Jr.

To radio station manager Roger Ingram, experience is what most readily opens the door to management. "While a degree is kind of like a union card in this day and age, a good track record is what wins the management job. You really must possess both."

Jane Duncklee began her ascent to station management by logging commercials for airplay, and eventually moved into other areas. "For the past seventeen years I have been employed by Champion Broad-

casting Systems. During that time I have worked in every department of the radio station, from traffic, where I started, to sales, programming, engineering, and finally management on both the local and corporate levels."

Many radio station managers are recruited from the sales area rather than programming. Since the general manager's foremost objective is to generate a profit, station owners usually feel more confident hiring someone with a solid sales or business background. Consequently, three out of four radio managers have made their living at some point selling airtime. It is a widely held belief that this experience best prepares an individual for the realities encountered in the manager's position. "I spent over a decade and a half in media sales before becoming a station manager. In fact, my experience on the radio level was exclusively confined to sales and then for only eight months. After that I moved into station management. Most of my radio-related sales experience took place on the national level with station rep companies," recalls Norm Feuer of Force Two Communications.

Station manager Carl Evans holds that a sales background is especially useful, if not necessary, to general managers. "I spent a dozen years as a station account executive, and prior to entering radio I represented various product lines to retailers. The key to financial success in radio exists in an understanding of retailing."

It is not uncommon for station managers to have backgrounds out of radio, but almost invariably their experience comes out of the areas of sales, marketing, and finance. Broadcaster Paul Aaron worked as a fundraiser for the United Way of America before entering radio, and contends that many managers come from other fields in which they have served in positions allied to sales, if not in sales itself. "Of those managers who have worked in fields other than radio, most have come to radio via the business sector. There are not many former biologists or glass blowers serving as station managers," says Aaron.

Although statistics show that the station salesperson has the best chance of being promoted to the station's head position (more general managers have held the sales manager's position than any other), a relatively small percentage of radio's managers come from the programming ranks. "I'm more the exception than the rule. I have spent all of my career in the programming side, first as a deejay at stations in Phoenix, Denver, and Pittsburgh, and then as program director for outlets in Kansas City and Chicago. I'll have to admit, however, that while it certainly is not impossible to become a GM [general manager] by approaching it from the programming side, resistance exists," admits station manager Randy Lane.

Many in the industry consider the programmer's role to be more an artistic function than one requiring a high degree of business savvy. However accurate or inaccurate this assessment is, the result is that fewer managers are hired with backgrounds exclusively confined to programming duties. Programmers have reason to be encouraged, however, since a trend in favor of hiring program directors (PDs) has surfaced in recent years, and predictions suggest that it will continue.

In its useful text pertaining to how PDs become station managers, *Up the Management Ladder: From Program Director to General Manager*, the NAB states:

The biggest obstacle facing the program director with an eye on management is image.

Programming is an operational expense. To create the "sound" of the station, the program director must spend money to pay staff salaries, to buy programming aids, and to maintain studio equipment. Where does the money come from? Sales.

And it used to be that only those who were in sales were considered for promotion. The reasoning? Those in sales, through the very nature of their jobs, had a solid understanding of the radio rule: Time = Money.

Those in sales, through the very nature of their jobs, also enjoyed the pursuit of more money.

"I get turned on," said one general sales manager, "when people tell me 'no.' I love getting them to say 'yes.'"

Program directors, it was believed, lacked that basic grounding. Concerned with creating the station's image, program directors inadvertently created an image for themselves as "creative" types without concern or respect for the "business" aspects of radio.

So how is the program director to compete?

By presenting skills you already possess in the most positive, business-oriented format and by getting the skills you don't already possess.

In reality, the most attractive candidate for a station management position is the one whose experience has involved both programming and sales responsibilities. No general manager can fully function without an understanding and appreciation of what goes into preparing and presenting the air product, nor can he or she hope for success without a keen sense of business and finance.

Today's highly competitive and complex radio market requires that the person aspiring to management have both formal training, preferably a college degree in broadcasting, and experience in all aspects of radio station operations, in particular sales and programming. Ultimately, the effort and energy an individual invests will bear directly on the dividends he or she earns, and there is not a single successful station manager who has not put in 15-hour days. The station manager is expected to know more and do more than anyone else, and rightfully so, since he or she is the person who stands to gain the most.

Radio group president Dan Mason relates the qualities he sees in the most successful station managers: "A keen sense of what is 'good business,' humility to take the blame in bad times and to give staff credit in good times, fairness and passion for all, responsiveness to situations (not reactionary), passion for the industry, recognition and knowledge of staff (know by first name), and ability to keep personal problems out of the station."

The Manager's Duties and Responsibilities

A primary objective of the station manager is to operate in a manner that generates the most profit, while maintaining a positive and productive attitude among station employees. This is more of a challenge than it may seem at first, claims radio broadcaster Cliff Shank. "In order to meet the responsibility that you are faced with daily, you really have to be an expert in so many areas: sales, marketing, finance, legal matters, technical, governmental, and programming. It helps if you're an expert in human nature, too." Jane Duncklee puts it this way: "Managing a radio station requires that you divide yourself equally into at least a dozen parts and be a 100 percent whole in each situation." In the new Telecommunications Act of 1996 environment, consultant Ed Shane observes, "The duties for station managers have changed radically. For example, Chris Wegmann, manager of the Capstar cluster at Baton Rouge, has responsibility for several AM and FM stations in other parts of Louisiana and Texas. Talk about dividing yourself."

In today's consolidated environment, this is more common than not; says Jay Williams, "Mike Glickenhaus, a Clear Channel vice president and market manager, originally oversaw 9 FM stations in the San Diego cluster."

Station owner Bill Campbell says that the theme that runs throughout the classic Tom Peters's book, *In Search of Excellence*, is one that is relevant to the station manager's task today. "The idea in Peters's book is that you must make the customer happy, get your people involved, and get rid of departmental waste and unnecessary expenditures. A station should be a lean and healthy organism."

Station managers themselves generally must answer to a higher authority. The majority of radio stations, roughly 90 percent, are owned by companies and corporations that both hire the manager and establish financial goals or projections for the station. It is the station manager's job to see that corporate expectations are met and, ideally, exceeded. Managers who fail to operate a facility in a way that satisfies the corporate hierarchy may soon find themselves looking for another job.

Fewer than 10 percent of the nation's stations are owned by individuals or partnerships. At these radio outlets the manager still must meet the expectations of the station owner(s). In some cases, the manager may be given more latitude or responsibility in determining the station's fate, whereas in others the owner may play a greater role in the operation of the station.

It is a basic function of the manager's position to formulate station policy and see that it is implemented. To ensure against confusion, misunderstanding, and possible unfair labor practices that typically impede operations, employees often receive a station policy manual. This manual states the station's positions on a host of issues, such as hiring, termination, salaries, raises, promotions, sick leave, vacation, benefits, and so forth. As standard practice a station may require that each new employee read and become familiar with the contents of the policy manual before actually starting work. Job descriptions, as well as organization flowcharts, commonly are outlined to make it abundantly clear to staff members who is responsible for what. A well-conceived policy book may contain a statement of the station's programming philosophy with an explanation of the format it employs. The more comprehensive a policy book, the less likely there will be confusion and disruption.

Hiring and retaining good people are other key managerial functions. "You have some pretty delicate egos to cope with in this business. Radio attracts some very bright and highly talented people, sometimes with erratic temperaments. Keeping harmony and keeping people are among the foremost challenges facing a station manager," claims Norm Feuer.

Steve Woodbury agrees with Feuer, adding, "You have to hire the right people and motivate them properly, and that's a challenge. You have to be capable of inspiring people. Actually, if you are unable to motivate your people, the station will fail to reach its potential. Hire the best people you can and nurture them."

Says cluster market manager Mike Glickenhaus, "You make sure you have a lot of great people. You need more key people who you can give lots of responsibility to because you don't have time to micromanage them. It's important to hire the right people and then clearly lay out the vision, goals, and many of the steps that will be necessary and agree on them. You need people who understand what it takes, what they have to do, and have the direction to get there. Then as manager you have to decide what (projects or problems) you're going to apply your time to."

As mentioned earlier, managers of small market radio stations are confronted with a unique set of problems when it comes to hiring and holding onto qualified people, especially on-air personnel. "In our case, finding and keeping a professional-sounding staff with our somewhat limited budget is an ongoing problem. This is true at most small market stations, however," observes station manager J.G. Salter.

The rural station is where the majority of newcomers gain their experience. Because salaries are necessarily low and the fledgling air person's ambitions are usually high, the rate of turnover is significant. Managers of small outlets spend a great deal of time training people. "It is a fact of the business that radio people, particularly deejays, usually learn their trade at the 'out-of-the-way,' low-power outlet. To be a manager at a small station, you have to be a teacher, too. But it can be very rewarding despite the

Chart toppers

2002 rank	2000 rank	Radio group	2001 rev. millions
1	1	Clear Channel	$3,265.4
2	2	Infinity	$2,081.1
3	3	Cox Radio	$431.4
4	5	Entercom	$407.9
5	4	ABC Radio	$403.9
6	6	Citadel	$312.6
7	7	Radio One	$287.6
8	11	Cumulus Media	$267.1
9	9	Univision*	$256.1
10	8	Emmis	$251.1
11	10	Susquehanna Radio	$224.0
12	12	Bonneville	$188.8
13	13	Greater Media	$153.4
14	17	Salem	$132.9
15	15	Jefferson-Pilot	$126.2
16	14	Spanish Broadcasting	$122.4
17	16	Beasley	$115.7
18	18	Saga	$100.1
19	20	Entravision	$69.4
20	19	Journal Broadcast	$69.2
21	24	Regent	$64.4
22	21	Sandusky Radio	$58.2
23	22	Inner City	$57.0
24	25	NextMedia	$52.8
25	NR	Lotus	$45.9

* Pending approval of Univision's purchase of Hispanic Broadcasting
NR = Not in the Top 25 last year
Source: BIA Financial

FIGURE 2.4

Radio is a huge money business run by top managers. Courtesy Broadcasting & Cable.

obvious problem of having to rehire to fill positions so often. We deal with many beginners. I find it exciting and gratifying, and no small challenge, to train newcomers in the various aspects of radio broadcasting," says Salter.

Randy Lane enjoys the instructor's role also, but notes that the high turnover rate affects product continuity. "With air people coming and going all the time, it can give the listening public the impression of instability. The last thing a station wants to do is sound schizophrenic. Establishing an image of dependability is crucial to any radio station. Changing air people every other month doesn't help. As a station manager, it is up to you to do the best you can with the resources at hand. In general, I think small market managers do an incredible job with what they have to work with."

Whereas managers of small market stations must wrestle with the problems stemming from diminutive budgets and high employee turnover, those at large stations must grapple with the difficulties inherent in managing larger budgets, bigger staffs, and, of course, stiffer competition. "It's all relative, really. While the small town station gives the manager turnover headaches, the metropolitan station manager usually is caught up in the ratings battle, which consumes vast amounts of time and energy. Of course, even larger stations are not immune to turnover," observes KGLD's Bremkamp.

It is up to the manager to control the station's finances. A knowledge of book-keeping and accounting procedures is necessary. "You handle the station's purse-strings. An understanding of budgeting is an absolute must. Station economics is the responsibility of the GM. The idea is to control income and expenses in a way that yields a sufficient profit," says Roger Ingram.

The manager allocates and approves spending in each department (in cluster operations this means each station). Heads of departments must work within the budgets they have helped establish. Budgets generally cover the expenses involved in the operation of a particular area within the station for a specified period of time, such as a 6- or 12-month period. No manager wants to spend more than is absolutely required. A thorough familiarity with what is involved in running the various departments within a station prevents waste and overspending. "A manager has to know what is going on in programming, engineering, sales, actually every little corner of the station, in order to run a tight ship and make the most revenue possible. Off course, you should never cut corners simply for the sake of cutting corners. An operation must spend in order to make. You have to have effective cost control in all departments. That doesn't mean damaging the product through under-nourishment either," says Evans.

David Saperstein, president of Metro Networks, observes that, "In the early days, radio was a mom-and-pop type of business. With the huge dollars in radio today, one mistake could cost a station hundreds of thousands or even millions of dollars in revenue."

To ensure that the product the station offers is the best it can be, the station manager must keep in close touch with every department. Since the station's sound is what wins listeners, the manager must work closely with the program director and engineer. Both significantly contribute to the quality of the air product. The program director is responsible for what goes on the air, and the engineer is responsible for the way it sounds.

Meanwhile, the marketing of the product is vital. This falls within the province of the sales department. Traditionally, the general manager works more closely with the station's sales manager than with anyone else.

An excellent air product attracts listeners, and listeners attract sponsors. It is as basic as that. The formula works when all departments in a station work in unison and up to their potential, contends Marlin R. Taylor. "In radio our product is twofold—the programming we send over our frequency and the listening audience we deliver to advertisers. A station's success is linked to customer/listener satisfaction, just like a retail store's. If you don't have what the consumer desires, or the quality doesn't meet his standards, he'll go elsewhere and generally won't return."

In a fast-moving, dynamic industry like radio, where both cultural and technological innovations have an impact on the way a station operates, the manager must stay informed and keep one eye toward the future. Financial projections must be based on data that include the financial implications of prospective and predicted events. An effective manager anticipates change and develops appropriate plans to deal with it. Industry trade journals (*Broadcasting and Cable, Radio and Records, The Radio Ink, Radio Business Report*) and conferences conducted by organizations such as the National Association of Broadcasters (NAB)

Volume Two, 1993-1994

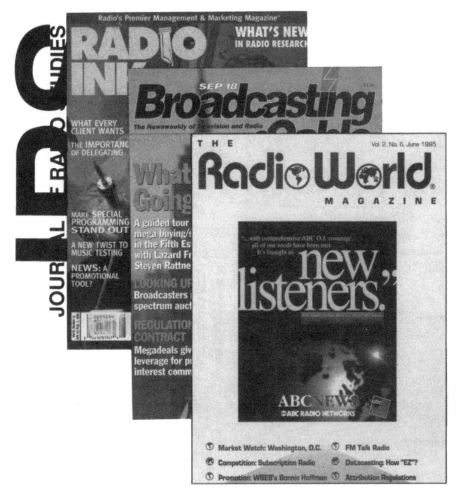

FIGURE 2.5
Publications such as these keep managers informed of industry developments and issues.

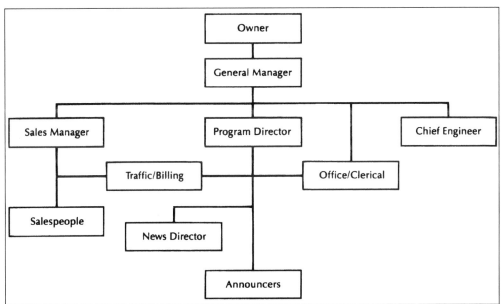

FIGURE 2.6
Organizational structure of a small market radio station.

and the Radio Advertising Bureau (RAB) help keep the station manager informed of what tomorrow may bring.

About industry trade journals, Ed Shane observes, "The consultant (not the comedian) George Burns once said 'Never has so much been written by so many about so few.' The differences in today's trades compared to just a few years ago are significant. *Inside Radio, Radio Only, Radio Business Report's Radio News Today, R&R's Hot Wax,* and *Alternative Radio Confidential* are all paperless papers. *Broadcasting* is now *Broadcasting and Cable.* What does that say to the student of radio as a career? *R&R* [*Radio and Records*] claims more company executives subscribe to it than any other trade, which was formerly *Broadcasting's* forte. Nonetheless, you have to read them to be up to date."

FIGURE 2.7
A cluster organizational chart.

Station consultants and "rep companies," which sell local station airtime to national advertising agencies, also support the manager in his or her efforts to keep on top of things. "A station manager must utilize all that is available to stay in touch with what's out there. Foresight is an essential ingredient for any radio manager. Hindsight is not enough in an industry that operates with one foot in the future," says Lynn Christian, who summarizes the duties and responsibilities of a station manager: "To me the challenges of running today's radio station include building and maintaining audience ratings, attracting and keeping outstanding employees, increasing gross revenues annually, and creating a positive community image for the station, not necessarily in that order." Richard Bremkamp is more laconic. "It boils down to one sentence: Protect the license and turn a profit."

Organizational Structure

Radio stations come in all sizes and generally are classified as being either small, medium, or large (metro) market outlets (see figures 2.6 and 2.7). The size of the community that a station serves usually reflects the size of its staff. That is to say, the station in a town of 5,000 residents may have as few as three or four full-time employees. It is a question of economics. However, some small market radio outlets have staffs that rival those of larger market stations because their income warrants it. Few small stations earn enough to have elaborate staffs, however. Out of financial necessity, an employee may serve in several capacities. The station's manager also may assume the duties of sales manager, and announcers often handle news responsibilities. Meanwhile, everyone, including the station's secretary, may write commercial copy. The key word at the small station is flexibility, since each member of the staff is expected to perform numerous tasks.

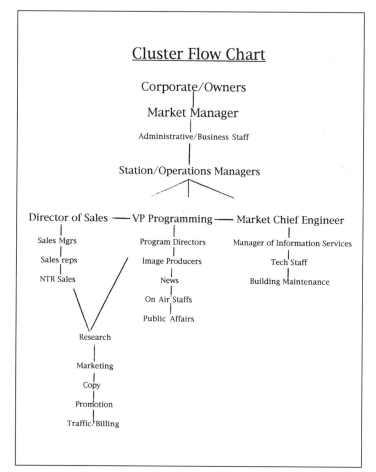

Cluster Flow Chart

Corporate/Owners
|
Market Manager
|
Administrative/Business Staff
|
Station/Operations Managers

Director of Sales —— VP Programming —— Market Chief Engineer
| | |
Sales Mgrs   Program Directors   Manager of Information Services
| | |
Sales reps   Image Producers   Tech Staff
| | |
NTR Sales   News   Building Maintenance
|
On Air Staffs
|
Public Affairs

Research
|
Marketing
|
Copy
|
Promotion
|
Traffic/Billing

Norman Feuer | The Qualities That Make a Station Manager

1. Smart/intelligent. This is something that I cannot teach or help someone with; they are either smart or they're not.
2. Organized. A GM or GSM [general sales manager] has a lot on his or her plate, especially with the limited time available to accomplish what has to be done. An unorganized person will waste that time.
3. Good communicator. As a group head, I too have a lot on my plate. I must rely on my managers to communicate with me quickly and efficiently. If they can do that, I have the comfort that they are able to communicate effectively with their staff on the station's missions and goals to be accomplished.
4. Strategic thinker. In today's world there's no such thing as a quick fix. Therefore, I need to have someone who can think through the long-term effects of each major decision that he or she makes.
5. Motivated. In my opinion, you cannot motivate people; they are either self-motivated or not. All I can do is set a work environment that motivates them to do their best.
6. Businesslike. I need a person who understands that this is a business, not a hobby, and that every decision that they make has a return on investment and will lead to a successful business conclusion.
7. Leader. I want a person who is a winner, for whom people want to work, with the ability to read personnel, hire the best people, and be able to maximize the potential of all his or her people.
8. Has a good track record. Although it is nice to be able to find someone who has a winning track record on all or most of his or her previous assignments, we also understand that no one is born a GM or GSM. Therefore, it is not always a criterion.
9. Has a high energy level. I've always felt that you can determine a successful person by watching the way he or she walks down the hallway. I believe a person with a high energy level tends to get his or her people to move at a higher level also.
10. Honest and has integrity. It is absolutely critical that you trust your manager, and trust that he or she won't try to make excuses and place blame on other people. This is a very hard ingredient to determine up front and may have to be acquired eventually.

Medium market stations are located in more densely populated areas. An outlet in a city with a population of between 100,000 and a half million may be considered medium sized. Albany, New York; Omaha, Nebraska; and Albuquerque, New Mexico, are typical medium markets. Greater competition exists in these markets, more than in the small market where only one or two stations may be vying for the listening audience. Each of the medium markets cited has over a dozen stations.

The medium market radio station averages 12 to 20 employees. Although an overlapping of duties does occur even in the larger station, positions usually are more limited to specific areas of responsibility. Seldom do announcers substitute as news people. Nor do salespeople fill airshifts as is frequently the case at small outlets. (Reexamine figure 1.30, a medium market flowchart.)

Large (also referred to as major or metro) market radio stations broadcast in the nation's most populated urban centers. New York, Los Angeles, and Chicago rank first, second, and third, respectively. The top 20 radio markets also include cities such as Houston, Philadelphia, Boston, Detroit, and San Francisco. Competition is greatest in the large markets, where as many as 70 stations may be dividing the audience pie.

When stations are purchased by large radio companies, positions are typically consolidated and centralized. For example, middle management slots (sales manager, program director, etc.) may be eliminated at the local station.

Ward Quaal

My Management Philosophy

1. To succeed, radio stations must rededicate themselves to "localism" and their involvement in every possible phase of activity within their respective community (this applies regardless of format).
2. Regardless of the size of the market involved, those people who are making the news, whether in the world of academia, government, politics in general, and civic leadership, must become a part of a radio station's total operation. In short, management must encourage and develop their participation so as to add to the richness and the superior culture of the property.
3. Basic to every radio operation and ultimate success is policy control over commercial material–its length, its acceptability to a station of the type involved, and passing of the "test" as to whether the commercial and the station complement one another.

FIGURE 2.8
Ward Quaal.

Major market stations employ as many as 50 to 60 people and as few as 20, depending on the nature of their format. Stations relying on automation, regardless of the size of their market, usually employ fewer people. Keep in mind, too, that station clustering and consolidation have changed the personnel landscape at many stations, as radio groups often concentrate the operation of several stations in one center. Station clusters often employ over 100 people.

The following brief descriptions of department head duties and responsibilities are explained more fully in later chapters. These individuals are regarded as station middle management and generally report directly to the station's manager. In cluster operations these positions are often expanded or eliminated all together.

Operations Manager

Second only to the general manager in level of authority, the operations manager (not all stations have such a slot) is sometimes considered the station's assistant manager. The operations manager's duties include the following:

- Supervising administrative (office) staff
- Helping to develop station policies and see that they are implemented
- Handling departmental budgeting
- Keeping abreast of government rules and regulations pertaining to the entire operation
- Working as the liaison with the community to ensure that the station provides appropriate service and maintains its "good guy" image

Duties tend to be more skewed toward programming and may even include the job of station programmer or, as in the age of station clustering, the operations manager may be responsible for a radio group's programming and direct its individual station PDs. In cases such as this, the operations manager's duties are designed with a primary emphasis on on-air operations. Assistant program directors commonly are appointed to work with the operations manager to accomplish programming goals. Not all stations have established this position, preferring the department head reporting to station manager approach.

Program Director

One of the three key department head positions at a radio station, the program director is responsible for the following:

- Developing and executing format
- Hiring and managing air staff
- Establishing the schedule of airshifts
- Monitoring the station to ensure consistency and quality of product
- Keeping abreast of competition and trends that may affect programming
- Maintaining the music library
- Complying with FCC rules and regulations
- Directing the efforts of the news and public affairs areas

Sales Manager

The sales manager's position (called Director of Sales in cluster operations) is a pivotal one at any radio station, and involves the following:

- Generating station income by directing the sale of commercial airtime
- Supervising sales staff
- Working with the station's rep company to attract national advertisers
- Assigning lists of retail accounts and local advertising agencies to salespeople
- Establishing sales quotas
- Coordinating on-air and in-store sales promotions
- Developing sales materials and rate cards

In cluster situations, a group general sales manager may direct the efforts of individual sales managers or account executives.

Chief Engineer

The chief engineer's job is a vital station function. Responsibilities include the following:

- Operating the station within prescribed technical parameters established by the FCC
- Purchasing, repairing, and maintaining equipment
- Monitoring signal fidelity
- Adapting studios for programming needs
- Setting up remote broadcast operations
- Working closely with the programming department

Human Resources

The management of station personnel constitutes one of the manager's greatest challenges. What follows is prominent radio executive Dick Oppenheimer's perspective on the subject: "One of the oldest sayings I can remember is that the more things change, the more they stay the same. Perhaps, but that adage certainly does not apply to the radio industry any longer.

"Before there were LMAs, duopolies, and super-duopolies, you were the manager of one or, at most, two radio stations. Now the norm is to manage at least six in your market. This is an industry where the inventory is time and the commodity is people. In fact, radio is a business totally driven by people.

"I can remember the days when almost anything was acceptable. The radio station was a totally male-dominated environment, except for the few female administrative assistants (clerks and secretaries). As a male manager you flattered, pampered, complimented, and cajoled the women employees. The station was a close-knit family whereby if you did not make notice of the appearance of a female worker she was insulted. If you did not put your arm around her, it meant you did not care. Likewise, if you did not insult or intimidate a male employee, something was wrong. Now, any and all of that can and probably will inspire a lawsuit–one you cannot win no matter what the outcome.

"The typical radio station had perhaps fifteen employees and although you had middle managers you were truly 'hands-on.' The manager was more than just the boss, he was priest, rabbi, psychologist, big brother, confidant, and so on. Today, with upward of 100 employees, you can no longer be 'hands-on.' You are now a corporate figurehead. You are responsible to and for your corporation for the day-to-day operations of your slew of radio stations.

"Today's radio station is far different from the one of ten or twenty years ago. Now there's a host of considerations you as manager must keep a watchful eye on, including sexual harassment, job discrimination, hostile work environment, disabilities acts, and race, religion, and gender issues. That's for starters.

"The first thing a manager must do is learn all the rules and laws concerning areas that impact human resources. You shouldn't attempt this yourself. Hire and retain an attorney who specializes in labor law. Have the attorney write an employee manual and establish the policies that are necessary for you to be a competent personnel manager. Once you have done this, have an initial meeting with your management staff and your attorney to convey the information necessary to assist your people in their management of other people.

"Next have your employees acknowledge receipt of the manual, and each and every quarter have reviews with your management staff regarding the various policies outlined in the manual as a means of detecting and assessing any potential problems.

"Document everything. *Remember, if it is not in writing, it did not occur.* When an employee comes to you with a complaint, have someone else present to verify the discussion and its content. Keep in mind that in a courtroom, you are the defendant. All

the employee has to say is that it happened. The burden of proof is yours.

"Of course, one of the best ways to prevent problems is through proper hiring. It has been my experience that, often times, the employee who files charges against you is a marginal or questionable employee. That is to say, an employee who should not have been hired in the first place. Unfortunately, it is not until a suit has been filed that you learn about an employee's history of filing complaints. However, there are times when a complaint is legitimate. Real problems can and do exist. You have to be mindful of this.

"Handling people is one of the significant challenges of any manager. It is also one of the most rewarding."

Whom Do Managers Hire?

Managers want to staff their stations with the most qualified individuals. Their criteria go beyond education and work experience to include various personality characteristics. "A strong resume is important, but the type of person is what really decides it for me. The goal is to hire someone who will fit in nicely with the rest of the station's members. A station is a bit like a family in that it is never too large and people are in fairly close contact with one another. Integrity, imagination, intelligence, and a desire to succeed are the basic qualities that I look for when hiring," says Maine station manager Christopher Spruce.

Ambition and a positive attitude are attributes that rank high among most managers. "People with a sincere desire to be the best, to win, are the kind who really bolster an operation. Our objective when I headed Viacom Radio was to be number one at what we did, so any amount of negativity or complacency was viewed as counterproductive," says Norm Feuer. Lynn Christian, who once served as Feuer's boss while manager of a Miami radio station, says that competitiveness and determination are among the qualities he, too, looks for, and adds loyalty and dedication to the list. "Commitment to the station's philosophy and goals must exist in every employee or there are soft spots in the operation. In today's marketplace you have to operate from a position of strength, and this takes a staff that is with you all the way."

Stability and reliability are high on any manager's list. Radio is known as a nomadic profession, especially the programming end. Deejays tend to come and go, sometimes disappearing in the night. "A manager strives to staff his station with dependable people. I want an employee who is stable and there when he or she is supposed to be," states Duncklee.

A station can ill afford to shut down because an air person fails to show up for his or her scheduled shift. When a no-show occurs, the station's continuity is disrupted both internally and externally. Within the station, adjustments must be made to fill the void created by the absent employee. At the same time, a substitute deejay often detracts from efforts to instill in the audience the feeling that they can rely on the station.

Managers are wary of individuals with fragile or oversized egos. "No prima donnas, please! I want a person who is able to accept constructive criticism and use it to his or her advantage without feeling that he is being attacked. The ability to look at oneself objectively and make the adjustments that need to be made is very important," observes manager Cliff Shank. Carl Evans echoes his sentiments. "Open-mindedness is essential. An employee who feels that he can't learn anything from anyone or is never wrong is usually a fly in the ointment."

Honesty and candor are universally desired qualities, says Bremkamp. "Every station manager appreciates an employee who is forthright and direct, one who does not harbor ill feelings or unexpressed opinions and beliefs. An air of openness keeps things from seething and possibly erupting.

I prefer an employee to come to me and say what is on his or her mind, rather than keep things sealed up inside. The lid eventually pops and then you have a real problem on your hands."

Self-respect and esteem for the organization are uniquely linked, claims J.G. Salter. "If an individual does not feel good about himself, he cannot feel good about the world around him. This is not a question of ego, but rather one of appropriate self-perception. A healthy self-image and attitude in an employee makes that person easier to manage and work with. The secret is identifying potential problems or weaknesses in prospective employees before you sign them on. It's not easy without a degree in Freud."

Other personal qualities that managers look for in employees are patience, enthusiasm, discipline, creativeness, logic, and compassion. "You look for as much as you can during the interview and, of course, fill in the gaps with phone calls to past employers. After that, you hope that your decision bears fruit," says Spruce.

The Manager and the Profit Motive

Earlier we discussed the unique nature of the radio medium and the particular challenges that face station managers as a consequence. Radio, indeed, is a form of show business, and both words of the term are particularly applicable since the medium is at once stage and store. Radio provides entertainment to the public and, in turn, sells the audience it attracts to advertisers.

The general manager or market manager is answerable to many: the station's owners and corporate heads, listeners, and sponsors. However, to keep his or her own job, the manager must first please the owner or corporate manager. More often than not, this person's number one concern is profit. As in any business, the more money the manager generates, the happier the owner.

Observes Ed Shane, "The new radio paradigm is 'manager as financial expert.' Pressure from corporate ownership to feed stock prices has changed the way managers think about their stations. Budgets, once an annual affair, are reevaluated quarterly and even monthly. Managers now must be prepared at a moment's notice to cancel planned advertising expenditures or to move the expenditures into another quarter if the local cluster (or the company's region) is not making budgets. 'Budgets' does not mean breaking even. It means achieving the percentage increase over the previous year's cash flow. Margins of 45 to 50 percent are not uncommon."

Critics have chided the medium for what they argue is an obsessive preoccupation with making money that has resulted in a serious shortage of high-quality, innovative programming. They lament too much sameness. Meanwhile, station managers often are content to air material that draws the kind of audience that advertisers want to reach.

Marlin Taylor observes that too many managers overemphasize profit at the expense of the operation. "Not nearly enough of the radio operators in this country are truly committed to running the best possible stations they can, either because that might cost them more money or they simply don't understand or care what it means to be the best. In my opinion, probably no more than 20 percent of the nation's stations are striving to become the IBM of radio, that is, striving for true excellence. Many simply are being milked for what the owners and managers can take out of them."

The pursuit of profits forces the station manager to employ the programming format that will yield the best payday. In several markets certain formats, such as classical and jazz, which tend to attract limited audiences, have been dropped in favor of those that draw greater numbers. In some instances, the actions of stations have caused outcries by unhappy and disenfran-chised listeners who feel that their programming needs are being disregarded. Several disgruntled listener groups have gone to court in an attempt to force stations to reinstate abandoned formats. Since the government currently avoids involvement in programming decisions, leaving it up to stations to do as they see fit, little has come of their protests.

The dilemma facing today's radio station manager stems from the complexity of having to please numerous factions while earning enough money to justify his or her continued existence at the station. Marlin Taylor has suggested that stations reinvest more of their profits as a method of upgrading the overall quality of the medium. "Overcutting can have deleterious effects. A station can be too lean, even anemic. In other words, you have to put something in to get something out. Too much draining leaves the operation arid and subject to criticism by the listening public. It behooves the station manager to keep this thought in mind and, if necessary, impress it upon ownership. The really successful operations know full well that money has to be spent to nurture and develop the kind of product that delivers both impressive financial returns and listener praise."

Although it is the manager who must deal with bottom-line expectations, it is also the manager who is expected to maintain product integrity. The effective manager takes pride in the unique role radio plays in society and does not hand it over to advertisers, notes station manager Bremkamp. "You have to keep close tabs on your sales department. They are out to sell the station, sometimes one way or the other. Overly zealous salespeople can, on occasion, become insensitive to the station's format in their quest for ad dollars. Violating the format is like mixing fuel oil with water. You may fill your tank for less money, but you're not likely to get very far. The onus is placed on the manager to protect the integrity of the product while making a dollar. Actually,

Paul Fiddick

What Makes a Successful Radio Manager?

FIGURE 2.9
Paul Fiddick.

In reflecting on "what qualities . . . make a radio manager successful," I've considered the dozens of managers who have worked for me in my stints running the Multimedia radio group (when they had one) and the last nine years with Heritage. And I've decided that there are two indicators that are essential (among others, I'm sure) for high performance. The first of these is a bias for action, or what industrial psychologists describe as task orientation. The concept of entrepreneurism is closely related to this, as is the quality of decisiveness. The radio manager must be innately tuned to the notion of taking the initiative if opportunities are to be exploited or—at a minimum—order is to be maintained.

The other quality is harder to describe. The term I have used is that successful managers take things personally. This may seem counterintuitive. Shouldn't managers retain a kind of cool objectivity with regard to their work?

What I've found is that the job is too demanding for that—at least at the highest levels. In order to overcome the frustrations that come from so many aspects of your performance being outside of your direct control (i.e., ratings, competitive changes, the fact that a music station's primary product is produced by someone else), the successful manager must be a driven personality, and that drive comes from an inner, personal need. I do not believe it coincidental that success and obsessiveness go hand in hand in the radio business.

doing the former usually takes care of the latter."

Conscientious station managers are aware of the obligations confronting them, and sensitive to the criticism that crass commercialism can produce a desert or "wasteland" of bland and uninspired programming. They are also aware that while gaps and voids may exist in radio programming and that certain segments of the population may not be getting exactly what they want, it is up to them to produce enough income to pay the bills and meet the ownership's expectations.

The Manager and the Community

In the early 1980s, the FCC reduced the extent to which radio stations must become involved in community affairs. (This deregulation process continued into the 1990s with the Republicans' creation of a sweeping telecommunications bill.) Ascertainment procedures requiring that stations determine and address community issues have all but been eliminated. If a station chooses to do so, it may spin the hits 24 hours a day and virtually divorce itself from the concerns of the community. However, a station that opts to function independently of the community to which it is licensed may find itself on the outside looking in. This is especially true of small market stations, which, for practical business reasons, traditionally have cultivated a strong connection with the community. Therefore, most stations do make an attempt to ascertain community issues and do so on a quarterly basis, maintaining the results of these surveys (often a list of the top-ten issues confronting the community of license) in their Public File to attest to their good citizenship. This looks particularly positive at license renewal time.

A station manager is aware that it is important to the welfare of his or her organization to behave as a good citizen and neighbor. Although the sheer number of stations in vast metropolitan areas makes it less crucial that a station exhibit civic mindedness, the small market radio outlet often finds that the level of business it generates is relative to its community involvement. Therefore, maintaining a relationship with the town leaders, civic groups, and religious leaders, among others, enhances a station's visibility and status and ultimately affects business. No small market station can hope to operate autonomously and attract the majority of local advertisers. Stations that remain aloof in the community in which they broadcast seldom realize their full revenue potential.

One of the nation's foremost figures in broadcast management, Ward Quaal, president of the Ward L. Quaal Company, observes, "A manager must not only be tied, or perhaps I should say 'married' to a station, but he or she must have total involvement in the community. This is very meaningful, whether the market is Cheyenne, Cincinnati, or Chicago. The community participation builds the proper image for the station and the manager and concurrently aids, dramatically, business development and produces lasting sales strength."

Cognizant of the importance of fostering an image of goodwill and civic mindedness, the station manager seeks to become a member in good standing in the community. Radio managers often actively participate in groups or associations, such as the local Chamber of Commerce, Jaycees, Kiwanis, Rotary Club, Optimists, and others, and encourage members of their staff to become similarly involved. The station also strives to heighten its status in the community by devoting airtime to issues and events of local importance and by making its microphones available to citizens for discussions of matters pertinent to the area. In so doing, the station becomes regarded as an integral part of the community, and its value grows proportionately.

Surveys have shown that over a third of the managers of small market radio stations are native to the area their signal serves. This gives them a vested interest in the quality of life in their community and motivates them to use the power of their medium to further improve living conditions.

Medium and large market station managers realize, as well, the benefits derived from participating in community activities. "If you don't localize and take part in the affairs of the city or town from which you draw your income, you're operating at a disadvantage. You have to tune in your audience if you expect them to do likewise," says Bremkamp.

The manager has to work to bring the station and the community together. Neglecting this responsibility lessens the station's chance for prosperity, or even survival. Community involvement is a key to success.

The Manager and the Government

Earlier in this chapter, station manager Richard Bremkamp cited protecting the license as one of the primary functions of the general manager. By "protecting" the license he meant conforming to the rules and regulations established by the FCC for the operation of broadcast facilities. Since failure to fulfill the obligations of a license may result in punitive actions such as reprimands, fines, and even the revocation of the privilege to broadcast, managers have to be aware of the laws affecting station operations and see to it that they are observed by all concerned.

An article in *Radio Ink* summarized the FCC's punitive actions against stations for rules violations. Here are some examples:

- Construction or operation without authorization–$20,000
- Unauthorized transfer of control–$20,000
- Failure to permit FCC inspections: $18,750
- Failure to respond to FCC communications: $17,500
- Exceeding power limits: $12,500
- EBS equipment broken or not installed: $12,500
- Broadcasting indecent/obscene material: $12,500
- Violation of EEO or political broadcast rules: $12,500
- Violation of main studio rule: $10,000
- Public file violations: $7,500
- Sponsor ID or lottery violations: $6,250

The manager delegates responsibilities to department heads who are directly involved in the areas affected by the commission's regulations. For example, the program director will attend to the legal station identification, station logs, program content, and myriad other concerns of interest to the government. Meanwhile, the chief engineer is responsible for meeting technical standards, and the sales manager is held accountable for the observance of certain business and financial practices. Other members of the station also are assigned various responsibilities applicable to the license. Of course, in the end it is the manager who must guaran-

tee that the station's license to broadcast is, indeed, protected.

All rules and regulations pertaining to radio broadcast operations are contained in Title 47, Part 73, of the *Code of Federal Regulations* (CFR). The station manager keeps the annual update of this publication accessible to all employees involved in maintaining the license. A copy of the CFR may be obtained through the Superintendent of Documents, Government Printing Office, Washington, D.C. 20402, for a modest fee. Specific inquiries concerning the publication can be addressed to the Director, Office of the Federal Register, National Archives and Records Service, General Services Administration, Washington, D.C. 20408.

To provide an idea of the scope of this document, as well as the government's dicta concerning broadcasters, the CFR's index to radio broadcast services is included as an appendix to this chapter. Immediately apparent from a perusal of the index is the preponderance of items that come under the auspices of the engineering department. Obviously, the FCC is concerned with many areas of radio operation, but its focus on the technical aspect is prodigious. Many other items involve programming and sales, and, of course, responsibilities also overlap into other areas of the station.

To reiterate, although the station manager shares the duties involved in complying with the FCC's regulations with other staff members, he or she holds primary responsibility for keeping the station out of trouble and on the air.

In Chapter 1 it was noted that many of the rules and regulations pertaining to the daily operation of a radio station have undergone revision or have been rescinded. Since the CFR is published annually, certain parts may become obsolete during that period. Martha L. Girard, director of the Office of the *Federal Register*, suggests that the *Federal Register*, from which the CFR derives its information, be consulted monthly. "These two publications must be used together to determine the latest version

☑ tactics:direct marketing
A Management Report from Shane Media

WWW.YOUR STATION

What's the first step in getting radio clients to spend money on your Web site? Getting them to accept the Web as a viable medium to reach customers, according to iRADIO, the Internet newsletter.

The advice: Let advertisers know that your Web site is part of your station's overall marketing artillery and that you have a reason for net surfers to check your site and come back for more.

Here are priorities iRADIO recommends for radio station Web sites:

- Station line-up and schedule
- Sound bites from station programming
- Live audio using Audio Net
- Monthly promotion calendars with event details
- Loyal listener club registration
- Station merchandise sales
- Contest information including tips on winning
- Station phone numbers, addresses, etc.
- E-mail feedback to personalities and management
- Listener testimonials
- Advertiser testimonials
- Promos for programs and features
- "Virtual Mall" of advertisers (by category)
- Weekly music charts
- New music releases and reviews
- Concert and entertainment calendar

Should your Web site include links to other sites? Yes, but be careful. Your Web site should be a promotional vehicle for your station. Links take your customer out of reach of your message and put someone else's message in front of them.

For example, a news station that links to CNN undermines its own news credibility. On the other hand, a Country station that links to the Garth Brooks fan club is doing its listeners a service. Avoid links to the competition.

Don't forget that your Web site is first and foremost -- a promotional vehicle for your station. The best use of the Internet is to motivate surfers to turn on the radio. Consider a "silent contest" that rewards net surfers when they log on to radio.

Another use for the Web: It's the ultimate "at work network." Set up regular e-mail to office workers with the same contest and event news you distribute through at-work faxes.

© SHANE MEDIA   HOUSTON, TX   (713) 952-9221

FIGURE 2.10
Sourcing nontraditional revenue is a management goal. Courtesy Shane Media.

of any given rule," says Byrne. A station may subscribe to the *Federal Register* or visit the local library.

Since the FCC may, at any time during normal business hours, inspect a radio station to see that it is in accordance with the rules and regulations, a manager makes certain that everything is in order. An FCC inspection checklist is contained in the CFR, and industry organizations, such as the National Association of Broadcasters (NAB), provide member stations with similar checklists. Occasionally, managers run mock inspections in preparation for the

real thing. A state of preparedness prevents embarrassment and problems. (See figure 2.12)

The Public File

Radio stations are required by the FCC to maintain a Public File. This, too, is ultimately the manager's responsibility. However, other members of a station's staff typically are required to update certain elements of the file.

The purpose of the file is to provide the general population with access to information pertaining to the way a station has conducted itself during a license period.

Interest in a station's Public File often increases around license renewal periods, when members of a community may choose to challenge a station's right to continue broadcasting.

The FCC expects a station's Public File to contain the following (this is subject to change as rules and regulations are revised):

- *The Public and Broadcasting—A Procedural Manual* (revised edition)
- Annual employment reports
- Copies of all FCC applications (power increases, original construction permit, facilities changes, license renewals)
- Ownership reports
- Political file
- Letters from the public
- Quarterly issues
- Local public notices

The Public File must be located in the community in which the station is licensed. Most stations keep the file at their main studio facility rather than at another public location, which is also permissible. The Public File is often the first place FCC agents look when they inspect a station. So it must be readily available. It is imperative that the file be kept up-to-date. As a general

FIGURE 2.11
FCC Ownership and License application form.

---

rule, files are retained for a period of seven years.

More detailed information pertaining to a station's Public File may be found in Section 73.3526 of the FCC's *Rules and Regulations*.

The Manager and Unions

The unions most active in radio are the American Federation of Television and Radio Artists (AFTRA), the National Association of Broadcast Employees and

FIGURE 2.11
continued

Federal Communications Commission
Washington, D.C. 20554

APPLICATION FOR NEW BROADCAST STATION LICENSE
(Carefully read instructions before filling out Form)
RETURN ONLY FORM TO FCC

Approved by OMB
3060-0029
Expires 9/30/90

For Commission Fee Use Only

FEE NO:

FEE TYPE:

FEE AMT:

ID SEQ:

For Applicant Fee Use Only

Is a fee submitted with this application? ☐ Yes ☐ No

If No, indicate reason therefor (check one box):

☐ Nonfeeable application

Fee Exempt (See 47 C.F.R. Section 1.1112)

☐ Noncommercial educational licensee

☐ Governmental entity

SECTION I – GENERAL DATA

For Commission Use Only

File No.

Legal Name of Applicant

Mailing Address

City   State   Zip Code

Telephone No. (include area code)

1. Facilities authorized by construction permit

This application is for: ☐ Commercial ☐ Noncommercial

☐ AM Directional ☐ AM Non-Directional ☐ FM Directional ☐ FM Non-Directional ☐ TV

Call Letters	Community of License	Construction Permit File No.	Modification of Construction Permit File No(s).	Expiration Date of Last Construction Permit

2. Is the station now operating pursuant to automatic program test authority in accordance with 47 C.F.R. Section 73.1620?   ☐ Yes ☐ No

   If No, explain.

3. Have all the terms, conditions, and obligations set forth in the above described construction permit been fully met?   ☐ Yes ☐ No

   If No, state exceptions.

4. Apart from the changes already reported, has any cause or circumstance arisen since the grant of the underlying construction permit which would result in any statement or representation contained in the construction permit application to be now incorrect?   ☐ Yes ☐ No

   If Yes, explain.

5. Has the permittee filed its Ownership Report (FCC Form 323) or ownership certification in accordance with 47 C.F.R. Section 73.3615(b)?   ☐ Yes ☐ No ☐ Does not apply

   If No, explain.

FCC 302
June 1988

Technicians (NABET), and the International Brotherhood of Electrical Workers (IBEW). Major market radio stations are the ones most likely to be unionized. The overwhelming majority of American stations are nonunion, and in fact, in recent years union memberships have declined.

Dissatisfaction with wages and benefits, coupled with a desire for greater security are often motivators that prompt station employees to vote for a union. Managers seldom encourage the presence of a union since many believe that unions impede and constrict their ability to control the destiny of their operations. However, a small percentage of managers believe that the existence of a union may actually stabilize the working environment and cut down on personnel turnover.

It is the function of the union to act as a bargaining agent working in good faith with station employees and management to upgrade and improve working conditions. The focus of union efforts usually is in the areas of salary, sick leave, vacation, promotion, hiring, termination, working hours, and retirement benefits, among others.

A unionized station appoints or elects a shop steward who works as a liaison between the union, which represents the employees, and the station's management. Employees may lodge complaints or grievances with the shop steward, who will then review the union's contract with the station and proceed accordingly. Station managers are obliged to work within the agreement that they, along with the union, helped formulate.

As stated, unions are a fact of life in many major markets. They are far less prevalent elsewhere, although unions do exist in some medium and even small markets. Most small operations would find it impractical, if not untenable, to function under a union contract. Union demands would quite likely cripple most marginal or small profit operations.

Managers who extend employees every possible courtesy and operate in a fair and reasonable manner are rarely affected by unions, whose prime objective is to protect and ensure the rights of station workers.

The Manager and Industry Associations

Every year the NAB and a variety of specialized and regional organizations conduct conferences and seminars intended to generate industry awareness and unity. At these gatherings, held at various locations throughout the country, radio managers and station personnel exchange ideas and share experiences, which they bring back to their stations.

The largest broadcast industry trade organization is the NAB, which was originally conceived out of a need to improve operating conditions in the 1920s. Initially only a lobbying organization, the NAB has maintained that focus while expanding considerably in scope. The primary objective of the organization is to support and promote the stability and development of the industry. (See figure 2.13)

In the mid-1990s, however, the National Radio Broadcaster's Association, which merged with the NAB in the 1980s, threatened to break from the organization for its alleged overemphasis on nonradio matters.

FY 2003 Radio Station Regulatory Fees						
Population Served	AM Class A	AM Class B	AM Class C	AM Class D	FM Classes A, B1 & C3	FM Classes B, C, C0, C1 & C2
<=25,000	0317 $600	0323 $450	0329 $325	0335 $400	0341 $475	0347 $625
25,001 - 75,000	0318 $1200	0324 $900	0330 $475	0336 $600	0342 $950	0348 $1,100
75,001 - 150,000	0319 $1,800	0325 $1,125	0331 $650	0337 $1,000	0343 $1,300	0349 $2,025
150,001 - 500,000	0320 $2,700	0326 $1,925	0332 $975	0338 $1,200	0344 $2,025	0350 $2,650
500,001 - 1,200,000	0321 $3,900	0327 $2,925	0333 $1,625	0339 $2,000	0345 $3,200	0351 $3,900
1,200,001 - 3,000,000	0322 $6,000	0328 $4,500	0334 $2,450	0340 $3,200	0346 $5,225	0352 $6,250
>3,000,000	0379 $7,200	0380 $5,400	0381 $3,100	0382 $4,000	0383 $6,650	0384 $8,125

Regulatory Fee Group or Category	Regulatory Fee	Payment Type Code
Broadcast Auxiliary Station License	$10	0369
Construction Permit for New AM Station	$455	0315
Construction Permit for New FM Station	$1,850	0316

VHF/UHF/Satellite TV Stations

Who Must Pay: Licensees of commercial VHF, UHF and satellite television stations, and holders of construction permits for new stations whose license or permit was granted on or before October 1, 2002. Commercial television station licensees who also hold auxiliary broadcast service licenses for stations operated in conjunction with the main TV station (e.g., remote pickup stations, intercity relay stations) will also be assessed a regulatory fee of $10 for each of these stations. Holders of construction permits (CPs) for new television stations for which a license to cover the CP had not been granted as of October 1, 2002, will be assessed $4,625 (VHF), $8,300 (UHF), or $515 (Satellite TV) for each permit held, regardless of market size.

Fee Requirement: Fees for commercial television stations are based upon the size of the Nielsen Designated Market Area (DMA) as listed in the 2003 Edition of the Television & Cable Factbook, Stations Volume No. 71, Warren Publishing, Inc. Fees will be assessed as follows:

FIGURE 2.12
A listing of annual FCC operating fees for radio stations. Fees vary depending on a station's category.

FIGURE 2.13
The NAB's Crystal Awards are presented to those stations with exemplary community service. Courtesy NAB.

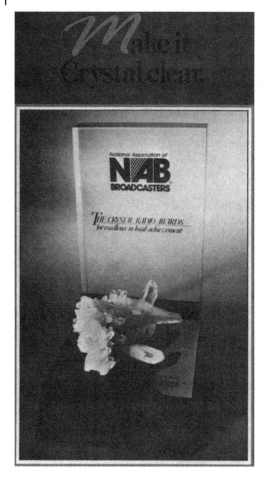

Thousands of radio stations also are members of the Radio Advertising Bureau (RAB), which was founded in 1951, a time when radio's fate was in serious jeopardy due to the rise in television's popularity. "The RAB is designed to serve as the sales and marketing arm of America's commercial radio industry. Members include radio stations, broadcast groups, networks, station representatives, and associated industry organizations in every market in all fifty states," explains RAB's Kenneth J. Costa.

Dozens of other broadcast trade organizations focus their attention on specific areas within the radio station, and regional and local broadcast organizations are numerous. The following list is a partial rundown of national organizations that support the efforts of radio broadcasters. A more comprehensive list may be found in *Broadcasting Yearbook*, the definitive industry directory, or by consulting local area directories.

- National Association of Broadcasters, 1771 N Street, N.W., Washington, DC 20036
- Radio Advertising Bureau, 304 Park Avenue, New York, NY 10010
- National Association of Farm Broadcasters, 26 E. Exchange Street, St. Paul, MN 55101
- American Women in Radio and Television, 1101 Connecticut Avenue, N.W., Suite 700, Washington, DC 20036
- Broadcast Education Association, 1771 N Street, N.W., Washington, DC 20036
- Broadcast Pioneers, 320 W. 57th Street, New York, NY 10019
- Clear Channel Broadcasting Service, 1776 K Street, N.W., Washington, DC 20006
- Native American Public Telecommunications, Box 83111, Lincoln, NE 68501
- National Association of Black Owned Broadcasters, 1730 M Street, N.W., Suite 412, Washington, DC 20036
- National Religious Broadcasters, 299 Webro Road, Parisippany, NJ 07054
- Radio Network Association, 1700 Broadway, 3rd floor, New York, NY, 10019
- Radio-Television News Directors Association, 1000 Connecticut Avenue, N.W., Washington, DC 20006
- Society of Broadcast Engineers, Box 20450, Indianapolis, IN 46220

NAB membership dues are based on a voluntary declaration of a station's annual gross revenues. The RAB and others take a similar approach. Some organizations require individual membership fees, which often are absorbed by the radio station as well.

Buying or Building a Radio Station

The process involved in the purchase of an existing radio facility is fairly complex. There is much to take into consideration. For one thing, it is rarely a quick and easy procedure because the FCC must approve of all station transfers (sales).

The FCC examines the background of any would-be station owner. Licensees must be U.S. citizens and must, among other things:

• Not have a criminal record
• Be able to prove financial stability
• Have a solid personal and professional history

Anyone interested in purchasing a radio property should employ the services of an attorney and/or broker who specializes in this area (consult *Broadcasting and Cable Market Place* for listings or contact the NAB).

The following points should be carefully considered before definitive action is taken to purchase a station:

• Analyze the market in which the station is located.
• Evaluate the facilities and assets.
• Hire a technical consultant.
• Assess existing contracts, leases, and agreements.
• Research financial records. Examine the Public File.
• Probe the FCC's file.

According to radio station acquisition expert Erwin G. Krasnow, "The due diligence process involved in the acquisition of a radio station typically includes a review of the general economic and operational conditions, as well as such areas as the financial and accounting systems, programming, technical facilities, legal matters, marketing, employee benefits, and personnel and environmental matters. The objective of due diligence is to obtain information that will (a) influence the decision of whether or not to proceed with the acquisition; and (b) have an effect on the purchase price or working capital adjustment."

Purchasing a broadcast property is unlike any other kind of acquisition because of the unique nature of the business. It is important to keep in mind that in the end a station owner does not own a frequency. An operator is merely granted permission (a license) to propagate a signal for a prescribed period of time (seven years) and then must reapply to continue broadcasting.

If an individual wishes to create a station from scratch, an application for a construction permit (CP) must be filled out and submitted to the FCC. This too is quite involved and requires special expertise; it is necessary to determine whether a new station can be accommodated on the existing broadcast bands in the area of proposed operation.

If it can be proven that an available frequency exists and that no interference will occur, a CP may be granted. The applicant is then given a specified amount of time

FCC judge moves to pull radio licenses

By Chris McConnell

An FCC administrative law judge has decided to revoke the license of a broadcaster convicted of

FIGURE 2.14
Job one: "Protect the license." Courtesy *Broadcasting and Cable*.

(usually 18 months) to commence and complete construction.

Before proceeding with a CP request, it is incumbent on the applicant to meet all of the criteria for station ownership set by the FCC. A new station must apply to the FCC for call letter acquisition. The station may request a particular set of calls, offer an existing station (possessing the calls it wants) a deal to transfer their calls to it, or take whatever the FCC issues it. Meanwhile, a station receives its frequency (KHz/MHz) from the FCC based on what is available in the allocation table for a particular market.

CHAPTER HIGHLIGHTS

1. Radio's unique character requires that station managers deal with a wide variety of talents and personalities.

2. The authoritarian approach to management implies that the general manager makes all of the policy decisions. The collaborative approach allows the general manager to involve other station staff in the formation of policy. The hybrid or chief-collaborator approach combines elements of both the authoritarian and collaborative management models. The chief-collaborator management approach is most prevalent in radio today.

3. To attain management status, an individual needs a solid formal education and practical experience in many areas of station operation–especially sales.

4. Key managerial functions include operating in a manner that produces the greatest profit, meeting corporate expectations, formulating station policy and seeing to its implementation, hiring and retaining good people, inspiring staff to do their best, training new employees, maintaining communication with all departments to ensure an excellent air product, and keeping an eye toward the future.

5. Station clustering and consolidation has changed the personnel landscape at stations as radio groups often concentrate the operation of several stations in one central location.

6. The operations manager, second only to the general manager at those stations that have established this position, supervises administrative staff, helps develop and implement station policy, handles departmental budgeting, functions as regulatory watchdog, and works as liaison with the community. The program director is responsible for format, hires and manages air staff, schedules airshifts, monitors air product quality, keeps abreast of competition, maintains the music library, complies with FCC rules, and directs the efforts of news and public affairs. The sales manager heads the sales staff, works with the station's rep company, assigns account lists to salespeople, establishes sales quotas, coordinates sales promotions, and develops sales materials and rate cards. The chief engineer operates within the FCC technical parameters; purchases, repairs, and maintains equipment; monitors signal fidelity; adapts studios for programming needs; sets up remote broadcasts; and works closely with programming.

7. Managers hire individuals who possess a solid formal education, strong professional experience, ambition, a positive attitude, reliability, humility, honesty, self-respect, patience, enthusiasm, discipline, creativity, logic, and compassion.

8. Says consultant Ed Shane, "The new radio paradigm is 'manager as financial expert.'"

9. Radio provides entertainment to the public and, in turn, sells the audience it attracts to advertisers. It is the station manager who must ensure a profit, but he or she must also maintain product integrity.

10. To foster a positive community image, the station manager becomes actively involved in the community and devotes airtime to community concerns–even though the FCC has reduced a station's obligation to do so.

11. Although the station manager delegates responsibility for compliance with FCC regulations to appropriate department heads, the manager is ultimately responsible for protecting the license. Title 47, Part 73, of the *Code of Federal Regulations* contains the rules pertaining to radio broadcast operations. Updates of regulations are listed monthly in the *Federal Register*.

12. Radio stations are required to maintain a Public File and to make it available to the public during normal business hours.

13. The American Federation of Television and Radio Artists (AFTRA), the National Association of Broadcast Employees and Technicians (NABET), and the International Brotherhood of Electrical Workers (IBEW) are the unions most active in radio.

14. The National Association of Broadcasters (NAB) and the Radio Advertising Bureau (RAB) are among the largest radio trade industry organizations.

15. A person must be a U.S. citizen to hold a broadcast license. The FCC investigates all would-be station owners. To put a new station on the air, a construction permit (CP) application must be submitted to the FCC.

16. Call letters and frequencies are issue by the FCC.

APPENDIX: *Code of Federal Regulations* Index

The index to the *Code of Federal Regulations*, Title 47, Part 73, Subparts A, B, G, and H, shown here, deals specifically with commercial radio operations. The department heads most affected by the sections listed in the index are noted in parentheses after each entry: GM = general manager, PD = program director, E = engineer, SM = sales manager. This CFR index dates to the mid-1990s.

Subpart A—AM Broadcast Stations

73.1 Scope. (All department heads)
73.14 AM broadcast definitions. (All)
73.21 Classes of AM broadcast channels and stations. (All)
73.22 Assignment of Class II-A stations. (GM, E)
73.24 Broadcast facilities; showing required. (GM, E)
73.25 Clear channels; Classes I and II stations. (GM, E)
73.26 Regional channels; Classes III-A and Ill-B stations. (GM, E)
73.27 Local channels; Class IV stations. (GM, E)
73.28 Assignment of stations to channels. (GM, E)
73.29 Class IV stations on regional channels. (GM, E)
73.30 Petition for authorization of an allotment in the 1605–1705 kHz band. (GM, E)
73.31 Rounding of nominal power specified on applications. (E)
73.33 Antenna systems; showing required. (E)
73.35 Multiple ownership. (GM)
73.37 Applications for broadcast facilities; showing required. (GM, E)
73.44 AM transmission system emission limitations. (E)
73.45 AM antenna systems. (E)
73.49 AM transmission system installation and safety requirements. (E)
73.51 Determining operating power. (E)
73.53 Requirements for type acceptance of antenna monitors. (E)
73.54 Antenna resistance and reactance measurements. (E)
73.57 Remote reading antenna and common point ammeters. (E)
73.58 Indicating instruments. (E)
73.61 AM directional antenna field measurements. (E)
73.62 Directional antenna system tolerances. (E)

73.68 Sampling systems for antenna monitors. (E)

73.69 Antenna monitors. (E)

73.72 Operating during the experimental period. (E)

73.88 Blanketing interference. (E)

73.93 AM operator requirements. (E, PD)

73.99 Presunrise service authorization (PSRA) and postsunset service authorization (PSSA). (E, GM, PD)

Other Operating Requirements

73.127 Use of multiplex transmission. (E, GM, PD)

73.128 AM stereophonic broadcasting. (E, PD)

73.132 Territorial exclusivity. (PD)

73.150 Directional antenna systems. (E)

73.151 Field strength measurements to establish performance of directional antennas. (E)

73.152 Modification of directional antenna data. (E)

73.153 Field strength measurements in support of applications or evidence at hearings. (E)

73.154 Directional antenna partial and skeleton proof of performance field strength measurements. (E)

73.157 Special antenna test authorizations. (E)

73.158 Directional antenna monitoring points. (E)

73.160 Vertical plane radiation characteristics, f(\gu). (E)

73.182 Engineering standards of allocation. (E)

73.183 Ground wave signals. (E)

73.184 Ground wave field strength charts. (E)

73.185 Computation of interfering signal. (E)

73.186 Establishment of effective field at one mile. (E)

73.187 Limitation on daytime radiation. (E)

73.189 Minimum antenna heights or field strength requirements. (E)

73.190 Engineering charts. (E)

Subpart B—FM Broadcast Stations

73.201 Numerical designation of FM broadcast channels. (E)

73.202 Table of Allotments. (E, GM)

73.203 Availability of channels. (E, GM)

73.204 International agreements and other restrictions of use of channels. (GM, E)

73.205 Zones. (E)

73.207 Minimum distance separation between stations. (GM, E)

73.208 Reference points and distance computations. (E)

73.209 Protection from interference. (E)

73.210 Station classes. (GM, E)

73.211 Power and antenna height requirements. (E)

73.212 Administrative changes in authorizations. (E)

73.213 Stations at spacings below the minimum separations. (E)

73.215 Contour protection for short-spaced assignments. (E)

73.220 Restrictions on use of channels. (GM, E)

73.232 Territorial exclusivity. (GM, PD)

73.239 Use of common antenna site. (E)

73.258 Indicating instruments. (E)

73.267 Determining operating power. (E)

73.277 Permissible transmissions. (E)

73.293 Use of FM multiplex subcarriers. (E)

73.295 FM subsidiary communications services. (GM, PD, E)

73.297 FM stereophonic sound broadcasting. (E, PD)

73.310 FM technical definitions. (E)

73.311 Field strength contours. (E)

73.312 Topographic data. (E)

73.313 Prediction of coverage. (E)

73.314 Field strength measurements. (E)

73.315 Transmitter location. (E)

73.316 FM antenna systems. (E)

73.317 Transmission system requirements. (E)

73.318 FM blanketing interference. (E)

73.319 FM multiplex subcarrier technical standards. (E)

73.322 FM stereophonic sound transmission standards. (E)

73.330 Use of modulation monitors at auxiliary transmitters. (E)

73.333 FM engineering charts. (E)

Subpart G—Emergency Broadcast System

Scope and Objectives

73.901 Scope of subpart. (GM, PD, E)

73.902 Objectives of subpart. (GM, PD, E)

Definitions

73.903 Emergency Broadcast System (EBS). (PD, E, GM)

73.904 Licensee. (GM, E)

73.905 Emergency Action Notification (EAN). (GM, PD, E)

73.906 Attention signal. (E, PD)

73.907 Emergency Action Termination. (E, PD)

73.908 EBS Checklist. (PD, E)

73.909 Standard Operating Procedures (SOPs). (E, PD)

73.910 Authenticator word lists. (PD, E)

SUGGESTED FURTHER READING

Agor, Weston H. *Intuitive Management.* Englewood Cliffs, N.J.: Prentice Hall, 1984.

Albrecht, Karl G. *Successful Management Objectives.* Englewood Cliffs, N.J.: Prentice Hall, 1979.

Appleby, Robert C. *The Essential Guide to Management.* Englewood Cliffs, N.J.: Prentice Hall, 1981.

Aronoff, Craig E., ed. *Business and the Media.* Santa Monica, Calif.: Goodyear Publishing Company, 1979.

Boyatzis, Richard E. *The Competent Manager.* New York: John Wiley and Sons, 1983.

Brown, Arnold. *Supermanaging.* New York: McGraw-Hill, 1984.

Coleman, Howard W. *Case Studies in Broadcast Management.* New York: Hastings House, 1978.

Cottrell, David, *Monday Morning Leadership.* New York: Cornerstone Leadership, 2002.

Creech, Kenneth C. *Electronic Media Law and Regulation*, 4nd ed. Boston: Focal Press, 2003.

Czech-Beckerman, Elizabeth Shimer. *Managing Electronic Media.* Boston: Focal Press, 1991.

Elimore, R. Terry. *Broadcasting Law and Regulation.* Blue Ridge Summit, Pa.: Tab Books, 1982.

Goodworth, Clive T. *How to Be a Super-Effective Manager: A Guide to People Management.* London: Business Books, 1984.

Kahn, Frank J., ed. *Documents of American Broadcasting*, 4th ed. Englewood Cliffs, N.J.: Prentice Hall, 1984.

Kobert, Norman. *The Aggressive Management Style.* Englewood Cliffs, N.J.: Prentice Hall, 1981.

Krasnow, Erwin G. and Werner, Eric T. *Radio Deals: A Step by Step Guide.* Springfield, VA: RBR Publications, 2002.

Lacy, Stephen, et al. *Media Management: A Casebook Approach.* Hillsdale, N.J.: Lawrence Erlbaum Associates, 1993.

McCormack, Mark H. *What They Don't Teach You at Harvard Business School.* New York: Bantam, 1984.

Miner, John B. *The Management Process: Theory, Research, and Practice.* New York: Macmillan, 1978. National Association of Broadcasters. *Up the Management Ladder: From Program Director to General Manager.* Washington, D.C.: NAB, 1991.

Pember, Don R. *Mass Media in America.* Chicago: Science Research Association, 1981.

Pringle, Peter K., Starr, Michael F., and McCavitt, William E. *Electronic Media Management*, 4rd ed. Boston: Focal Press, 1999.

Quaal, Ward L., and Brown, James A. *Broadcast Management*, 2nd ed. New York: Hastings House, 1976. Rhoads, B. Eric, et al., eds. *Management and Sales Management.* West Palm Beach, Fla.: Streamline Press, 1995.

Routt, Ed. *The Business of Radio Broadcasting.* Blue Ridge Summit, Pa.: Tab Books, 1972.

Schwartz, Tony. *Media, The Second God.* New York: Praeger, 1984.

Shane, Ed. *Cutting Through: Strategies and Tactics for Radio.* Houston, Tex.: Shane Media, 1990.

—. *Selling Electronic Media.* Boston: Focal Press, 1999.

Townsend, Robert. *Further Up the Organization.* New York: Knopf, 1984.

3 Programming

Program Formats

Programming a radio station continues to be an increasingly complex task, even as large radio companies cluster their outlets in the age of station consolidation. There are twice the number of stations today competing for the audience's attention than existed in the 1960s, and more continue to enter the fray. Other media have proliferated as well, resulting in a further distraction of radio's customary audience. The government's laissez-faire, "let the marketplace dictate" philosophy concerning commercial radio programming gives the station great freedom in deciding the nature of its air product, but determining what to offer the listener, who is often presented with dozens of alternatives, involves intricate planning.

The basic idea, of course, is to air the type of format that will attract a sizable enough piece of the audience demographic to satisfy the advertiser. Once a station decides on the format it will program, it then must know how to effectively execute it.

Brief descriptions of some of the most frequently employed formats in radio today follow. There are a host of other formats, or subformats—more than 100, in fact. Many are variations of those listed.

Adult Contemporary (AC)

In terms of the number of listeners, Adult Contemporary (also referred to as The Mix, Hot AC, Triple A, Urban AC, Soft AC, Spectrum AC, and Lite AC) was the most popular format in the 1980s and continues to draw impressive audiences in the new millennium, although some subcategories have lost ground since the last edition of this book. Says consultant Ed Shane, "Because the AC target audience is so diverse, the format has been most prone to fragmentation and competition."

AC is very strong in the 25- to 49-year-old age group, which makes it particularly appealing to advertisers, since this demographic group has significant disposable income. Also, some advertisers spend money on AC stations simply because they like the format themselves. The Adult Contemporary format is also one of the most effective in attracting female listeners.

AC outlets emphasize current and not so current (all the way back to the 1970s at some AC stations) pop standards, sans raucous or pronounced beats—in other words, no hard rock. Some AC stations could be described as soft rockers. However, the majority mix in enough ballads and easy listening sounds to justify their title. The main thrust of this format's programming is the music. More music is aired by deemphasizing chatter. Music is commonly presented in uninterrupted sweeps or blocks, perhaps 10 to 12 minutes in duration, followed by a brief recap of artists and song titles. High-profile morning talent or teams became popular at AC stations in the 1980s and remain so today. Commercials generally are clustered at predetermined times, and midday and evening deejay talk often is limited to brief informational announcements. News and sports are secondary to the music.

Contemporary Hit Radio (CHR)

Once known as Top 40, CHR stations play only those records that currently are the fastest selling. CHR's narrow playlists are designed to draw teens and young adults. The heart of this format's demographic is the 12- to 18-year-old, although in the mid1980s it enjoyed a broadening of its core audience. Like AC, it too has experienced erosion in its numbers in recent years. In the *Journal of Radio Studies* (1995–1996), Ed Shane observed that the format "was a statistical loser in the 1990s. What futurist Alvin Toffler called 'the demassification of media' affected CHR the most. . . . There were too many types of music to play. No one radio station could create a format with elements as diverse as rapper Ice T, rockers like Nirvana, country artists like George Strait and Randy Travis, or jazz musicians like Kenny G or David Benoit. Each of those performers fits someone's definition of 'contemporary hit radio.' CHR lost its focus."

Consultant Jeff Pollack believed that CHR had lost ground because it was not in tune with what he called the "streets," and predicted the format would embrace a more dance-rap sound as well as develop more appreciation for alternative rock hits. The format is characterized by its swift, often unrelenting pace. Silence, known as "dead air," is the enemy. The idea is to keep the sound hot and tight to keep the kids from station hopping, which is no small task since many markets have at least two hit-oriented stations.

In a 1995 interview in *Radio Ink*, programmer Bill Richards predicted that the high-intensity jock approach would give way to a more laid back, natural sound. "The days of the 'move over and let the big dog eat' sweepers are over. Top 40 will look

Radio's Most Popular Formats

Rank	Format	#Stations
1	Country	2133
2	News/Talk	1177
3	Oldies	814
4	Adult Contemporary	716
5	Hispanic	596
6	Adult Standards	559
7	Top 40	472
8	Hot AC	395
9	Sports	380
10	Classic Rock	378
11	Soft Adult Contemporary	346
12	Religion (Teaching, Variety)	335
13	Rock	279
14	Black Gospel	257
15	Classic Hits	255
16	Southern Gospel	239
17	R&B	194
18	Contemporary Christian	164
19	Modern Rock	146
20	Urban AC	118
21	Ethnic	99
22	Alternative Rock	97
23	Jazz	82
24	R&B Adult/Oldies	78
25	Modern AC	59
26	Gospel	52
27	Pre-Teen	50
28	Variety	42
29	Classical	32
30	Easy Listening	21
31	Other/Not Available	6

Source: M Street Corp., © 2002

FIGURE 3.1
Format chart shows the popularity of formats around the country. The chart changes with each ratings sweep. Courtesy RAB.

for more jocks who sound like real people and shy away from the hyped deejay approach." CHR deejays have undergone several shifts in status since the inception of the chart music format in the 1950s. Initially, pop deejay personalities played an integral role in the air sound. However, in the mid-1960s the format underwent a major change when deejay presence was significantly reduced. Programming innovator Bill Drake decided that the Top 40 sound needed to be refurbished and tightened. Thus, deejay talk and even the number of commercials scheduled each hour were cut back in order to improve flow. Despite criticism that the new sound was too mechanical, Drake's technique succeeded at strengthening the format's hold on the listening audience.

In the mid- and late-1970s the deejay's role on hit stations began to regain its former prominence, but in the 1980s the format underwent a further renovation (ini-

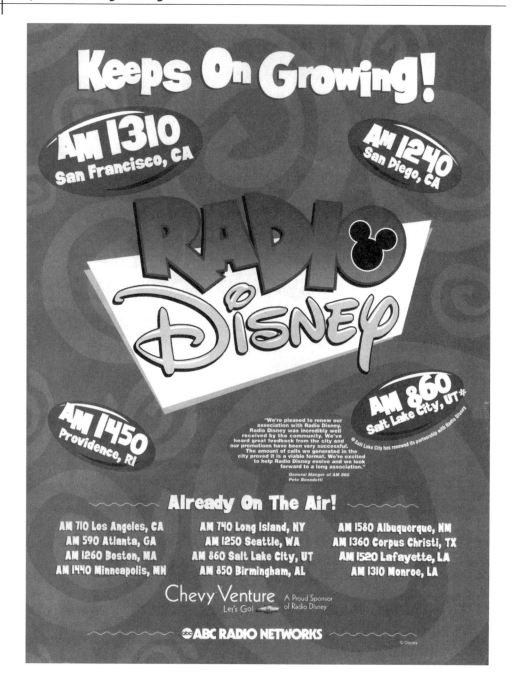

tiated by legendary consultant Mike Joseph) that resulted in a narrowing of its playlist and a decrease in deejay presence. Super or Hot Hit stations, as they also are called, were among the most popular in the country and could be found either near or at the top of the rating charts in their markets.

At the moment, at least, CHR has a bit less of a frenetic quality to it, and perhaps (it could be said) a more mature sound. Undergoing an image adjustment, the format is keying in on improving overall flow while pulling back on jumping aboard the fad bandwagon. The continued preening of the playlist will keep the format viable, say the experts.

News is of secondary importance on CHR stations. In fact, news programming is considered by many program directors to be a tune-out factor. "Kids don't like news," they claim. However, despite deregulation, which has freed stations of nonentertainment program requirements, most retain at least a modicum of news out of a sense of obligation. CHR stations are very promotion minded and contest oriented.

Fewer than 500 stations (nearly all FM) call themselves CHR. Many of these stations preferred to be called Rhythm Hits (Churban fell out of favor in the late 1990s), which combines urban and rock hits, or Modern Hits, a narrower-based version of Top 40 that draws its playlist from MTV and college stations.

Country

Since the 1970s the Country format has been adopted by more stations than any other. Although seldom a leader in the ratings race, its appeal is exceptionally broad. An indication of country music's rising popularity is the fact that there are over 10 times as many full-time Country stations today than there were 20 years ago. Although the format is far more prevalent in the south and midwest, most medium and large markets in the north have Country stations. Due to the diversity of approaches within the format—for example, traditional, middle-of-the road, contemporary hit, and so on—the Country format attracts a broad age group, appealing to young as well as older adults. "The Country format has scored very high among 25- to 54-year-olds," adds Burkhart.

Says Shane, "In spite of predictions, Country has not fragmented. There are ways to skew the format for older or younger demos, but each group demands essentially the same music. The difference is in presentation and content between the songs."

Country radio has always been particularly popular among blue-collar workers. According to the Country Music Association and the Organization of Country Radio Broadcasters, the Country music format is drawing a more upscale audience today than it has in the past. As many FM as AM stations are programming the Country sound in the 1990s, which was not the case just a few years ago. Until the 1980s, Country was predominantly an AM offering. Depending on the approach they employ, Country outlets may emphasize or de-emphasize air personalities, include news and public affairs features, or confine their programming almost exclusively to music.

According to some programming experts, the Country format peaked in the mid-1990s, and there will be little further growth, at least for the time being. A recent *M Street Journal* survey concluded that over 2,600 stations air some form of country music.

Easy Listening/Smooth Jazz

The Beautiful Music station of the 1960s became the Easy Listening or Smooth Jazz station of the 1990s. Playlists in this format have been carefully updated in an attempt to attract a somewhat younger audience. The term *Beautiful Music* was exchanged for *Easy Listening* in an effort to dispel the geriatric image the former term seemed to convey. Easy Listening is the ultimate "wall-to-wall" music format. Talk of any type is kept minimal, although many stations in this format concentrate on news and information during morning drivetime.

Instrumentals and soft vocals of established songs are a mainstay at Easy Listening stations, which also share a penchant for lush orchestrations featuring plenty of strings. These stations boast a devoted audience.

Station hopping is uncommon. Efforts to draw younger listeners into the Easy Listening fold have been moderately successful,

PROGRAMMING PROFILES
Tuning around the Orlando Radio Dial

AM	540	580	740	990	1030	1140	1270	1440	1600
	WQTM	WDBO	WWNZ	WHOO	WONQ	WRMQ	WRLZ	WPRD	WOKB

FM	92.3	93.1	94.5	95.3	96.5	97.5	98.1	98.9	100.3	101.1	101.9	103.1	104.1	105.1	105.9	106.7	107.7
	WWKA	WKRO	WCFB	WTLN	WHTQ	WPCV	WGNE	WMMO	WSHE	WJRR	WJHM	WLOQ	WTKS	WOMX	WOCL	WXXL	WMGF

JAMMIN OLDIES	COUNTRY	ADULT CONTEMPORARY	SPANISH	CLASSIC ROCK
WOCL	WWKA WPCV WGNE	WOMX	WONQ WRMQ WRLZ WOKB WPRD	WHTQ

OLDIES				SOFT ROCK
WSHE				WMMO

ROCK	NEWS/TALK	URBAN	CHURBAN	LITE ROCK
WJRR	WWNZ WTKS WDBO	WJHM WCFB	WTLN	WMGF

ADULT STANDARD	CHR	JAZZ	SPORTS	ALTERNATIVE
WHOO	WXXL	WLOQ	WQTM	WKRO

FIGURE 3.3
Market format breakdown. Courtesy Mix 105.1.

but most of the format's primary adherents are over 50. Music syndicators provide prepackaged (canned) programming to approximately half of the nation's Easy Listening/Smooth Jazz stations, and over three-quarters of the outlets within this format utilize automation systems to varying degrees. Easy Listening has held strong in several markets, although the format lost some ground in the 1980s and 1990s to Adult Contemporary and other adult-appeal formats such as New Age, which has been referred to by some media critics as Easy Listening for Yuppies.

Soft Adult, Lite and Easy, and Smooth Jazz have become replacement nomenclatures for Easy Listening, which, like its pre-decessor, Beautiful Music, began to assume a geriatric connotation.

Rock and Alternative

The birth of the Album Oriented Rock (AOR) format in the late 1960s was the result of a basic disdain for the highly formulaic Top 40 sound that prevailed at the time. In the summer of 1966, WOR-FM, New York, introduced Progressive radio, the forerunner of AOR. As an alternative to the superhyped, ultracommercial sound of the hit song station, WOR-FM programmed an unorthodox combination of nonchart rock, blues, folk, and jazz. In the 1970s the format concentrated its attention almost exclusively on album rock, while becoming less free-form and more formulaic and systematic in its programming approach.

Today AOR often is simply called Rock, or more specifically Modern Rock or Classic Rock, and while it continues to do well in garnering the 18- to 34-year-old male, this format has always done poorly in winning female listeners, especially when it emphasizes a heavy or hard-rock playlist. This has proven to be a sore spot with certain advertisers. In the 1980s, the format lost its prominence due, in part, to the meteoric rebirth of hit radio. However, as the decade came to an end, AOR had regained a chunk of its numbers, and in the 1990s it renamed itself Modern Rock.

Generally, Rock stations broadcast their music in sweeps, or at least segue two or three songs. A large airplay library is typical, in which 300 to 700 cuts may be active. Depending on the outlet, the deejay may or may not have "personality" status. In fact, the more-music/less-talk approach particularly common at easy listening stations is emulated by many album rockers. Consequently, news plays a very minor part in the station's programming efforts.

Rock (also called Active Rock) stations are very lifestyle-oriented and invest great time and energy developing promotions relevant to the interests and attitudes of their listeners.

Reflecting the considerable drift away from the AOR nomenclature and model, WBCN's long-time program director, Oedipus, declared to the world in 1995, "We're Modern Rock!"

The Alternative Rock format tries for distinctiveness. That is to say, it attempts to provide a choice that is in contrast to the other Rock radio approaches. Creating this alternative sound is a challenge, says Stephanie Hindley, PD of Buzz 99.9, "The Alternative format is a great challenge for programmers. Think of the music you liked and the things you did when you were 18. Now think of the music you liked (or will like) and the things you did (or will do) at age 34. Despite the vast differences in taste in the 18–34 demographic, we need to play music that will appeal to as many people as possible within this diverse group. It's a constant balancing act. We have to play a lot of new music without sounding too unfamiliar. We have to be cool and hip without sounding exclusive. We have to be edgy without being offensive. Be smart without sounding condescending. Young and upbeat without sounding immature. As long as those balances are maintained on a daily basis, we will continue to have success in this format."

News, Talk, and Sports

There are News, News/Talk, News Sports, News Plus, and Talk formats, and each is distinct and unique unto itself. News stations differ from the others in that they devote their entire air schedule to the presentation of news and news-related stories and features. The All-News format was introduced by Gordon McLendon at XETRA (known as XTRA) in Tijuana, Mexico, in the early 1960s. Its success soon inspired the spread of the format in the United States. Due to the enormous expense involved in the presentation of a purely News format, requiring three to four times the staff and budget of most music operations, the format has been confined to larger markets able to support the endeavor.

The News/Talk format is a hybrid. It combines extensive news coverage with blocks of two-way telephone conversations. These stations commonly "daypart" or segmentalize their programming by presenting lengthened newscasts during morning and afternoon drivetime hours and conversation in the midday and evening periods. The News/Talk combo was conceived by KGO in San Francisco in the 1960s and has gradually gained in popularity so that it now leads both the strictly News and the Talk formats. Talk radio began at KABC-AM, Los Angeles, in 1960. However, talk shows were familiar to listeners in the 1950s, since a number of adult music stations devoted a few hours during evenings or overnight to call-in programs. The motivation behind most early Talk· programming stemmed from a desire to strengthen weak time slots while satisfying public affairs programming requirements. Like its nonmusic siblings, Talk became a viable format in the 1960s and does well today, although it too has suffered due to greater competition. In contrast to All-News, which attracts a slightly younger and more upscale audience, All-Talk amasses a large following among blue-collar workers and retirees.

One of the recent news and information-oriented formats calls itself News Plus. Even though its emphasis is on news, it fills periods with music, often Adult Contemporary in flavor. News Plus stations also may carry a heavy schedule of sporting events. This combination has done well in several medium and large markets, but has apparently plateaued as this book goes to press.

News and/or Talk formats are primarily located on the AM band, where they have become increasingly prevalent since FM has captured all but a few of radio's music listeners. Meanwhile, the number of non-music formats is significantly increasing on FM.

In the late 1990s, over 1,000 stations offered the information and/or news format. This was up nearly 300 percent since the late 1980s. Over 100 stations alone concentrated on sports exclusively, and dozens of others were beginning to splinter and compartmentalize into news/info niches, such as auto, health, computer, food, business, tourism, entertainment, and so on.

According to a recent survey conducted by *Radio & Records*, News/Talk stations were the most tuned format in the United States. National talk networks and syndicated talk shows were proliferating as well in the latter part of the 1990s, as more and more Baby Boomers became engaged in the political and social dialogues of the day.

An indication that the News format is achieving broader appeal among younger listeners is the recent emergence on the FM dial of a new hybrid called Talk 'n' Rock.

The trend in the last few years in the proliferation of the All-Sports format has boosted the popularity of nonmusic radio and significantly contributed to the dominance of "chatter" radio in the ratings. Today several hundred stations offer round the clock sports talk, among them WFAN and WEEI in the northeast. In addition several sports networks now appear across the radio band. Since the mid-1990s, ESPN Radio Network, Fox Sports Radio, and Sporting News Radio have emerged and are now carried by stations throughout the country. If AM radio is able to claim a younger demographic at all it is because males 18–29 are big fans of sports radio.

FM Talk

Perhaps the most unique manifestation in nonmusic radio is the growing presence of talk on FM. Jason Insalaco, an executive producer at Los Angeles' KLSX, gives his perspective on the rise of the *discourse* format on what has always been the dial for music: "While traditional AM talk has been profiled in recent years for its explosion onto the radio landscape, FM talk radio has become a popular format for an audience previously ignored by talk programmers. FM talk's primary audience is 25 to 44 years old. This demographic likely did not grow up listening to AM talk radio. In fact, the FM talk audience has very likely tuned AM very little during its lifetime. FM talk does not program itself like a traditional full-service AM talk outlet. There is not the emphasis on news and traffic, which is a staple of the AM talkers. Rather FM talk's focus is personality driven, aka Howard Stern, Tom Leykis, and Jonathan Brandmeier. These FM talk stalwarts do incorporate some news into their programs, but the main focus is entertainment. FM

FIGURE 3.4
Popular personalities
bring in the big
numbers. Courtesy
KRLA-FM.

97.1 FM TALK

HOWARD STERN

PERSONS

| 25-49 | #1 |
| 25-54 | #1 |

MEN

12+	#1
18+	#1
18-49	#1
25-49	#1
25-54	#1
35-54	#1

Source: Winter `99 ARB AQH, Metro, Mon-Fri 6a-10a
(English-Language Stations)

talk programs itself more like an FM music station than an AM talk station. It features shorter segments covering a variety of issues in contrast to the one hour AM talk sweep. Issues discussed typically come from sources like *Rolling Stone* and *People* magazine and the local sports and entertainment section of the newspaper. Topics are not necessarily caller intensive as with most AM talkers. Listener participation is a part of FM talk radio; however, there is not the typical topic-monologue-caller participation cycle of AM talkers. Moreover, the 'bumper music' played to intro segments of FM talk come from the latest alternative and rock artists found on the competing music stations. This gives the station a youthful sound and grabs the potential talk listener who is scanning the dial. FM talk's competition comes from Alternative/Modern Rock/AOR and

FIGURE 3.4
continued

DON IMUS
Monday-Friday 5am-9am

Time Magazine labeled him as "One of the most influential people in America." His radio show is heard in over 90 markets across the U.S. His best-selling novel **God's Other Son** spent 3 months on The New York Times Best Seller's List. His charitable efforts have raised nearly 13 million dollars to benefit the C.J. Foundation for SIDS and The Tomorrow's Children Fund. And as host of America's Best Morning Show...Don Imus has only just begun!

Don is **SERIOUS!**...A show blending news, music, sports and bawdy humor...where politicians and journalists mingle to be heard by an audience of chattering peers. His guests have included President Clinton, CBS News Anchors Dan Rather and Walter Cronkite, Senators Bob Dole and Alfonse D'Amato, Comedian George Carlin, NBC's News Anchors Tom Brokaw and Jane Pauley, Former Pittsburgh Steeler's Quarterback Terry Bradshaw and countless others.

Winner of 4 Marconi Awards, an inductee into the NAB and Emerson Radio Hall of Fame and recognized by Billboard Magazine as Major Market Personality of the Year...there is nobody like Don Imus. His goal..."To goad my guests into saying something that will ruin their life!"

Yes...the **I-MAN COMETH**...and he's **Don Imus.** Hear him every weekday morning from 5 to 9am on the new **LA TALK 1110!**

Classic Rock stations. The future of FM talk looks bright. Expect the format to become more widespread in the coming years."

Indeed, the number of FM talk outlets in major markets is on the increase. A good example is 96.9 FM in Boston, which has made serious inroads into the nonmusic radio arena. In recent surveys it has challenged the city's long-standing talk-oriented stations on AM, and this feat is being duplicated in other markets around the country.

Classic/Oldies/Nostalgia

Although these formats are not identical, they derive the music they play from years gone by. Whereas the Nostalgia station, sometimes referred to as *Big Band*, constructs its playlist around tunes popular as far back as the 1940s and 1950s, the Oldies outlet focuses its attention on the pop tunes of the late 1950s and 1960s. A typical oldies quarter-hour might consist of songs by Elvis Presley, the Everly Brothers, the Beatles,

Brian Hyland, Three Dog Night, and the Ronettes. In contrast, a Nostalgia quarter-hour might consist of tunes from the prerock era performed by artists like Frankie Lane, Les Baxter, the Mills Brothers, Tommy Dorsey, and popular ballad singers of the last few decades.

Nostalgia radio caught on in the late 1970s, the concept of programmer Al Ham. Nostalgia is a highly syndicated format, and most stations go out-of-house for programming material. Because much of the music predates stereo processing, AM outlets are most apt to carry the Nostalgia sound. Music is invariably presented in sweeps and, for the most part, deejays maintain a low profile. Similar to Easy Listening, Nostalgia pushes its music to the forefront and keeps other program elements at an unobtrusive distance. In the 1980s, Easy Listening/Beautiful Music stations lost some listeners to this format, which claimed a viable share of the radio audience.

The Oldies format was first introduced in the 1960s by programmers Bill Drake and Chuck Blore. Although Nostalgia's audience tends to be over the age of 50, most Oldies listeners are somewhat younger. Unlike Nostalgia, most Oldies outlets originate their own programming, and very few are automated. In contrast with its vintage music cousin, the Oldies format allows greater deejay presence. At many Oldies stations, air personalities play a key role. Music is rarely broadcast in sweeps, and commercials, rather than being clustered, are inserted in a random fashion between songs.

Consultant Kent Burkhart noted that in the early 1990s, "Oldies stations are scoring very big in a nice broad demographic. These stations are doing quite well today, and this should hold for a while." At the same time, Nostalgia has not been shown as having much growth but remains fairly solid in some markets. In the 1990s, Oldies outlets have lost audience ground. However, over 700 stations still call themselves Oldies or Nostalgia. Meanwhile a more dance/contemporary approach, called "Jammin' Oldies," has attracted additional listeners.

Meanwhile Classic Rock and Classic Hit stations emerged as the biggest winners in the late 1980s and early 1990s. These vintage music stations draw their playlists from the chart toppers (primarily in the rock music area) of the 1970s and 1980s (and early 1990s) and often appear in the top 10 ratings.

Classic Rock concentrates on tunes essentially featured by former AOR stations over the past two decades, whereas Classic Hit stations fill the gap between Oldies and CHR outlets with playlists that draw from 1970s' and 1980s' Top 40 charts.

Urban Contemporary (UC)

Considered the "melting pot" format, Urban Contemporary, attracts large numbers of Hispanic and Black listeners, as well as white. As the term suggests, stations employing this format usually are located in metropolitan areas with large, heterogeneous populations. UC was born in the early 1980s, the offspring of the short-lived Disco format, which burst onto the scene in 1978. What characterizes UC the most is its upbeat, danceable sound and deejays who are hip, friendly, and energetic. Although UC outlets stress danceable tunes, their playlists generally are anything but narrow. However, a particular sound may be given preference over another, depending on the demographic composition of the population in the area that the station serves. For example, UC outlets may play greater amounts of music with a Latin or rhythm-and-blues flavor, whereas others may air larger proportions of light jazz, reggae, new rock, or hip hop. Some AM stations around the country have adopted the UC format; however, it is more likely to be found on the FM side, where it has taken numerous stations to the forefront of their market's ratings.

UC has had an impact on Black stations, which have experienced erosion in their youth numbers. Many Black stations have countered by broadening their playlists to include artists not traditionally programmed. Because of their high-intensity, fast-paced sound, UC outlets can give a Top 40 impression, but in contrast they commonly segue songs or present music in sweeps and give airplay to lengthy cuts, sometimes six to eight minutes long. Although Top 40 or CHR stations seldom program cuts lasting more than four minutes, UC outlets find long cuts or remixes compatible with their programming approach. Remember, UCs are very dance oriented. Newscasts play a minor role in this format, which caters to a target audience aged 18 to 34. Contests and promotions are important program elements.

As noted earlier, several CHR stations have adopted urban artists in order to offer the hybrid Churban or Rhythm Hits sound. Likewise, many Urban outlets have drawn from the more mainstream CHR playlist in an attempt to expand their listener base.

Classical

Although there are fewer than three-dozen full-time commercial Classical radio stations in the country, no other format can claim a more loyal following. Despite small numbers and soft ratings, most Classical stations do manage to generate a modest to good income. Over the years, profits have remained relatively minute in comparison to other formats. However, member stations of the Concert Music Broadcasters Association reported ad revenue increases of up to 40 percent in the 1980s with more growth in the 1990s and beyond. Due to its upscale audience, blue-chip accounts find the format an effective buy. This is first and foremost an FM format, and it has broadcast over the megahertz band for almost as long as it has existed.

In many markets, commercial Classical stations have been affected by public radio outlets programming classical music. Since commercial Classical stations must break to air the sponsor messages that keep them operating, they must adjust their playlists accordingly. This may mean shorter cuts of music during particular dayparts—in other words, less music. The noncommercial Classical outlet is relatively free of such constraints and thus benefits as a result. A case in point is WCRB-FM in Boston, the city's only full-time Classical station. Although it attracts most of the area's Classical listeners throughout the afternoon and evening hours, it loses many to public radio WGBH's classical segments. At least in part, public radio's success consists of having fewer interruptions in programming.

Classical stations target the 25- to 49-year-old, higher income, college-educated listener. News is typically presented at 60- to 90-minute intervals and generally runs from 5 to 10 minutes. The format is characterized by a conservative, straightforward air sound. Sensationalism and hype are avoided, and on-air contests and promotions are as rare as announcer chatter.

Religious/Christian

Live broadcasts of religious programs began while the medium was still in its experimental stage. In 1919 the U.S. Army Signal Corps aired a service from a chapel in Washington, D.C. Not long after that, KFSG in Los Angeles and WMBI in Chicago began to devote themselves to religious programming. Soon dozens of other radio outlets were broadcasting the message of God. In the 1980s, over 600 stations broadcast religious formats on a full-time basis, and another 1,500 air at least six hours of religious features on a weekly basis. *M Street Journal* reports that over 900 stations air the Religious format today.

Religious broadcasters typically follow one of two programming approaches. One includes music as part of its presentation, and the other does not. The Religious station that features music often programs contemporary tunes containing a Christian

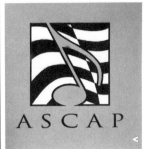

Essentials

THE AMERICAN SOCIETY OF COMPOSERS, AUTHORS AND PUBLISHERS

ASCAP is ▷

a **performing-rights organization** whose function is to protect the **rights** of our members by licensing and collecting royalties for the public performance of their copyrighted musical works.

the only U.S. society **created and controlled** by songwriters and publishers.

the only U.S. society that gives writers and publishers **a voice.** ASCAP conducts open membership meetings, issues financial reports to its members, has writer and publisher member advisory committees.

the only U.S. society that gives writers and publishers **a vote.** ASCAP is governed by an experienced Board of Directors composed of knowledgeable songwriters, composers and music publishers, each of whom is elected by the membership.

the **largest** performing-rights society in the world in terms of **license-fee collections** and writer and publisher **performance-royalty payments.** 1995 income: more than $435 million.

the **largest** performing-rights society in the world in terms of **constituency.** ASCAP has more than **75,000** U.S. writer and publisher members. Additionally, it represents more than **200,000** foreign-society writers and publishers.

the industry **leader** since 1914 in negotiating license fees with the users of music.

one of the most effective protectors of the rights of creators and music publishers. ASCAP **lobbies** in Congress and **litigates** in the courts, if necessary, on behalf of its constituents.

the only society where writers and publishers sign **identical contracts,** with **the right to resign** every year of the contract.

the only U.S. society with specific written rules covering **all types of performances on all types of media,** with all royalties distributed solely on that basis.

the only U.S. society where payment **changes have to be approved** by the Board of Directors, the Department of Justice and in some cases by a U.S. Federal Court after an open court hearing. No changes are made without notice to the membership, and rates are not subject to arbitrary change at any time, as they are at other performing-rights organizations.

the only U.S. society where your **royalties are determined objectively** over their entire copyright life and not by discretionary voluntary payments, short-term special deals or management discretion.

FIGURE 3.5
Radio stations pay an annual fee to music licensing services such as BMI and ASCAP.

or life-affirming perspective. Observes broadcast educator Janet McMullen, programming Contemporary Christian is a challenge for a number of reasons. "With the broad scope of denominations possessing varying beliefs, it is sometimes very hard to keep the listening public happy. It is a very fine line to walk. You have to be careful not to offend or alienate listeners, even in our format. This requires careful and thoughtful programming." The religious format approach also includes the scheduling of blocks of religious features and programs. Nonmusic Religious outlets

Some Format Debuts						
Prior to 1950	1950s	1960s	1970s	1980s	1990s	2000s
Classical	Middle-of-	News	Adult	Arena Rock	Mix	Jammin' Oldies
Country	the-Road	Talk	Contemporary	Hot Adult	All-Children	Rhythm Hits
Hit Parade	Top 40	News/Talk	Album	Contemporary	Arrow	Active Rock
Religious	Beautiful Music	Progressive	Oriented Rock	Hit/Radio	Rap/Hip Hop	Adult Hits
Black		Acid/	Easy Listening	Urban	Digital Hits	FM Talk
Hispanic		Psychedelic	Contemporary	Contemporary	Gen X	Diversity
		Jazz	Country	New Age	Tourist Radio	Christian
		All Request	Urban Country	Eclectic	Triple A	Contemporary
		Oldies	Mellow Rock	Oriented/Rock	NAC	Rhythmic Oldies
		Diversified	Disco	All Sports	Modern Rock	Acoustic
			Nostalgia	All Motivation	Churban	Spectrum AC
			British Rock	All Comedy	Boomer Rock	
			New Wave	All Beatles	Coupon Radio	
			Public Radio	Classic Hits		
				Classic Rock		
				Male Adult		
				Contemporary		

FIGURE 3.6
Dozens of other formats (often variations on those listed) have emerged since the start of program specialization in the 1950s.

concentrate on inspirational features and complementary talk and informational shows.

Religious broadcasters claim that their spiritual messages reach nearly half of the nation's radio audience, and the American Research Corporation in Irvine, California, contends that over 25 percent of those tuned to Religious stations attend church more frequently. Two-thirds of the country's Religious radio stations broadcast over AM frequencies.

An indication of the continued popularity of Religious radio in the latter part of the 1990s was the launch of ChristianNet, a network that offers talk shows from some of the biggest names in conservative chatter.

Ethnic (Black and Hispanic)

African-Americans constitute the largest minority in the nation, thus making Black one of the most prominent ethnic formats. Over 300 radio stations gear themselves to the needs and desires of Black listeners. WDIA-AM in Memphis claims to be the first station to program exclusively to a non-white audience. It introduced the format in 1947. Initially growth was gradual in this format, but in the 1960s, as the Motown sound took hold of the hit charts and the

Black Pride movement got under way, more Black stations entered the airways.

At its inception, the Disco craze in the 1970s brought new listeners to the Black stations, which shortly saw their fortunes change when All-Disco stations began to surface. Many Black outlets witnessed an exodus of their younger listeners to the Disco stations. This prompted a number of Black stations to abandon their more traditional playlists, which consisted of rhythm and blues, gospel, and soul tunes, for exclusively Disco music. When Disco perished in the early 1980s, the Urban Contemporary format took its place. Today, Progressive Black stations, such as WBLS-FM, New York, combine dance music with soulful rock and contemporary jazz, and many have transcended the color barrier by including certain white artists on their playlists. In fact, many Black stations employ white air personnel in efforts to broaden their demographic base. WILD-AM in Boston, long considered the city's Black station, is an example of this trend. "We have become more of a general appeal station than a purely ethnic one. We've had to in order to prosper. We strive for a distinct, yet neuter or deethnicized, sound on the air. The Black format has changed considerably over the years," notes WILD program director

Elroy Smith. The old-line R&B and gospel stations still exist and can be found mostly in the south.

Hispanic or Spanish-language stations constitute another large ethnic format. KCOR-AM, San Antonio, became the first All-Spanish station in 1947, just a matter of months after WDIA-AM in Memphis put the Black format on the air. Cities with large Latin populations are able to support the format, and in some metropolitan areas with vast numbers of Spanish-speaking residents, such as New York, Los Angeles, and Miami, several radio outlets are devoted exclusively to Hispanic programming.

Programming approaches within the format are not unlike those prevalent at Anglo stations. That is to say, Spanish-language radio stations also modify their sound to draw a specific demographic. For example, many offer contemporary music for younger listeners and more traditional music for older listeners.

Ed Shane views Hispanic radio as very diverse and vibrant. "An impressive multiplicity of programming styles and approaches are found in this format. Here in Houston, for example, we have two brands of Tejano, one of Exitos (hits), a lot of Ranchera, and a couple of Talk stations. In the Rio Grande Valley of Texas, there's a lush, instrumental-and-vocal 'Easy Listening' station in Spanish. The L.A. dial is full of Hispanic nuance. Miami, likewise, and it has a totally different slant."

Many Hispanic females are drawn to an approach called The Groove, which mixes Motown and Latin pop artists. The format is marketed by Interstar Programming.

Spanish media experts predicted that there would be a significant increase in the number of Hispanic stations through the 1990s, and they were right. Much of this growth occurred on the AM band but later spread rapidly on FM.

Hundreds of other radio stations countrywide apportion a significant piece of their air schedules (over 20 hours weekly), if not all, to foreign-language programs in Por-

tuguese, German, Polish, Greek, Japanese, and so on.

Around 30 stations broadcast exclusively to American Indians and Eskimos and are licensed to Native Americans. Today these stations are being fed programming from American Indian Radio on Satellite (AIROS), and the Indigenous Communications Association predicts over 100 Indian-operated stations by the end of the next decade. Meanwhile, the number of stations broadcasting to Asians and other nationalities is rising.

Full Service (FS)

The Full Service format (also called Variety, General Appeal, Diversified, etc.) attempts to provide its mostly middle-age listeners a mix of all programming genres—music, news, sports, and information features. Known for years as Middle-of-the Road (MOR), the format has attempted to

Radio Reaches Upscale Consumers

Radio reaches adults with incomes of $50,000+

	Weekly Reach	Avg. Daily Time Spent Listening Hrs:Min
Adults		
• 18+	99.3%	3:18
Men		
• 18+	99.6%	3:26
Women		
• 18+	98.9%	3:08

Radio reaches college graduates

	Weekly Reach	Avg. Daily Time Spent Listening Hrs:Min
Adults		
• 18+	97.0%	3:01
Men		
• 18+	96.8%	3:00
Women		
• 18+	97.3%	3:02

Radio reaches professionals/managers

	Weekly Reach	Avg. Daily Time Spent Listening Hrs:Min
Adults		
• 18+	96.3%	3:05
Men		
• 18+	96.2%	3:06
Women		
• 18+	96.3%	3:03

Source: RADAR ® 71, Fall 2001, © Copyright Arbitron
(Monday-Sunday, 24 hours, based on weekly cume, daily time spent listening)

FIGURE 3.7
Radio programming offers advertisers lifestyle targeting. Courtesy RAB.

strengthen its public service aspect through increased information programming. It is really one-stop shopping for listeners who would like a little bit of everything. Today this type of station exists mostly in small markets where stations attempt to be good-citizen radio for everyone. It has been called the *bridge* format because of its "all things to all people" programming approach. However, its large market audience has decreased over the years, particularly since 1980, due to the rise in popularity of more specialized formats. According to radio program specialist Dick Ellis, Full Service now has a predominantly over-40 age demographic, several years older than just a decade ago. In some major markets the format continues to do well in the ratings mainly because of strong on-air personalities. But this is not the format that it once was. Since its inception in the 1950s, up through the 1970s, stations working the MOR sound often dominated their markets. Yet the Soft Rock and Oldies formats in the 1970s, the updating of Easy Listening (Smooth Jazz), and particularly the ascendancy of Adult Contemporary and Talk formats have conspired to significantly erode MOR (now FS), numbers. For instance, *M Street Journal* cites fewer than 100 of these stations today.

Full Service is the home of the on-air personality. Perhaps no other format gives its air people as much latitude and freedom. This is not to suggest that FS announcers may do as they please. They, like any other, must abide by format and programming policy, but FS personalities often serve as the cornerstone of their station's air product. Some of the best-known deejays in the country have come from the FS (MOR) milieu. It would then follow that the music is rarely, if ever, presented in sweeps or even segued. Deejay patter occurs between each cut of music, and announcements are inserted in the same way. News and sports play another vital function at these stations. During drive periods, FS often presents lengthened blocks of news, replete with frequent traffic reports, weather updates, and the latest sports information. Many FS outlets are affiliated with major-league teams. With few exceptions, FS is an AM format. Although it has noted slippage in recent years, it will likely continue to bridge whatever gaps may exist in a highly specialized radio marketplace.

Niche Formats

Experts say that the Alternative formats, with their narrower focus on specific demographic segments, will enjoy greater success in the coming years. In an interview in *Broadcasting and Cable*, Jeff Pollack predicted formats offering more nontraditional approaches to mainstream music (Modern Rock, for example) would be the ratings winners of the next few years. The intense fragmentation of the listening pool means that the big umbrella formats are going to lose out to the ultra-specific ones.

Alternative Rock, which has never fully enjoyed star status, was expected to move up toward the front of the pack in the new millennium. Of course, when it comes to format prognostication the term *unpredictable* takes on a whole new meaning. Indeed, there will be a rash of successful niche formats in the coming years, due to the ever-increasing fragmentation of the radio audience, but exactly what they will be is anyone's guess.

A few years back, no one thought that All-Children's Radio (Disney, Radio Aahs) would draw an economically attractive segment of the listening public, but today it is one of the more successful niches on the dial (mostly on AM at this writing), and there are many other wannabes entering the cluttered airwaves. New niche or splinter formats emerge frequently—Active Rock and Christian Talk are good examples—in an industry always on the lookout for the next best thing and competing with a myriad of other listening options. In an MP3 world, staying fresh and current gives radio an edge—one that is more and more necessary as the audio landscape changes.

At best, the preceding is an incomplete list of myriad radio formats that serve the listening public. The program formats mentioned constitute the majority of the basic format categories prevalent today. Tomorrow? Who knows? Radio is hardly a static industry, but one subject to the whims of popular taste. When something new captures the imagination of the American public, radio responds, and often a new format is conceived.

Radio Theater

Poet Stephen Vincent Benet called radio the "theater of the mind." His description was coined during the medium's heyday in the 1930s and 1940s when a myriad of original prose and verse plays were being produced and aired by the networks. The foremost radiowright of the time was Norman Corwin, whose works soared to literary heights and were tuned and admired by millions. He was joined by many writers whose efforts were traditionally geared to the print media. These writers saw in the audio medium a chance to reach larger audiences with their works and so they generated a significant amount of original material for it. Among the most famous print authors to ply their craft to the ethereal page were W. H. Auden, Arthur Miller, Pearl S. Buck, Archibald MacLeish, Irwin Shaw, and Edna St. Vincent Milay. The medium itself engendered other great writers besides Corwin. A close rival was Arch Oboler, whose popular thrillers brought chills and thrills to the listening audience. Perhaps the most famous of all radio dramas was Orson Welles's adaptation of H. G. Wells's "War of the Worlds." So brilliantly evocative in its performances, writing, and production values, it quite literally sent its audience into a panic.

Following the arrival of television, radio dramas all but vanished from the airwaves. The networks were gone and local stations could ill-afford their manufacture. Over the decades since, there have been attempts to revive the art form (CBS and Mutual radio networks offered short-lived series), but the radio drama was and continues to be of only passing interest to an audience with a rapidly diminishing attention span and visual orientation. In recent years Public radio has become engaged in radio theater, and it is there that the medium's greatest artistic rendering makes occasional appearances.

The Programmer

Program directors (PDs) are radiophiles. They live the medium. Most admit to being smitten by radio at an early age. "It's something that is in your blood and grows to consuming proportions," admits programmer Peter Falconi. Long-time PD Brian Mitchell recalls an interest in the medium as a small child, and for good reason. "I was born into a broadcasting family. My father is a station owner and builder. During my childhood, radio was the primary topic at the dinner table. It fed the flame that I believe was already ignited anyway. Radio fascinated me from the start."

The customary route to the programmer's job involves deejaying and participation in other on-air-related areas, such as copywriting, production, music, and news. It would be difficult to state exactly how long it takes to become a program director. It largely depends on the individual and where he or she happens to be. In some instances, newcomers have gone into programming within their first year in the business. When this happens it is likeliest to occur in a small market where turnover may be high. On the other hand, it is far more common to spend years working toward this goal, even in the best of situations. "Although my father owned the station, I spent a long time in a series of jobs before my appointment to programmer. Along the way, I worked as station janitor, and then got into announcing, production, and eventually programming," recounts Mitchell.

One of the nation's foremost air personalities, Dick Fatherly, whom *Billboard Magazine* has described as a "long-time legend," spent years as a deejay before making the transition. "In the twenty-five years that I've been in this business, I have worked as a jock, newsman, production director, and even sales rep. Eventually I ended up in program management. During my career I have worked at WABC, WICC, WFUN, WHB, to mention a few. Plenty of experience, you might say," comments Fatherly.

Experience contributes most toward the making of the station's programmer. However, individuals entering the field with hopes of becoming a PD do well to acquire as much formal training as possible. The programmer's job has become an increasingly demanding one as a result of expanding competition. "A good knowledge of research methodology, analysis, and application is crucial. Programming is both an art and a science today," observes general manager Jim Murphy.

Programmer Andy Bloom concurs with Murphy, adding, "A would-be PD needs to school him- or herself in marketing research particularly. Little is done anymore that is not based on careful analysis."

Publisher B. Eric Rhoads echoes this stance. "The role has changed. The PD used to be a glorified music director with some background in talent development. Today the PD must be a marketing expert. Radio marketing has become very complex, what with telemarketing, database marketing, direct mail, interactive communication (fax, computer bulletin boards), and so forth. Radio is changing, and the PD must adapt. No longer will records and deejays make the big difference. Stations are at parity in music, so better ways must be found to set stations apart."

Says Shane, "The ultimate analogy for the PD is 'brand manager,' overseeing not only the product, but also the image and perception of the product. Since program-

mers now must work hand in hand with sellers to maximize station revenues, there's a new awareness of the marketing dimension."

Cognizant of this, schools with programs in radio broadcasting have begun to emphasize courses in audience and marketing research, as well as other programming-related areas. An important fact for the aspiring PD to keep in mind is that more people entering broadcasting today have college backgrounds than ever before. Even though a college degree is not necessarily a prerequisite for the position of PD, it is clearly regarded as an asset by upper management. "It used to be that a college degree didn't mean so much. A PD came up through the ranks of programming, proved his ability, and was hired. Not that that doesn't still happen. It does. But more and more the new PD has a degree or, at the very least, several years of college," contends Joe Cortese, air personality, WBMX-FM, Boston. "I majored in Communication Arts at a junior college and then transferred to a four-year school. There are many colleges offering communications courses here in the Boston area, so I'll probably take some more as a way of further preparing for the day when I'll be programming or managing a station. That's what I eventually want to do," says Cortese, adding that experience in the trenches is also vital to success.

His point is well taken. Work experience does head the list on which a station manager bases his or her selection for program director. Meanwhile, college training, at the very least, has become a criterion to the extent that if an applicant does not have any, the prospective employer takes notice.

Beyond formal training and experience, Chuck Ducoty, major market station manager, says a PD must possess certain innate qualities. "Common sense and a good sense of humor are necessary attributes and are in rather short supply, I think." Dick Fatherly adds sensitivity, patience, compassion, and drive to the list.

THE MIX LOUNGE

The Mix Lounge showcases approximately 20-25 performances each year, and has seen some of the brightest faces in music today. Recent visits include Dave Matthews, Barenaked Ladies, Guster, The Cranberries, Alanis Morrissette, Macy Gray, Sting, Vertical Horizon, Third Eye Blind and Natalie Merchant. Approximately 50 consumers attend each exclusive performance. The Mix Lounge is a true testament to the clout Mix 98-5 has in the music industry. Check out some inside pictures of past Mix Lounge performances below!

Source: Arbitron Spring 2002/Scarborough 2002

The Program Director's Duties and Responsibilities

Where to begin this discussion poses no simple problem, because the PD's responsibilities and duties are so numerous and wide-ranging. Second in responsibility to the general manager, the program director is the individual responsible for everything that goes over the air. This involves working with the manager in establishing programming and format policy and overseeing their effective execution. In addition, he or she

FIGURE 3.9
Sports shows are popular in many formats, including those featuring music. Courtesy Infinity.

"Head and shoulders above the competition."

Good Sports?
Goose was There!

✈ Superbowl XXX

✈ The Penguins' Stanley Cup wins in '91 and '92

✈ The Pirates' postseason games, '91 through '93.

✈ Pirates' Spring Training, '84 through '96

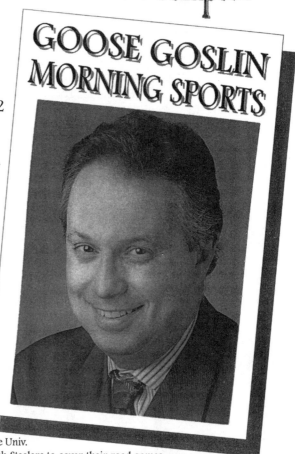

GOOSE GOSLIN MORNING SPORTS

For over 12 years, Goose Goslin has worked as KDKA Radio 1020 Morning Sports Anchor and Sports Director. He has won seven straight Associated Press awards as Best Major Market Radio Sportscaster in Pennsylvania.

Among the judge's comments from the 1995 ceremonies: "It wasn't even close. He was clearly head and shoulders above the competition." In addition, Goslin has won three Golden Quill awards from the Pittsburgh Press Club and several other broadcast awards.

Goslin has served as color analyst for Old Dominion University and Duquesne Univ. Basketball and travelled with the Pittsburgh Steelers to cover their road games for the past 15 seasons. He currently serves as color analyst for Indiana University of Pennsylvania's national ranked Division II football program and previously hosted "Goose Goslin's Hockey Talk" prior to Penguins broadcasts on KDKA.

Since 1991 Goose has been featured as the principal columnist of the Sunday sports editorial page of the Pittsburgh Tribune-Review, one of Pittsburgh's two major daily papers with a Sunday supplement circulation in excess of 100,000.

hires and supervises on-air music and production personnel, plans various schedules, handles the programming budget, develops promotions, monitors the station and its competition, assesses research, and may even pull a daily airshift. The PD also is accountable for the presentation of news, public affairs, and sports features, although a news director often is appointed to help oversee these areas.

The program director alone does not determine a station's format. This is an upper management decision. The PD may be involved in the selection process but, more often than not, the format has been chosen before the programmer has been hired. For example, WYYY decides it must switch from MOR to CHR in order to attract a more marketable demographic. After an in-depth examination of its own market, research on the effectiveness of CHR nationally, and advice from a program consultant and rep company, the format change is deemed appropriate. Reluctantly the station manager concludes that he must bring in a CHR specialist, which means that he must terminate the services of his present programmer, whose experience is limited to MOR. The station manager places an ad in an industry trade magazine, interviews several candidates, and hires the person he feels will take the station to the top of the ratings. When the new program director arrives, he or she is charged with the task of preparing the CHR format for its debut. Among other things, this may involve hiring new air people, the acquisition of a new music library or the updating of the existing one, preparing promos and purchasing jingles, and working in league with the sales, traffic, and engineering departments for maximum results.

On these points, Corinne Baldasano, vice president of SW programming, observes, "First of all, of course, you must be sure that the station you are programming fills a market void, i.e., that there is an opportunity for you to succeed in your geographic area with the format you are programming. For example, a young adult alternative rock station may not have much chance for success in an area that is mostly populated by retirees. Once you have determined that the format fills an audience need, you need to focus on building your station. The basic ingredients are making sure your music mix is correct (if you are programming a music station) and that you've hired the on-air talent that conveys the attitude and image of the station you wish to build. At this stage, it is far more important to focus inward than outward. Many stations have failed because they've paid more attention to the competition's product than they have their own."

Once the format is implemented, the program director must work at refining and maintaining the sound. After a short time, the programmer may feel compelled to modify air schedules either by shifting deejays around or replacing those who do not enhance the format. Says Metro Networks president David Saperstein, "You've got to continually fine-tune the station's sound. You must remove any and all negatives, like excessive talk, annoying commercials, technical weaknesses, and so forth. The most critical rule of thumb is that stations should always concentrate on bringing listeners to the station, keeping them tuned in, and providing the right balance of music, personalities, talk, information, and commercials so listeners do not have any reason to tune elsewhere."

The PD prepares weekend and holiday schedules as well, and this generally requires the hiring of part-time announcers. A station may employ as few as one or two part-timers or fill-in people, or as many as eight to ten. This largely depends on whether deejays are on a five- or six-day schedule. At most stations, air people are hired to work a six-day week. The objective of scheduling is not merely to fill slots but to maintain continuity and consistency of sound. A PD prefers to tamper with shifts as little as possible and fervently hopes that he has filled weekend slots with people who are reliable. "The importance of dependable, trustworthy air people cannot be overemphasized. It's great to have talented deejays, but if they don't show up when they are supposed to because of one reason or another, they don't do you a lot of good. You need people who are cooperative. I have no patience with individuals who try to deceive me or fail to live up to their responsibilities," says Brian Mitchell. A station that is constantly introducing new air personnel has a difficult time establishing listener habit. The PD knows that in order to succeed he or she must present a stable and dependable sound, and this is a significant programming challenge.

Production schedules also are prepared by the programmer. Deejays are usually tapped for production duties before or after their airshifts. For example, the morning person who is on the air from six to ten may be assigned production and copy chores from ten until noon. Meanwhile, the midday deejay who is on the air from ten until three is given production assignments from three to five, and so on. Large radio stations frequently employ a fulltime production person. If so, this individual handles all production responsibilities and is supervised by the program director.

A program director traditionally handles the department's budget, which generally constitutes 30 to 40 percent of the station's operating budget. Working with the station manager, the PD ascertains the financial needs of the programming area. The size and scope of the budget vary from station to station. Most programming budgets include funds for the acquisition of program materials, such as albums, features, and contest paraphernalia. A separate promotional budget usually exists, and it too may be managed by the PD. The programmer's budgetary responsibilities range from monumental at some outlets to minuscule at others. Personnel salaries and even equipment purchases may fall within the province of the program department's budget. Brian Mitchell believes that "an understanding of the total financial structure of the company or corporation and how programming fits into the scheme of things is a real asset to a programmer."

Devising station promotions and contests also places demands on the PD's time. Large stations often appoint a promotion director. When this is the case, the PD and promotion director work together in the planning, development, and execution of the promotional campaign. The PD, however, retains final veto power should he or she feel that the promotion or contest fails to complement the station's format. When the PD alone handles promotions and contests, he or she may involve other members of the programming or sales department in brainstorming sessions designed to come up with original and interesting concepts. The programmer is aware that the right promotion or contest can have a major impact on ratings. Thus, he or she is constantly on the lookout for an appropriate vehicle. In the quest to find the promotion that will launch the station on the path to a larger audience, the PD may seek assistance from one of dozens of companies that offer promotional services.

The program director's major objective is to program for results. If the station's programming fails to attract a sufficient following, the ratings will reflect that unhappy fact. All medium and larger markets are surveyed by ratings companies, primarily Arbitron. Very few small rural markets, with perhaps one or two stations, are surveyed. If a small market station is poorly programmed, the results will be apparent in the negative reactions of the local retailers. Simply put, the station will not be bought by enough advertisers to make the operation a profitable venture. In the bigger markets, where several stations compete for advertising dollars, the ratings are used to determine which is the most effective or cost-efficient station to buy. "In order to make it to the top of the ratings in your particular market, you have to be doing the best job around. It's the PD who is going to get the station the numbers it needs to make a buck. If he doesn't turn the trick, he's back in the job market," observes Dick Fatherly.

Program directors constantly monitor the competition by analyzing the ratings and by listening. A radio station's programming is often constructed in reaction to a direct competitor's. For example, rock stations in the same market often counterprogram newscasts by airing them at different times in order to grab up their competitor's tune-outs. However, rather than contrast with each other, pop stations tend to reflect one another. This, in fact, has been the basis of arguments by critics who object to the so-called mirroring effect. What happens is easily understood. If a station does well by presenting a particular format, other stations are going to exploit the sound in the hopes of doing well also. WYYY promotes commercial-free sweeps of music and captures big ratings, and soon its competitor programs likewise. "Program directors use what has proven to be effective. It is more a matter of survival than anything. I think most of us try to be original to the degree that we can be, but there is very little new under the sun. Programming moves cyclically. Today we're all doing this. Tomorrow we'll all be doing that. The medium reacts to trends or fads. It's the nature of the beast," notes programmer Mitchell. Keeping in step with, or rather one step ahead of, the competition requires that the PD know what is happening around him or her at all times.

Probably 60 percent of the nation's PDs pull an airshift (go on the air themselves) on either a full-time or part-time basis. A difference of opinion exists among programmers concerning their on-air participation. Many feel that being on the air gives them a true sense of the station's sound, which aids them in their programming efforts. Others contend that the three or four hours that they spend on the air take them away from important programming duties. Major market PDs are less likely to be heard on the air than their peers in smaller markets because of additional duties created by the size and status of the station. Meanwhile, small and medium market stations often expect their PDs to be seasoned air people capable of filling a key shift. "It has been my experience when applying for programming jobs that managers are looking for PDs with excellent announcing skills. It is pretty rare to find a small market PD who does not have a daily airshift. It comes with the territory," says Gary Begin.

Whether PDs are involved in actual airshifts or not, almost all participate in the production of commercials, public service announcements, and promos. In lieu of an airshift, a PD may spend several hours each day in the station's production facilities. The programmer may, in fact, serve as the primary copywriter and spot producer. This is especially true at nonmajor market outlets that do not employ a full-time production person.

In summation, the program director must possess an imposing list of skills to perform effectively the countless tasks confronting

FIGURE 3.10
Syndicated programming services promise to increase station audience size. Courtesy Broadcast Programming.

him or her daily. There is no one person, other than the general manager, whose responsibilities outweigh the programmer's. The program director can either make or break the radio station.

Elements of Programming

Few programmers entrust the selection and scheduling of music and other sound elements to deejays and announcers. There is too much at stake and too many variables, both internal and external, that must be

considered in order to achieve maximum results within a chosen format.

It has become a very complex undertaking, observes Bloom. "For instance, all of our music is tested via call-out. At least one or two perceptual studies are done every year, depending on what questions we need answered. Usually a couple of sets of focus groups per year, too. Everything is researched, and nothing is left to chance." In most cases, the PD determines how much music is programmed hourly and in what rotation, and when news, public affairs features, and commercials are slotted. Program wheels, also variously known as sound hours, hot clocks, and format disks, are carefully designed by the PD to ensure the effective presentation of on-air ingredients. Program wheels are posted in the control studio to inform and guide air people as to what is to be broadcast and at what point in the hour. Although not every station provides deejays with such specific programming schemata, today very few stations leave things up to chance since the inappropriate scheduling and sequencing of sound elements may drive listeners to a competitor. Radio programming has become that much of an exacting science. With few exceptions, stations use some kind of formula in the conveyance of their programming material.

At one time, Top 40 stations were the unrivaled leaders of formula programming. Today, however, even Full Service and Classic Rock outlets, which once were the least formulaic, have become more sensitive to form. The age of free-form commercial radio has long since passed, and it is doubtful, given the state of the marketplace, that it will return. Of course, stranger things have happened in radio. Depending on the extent to which a PD prescribes the content of a sound hour, programming clocks may be elaborate in their detail or quite rudimentary. Music clocks are used to plot out elements. Clocks reflect the minutes of the standard hour, and the PD places elements

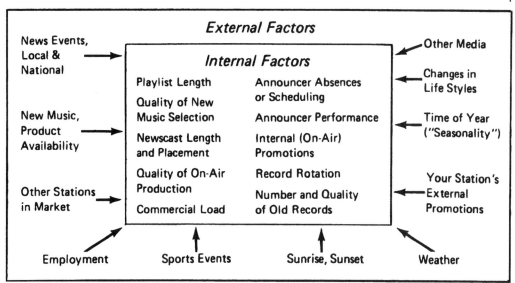

FIGURE 3.12
A model of a station's competitive environment as conceived by Arbitron. Courtesy Arbitron.

where they actually are to occur during the hour. Many programmers use a set of clocks, or clocks that change with each hour. (See figure 3.14 and 3.16)

Observes Ed Shane, "When I speak at college classes, there's always a question about why format clock hours are structured the way they are, so let me call what follows 'Clock Construction 101.' Arbitron entries show that the first quarter hour (:00–:15) gets the largest number of new entries, that is, when the radio is turned on for the first time or switched to a new station. The third quarter hour (:30–:45) gets the second largest number. The second quarter hour (:15–:30) gets the third largest number, and the fourth quarter hour (:45–:00) gets the fewest new tune-ins. That pattern is why many stations load their commercial content in the final or fourth quarter hour–trying to prevent a new listener from hearing a commercial as the first thing when tuning. Since the first quarter hour is so valuable in terms of new tune-ins, the most valuable programming elements should be placed in that segment. A music station is advised to load the first quarter hour with Power Current or Power Gold

songs, songs that test the best or are the biggest hits."

Indeed program clocks are set up with the competition and market factors in mind. For example, programmers will devise a clock that reflects morning and afternoon drive periods in their market. Not all markets have identical commuter hours. In some cities morning drive may start as early as 5:30 a.m.; in others it may begin at 7:00 a.m. The programmer sets up clocks accordingly. A clock parallels the activities of the community in which the station operates.

Music stations are not the only ones that use program wheels. News and Talk stations do so as well. News stations, like music outlets, use key format elements in order to maintain ratings through the hour. Many news stations work their clocks in 20-minute cycles. During this segment news is arranged according to its degree of importance and geographic relevance, such as local, regional, national, and international. Most news stations lead with their top local stories. News stories of particular interest are repeated during the segment. Sports, weather, and other news-related information, such as traffic and stock market reports,

THE FREQUENCY BASED MUSIC TEST.

Exclusively From The Benchmark Company

WHO DO YOU LIKE?

That's long been the dominant issue in auditorium music testing. Most tests are based on perceived *liking* of a "hook" of a record.

But that causes a problem! For most listeners, there's quite a gap between how much they *"like"* something and how frequently they want to hear it on the radio. Case in point: you play a "hook" of the *"Wind Cries Mary"* for a listener. He gives it the highest score for *"liking."*

But did he give it that score because he hasn't heard it in ten years, or because it's truly one of his favorites? Moreover, that kind of rating doesn't tell you how frequently he wants to hear it on the radio.

FREQUENCY OF AIR PLAY THE TRUE MEASURE

The Benchmark Company has developed a new frequency based music test system based not solely on *"liking"* of a record, but on the more reliable measure of "how often would you like to hear this record." Listeners can respond much more accurately to this type of question—hence, program directors have more reliable data with which to construct play lists and rotations.

The FBMT provides realistic answers for burnout too. While often difficult to measure in the common like-dislike test, burnout evaluation is built right into the FBMT.

CLUSTER ANALYSIS

There continues to be a lot of confusion with some broadcasters about multivariate techniques for analyzing music data. At Benchmark we make it simple to understand and use—after all, we pioneered the technique *ten* years ago!

Simply put, *cluster analysis* is a tool for data reduction. It allows you to identify groups of listeners who "cluster" together in their musical preferences. *Factor analysis* allows you to see how individual songs and artists can be grouped to improve rotations. The FBMT provides the perfect approach to use for cluster and factor analysis. Your FBMT results are turned around quickly and the reports (including cluster and factor analysis) are broadcaster friendly.

The Benchmark Company

*"The FBMT is the **best** new approach I've seen in auditorium research."*
Robb Stewart, PD
WMXC, Charlotte
Format: AC

"The FBMT represents a significant step forward in auditorium music research."
Chris Brodie, PD
KTWV, Los Angeles
Format: NAC

"The FBMT is light years ahead of the field. It really delivered for us at KVIL."
Tom Watson
Adult Contemporary Concepts
(Former PD at KVIL, Dallas)

For More Information on the Frequency Based Music Test™, Contact:
Paige Blount, Director of Research at 1-800-274-5164
1705 S. Capital of Texas Hwy. • Suite 305 • Austin, Texas 78746

constitute a part of the segment. Elements may be juggled around or different ones inserted during successive 20-minute blocks to keep things from sounding repetitious.

In the Talk format, two-way conversation and interviews fill the space generally allot-ted to songs in the music format. Therefore, Talk wheels often resemble music wheels in their structure. For example, news is offered at the top of the hour followed by a talk sweep that precedes a spot set. This is done in a fashion that is reminiscent of Easy Listening.

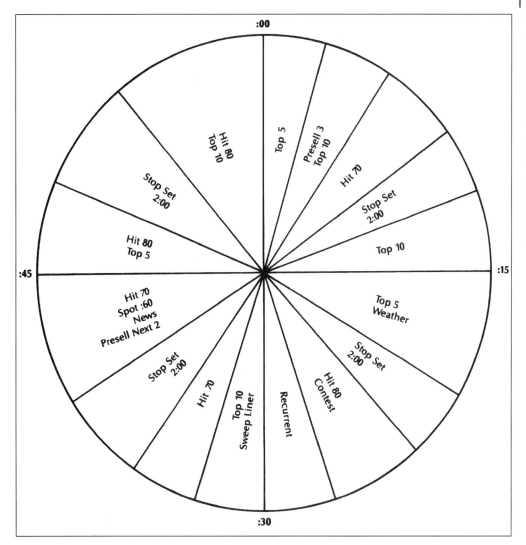

FIGURE 3.14
A typical morning drivetime CHR clock. It reflects a nine-minute commercial load maximum per hour. Notice the way the stop sets occur away from the quarter-hour. A Top 5 record is often aired on the quarter-hour to give the station the best ratings advantage. This is called "quarter-hour maintenance."

Of course, not all stations arrange their sound hours as depicted in these pages. Many variations exist, most inspired by computers, but these examples are fairly representative of some of the program schematics used in today's radio marketplace.

Program wheels keep a station on a preordained path and prevent wandering. As stated, each programming element—commercial, news, promo, weather, and so on—is strategically located in the sound hour to enhance flow and optimize impact. Balance is imperative: too much deejay patter on a station promoting more music and less talk, listeners become disenchanted; too little news and information on a station targeting the over-30 male commuter, the competition benefits. "When constructing or arranging the program clock, you have to work forward and backward to make sure that everything fits and is positioned correctly. One element out of place can become that proverbial hole in the dam. Spots, jock breaks, music—it all must be weighed before clocking. A lot of experimentation, not to mention research, goes into this," observes radio executive Lorna Ozman.

It was previously pointed out that a station with a more-music slant limits announcer discourse in order to schedule additional tunes. Some formats, in particular Easy Listening/Smooth Jazz, have reduced the role of the announcer to not much more than occasional live promos and IDs, which are written on liner or flip cards. Nothing is left to chance. This also is true of stations airing the super-tight hit music format. Deejays say what is written and move the music. At stations where deejays are given more control, wheels play a less crucial function. Outlets where a particular personality has ruled the ratings for years often let that person have more input as to what music is aired. However, even in these cases, playlists generally are provided and followed.

The radio personality has enjoyed varying degrees of popularity since the 1950s. Over the years, Top 40, more than any other format, has toyed with the extent of deejay involvement on the air. The pendulum has swung from heavy personality presence in the 1950s and early 1960s to a drastically reduced role in the mid- and later 1960s. This dramatic shift came as the result of programmer Bill Drake's attempt to streamline Top 40. In the 1970s, the air personality regained some of his status, but in the 1980s the narrowing of hit station playlists brought about a new leanness and austerity that again diminished the jock's presence. In the mid-1980s, some pop music stations began to give the deejay more to do. "There's sort of a pattern to it all. For a while, deejays are the gems in the crown, and then they're just

FIGURE 3.15
Keeping the station going weekends. Courtesy Infinity.

Weekend Program Schedule

Featuring Award-Winning Local & National News On The Hour & Half-Hour

Times	Saturday	Times	Sunday
12:01am	The Mary Anne Lewis Show	12:01am	The Mary Anne Lewis Show
6:00am	Breakfast Line with Rob Pratte	6:00am	Breakfast Line with Rob Pratte
10:00am	KDKA's Home Improvement Show	8:00am	Prudential Ask the Realtor
11:00am	Talking Travel	9:00am	Your Money & You
Noon	Sports Saturday with Rob Pratte	11:00am	Sports Sunday with Rob Pratte
1:00pm	KDKA Radio Talk	1:00pm	The Susie Barbour Show
4:00pm	Sports Saturday with Ron Cook	4:00pm	The Chris Moore Show
7:00pm-11:00pm	The Chris Moore Show	9:00pm-11:00pm	Amplify with Father Ron Lenguin

the metal holding the precious stones in place for another period of time. What went on in the mid-1970s with personality began to recur in the latter part of the 1980s. Of course, there are a few new twists in the tiara, but what it comes down to is the temporary restoration of the hit radio personality. It's a back and forth movement, kind of like a tide. It comes in, then retreats, but each time something new washes up. Deejays screamed at the teens in the 1950s, mellowed out some in the 1960s and 1970s, went hyper again in the 1980s, but conservatism seems to be gaining favor once again," observes Brian Mitchell.

In addition to concentrating on the role deejays play in the sound hour, the PD pays careful attention to the general nature and quality of other ingredients. Music is, of course, of paramount importance. Songs must fit the format to begin with, but beyond the obvious, the quality of the artistry and the audio mix must meet certain criteria. A substandard musical arrangement or a disc with poor fidelity detracts from the station's sound. Jingles and promos must effectively establish the tone and tenor of the format, or they have the reverse effect of their intended purpose, which is to attract and hold listeners. Commercials, too, must be compatible with the program elements that surround them.

In all, the program director scrutinizes every component of the program wheel to keep the station true to form. The wheel helps maintain consistency, without which a station cannot hope to cultivate a following. Erratic programming in today's highly competitive marketplace is tantamount to directing listeners to other stations.

The Program Director and the Audience

The programmer must possess a clear perception of the type of listener the station management wants to attract. Initially, a station decides on a given format because it is convinced that it will make money with the new-found audience, meaning that the people who tune in to the station will look good to prospective advertisers. The purpose of any format is to win a desirable segment of the radio audience. Just who these people are and what makes them tick are questions that the PD must constantly address in order to achieve reach and retention. An informed programmer is aware that different types of music appeal to different types of people. For example, surveys have long concluded that heavy rock appeals more to men than it does to women, and that rock music, in general, is more popular among teens and young adults than it is with individuals over 40. This is no guarded secret, and certainly the programmer who is out to gain the over-40 crowd is doing himself and his station a disservice by programming even an occasional hard rock tune. This should be obvious.

A station's demographics refer to the characteristics of those who tune in: sex, age, income, and so forth. Within its demographics a station may exhibit particular strength in specific areas, or *cells* as they have come to be termed. For example, an Adult Contemporary station targeting the 24- to 39-year-old group may have a prominent cell in females over 30. The general information provided by the major ratings surveys indicate to the station the age and sex of those listening, but little beyond that. To find out more, the PD may conduct an in-house survey or employ the services of a research firm.

Since radio accompanies listeners practically everywhere, broadcasters pay particular attention to the lifestyle activities of their target audience. A station's geographic locale often dictates its program offerings. For example, hoping to capture the attention of the 35-year-old male, a radio outlet located in a small coastal city along the Gulf of Mexico might decide to air a series of one-minute informational tips on outdoor activities, such as tennis, golf, and deep-sea

FIGURE 3.16
Program clock for a
network syndicated
format. Courtesy ABC.

FIGURE 3.16 Program clock for a network syndicated format. Courtesy ABC.

fishing, that are exceptionally popular in the area. Stations have always catered to the interests of their listeners, but in the 1970s audience research became much more lifestyle oriented.

In the 1990s, broadcasters delved further into audience behavior through psychographic research, which, by examining motivational factors, provides programmers with information beyond the purely quantitative. Perhaps one of the best examples of a station's efforts to conform to the lifestyle of its listeners is *dayparting*, a topic briefly touched on in the discussion of program wheels. For the sake of illustration, let us discuss how an AC station may daypart (segmentalize) its broadcast day. To begin with, the station is targeting an over-40 audience, somewhat skewed toward males. The PD concludes that the station's biggest listening hours are mornings between seven and nine and afternoons between four and six, and that most of those tuned in during these periods are in their cars commuting to or from work. It is evident to the programmer that the station's programming approach must be modified during drivetime to reflect the needs of the audience. Obviously traffic reports, news and sports updates, weather forecasts, and frequent time checks are suitable fare for the station's morning audience. The interests of homebound commuters contrast slightly with those of work-bound commuters. Weather and time are less important, and most sports information from the previous night is old hat by the time the listener heads for home. Stock market reports and information about upcoming games and activities pick up the slack. Midday hours call for further modification, since the lifestyle of the station's audience is different. Aware that the majority of those listening are homemakers (in a less enlightened age this daypart was referred to as "housewife" time), the PD reduces the amount of news and information, replacing them with music and deejay conversation designed specifically to complement the activities of those tuned. In the evening, the station redirects its programming and schedules sports and talk features, going exclusively talk after midnight. All of these adjustments are made to attract and retain audience interest.

The program director relies on survey information and research data to better gauge and understand the station's audience. However, as a member of the community that the station serves, the

programmer knows that not everything is contained in formal documentation. He or she gains unique insight into the mood and mentality of the area within the station's signal simply by taking part in the activities of day-to-day life. A programmer with a real feel for the area in which the station is located, as well as a fundamental grasp of research methodology and its application, is in the best possible position to direct the on-air efforts of a radio station. Concerning the role of audience research, Peter Falconi says, "You can't run a station on research alone. Yes, research helps to an extent, but it can't replace your own observations and instincts." Brian Mitchell agrees with

FIGURE 3.17
Many stations have replaced local deejays with national personalities. Tom Joyner is among the most popular. Courtesy ABC.

```
Page No.      1              CITISTAT - Chicago
                                 WKQX-FM/AC
91.01.18
                      TUNED IN-ALPHABETICAL LIST BY ARTIST

Artist                    Song Title                    Time
--------------------      ------------------------      ----


** 1
  10CC                    The Things We Do For Love      12m

** A
  ADAMS, OLETA            Get Here                       02a
  ADAMS, OLETA            Get Here                       06a
  ADAMS, OLETA            Get Here                       10a
  ADAMS, OLETA            Get Here                       02p
  ADAMS, OLETA            Get Here                       07p
  ADAMS, OLETA            Get Here                       11p
  ALIAS                   More Than Words Can Say        01a
  ALIAS                   More Than Words Can Say        12n
  ALIAS                   More Than Words Can Say        10p
  ASTLEY, RICK            It Would Take A Strong Strong  01p
  AUSTIN/INGRAM           Baby, Come To Me               02a

** B
  BAD ENGLISH             When I See You Smile           01a
  BANGLES                 Eternal Flame                  01a
  BANGLES                 Manic Monday                   04p
  BEACH BOYS              Kokomo                         07p
  BERLIN                  Take My Breath Away            01a
  BERLIN                  Take My Breath Away            08p
  BOLTON, MICHAEL         (Sittin' On) The Dock Of The.. 08p
  BRANIGAN, LAURA         Self Control                   01a
  BROWNE, JACKSON         Doctor My Eyes                 01p
  BROWNE, JACKSON         Running On Empty               09p
  BROWNE, JACKSON         Somebody's Baby                09a

** C
  CAFFERTY, JOHN & BBB    On The Dark Side               06a
  CARA, IRENE             Flashdance (What A Feeling)    01p
  CAREY, MARIAH           Love Takes Time                01a
  CAREY, MARIAH           Love Takes Time                05a
  CAREY, MARIAH           Love Takes Time                11a
  CAREY, MARIAH           Love Takes Time                04p
  CAREY, MARIAH           Love Takes Time                10p
  CAREY, MARIAH           Vision Of Love                 10p
  CARLISLE, BELINDA       Heaven Is A Place On Earth     02a
  CARLISLE, BELINDA       Heaven Is A Place On Earth     11p
  CARLISLE, BELINDA       I Get Weak                     06p
  CARMEN, ERIC            Hungry Eyes                    09p
  CHER                    If I Could Turn Back Time      12m
  CHER                    The Sh
  CHER                    The Sh   ┌──────────────────────────────────────┐
  CHER                    The Sh   │ Music is broken our alphabetically by artists with the │
  CHICAGO                 Feelir   │ exact hour of air noted                │
  CHICAGO                 Hard 1   └──────────────────────────────────────┘
  CHICAGO                 Look Away                      11p
  CHICAGO                 Old Days                       08p
```

FIGURE 3.18
Keeping track of a song's performance is a vital element in retaining the edge in music programming. Courtesy Mediabase.

Falconi. "I feel research is important, but how you react to research is more important. A PD also has to heed his gut feelings. Gaps exist in research, too. If I can't figure out what to do without data to point the way every time I make a move, I should get out of radio. Success comes from taking chances once in a while, too. Sometimes it's wiser to turn your back on the tried and tested. Of course, you had better know who's out there before you try anything. A PD who doesn't study his audience and community is like a racecar driver who doesn't familiarize himself with the track. Both can end up off the road and out of the race."

The Program Director and the Music

Not all radio stations have a music director. The larger the station, the more likely it is to have such a person. In any case, it is the PD who is ultimately responsible for the music that goes over the air, even when the position of music director exists. The duties of the music director vary from station to station. Although the title suggests that the individual performing this function would supervise the station's music programming from the selection and acquisition of records to the preparation of playlists, this is not always the case. At some stations, the position is primarily administrative or clerical in nature, leaving the PD to make the major decisions concerning airplay. In this instance, one of the primary duties of the music director might be to improve service from record distributors to keep the station well supplied with the latest releases. A radio station with poor record service may actually be forced to purchase music. This can be prevented to a great extent by maintaining close ties with the various record distributor reps.

Over the years the music industry and the radio medium have formed a mutually beneficial alliance. Without the product provided by the recording companies, radio would find itself with little in the way of programming material, since 90 percent of the country's stations feature recorded music. At the same time, radio serves as the principal means by which the recording industry gets word of its new releases to the general public. Succinctly put, radio sells records.

Although radio stations seldom pay for their music (cassettes, CDs)—recording companies send demos of their new product to most stations—it must pay annual licensing fees to ASCAP (American Society of Composers, Authors, and Publishers), BMI (Broadcast Music, Inc.), or SESAC (Society of European Stage Authors and Composers) for the privilege of airing recorded music.

These fees range from a few hundred dollars at small, noncommercial, educational stations, to tens of thousands of dollars at large, commercial, metro market stations. The music licensing fees paid by stations are distributed to the artists and composers of the songs broadcast.

When music arrives at the station, the music director (sometimes more appropriately called the music librarian or music assistant) processes them through the system. This may take place after the program director has screened them. Records are categorized, indexed, and eventually added to the library if they suit the station's format. Programmer Jon Lutes designates music categories in the following manner: New Music, Medium Current, Hot Current, Hot Recurrent, Medium Recurrent, Bulk Recurrent, Power Gold, Secondary Gold, Tertiary Gold, and so forth. Each station approaches cataloguing in its own fashion. Here is a simple example: an Adult Contemporary outlet receives an album by a popular female vocalist whose last name begins with an L. The program director auditions the album and decides to place three cuts into regular on-air rotation. The music director then assigns the cuts the following catalog numbers: L106/U/F, L106/D/F, and L106/M/F. L106 indicates where the album may be located in the library. In this case, the library is set up alphabetically, then numerically within the given letter that represents the artist's last name. In other words, this would be the 106th album found in the section reserved for female vocalists whose names begin with an L. The next symbol indicates the tempo of the cut: U(p) tempo, D(own) tempo, and M(edium) tempo. The F that follows the tempo symbol indicates the artist's gender: Female.

When a station is computerized (and in this day and age, few are not), this information, including the frequency or rotation of airplay as determined by the PD, will be entered accordingly.

Playlists are then assembled and printed by the computer. The music director sees that these lists are placed in the control room for use by the deejays. This last step is eliminated when the on-air studio is equipped with a computer terminal. Deejays then simply punch up the playlists designed for their particular airshifts. Offers Ed Shane, "To hone the music mix for proper balance and rotation, stations use music rotation software from a variety of suppliers. The most used software program is Selector from Radio Computing Services (which also supplies music test analysis software, traffic software, and a digital studio operation system). Other popular music rotation software is PowerGold and Music Master." (See figure 3.18)

Without a doubt the use of computers in music programming has become standard, especially in larger markets where the cost of computerization is absorbed more easily. The number of computer companies selling both hardware and software designed for use by programmers has soared. Among others providing computerized music systems are Halper and Associates, Jefferson Pilot Data Systems, and Columbine Systems. Also, some journals, such as *Billboard* and *Radio and Records*, provide up-to-date computerized music research on new singles and albums to assist station programmers.

FIGURE 3.19
Radio reflects the lifestyle of its users. Courtesy of Westinghouse Electric.

FIGURE 3.20
A host of
computerized music
programming services
are used by stations.
Courtesy RCS.

In light of the extensive reliance on computers, Jon Lutes and Shane Media caution that, "Music scheduling involves more than punching a few buttons on your computer keyboard. It helps to have a basic understanding of how the computer actually operates and what the particular software you are using will and will not do."

At those radio stations where the music director's job is less administrative and more directorial, this individual will actually audition and select what songs are to be designated for airplay. However, the music director makes decisions based on criteria established by the station's programmer. Obviously, a music director must work within the station's prescribed format. If the PD feels that a particular song does not fit the station's sound, he will direct the music director to remove the cut from rotation. Since the PD and music director work closely together, this seldom occurs.

A song's rotation usually is relative to its position on national and local record sales charts. For instance, songs that enjoy top ranking, say those in the Top 10, will get the most airplay on hit-oriented stations. When songs descend the charts, their rotation decreases proportionately. Former chart toppers are then assigned another rotation configuration that initially may result in one-tenth of their former airplay, and eventually even less. PDs and music directors derive information pertaining to a record's popularity from various trade journals, such as *Billboard*, *Radio and Records*, and *Monday Morning Replay*, as well as listener surveys, area record store sales, and numerous other sources. Stations that do not program from the current charts compose their playlists of songs that were popular in years gone by. In addition, these stations often remix current hit songs to make them adaptable to their more conservative sound. While Easy Listening stations do not air popular rock songs, they do air softened versions by other artists, usually large orchestras. Critics of this technique accuse the

```
**REMEMBER: FORWARD MOMENTUM!! WHY SHOULD THE LISTENER KEEP LISTENING?**

                    *******************************
                    *             WIZN-FM          *
                    *  10 AM  Wednesday  10-23-02  *
                    *******************************
ARTIST/ALBUM                    TITLE                        RUNTIME  YR   CAT
================================================================================

------------------------------------------------------------------------------
  00:00  LEGAL I.D.                                 5025   :08
------------------------------------------------------------------------------
STEVE MILLER BAND               TAKE THE MONEY AND RUN              E/ 2:51
FLY LIKE AN EAGLE
------------------------------------------------------------------------------
  02:59  SHOTGUN                                    5050   :05
------------------------------------------------------------------------------
TOM PETTY                       RUNNING DOWN A DREAM               F/ 4:23
FULL MOON FEVER                      54.00
------------------------------------------------------------------------------
  07:27  SPEED BREAK                                5605   :08
------------------------------------------------------------------------------
J. GEILS BAND                   MUST OF GOT LOST                  D/ 6:34
LIVE BLOW YOUR FACE OUT (ON CD)      50.00
------------------------------------------------------------------------------
  14:09  POSITIONER                                 5035   :08
------------------------------------------------------------------------------
PRETENDERS                      BRASS IN POCKET(I'M SPECI         E/ 3:01
THE PRETENDERS                       50.00
------------------------------------------------------------------------------
  17:18  SHOTGUN                                    5050   :05
------------------------------------------------------------------------------
HEART                           CRAZY ON YOU                      D/ 4:54
DREAMBOAT ANNIE                      69.00
------------------------------------------------------------------------------
  22:17  BOTTOM HOUR                                5016   :08
------------------------------------------------------------------------------
CLASH                           TRAIN IN VAIN                     E/ 3:13
LONDON CALLING                       43.00
------------------------------------------------------------------------------
  25:38  BREAK ONE/BACKSELL/LIVE PROMO              5606  1:00
------------------------------------------------------------------------------
ERIC CLAPTON                    FOREVER MAN                       F/ 3:12
BEHIND THE SUN
------------------------------------------------------------------------------
  29:50  BOTTOM HOUR                                5016   :08
------------------------------------------------------------------------------
MANFRED MANN'S EARTH BAND       BLINDED BY THE LIGHT              E/ 7:07
HIGHS OF 70'S CD                     80.00
------------------------------------------------------------------------------
  37:05  BREAK TWO/PRE-SELL 10-IN-A-ROW             5607  1:00
------------------------------------------------------------------------------
DEEP PURPLE                     HUSH                              D/ 4:26
WHEN WE ROCK WE ROCK, WHEN WE ROLL   49.00
------------------------------------------------------------------------------
  42:31  SHOTGUN                                    5050   :05
------------------------------------------------------------------------------
```

FIGURE 3.21
Computerized logging has made station programming even more exacting a science. Courtesy WIZN-FM.

Frank Bell

Advice to Programmers

FIGURE 3.22
Frank Bell.

Rule 1: *Follow the listeners, not the format.* So many people in radio get caught up in terms like *CHR, New AC, Alternative,* and *AAA* that they lose track of their goal: finding listeners.

Consumers of radio think in terms of "what I like" and "what I don't like." By researching your listeners' tastes and giving them what they want (as opposed to what fits the industry's definition of what

they should have), you'll maximize your chances for success.

Rule 2: *Think outside in, not inside out.* The fact that one company may now own several stations in a market and is capable, for example, of skewing one FM toward younger females and the other toward older females does not mean that you will automatically "dominate females."

The only reality that counts is that of the listener. If listeners feel your station serves a meaningful purpose for them, they will happily cast their Arbitron vote in your favor. If they believe you are simply duplicating what is already available elsewhere on the dial, you will be doomed to ratings obscurity.

Rule 3: *Early to bed, early to rise, Advertise, Advertise, Advertise.* In the Arbitron game of unaided recall, the dominant issue is Top-of-Mindness.

The best way to get that is through advertising your name and your station's benefits on your own

air and on any other medium you can afford. Just for fun, here's a diagram I sometimes use to show first-time PD's the various factors that influence their station's ratings:

$$\frac{X - Y}{A} \times B = \text{Your Ratings}$$

X is what your station does.
Y is what your direct competitors do.
A represents "environmental" factors in the market, such as what's on TV during the survey, riots, floods, earthquakes, and (in some cases) the OJ trial.
B is what the rating service does. In the case of Arbitron, this would include the response rate, editing procedures, and distribution of diaries by race, age, and sex.

The most important thing to understand is that as program director, the only part of the equation you can control is X. Do the best you can to keep your station sounding compelling, entertaining, and focused on its target audience, and don't get an ulcer over those elements you can't control.

producers of lobotomizing songs to bring them into the fold. In nonhit formats there are no "power-rotation" categories or hit positioning schemata; a song's rotation tends to be more random, although program wheels are used.

On the CHR front, Shane notes that, "There's a major change in the way charts are constructed. The original *Billboard* Hot 100 chart was based substantially on record sales. *The Gavin Report* and other 'tipsheets' used reports from radio station music direc-

tors who fed information on the positions on their own local charts, some validated by record sales and requests—some not.

"When *R&R* was launched in 1974, its charts were also compiled from reports from radio station programmers. *R&R*, however, mixed industry news and commentary to create a niche for itself as the most important of the music trade publications in the eyes of the music (record) industry. Because the charts were based on verbal reports from local stations, the system was too easily manipulated by a station programmer who might report play but not actually play the song. This practice was known as a 'paper add' because the record was added to the playlist only on paper and did not receive airplay. In 1989, *Billboard* became the first trade publication to track radio airplay as it happened and to count 'spins,' or plays, in compiling charts. *Billboard* and its companion publication, *Airplay Monitor*, used Broadcast Data Systems (BDS) to electronically detect airplay by matching segments of songs called 'footprints' to actual play on stations monitored over the air. The practice of paper adds decreased because a song reported to *R&R* could be tracked in BDS detections. In mid-1999 both *R&R* and *The Gavin Report* (now defunct) began using charts based on airplay detection with information compiled by MediaBase, a monitoring service owned by Premiere Radio Networks."

Constructing a station playlist is the single most important duty of the music programmer. What to play, when to play it, and how often are some of the key questions confronting this individual. The music director relies on a number of sources, both internal and external, to provide the answers, but also must cultivate an ear for the kind of sound the station is after. Some people are blessed with an almost innate capacity to detect a hit, but most must develop this skill over a period of time.

The Program Director and the FCC

The government is especially interested in the way a station conducts itself on the air. For instance, the program director makes certain that his or her station is properly identified once an hour, as close to the top of the hour as possible. The ID must include the station's call letters and the town in which it has been authorized to broadcast. Failure to properly identify the station is a violation of FCC rules.

Other on-air rules that the PD must address have to do with program content and certain types of features. For example, profane language, obscenity, sex- and drug-related statements, and even innuendos in announcements, conversations, or music lyrics jeopardize the station's license. Political messages and station editorials are carefully scrutinized by the programmer. On-air contests and promotions must not resemble lotteries in which the audience must invest to win. A station that gets something in return for awarding prizes is subject to punitive actions. Neither the deejays, PD, music director, nor anyone associated with the station may receive payment for plugging a song or album on the air. This constitutes "payola" or "plugola" and was the cause of great industry upheaval in the 1950s. Today, PDs and station managers continue to be particularly careful to guard against any recurrence, although there have been charges that such practices still exist.

The program director must monitor both commercial and noncommercial messages

FIGURE 3.23

A station's music library in a box. Courtesy WIZN-FM.

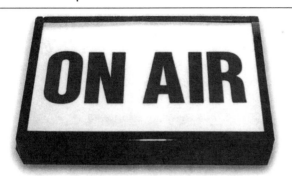

In Spanish...

Radiolandia 1330 AM (WRCA)

408 South Huntington Ave., Boston, MA 02130
(617) 522-5060 (617) 524-5886-fax

Radiolandia Broadcasting was established in 1973, as a Spanish-language radio format programmer for the purpose of serving the growing Hispanic population of Metropolitan Boston. Coupled with the backing of EL MUNDO SPANISH NEWSPAPER, Massachusetts' oldest and most respected Hispanic publication, (another division of CARIBE COMMUNICATIONS) it is recognized as one of New England's most consistent and credible broadcasters of quality ethnic programming.

FORMAT:

RADIOLANDIA provides the Latino community of Massachusetts with the very best in music, news, entertainment, sports and public affair programming...*all in Spanish!* The focus of RADIOLANDIA's varied programming allows it to reach listeners in *virtually every age group*.

AUDIENCE:

RADIOLANDIA targets its programming to adults 18+ with a concentration in the 18-59 year segment. Our audience is Spanish-speaking, representing over 20 Latin-American countries, from the Caribbean, Central and South America and Spain.

FACILITIES:

WRCA AM, 5000 watts, 1330 KHZ, (6AM-7PM)

COMMERCIAL POLICY

:30 and :60 spots available. Must air in Spanish.

FIGURE 3.24
The Hispanic radio format attracts large and loyal audiences. Courtesy Radiolandia.

to ensure that no false, misleading, or deceptive statements are aired, something the FCC staunchly opposes. This includes any distortion of the station's ratings survey results. A station that is not number one and claims to be is lying to the public as far as the FCC is concerned, and such behavior is not condoned.

License renewal programming promises must be addressed by the PD. The proportion of nonentertainment programming, such as news and public affairs features, pledged in the station's renewal application must be adhered to, even though such requirements have been all but eliminated. A promise is a promise. If a station claims that it will do something, it must abide by its word.

The PD helps maintain the station's Emergency Alert System (EAS), making certain that proper announcements are made on the air and that the EAS checklist containing an authenticator card is placed in the control room area. PDs also instruct personnel in the proper procedures used when conducting on-air telephone conversations to guarantee that the rights of callers are not violated.

The station log (which ultimately is the chief engineer's responsibility) and program log (no longer required by the FCC but maintained by most stations anyway) are examined by the PD for accuracy, and he or she also must see to it that operators have permits and that they are posted in the on-air studio. In addition, the station manager may assign the PD the responsibility for maintaining the station's Public File. If so, the PD must be fully aware of what the file is required to contain. The FCC and many broadcast associations will provide station operators with a Public File checklist upon request. This information is available in the *Code of Federal Regulations* (73.3526) as well.

Additional programming areas of interest to the FCC include procedures governing rebroadcasts, simulcasts, and subcarrier activities. The program director also must be aware that the government is keenly interested in employment practices. The programmer, station manager, and other department heads are under obligation to familiarize themselves with equal employment opportunity (EEO) and affirmative action rules. An annual employment report must be sent to the FCC.

The preceding is only a partial listing of the concerns set forth by the government relative to the program director's position. For a more comprehensive assessment, refer to the CFR appendix at the end of Chapter 2.

The Program Director and Upper Management

The pressures of the program director's position should be apparent by now. The station or cluster programmer knows well that his or her job entails satisfying the desires of many—the audience, government, air staff, and, of course, management. The relationship between the PD and the station or corporation's upper echelon is not always serene or without incident. Although usually a mutually fulfilling and productive alliance, difficulties can and do occur when philosophies or practices clash. "Most inhibiting and detrimental to the PD is the GM who lacks a broad base of experience but imposes his opinions on you anyway. The guy who has come up through sales and has never spent a minute in the studio can be a real thorn in the side. Without a thorough knowledge of programming, management should rely on the expertise of that person hired who does. I don't mean, 'Hey, GM, get out of the way!' what I'm saying is, don't impose programming ideas and policies without at least conferring with that individual who ends up taking the heat if the air product fails to bring in the listeners," says Dick Fatherly.

WPAT 930 AM Metro NY	
****ALL JEWISH ALL THURSDAY NIGHT****	
10:00–10:30 PM	**INNER MEANING WITH KIM CHEROVSKY** Interviews on Judaism and spirituality with special guest Rabbi Jacob Jungreis
10:30–11:00 PM	**THE TOP TEN JEWISH MUSIC COUNTDOWN** FAVORITE Jewish music of the week.
11:00–12:00 AM	**TALKLINE WITH ZEV BRENNER.** *AMERICA'S LEADING JEWISH PROGRAM. LIVE CALL IN WITH NEWSMAKER GUESTS AND CELEBRITIES MAKING HEADLINES IN THE JEWISH WORLD.*
12:00–12:30 PM	**BETWEEN THE LINES: THE TORAH CODES.** With Dr. Robert Wolf and Joel Gallis.
12:30–2:00 AM	**THE VOICE OF JERUSALEM WITH AVI. THE LATEST NEWS, SHMOOZ, AND CONTESTS LIVE FROM ISRAEL.**
2:00–3:00 AM	**THE TED SMITH SHOW.** Interview show on health and social issues.
3:00–4:30 AM	**THE TOP TEN JEWISH MUSIC COUNTDOWN.**
4:30–5:00 AM	**LIVE FROM ISRAEL.** The latest up to date news from Israel with Dov Shurin.

FIGURE 3.25
Many stations ultra-niche (position) their programming. Courtesy WPAT.

Station manager Chuck Ducoty contends that managers can enhance as well as inhibit the style of programmers. "I've worked for some managers who give their PDs a great deal of space and others who attempt to control every aspect of programming. From the station manager's perspective, I think the key to a good experience with those who work for you is to find excellent people from the start and then have enough confidence in your judgment to let them do their job with minimal interference. Breathing down the neck of the PD is just going to create tension and resentment."

Programmer Peter Falconi believes that a sincere effort to get to know and understand one another should be exerted by both the PD and manager. "You have to be on the same wavelength, and there has to be an excellent line of communication. When a manager has confidence and trust in his PD, he'll generally let him run with the ball. It's a two-way street. Most problems can be resolved when there is honesty and openness."

Programmer Andy Bloom offers this observation: "Great upper management hires the best players, gives them the tools to do their job, and then leaves them alone. A winning formula."

An adversarial situation between the station's PD and upper management does not have to exist. The station that cultivates an atmosphere of cooperation and mutual respect seldom becomes embroiled in skirmishes that deplete energy—energy better spent raising revenues and ratings.

CHAPTER HIGHLIGHTS

1. The Adult Contemporary (AC) format features recent (since the 1970s) and current pop standards. It appeals to the 25- to 49-year-old age group, which attracts advertisers. It often utilizes music sweeps and clustered commercials.

2. Contemporary Hit Radio (CHR) features current, fast-selling hits from the Top 40. It targets teens, broadcasts minimal news, and is very promotion/contest oriented. Some CHRs have redirected their playlists to create a Modern Hit or Churban sound.

3. Country is the fastest growing format since the 1970s. More prevalent in the south and midwest, it attracts a broad age group and offers a variety of subformats.

4. Easy Listening/Smooth Jazz stations evolved from the Beautiful Music stations of the 1960s and 1970s. Featuring mostly instrumentals and minimal talk, many stations have become automated and use prepackaged programming from syndicators. The primary audience is over age 50. Its following has dwindled in recent years due to myriad softer AC formats.

5. Rock or Album-Oriented Rock (AOR) stations began in the mid-1960s to counter Top 40 stations. They featured music sweeps with a large airplay library, and they played rock album cuts. News was minimal. The format attracted a predominantly male audience aged 18 to 34. Today these stations are usually referred to simply as Rock stations.

6. All-News stations rotate time blocks of local, regional, and national news and features to avoid repetition. The format requires three to four times the staff and budget of most music operations.

7. All-Talk combines discussion and call-in shows. It is primarily a medium and major market format. Like All-News, All-Talk is mostly found on AM but is now finding a home on the FM band. All-Sports has boosted the nonmusic format's numbers and now is offered by several networks.

FIGURE 3.26
Payola statement signed by a station employee. Courtesy Michael Napoilitano and Capital Cities/ABC, Inc.

8. The Nostalgia playlist emphasizes popular tunes from the 1940s and prerock 1950s, presenting its music in sweeps with a relatively low deejay profile.

9. The Oldies playlist includes hits from the 1950s and 1960s, relying on fine air personalities. Commercials are placed randomly and songs are spaced to allow deejay patter.

10. Classic Rock concentrates on tunes once primarily featured by AOR stations. Meanwhile, Classic Hit stations fill the gap between Oldies and CHR outlets with playlists that draw from 1970s' and 1980s' Top 40 charts.

11. Urban Contemporary (UC) is the "melting pot" format, attracting a heterogeneous audience. Its upbeat, danceable sound and hip, friendly deejays attract the 18- to 34-year-old age group. Contests and promotions are important.

12. Classical commercial outlets are few, but they have a loyal audience. Primarily an FM format appealing to a higher income,

tactics:programming

Programming Report from Shane Media Services

PROGRAM DIRECTOR - TEN TACTICS FOR SUCCESS

There are no schools to attend to become a Program Director. Many people fall into the job without a clue as to what the job really entails. Here are 10 basic points for PD success:

1. <u>Show up.</u> Not just for work. Show up at 2AM and visit with the overnight jock. Get to know that person in their time zone. Show up at remotes. Know how your airstaff and promotions people put on a show. Be visible both in and out of the station.

2. <u>Listen up.</u> You can't listen 24 hours a day, but you can tape when you must sleep. Tape the competition when you're monitoring your own shop. Don't listen as a programmer all the time. Try to slip into the attitude of your average listener to determine how well your station is delivering the format and serving your town.

3. <u>Clean up.</u> If you notice something wrong, why wait to make an adjustment? Eliminate small problems before they become large ones.

4. <u>Take notes.</u> Who's doing what in your town? Be aware of the "big picture" in your market, like an air traffic controller. If you need to make an instant adjustment, you'll be prepared.

5. <u>Make notes.</u> How many times have you had a brilliant idea in the middle of the night, and forgotten it by morning? Keep a note pad and pencil or mini recorder by your bed, in your car, wherever you go. A simple phrase or word jotted down quickly can bring back that concept when you've got time to develop the idea.

6. <u>Leave notes.</u> We are in the business of communicating, yet often do a poor job of getting a message from one end of the station to the other. Leave notes on the music log, a discrepancy sheet, a slip of paper in the phone message slot. Get in the habit of noting your thoughts to others, and watch your effectiveness as a manager improve.

©SHANE MEDIA SERVICES   HOUSTON, TX   (713) 952-9221

FIGURE 3.27
Rules for success.
Courtesy Shane
Media.

college-educated (upscale, 25 to 49 years old) audience, Classical features a conservative, straightforward air sound.

13. Religious stations are most prevalent on the AM band. Religious broadcasters usually approach programming in one of two ways. One includes music as a primary part of its presentation, whereas the other does not.

14. Ethnic stations serve the listening needs of minority groups. Black and Hispanic listeners constitute the largest ethnic audiences.

15. Full Service stations (formerly MOR) rely on the strength of air personalities and features. Mostly an AM format, FS attempts to be all things to all people, attracting an over-40 audience.

16. Niche formats, like All-Children, Business, and Tourist Radio, are popping up all over the dial as the listening audience becomes more diffused.

17. Program directors (PDs) are hired to fit whatever format the station management has selected. They are chosen for their experience, primarily, although education level is important.

18. The PD is responsible for everything that is aired. Second in responsibility to the general manager (when no operations manager position exists), the PD establishes programming and format policy; hires and supervises on-air, music, and production personnel; handles the programming budget; develops promotions; monitors the station and its competitors and assesses research; is accountable for news, public affairs, and sports features; and may even pull an airshift.

19. The PD's effectiveness is measured by ratings in large markets and by sales in smaller markets.

20. The PD determines the content of each sound hour, utilizing program clocks to ensure that each element—commercial, news, promo, weather, music, and so on—is strategically located to enhance flow and optimize impact. Even News/Talk stations need program clocks.

21. PDs must adjust programming to the lifestyle activities of the target audience. They must develop a feel for the area in which the station is located, as well as an understanding of survey information and research data.

22. Finally, the PD must ensure that the station adheres to all FCC regulations pertaining to programming practices, anticipating problems before they occur.

APPENDIX: A Station Owner Airchecks His Programming

To: Steve
Fr: Jay
Re: WLKZ Programming

In listening over the past few days, but only to an hour or two total, it appears that much of the "big picture" programming philosophy has been lost. Perhaps Joe hasn't reviewed the old operations manual. But some mechanical changes could dramatically help the sound of the station until the philosophy is recreated or changed.

1.   One part-timer's mike was way too hot compared to the music. Music should always be dominant; personalities should never overwhelm it. The voice should be "in" the music.

2.   Song titles were often announced. Oldies listeners know the song titles, and a lot more than our own people do about every record. There is also the danger that our mostly young talent will say something that reveals their age/lack of knowl-edge when talking about music. This is unnecessary talk and should be eliminated.

3.   Conversely, there is almost no local content. This does not mean PSAs about bean suppers; this means the progress on the new building in downtown Wolfeboro, or the time the town Christmas lights will be turned on, for example. It takes more work than announcing a song title, but it's a much better reason to listen.

4.   After the weather was given, the personality commented, "At least that's what it says here." Weather is one of the principal reasons people choose a radio station. The forecast (or the Radar Weather franchise) is only as credible as we make it (the information all comes from the same place).

5.   Talk between records. The music should never stop unless it has to (commercials). Stopping it down to talk, even for a liner that can be delivered over an intro, kills the momentum.

6.   There are literally no prepromotes going into stop sets. The listener is not given any reasons to stick around (and forward momentum again stops).

7.   There are recorded PSAs (a corporate no-no). The one I heard tells us to wear seat

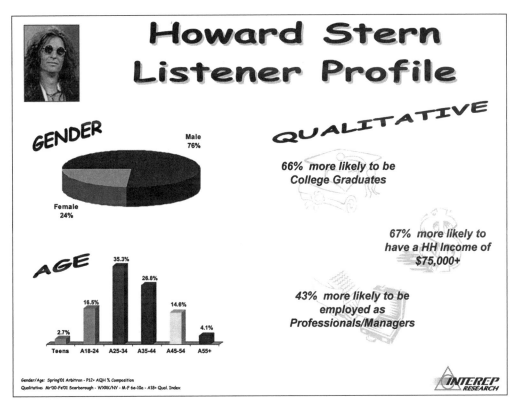

FIGURE 3.28
Radio stars keep the medium in the foreground. Courtesy Infinity.

PRESS RELEASE
DATE: 25th March 2002 (Embargo)

Global Radio News Ltd. Announces Distribution Deal With Sky News Radio

Sky News Radio audio programme content will be available for distribution to radio stations outside the UK and South Africa via the Global Radio News network from Monday 25th March 2002.

Stations will be able to browse correspondent reports and a wide variety of material from Sky News Radio through the website (www.globalradionews.com) on a story-by-story basis. There is no subscription obligation and editors can use material that will suit their listener demographic. Stations just pay for what they use.

Henry Peirse, Director of Global Radio News Ltd. says 'this is an exciting development; stations now have the option to pick from Global Radio News correspondent reports and Sky News stories. The two complement each other well providing a comprehensive and detailed list of stories for our affiliates'.

Andy Ivy, Editor of Sky News Radio says 'the quality of our service is proving a big hit with radio newsrooms in the UK and Global Radio News allows us to make our audio available to stations worldwide.'

Global Radio News is a web-based audio content agency and distribution service with a network of more than 400 correspondents worldwide.

Sky News Radio is a division of Sky News. A dedicated team of radio journalists provides a news service to around 30 UK radio stations including talkSPORT, the Wireless Group and Chrysalis Radio, making it the second biggest supplier of national and international news to commercial radio stations in the UK.

Please contact: Henry Peirse at Global Radio News Ltd. – 020 7242 9192 or henry@globalradionews.com or Andy Ivy at Sky News Radio – 020 7705 3000 or andy.ivy@bskyb.com.

Note to editors:

Pictures of the Sky News Radio newsroom are available on Image Net or from the Sky Stills department on 020 7800 4271. Please contact Global Radio News Ltd. on 020 7242 9192 for pictures.

FOR IMMEDIATE RELEASE ON OR AFTER 25th MARCH 2002

FIGURE 3.29

News release. In the global world, there is a need for global radio news. Courtesy Sky News.

belts. Every media, every politician, every do-gooder is trying to tell other people what to do. Let's just be the medium that informs and entertains. Let's be an escape from all the other pointed fingers. . . .

8. Joe signs off his show and also refers to his listener as "everybody." We should talk to only one listener at a time. And we should never end anything—keep it going, part of forward momentum. Talk about the guy coming up next. . . .

9. Could you send Joe a memo or talk with him on a visit soon? I want to keep that station tight and happening; it's important.

10. Also, what do you think about adding some Beatles songs (over and above what we have) for the next month or so? And trading/giving away some anthology CDs? Thanks.

FIGURE 3.30
Employment
application with EEO
policy statement.
Courtesy of WHDH-
AM.

RADIO 85

FOUR FORTY-ONE STUART STREET
BOSTON, MASSACHUSETTS 02116
TELEPHONE (617)267-3302

APPLICATION FOR EMPLOYMENT

"Employment discrimination because of race, color, religion, national origin, sex or age is prohibited. Anyone who believes that he or she has been a victim of discrimination in seeking employment at this station is urged to report the matter promptly to the President of WHDH and may notify the Federal Communications Commission or other appropriate agency."

This application will be given every consideration. Its acceptance, however, does not imply that the applicant will be employed. If an applicant is not employed, it will be retained in our active file for one year.

All appointments to positions are on trial and subject to satisfactory work. If it is found that an employee is not adapted to radio work or is likely to prove useful, he or she may be dismissed.

WHDH CORPORATION
EQUAL EMPLOYMENT OPPORTUNITY POLICY

Equal employment opportunity is the policy of WHDH Corporation (WHDH). Prejudice or discrimination, based upon race, color, religion, national origin, or sex, is strictly prohibited by WHDH in recruitment, selection and hiring, placement and promotion, pay, working conditions, demotion, termination, and in all employment practices generally. All personnel are required diligently and affirmatively to observe this policy and are absolutely forbidden to violate, frustrate or diminish that policy. Any applicant for employment, any employee or any other person having reason to believe that there exists any prejudice or discrimination based upon race, color, religion, national origin, or sex, in any area of WHDH's employment practices, is urged to report the matter promptly to the President of WHDH or any other officer, executive or supervisor employed by WHDH Corporation. Any person believing himself to have been a victim of prohibited discrimination in any area of WHDW's employment practices also has the right to notify the Federal Communications Commission or other appropriate federal or state agencies, or all of these, of such incident or incidents. It is requested that all employees and applicants for employment make this policy of equal employment opportunity known to others, whenever appropriate.

FIGURE 3.30
continued

EDUCATIONAL RECORD	IN THE UNITED STATES (Names of Schools attended)	CITY/TOWN	No. of Years Completed	If Grad. give Mo. and Yr.	If not Grad. give date of leaving
High or Preparatory School					
Commercial School					
College					
Graduate School					

If you did not graduate from school or college, state reason for leaving: _____

Were you ever suspended or expelled from any of the institutions above? _____ If so, state the reason fully:

What educational courses are you now taking? _____

PERSONAL RECORD

Date of Birth (OPTIONAL) _____ Are you a citizen of the United States? _____

Have you ever been arrested or convicted for an offense other than a minor traffic violation? _____ If yes, explain

Give number of persons in immediate family _____ Does this include (if living) both father and mother? _____

If not living at home, with whom do you live? Relatives _____ Friends _____ Alone _____ Board _____

Number of persons financially dependent upon you? Fully _____ Partially _____

What is your present selective service classification? _____

Have you served in the armed forces of the United States? _____ Branch of service _____

Month and year of induction _____ Date of discharge or transfer to reserve _____

Rank at time of discharge _____

HEALTH RECORD

How much time have you lost from work or school during the last three years on account of illness? _____

What was the nature of the illness? _____

Are you related to any director, officer or employee of WHDH? _____ Relatives name _____

Describe your outside interests or hobbies _____

Please describe any special assets you bring to WHDH _____

List below, five personal references (not relatives, former employers or fellow employees) who have known you well during the past five or more years.

Print Name in Full	Address (Street / City)	No of Years Known	Occupation

THIS SECTION TO BE FILLED OUT ONLY BY APPLICANTS FOR CLERICAL POSITIONS:

What shorthand method do you use? _____ Words per minute _____ Do you type? _____

Words per minute _____ List office machines that you have operated _____

I hereby affirm that my answers to the foregoing questions are true and correct, and that I have not knowingly withheld any fact or circumstance that would, if disclosed, affect my application unfavorably.

Please sign HERE _____

On a separate sheet of paper you may give any further information you desire to explain your qualifications.

FIGURE 3.31
Radio illustrates its music format variety. Courtesy Mix 98.5, WDEZ-FM, and KSSJ-FM.

SUGGESTED FURTHER READING

Adams, Michael H., and Massey, Kimberly K. *Introduction to Radio: Production and Programming*. Madison, Wisc.: Brown and Benchmark, 1995.

Armstrong, Ben. *The Electronic Church*. Nashville: J. Nelson, 1979.

Busby, Linda, and Parker, Donald. *The Art and Science of Radio*. Boston: Allyn & Bacon, 1984.

Carroll, Raymond L., and Davis, Donald M. *Electronic Media Programming: Strategies and Decision Making*. New York: McGraw-Hill, 1993.

Chapple, Steve, and Garofalo, R. *Rock 'n' Roll Is Here to Pay*. Chicago: Nelson-Hall, 1977.

Cliff, Charles, and Greer, A. *Broadcasting Programming: The Current Perspective*. Washington, D.C.: University Press of America, 1974 to date, revised annually.

Coddington, R.H. *Modern Radio Programming*. Blue Ridge Summit, Pa.: Tab Books, 1970.

DeLong, Thomas, A. *The Mighty Music Box*. Los Angeles: Amber Crest Books, 1980.

Denisoff, R.S. *Solid Gold: The Popular Record Industry*. New York: Transaction Books, 1976.

Dingle, Jeffrey L. *Essential Radio*. Marblehead, Mass.: Peregrine Books, 1995.

Eastman, Susan Tyler. *Broadcast/Cable Programming: Strategies and Practices*, 6th ed. Belmont, Calif.: Wadsworth Publishing, 2001.

Hall, Claude, and Hall, Barbara. *This Business of Radio Programming*. New York: Billboard Publishing, 1977.

Halper, Donna. *Full-Service Radio*. Boston: Focal Press, 1991.

—. *Radio Music Directing*. Boston: Focal Press, 1991.

Hilliand, Robert and Keith, Michael. *Diety Discourse: Sex and Indecency in American Radio*. Ames, IA: Iowa State Press, 2003.

Johnson, Tracy and Burns, Alan. *Morning Radio*. Washington: Johnson Publishing, 1999.

Keirstead, Phillip A. *All-News Radio*. Blue Ridge Summit, Pa.: Tab Books, 1980.

Keith, Michael C. *Radio Programming: Consultancy and Formatics*. Stoneham, Mass.: Focal Press, 1987.

—. *Signals in the Air: Native Broadcasting in America*. Westport, Conn.: Praeger Publishing, 1995.

—. *Sounds in the Dark: All Night Radio in American Life*. Ames. IA: Iowa State Press, 2001.

Land, Jeff. *Active Radio: Pacifica's Brash Experiment*. Minneapolis: University of Minnesota Press, 1999.

Lynch, Joanna and Gillispie, Greg. *Process and Practice of Radio Programming*. Lanham, MD: University Press of America, 1998.

Lujack, Larry, and Jedlicka, D.A. *Superjock: The Loud, Frantic, NonStop World of Rock Radio Deejays*. Chicago: Regnery, 1975.

MacFarland, David T. *The Development of the Top 40 Format*. New York: Arno Press, 1979.

—. *Contemporary Radio Programming Strategies*. Hillsdale, N.J.: Lawrence Erlbaum, 1990.

Maki, Val, and Pederson, Jill. *The Radio Playbook*. St. Louis, Mo.: Globe Mack, Inc., 1991.

Matelski, Marilyn J. *Broadcast Programming and Promotion Worktext*. Boston: Focal Press, 1989.

McCoy, Quincy. *No Static: A Guide to Creative Programming*. Chicago: Miuller Freeman Books, 1999.

Morrow, Bruce. *Cousin Brucie*. New York: Morrow and Company, 1987.

Norberg, Eric. *Radio Programming: Tactics and Strategies*. Boston: Focal Press, 1996.

Passman, Arnold. *The Deejays*. New York: Macmillan, 1971.

Rhoads, B. Eric, et al., eds. *Programming and Promotion*. West Palm Beach, Fla.: Streamline Press, 1995.

Routt, Ed, McGrath, James B., and Weiss, Frederic A. *The Radio Format Conundrum*. New York: Hastings House, 1978.

Sklar, Rick. *Rocking America: How the All-Hit Radio Stations Took Over*. New York: St. Martin's Press, 1984.

Vane, Edwin T., and Gross, Lynne S. *Programming for TV, Radio, and Cable*. Boston: Focal Press, 1994.

Warren, Steve. *Radio: The book*, 3rd ed. Washington, D.C.: NAB Books, 1999.

4 Sales

Commercialization: a Retrospective

In the 21st century selling commercials keeps the majority of radio stations on the air. It is that simple—yet not so simple. In the 1920s broadcasters realized the necessity of converting the medium into a sponsor-supported industry. It seemed to be the most viable option and the key to growth and prosperity. Not everyone approved of the method, however. Opponents of commercialization argued that advertising would decrease the medium's ability to effectively serve the public's good, and one U.S. senator voiced fears that advertisers would turn radio into an on-air pawnshop. These predictions would prove to be somewhat accurate. By the mid-1920s, most radio outlets sold airtime, and few restrictions existed pertaining to the substance and content of messages. Commercials promoting everything from miracle pain relievers to instant hair-growing solutions filled the broadcast day. It was not until the 1930s that the government developed regulations that addressed the issue of false advertising claims. This resulted in the gradual elimination of sponsors peddling dubious products.

Program sponsorships were the most popular form of radio advertising in the 1920s and early 1930s. Stations, networks, and advertising agencies often lured clients onto the air by naming or renaming programs after their products, such as *Eveready Hour, Palmolive Hour, Fleischmann Hour, Clicquot Club Eskimos, The Coty Playgirl*, and so on. Since formidable opposition to commercialization existed in the beginning, sponsorships, in which the only reference to a product was in a program's title, appeared the best path to take. This approach was known as *indirect* advertising.

As the outcry against advertiser-supported radio subsided, stations became more blatant or *direct* in their presentation of commercial material. Parcels of time, anywhere from 1 to 5, even 10 minutes, were sold to advertisers eager to convey the virtues of their labors. Industry advertising revenues soared throughout the 1930s, despite the broken economy. Radio salespeople were among the few who had a salable product. World War II increased the rate of sales revenues twofold. As it became the foremost source of news and information during that bleak period in American history, the value of radio's stock reached new highs, as did the incomes of salespeople. The tide would shift, however, with the advent of television in the late 1940s.

When television unseated radio as the number one source of entertainment in the early 1950s, time sellers for the deposed medium found their fortunes sagging. In the face of adversity, as well as opportunity, many radio salespeople abandoned the old in preference for the new, opting to sell for television. Radio was, indeed, in a dilemma of frightening proportions, but it soon put itself back on course by renovating its programming approach. By 1957 the medium had undergone an almost total transformation and was once again enjoying the rewards of success. Salespeople concentrated on selling airtime to advertisers interested in reaching specific segments of the population. Radio became extremely localized and, out of necessity, the networks diverted their attention to television.

Competition also became keener. Thousands of new outlets began to broadcast between 1950 and 1970. Meanwhile, FM started to spread its wings, preparing to surpass its older rival. AM music stations experienced great difficulties in the face of the mass exodus to FM, which culminated in 1979 when FM exceeded AM's listenership. FM became the medium to sell.

In the first half of the 1980s, radio programming was easily divisible. Talk was found on AM and music on FM. Today, hundreds of AM stations have become stereo in an attempt to improve their marketing potential, and some FM outlets have taken to airing nonmusic formats as a way of surviving the ratings battles.

Selling time in the new millennium is a far cry from what it was like during the medium's heyday. Observes general manager Ted Jordan, "Five years ago salespeople on a call spent a lot of time separating their stations from competitors. For example 'We're the contest station,' 'We're the office station,' etc. Now, with consolidation, we gloss over the differences. 'Here's what it will cost you and here's what we're willing to add' comes up much faster."

Station account executives no longer search for advertisers willing to sponsor half-hour sitcoms, quiz shows, or mysteries. Today, the advertising dollar generally is spent on spots scheduled for airing during specific dayparts on stations that attract a particular piece of the highly fractionalized radio audience pie. The majority of radio outlets program prerecorded music, and it is that which constitutes the station's product. The salesperson sells the audience, which the station's music attracts, to the advertiser or time buyer.

Selling Airtime

Airtime is intangible. You cannot see it or hold it in your hand. It is not like any other form of advertising. Newspaper and magazine ads can be cut out by the advertiser and pinned to a bulletin board or taped to a window as tangible evidence of money spent. Television commercials can be seen, but radio commercials are sounds flitting through the ether with no visual component to attest to their existence. They are ephemeral, or fleeting, to use words that are often associated with radio advertising. However, any informed account executive will respond to such terms by stating the simple fact that an effective radio commercial makes a strong and lasting impression on the mind of the listener in much the same way that a popular song tends to permeate the gray matter. "The so-called intangible nature of a radio commercial really only means you can't see it or touch it. There is little doubt, however, that a good spot is concrete in its own unique way. Few of us have gone unaffected or, better still, untouched by radio commercials. If a spot is good, it is felt, and that's a tangible," says radio sales manager Charles W. Friedman.

Initially considered an experimental or novel way to publicize a product, it soon became apparent to advertisers that radio was far more. Early sponsors who earmarked a small portion of their advertising budgets to the new electronic "gadget," while pouring the rest into print, were surprised by the results. Encouraged by radio's performance, advertisers began to spend more heavily. By the 1930s many prominent companies were reallocating substantial portions of their print advertising budgets for radio. To these convinced advertisers, radio was, indeed, a concrete way to market their products.

Yet the feeling that radio is an unconventional mode of advertising continues to persist to some extent even today, especially among small, print-oriented retailers.

Usually, the small market radio station's prime competitor for ad dollars is the local newspaper. Many retailers have used papers for years and perceive radio as a secondary or even frivolous means of advertising, contends Friedman. "Retailers who have used print since opening their doors for business are reluctant to change. The toughest factor facing a radio salesperson is the notion that the old way works the best. It is difficult to overcome inertia."

Radio is one of the most effective means of advertising when used correctly. Of course, there is a right way and a wrong way to utilize the medium, and the salesperson who knows and understands the unique character of his or her product is in the best position to succeed. To the extent that a radio commercial cannot be held or taped to a cash register, it is intangible.

However, the results produced by a carefully conceived campaign can be seen in the cash register. Consistent radio users, from the giant multinational corporations to the so-called mom-and-pop shops, know that a radio commercial can capture people's attention as effectively as anything crossing their field of vision. A 1950s promotional slogan says it best: "Radio gives you more than you can see."

On a final note, Ed Shane says that although over-the-air advertising remains the primary source of income for most stations, "non-traditional revenue (NTR) streams (such as a web site or special events) help stations realize financial goals."

Becoming an Account Executive

A notion held by some sales managers is that salespeople are born and not made. This position holds that a salesperson either "has it" or does not, "it" being the innate gift to sell, without which all the schooling and training in the world means little. Although not all sales managers embrace this theory, many agree with the view that anyone attempting a career in sales should first and foremost possess an unflagging desire to make money, because without it, failure is almost assured.

According to RAB figures, 70 percent of the radio salespeople hired by stations are gone within three years; another study reveals that 73 percent of new radio salespeople leave the business within a year. Although this sounds less than encouraging, it also must be stated that to succeed in broadcast sales invariably means substantial earnings and rapid advancement. True, the battle can be a tough one and the dropout rate is high, but the rewards of success are great.

The majority of newly hired account executives have college training. An understanding of research, marketing, and finance is important. Formal instruction in these areas is particularly advisable for persons considering a career in broadcast sales. Broadcast sales has become a familiar course offering at many schools with programs in electronic media. Research and

FIGURE 4.1
Sales bullpen area. Courtesy Clear Channel.

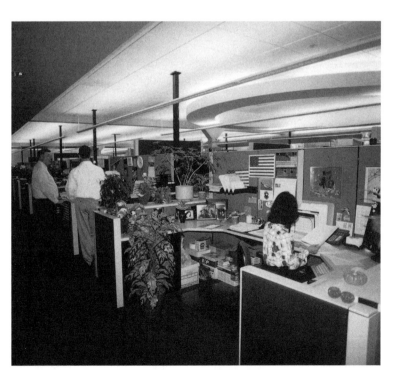

marketing courses designed for the broadcast major also have become more prevalent since the 1970s. "Young people applying for sales positions here, for the most part, have college backgrounds. A degree indicates a certain amount of tenacity and perseverance, which are important qualities in anyone wanting to sell radio. Not only that, but the candidate with a degree often is more articulate and self-assured. As in most other areas of radio, ten or fifteen years ago fewer people had college diplomas, but the business has become so much more sophisticated and complex because of the greater competition and emphasis on research that managers actually look for salespeople with college training," says general manager Richard Bremkamp.

Whether a candidate for a sales position has extensive formal training or not, he or she must possess a knowledge of the product in order to be hired. "To begin with, an applicant must show me that she knows something about radio; after all, that is what we're selling. The individual doesn't necessarily have to have a consummate understanding of the medium, although that would be nice, but she must have some product knowledge. Most stations are willing to train to an extent. I suppose you always look for someone with some sales experience, whether in radio or in some other field," says general sales manager Bob Turley.

Stations do prefer a candidate with sales exposure, be it selling vacuum cleaners door-to-door or shoes in a retail store. "Being out in front of the public, especially in a selling situation, regardless of the product, is excellent training for the prospective radio sales rep. I started in the transportation industry, first in customer service, then in sales. After that I owned and operated a restaurant. Radio sales was a whole new ball game for me when I went to work for WCFR in Springfield, Vermont, in the mid-1970s. Having dealt with the public for two decades served me well. In two years I rose to be the station's top biller,

WHY RADIO?

▸ Radio has transcended current lifestyles...people today are money-rich and time-poor. 85% of all Americans are two income households complaining that they have no time to read the newspaper. Radio is the go ANYWHERE at ANYTIME medium:

  ▸ 99% of all households have radios

  ▸ 95% of all motor vehicles have radios

  ▸ 61% of all adults have radios at work

  ▸ Radio reaches people everywhere...in cars, at home, at work, on the way to and from anywhere!

  ▸ Radio appeals to each individuals own imagination...it's theater of the mind!

  ▸ Radio appeals to human emotions

  ▸ Radio convinces listeners to take action

  ▸ Radio is the IMMEDIATE medium...you can have a spot produced and be on the air with your message in as little as a few hours!

  ▸ Radio's message is easily changed...production costs are low

The 50/50 Music Mix of Yesterday & Today

FIGURE 4.2
Courtesy Mix 105.1.

concentrating mainly on direct retail sales. In 1979, WKVT in Brattleboro hired me as sales manager," recalls Charles W. Friedman.

Hiring inexperienced salespeople is a gamble that a small radio station generally must take. The larger outlets almost always require radio sales credentials, a luxury that lesser stations cannot afford. Thus, they must hire untested salespeople, and there are no guarantees that a person who has sold lawn mowers can sell airtime, that is, assuming that the newly hired salesperson has ever sold anything at all. In most cases, he or she comes to radio and sales without experience, and the station must provide at least a modicum of training. Unfortunately, many stations fail to provide adequate training, and this too contributes to the high rate of turnover. New salespeople commonly are given two to three months to display their wares and exhibit their potential. If they prove themselves to the sales manager by generating new business, they are asked to stay. On the other hand, if the sales manager is not convinced that the apprentice salesperson has the ability to bring in the accounts, then he or she is shown the door.

During the trial period, the salesperson is given a modest draw against sales, or a "no-strings" salary on which to subsist. In the former case, the salesperson eventually must pay back, through commissions on sales, the amount that he or she has drawn. Thus, after a few months, a new salesperson may well find him- or herself in debt for $2,000 or $3,000. As a show of confidence and to encourage the new salesperson who has shown an affinity for radio sales, management may erase the debt. If a station decides to terminate its association with the new salesperson, it must absorb the loss of time, energy, and money invested in the employee.

Characteristics that managers most often look for in prospective salespeople include ambition, confidence, energy, determination, honesty, and intelligence. "Ambition is the cornerstone of success. It's one of the first things I look for. Without it, forget it. You have to be hungry. It's a great motivator. You have to be a quick thinker—be able to think on your feet, under pressure, too. Personal appearance and grooming also are important," says sales manager Gene Etheridge.

Station sales manager Joe Martin places a premium on energy, persistence, creativity, and organization. "Someone who is a self-starter makes life a lot easier. No manager likes having to keep after members of his sales team. A salesperson should take initiative and be adept at planning his day. Too many people make half the calls they should and could. A salesperson without organizational skills is simply not going to bring in the same number of orders as the person who does. There is a correlation between the number of pitches and the number of sales."

Metro market general sales manager Peg Kelly values people skills. "Empathy is right up there. I need someone who possesses the ability to get quick answers, learn the client's business quickly, and relate well to clients. It's a people business, really." Charles W. Friedman also looks for sales personnel who are people oriented. "My experience has proven that a prospective salesperson had better like people. In other words, be gregarious and friendly. This is something that's hard to fake. Sincerity, or the lack of it, shows. If you're selling airtime, or I guess anything for that matter, you had better enjoy talking with people as well as listening. A good listener is a good salesperson. Another thing that is absolutely essential is the ability to take rejection objectively. It usually takes several 'no's' to get to the 'yes.'"

Friedman believes that it is important for a salesperson to have insight into human nature and behavior. "You really must be adept at psychology. Selling really is a matter of anticipating what the prospect is thinking and knowing how best to address his concerns. It's not so much a matter of outthinking the prospective client, but rather being cognizant of the things that play a significant role in his life. Empathy requires the ability to appreciate the experiences of others. A salesperson who is insensitive to a client's moods or states of mind usually will come away empty handed."

In recent years, sales managers have recruited more heavily from within the radio station itself rather than immediately looking elsewhere for salespeople. For decades, it was felt that programming people were not suited for sales. An inexplicable barrier seemed to separate the two areas. Since the 1970s, however, this attitude has changed to some degree, and sales managers now give serious consideration to on-air people who desire to make the transition into sales. Consolidation and downsizing in the 1990s also inspired multiple role playing at stations. That is to say, the morning deejay may become the afternoon salesperson. The major advantage of hiring programming people to sell the station is that they have a practical understanding of the product. "A lot of former deejays make good account reps because they had to sell the listener on the product. A deejay really is a salesperson, when you get right down to it," observes broadcaster Joe Martin.

Realizing, too, that sales is the most direct path into station management, programming people often are eager to make the shift. Since the 1980s, the trend has been greater than ever to recruit managers from the programming ranks. However, a sales background is still preferred.

The salesperson is invariably among the best-paid members of a station. How much a salesperson earns is usually left up to the individual to determine. Contrary to popular opinion, the salesperson's salary generally exceeds the deejay's, especially in the smaller markets. In the larger markets, certain air personalities' salaries are astronomical and even surpass the general manager's income, but major market sales salaries are commonly in the five- and even six-figure range.

Entry-level sales positions are fairly abundant (although station consolidation has reduced these opportunities), and stations are always on the lookout for good people. Perhaps no other position in the radio station affords an individual the opportunities that sales does, but most salespeople will never go beyond entry level in sales. Yet for those who are successful, the payoff is worthwhile. "The climb itself can be the most exhilarating part, I think. But you've got to have a lot of reserve in your tanks, because the air can be pretty thin at times," observes Etheridge.

50 Ways to Leave Your Loser

The attributes, habits and characteristics America's top local Radio salespeople say make them winners.

1. Discipline	28. Insistence on doing the best possible job — not just "good enough"
2. Attention to detail	
3. Follow-through	29. Deliver on promises
4. Honesty	30. Very presentable personal appearance
5. Listening	31. Open minded — never stop growing
6. Timeliness, promptness	32. Advance preparation — no winging it
7. Determination	33. Rarely forget to ask for the order (as opposed to rarely remembering)
8. Thoroughness	34. Regular self-improvement. Read a lot, listen to tapes. Attend seminars
9. Always prospecting	
10. Creativeness	35. Strong communication skills: intra-office and with clients mail/phone/in-person
11. Consistently (re)discovering and fulfilling prospect/client needs	
12. Flexibility	36. Aggressiveness — stay with prospect/client until the job is done right
13. Love the business	
14. Sincerely want their clients to succeed	37. Empathy/sincere caring for client's results
15. Knowledge	38. Results oriented
16. Strong work ethic	39. Do-it-now attitude
17. 50-plus-hour workweek	40. Keep good records
18. Organized	41. In office/on street early and stay late
19. Effective time/territory management	42. Under-promise and over-deliver
20. Priority management/crisis avoidance techniques	43. Get into the client's shoes, view things from client's perspective
21. Accessible to clients/peers/management	44. Anticipate and eliminate problems before they develop
22. Faith in God, self, product	45. Don't make assumptions
23. Unwavering enthusiasm	46. Don't take anything for granted, especially your station's place in the buy
24. Total personal acceptance of successes and failures	47. Loyalty to company, clients, self
25. Focus-focus-focus. Know what you want, what you need to do, do it.	48. Keep in touch with clients, especially during their schedules
26. Understanding and application of the basics of selling	49. Don't take rejection personally
27. Persistence	50. Sell ideas and solutions, not spots, flights, or packages

FIGURE 4.3
Some cogent advice. Courtesy Radio Ink.

The Sales Manager

The general sales manager (also called director of sales (DOS) in cluster operations) supervises the marketing of a station's or cluster's airtime. This person is responsible for moving inventory, which in the case of the radio outlet constitutes the selling of spot and feature schedules to advertisers. To achieve this end, the sales manager directs the daily efforts of the station's account executives, establishes sales department policies, develops sales plans and materials, conceives of sales and marketing campaigns and promotions, sets quotas, and also may sell as well.

A station's sales department customarily includes an emphasis on national, regional, and local sales. The station's or the cluster's general sales manager usually handles national responsibilities. This includes working with the station's rep company to stimulate business from national advertisers. The regional sales manager is given the responsibility of exploring sales possibilities in a broad geographical area surrounding the station or stations. For example, the regional person for an outlet in New York City may be assigned portions of Connecticut, New Jersey, and Long Island. The local sales manager at the same station would concentrate on advertisers within the city proper. The general sales manager oversees the efforts of each of these individuals.

The size of a station's sales staff varies according to its location and reach. A typical small market radio station employs between two and four account executives, and the medium market station averages about five. Large, top-ranked metropolitan outlets employ as many as 8 to 10 salespeople, although it is more typical for the major market station to have about a half dozen account executives. Of course, in cluster operations where team selling often exists, these numbers will vary, as a salesperson may be selling the airtime of several stations. In cluster operations it is not uncommon for there to be dozens of sales personnel.

The general sales manager/director of sales reports directly to the station or station cluster's general manager and works closely with the programming department in developing salable features. Regular daily and weekly sales meetings are scheduled and headed by the sales manager, during which time goals are set and problems addressed. The sales manager also assigns account lists to members of his or her staff and helps coordinate trade and co-op deals.

As mentioned earlier, the head of the sales department usually is responsible for maintaining close contact with the station's rep company as a way of generating income from national advertisers who are handled by advertising agencies. The relationship of the sales manager and rep company is a particularly important one and will be discussed in greater detail later in this chapter. In addition, the sales manager must be adept at working ratings figures to the station's advantage for inclusion in sales promotional materials that are used on both the national and local level.

All sales come under the scrutiny of the sales manager, who determines if an account is appropriate for the station and whether conditions of the sale meet established standards. In addition, the sales manager may have a policy that requires credit checks to be made on every new account and that new clients pay for a portion of their spot schedule up front as a show of good faith. Again, policies vary from station to station.

It is up to the head of sales to keep abreast of local and national sales and marketing trends that can be used to the station's advantage. This requires the sales manager to constantly survey trade magazines like *Radio Ink*, *Radio Business Report*, and *ADWEEK*, and attend industry seminars such as those conducted by the Radio Advertising Bureau. No sales department can operate in a vacuum and hope

FIGURE 4.4
Stats make the pitch.
Courtesy RAB.

MAXIMIZE YOUR ADVERTISING WITH RADIO

Why? Because every day your current and potential customers take their favorite Radio station into their cars, their homes, and the workplace. They even include Radio as part of their leisure time activities. To listeners, Radio is more than a medium, it's a special companion with whom they spend nearly three hours each day and more than four hours each weekend.

For the contemporary marketer, there's no other advertising medium that can build personal, one-to-one relationships that can reach and motivate consumers like Radio. Your best potential prospects for each of your most important products and services can be accurately targeted by age, income, gender, race, geography and lifestyle with effective frequency through a system of easily identifiable Radio formats.

YOU'LL REACH ALL YOUR BEST PROSPECTS WITH RADIO

WEEKLY REACH: Virtually every American listens to Radio! Not only do they tune in, they stay tuned — averaging 2 hours and 43 minutes of Radio listening every day.

AT WORK: Radio allows you to influence your best prospects all day long where other media can't: at work. Radio's varied formats appeal to people of all professional backgrounds.

RADIO'S WEEKLY REACH BY AGE AND SEX [28]	
MEN 18+	97%
WOMEN 18+	95%
TEENS 12-17	99%

RADIO'S MIDDAY REACH BY OCCUPATION [29]	
PROFESSIONAL/MANAGERIAL	76.1%
TECH./SALES/CLERICAL	80.3%
OTHER WORKERS	79.4%

YOU'LL MOTIVATE CONSUMERS EVERYWHERE WITH RADIO

AT HOME AND VIRTUALLY EVERYWHERE: Radio reaches your customers no matter where they are at work, shopping or just relaxing at home. Radio's in-car reach is also outstanding, reaching 86% of commuters each week. [30]

Share of Total Radio Listening by Location [31]

AT HOME 41.3%
OTHER PLACES 29.1%
IN CARS 29.6%

SHARE OF MEDIA TIME: Customers spend more time with Radio than any other media — up to 40% of total time spent with media.

Share of Time Spent With Media
(Total hours per year — Adults 18+)[32]

MAGAZINES 3.0%
NEWSPAPERS 6.0%
TV 38.4%
RADIO 40.0%
CABLE 12.7%

YOU'LL ENJOY THESE BENEFITS WITH RADIO

- *Total Market Reach*
- *Effective Message Frequency*
- *Targetability by Format Options*
- *Positive Advertising Environment*
- *Uncluttered Commercial Platform*
- *Complete Flexibility*
- *Sufficient Competitive Separation*
- *Unparalleled Cost Efficiency* • *Pro-active Promotional Opportunities*

to succeed in today's dynamic radio marketplace.

Statistics continue to bear out the fact that sales managers are most often recruited to fill the position of general manager. It is also becoming more commonplace for sales managers to have experience in other areas of a station's operations, such as programming and production, a factor that has become increasingly important to the person who hires the chief account executive.

FIGURE 4.5
Coverage maps are
used to sell those areas
within the station's
signal. Courtesy
KDKA.

FIGURE 4.5
continued

MIX 105.1 FM
Picking You Up And Making You Feel Good

Coverage Map

WOMX-FM / MIX 105.1
100,000 Watts
1,597 Feet
34 DBU Contour

	12+ POPULATION*
Metro Survey Area	1,104,600
Total Survey Area	2,512,900
Designated Market Area	2,331,100

COUNTY	POPULATION*	COUNTY	POPULATION*
Orange	688,500	Lake	172,100
Seminole	290,900	Marion	210,600
Osceola	125,200	Flagler	38,700
Volusia	366,500	Polk	392,400
Brevard	397,400	Sumter	41,200

*Source: WI '00, Arbitron

am·fm

Radio Sales Tools

The fees that a station charges for airtime are published in its rate card. Rates for airtime depend on the size of a station's listenership—the bigger the audience the higher the rates. At the same time, the unit cost for a spot or a feature is affected by the quantity or amount purchased—the bigger the "buy," the cheaper the unit price.

Clients also get discounts for consecutive-week purchases over a prescribed period of time—say, 26 or 52 weeks.

The sales manager and station manager (director of sales and market manager in cluster setups) work together in designing the rate card, basing their decisions on ratings and what their market can support. A typical rate card will include a brief policy statement concerning terms of payment and

2002 Rate Card

Monday - Sunday
BTA (Best Time Available), 6a-midnight*...$40
TAP (Total Audience Plan), 6a-midnight**....$46
6a-8p...$50

Monday - Friday
Morning Drive (6-10a).....$60
Midday (10a-3p)....$50
Afternoon Drive (3-7p)....$55
11a-8p...$52
Evenings (7p-mid)....$30
Overnights (Mid-5a)....$5

Weekends
Mornings/Evenings....$30
Middays/Afternoons....$40

BTA and TAP - add 10% to rate for Wednesday - Friday placement
Live reads by on-air talent - add 40% to rate
Live reads by Howard Stern - add 50% to rate, plus $2,000 fee for production

* BTA = Best Time Available, random placement by computer
** TAP = Total Audience Plan, 50% drives, 50% middays/evenings
All rates NET to station. Rates are for :30 or :60 commercials.
There is a premium for fixed positions or narrowed dayparts. Rates are subject to change without notice.

FIGURE 4.6
Station rate card with BTA and TAP features. Courtesy WIZN.

commission: "Bills due and payable when rendered. Without prior credit approval, cash in advance required. Commission to recognized advertising agencies on net charges for station time—15%." A statement pertaining to the nature of copy and when it is due at the station also may be included in the rate card: "All programs and announcements are subject to removal without notice for any broadcast which, in our opinion, is not in the public's interest. Copy must be at the station 48 hours prior to broadcast date and before noon on days preceding weekends and holidays." A station's approach to discounting must, of practical necessity, be included in the rate card: "All programs, features, and announcements are provided a 5% discount if on the air for 26 consecutive weeks and a 10% discount if on the air for 52 weeks." (See figure 4.7)

It is important to state as emphatically and clearly as possible the station's position on all possible topics affecting a sale. Most stations provide clients with rate protection for a designated period of time should fees for airtime change. This means that if a client purchases a three-month spot schedule in May, and the station raises its rates in June, the advertiser continues to pay the original rates until the expiration of its current contract.

The rate card also contains its feature and spot rates (see figure 4.9). Among the most prevalent features that stations offer are traffic, sports, weather, and business reports. Newscasts also are available to advertisers. Features generally include an open (introduction) and a 30- or 60-second announcement. They are particularly effective advertising vehicles because listeners tend to pay greater attention. Conditions pertaining to feature buys usually appear in the rate card: "All feature sales are subject to four weeks' notice for renewal and cancellation." A station wants to establish credibility with its features and therefore prefers to maintain continuity among its sponsors. A feature with a regular sponsor conveys stability, and that is what a station seeks.

Since the size of a radio station's audience generally varies depending on the time of day, rates for spots (commercials) or features must reflect that fact. Thus, the broadcast day is divided into time classifications: 6 to 10 a.m. weekdays is typically a station's prime selling period and therefore may be designated AAA; afternoon drivetime, usually 3 to 7 p.m., may be called AA because of its secondary drawing power. Under this system, the midday segment, 10 to 3 p.m., would be given a single A designation, and evenings, 7 to midnight, a B. Overnights, midnight to 6 a.m., may be classified as C time. Obviously, the fees charged for spots are established on an ascending

FIGURE 4.7
Rate card using a grid
structure.

scale from C to AAA. A station may charge $300 for an announcement aired at 8 a.m. and $45 for one aired at 2 a.m. The difference in the size of the station's audience at those hours warrants the contrast.

As previously mentioned, the more airtime a client purchases, the less expensive the cost for an individual commercial or unit. For instance, if an advertiser buys 10 spots a week during AAA time, the cost of each spot would be slightly less than if the sponsor purchased two spots a week. A client must buy a specified number of spots in order to benefit from the frequency discount. A 6X rate, meaning six spots per week, for AAA 60s (60-second announcements) may be $75; the 12X rate may be $71 and the 18X rate $68, and so forth. Thirty-second spots are usually priced at two-thirds the cost of a 60-second spot. Should a client desire that a spot be aired at a fixed time—say, at 7:10 a.m. daily—the station will tack on an additional charge, possibly 20 percent. Fixed position drivetime spots are among the most expensive in a station's inventory.

Many stations use a grid structure. This gives stations a considerable degree of rate flexibility. For example, if a station has five rate-level grids, it may have a range between $20 and $50 for a 60-second spot. Clients would then be given rates at the lower grid if the station had few sponsors on the air, thus creating many availabilities (places to insert commercial messages). As business increased at the station and availabilities became scarcer, the station would ask for rates reflected in the upper grids. Gridding is based on the age-old concept of supply and demand. When availabilities are tight and airtime is at a premium, that time costs more.

Grids are inventory sensitive; they allow a station to remain viable when business is at a low ebb. Certainly when inventory prices reach a bargain level, this encourages business. For instance, during a period when advertiser activity is sluggish, a station that can offer spots at a considerable reduction stands a chance of stimulating buyer interest.

When business is brisk at a station, because of holiday buying, for example, the situation may be exploited in a manner positive to the revenue column. Again the supply-and-demand concept is at work (one idea on which capitalism is based).

Not all stations grid their rate cards, however. Since the late 1970s, this system has gained considerable popularity because of its relevance to the ever fluctuating economy. As apparent in the rate cards exhibited in this chapter, grids are delineated by some sort of scale, usually alphabetical or numerical.

Clients are offered several spot schedule plans suited for their advertising and budgetary needs. For advertisers with limited funds, run-of-station (ROS) or best-time-available (BTA) plans are usually an option. Rates are lower under these plans since no guarantee is given as to what times the spots will be aired. However, most stations make a concerted effort to rotate ROS and BTA spots as equitably as possible, and during periods when commercial loads are light they frequently are scheduled during premium times. Of course, when a station is loaded down with spot schedules, especially around holidays or elections, ROS and BTA spots may find themselves buried. In the long run, advertisers using these plans receive a more than fair amount of choice times and at rates considerably lower than those clients who buy specific dayparts.

In *Radio Advertising's Missing Ingredient: The Optimum Effective Scheduling System* by Pierre Bouvard and Steve Marx, an innovative system is presented that improves the might of a spot schedule. According to the authors, "Optimum effective scheduling ensures that the effective reach, those hit three or more times, is at least 50 percent of the total reach." The idea behind optimum effective scheduling (OES) is to strengthen the impact of client buys. The OES formula is designed to heighten the efficiency of a spot buy through a system of scheduling based on ratings performance. This is accomplished by factoring a station's turnover ratio and cume.

Total audience plan (TAP) is another popular package offered clients by many stations. It is designed to distribute a client's spots among the various dayparts for maximum audience penetration, while costing less than an exclusive prime-time schedule. The rate for a TAP spot is arrived at by averaging the cost for spots in several time classifications. For example, AAA = $80, AA = $70, A = $58, B = $31; thus, the TAP rate per spot is $59. The advantages are obvious. The advertiser is getting a significant discount on the spots scheduled during morning and afternoon drive periods. At the same time, the advertiser is paying more for airtime during evenings. However, TAP is very attractive because it does expose a client's message to every possible segment of a station's listening audience with a measure of cost effectiveness.

Bulk or annual discounts are available to advertisers who buy a heavy schedule of commercials over the course of a year. Large companies in particular take advantage of volume discounts because the savings are significant.

Announcements are rotated or "orbited" within time classifications to maximize the number of different listeners reached. If a client buys three drivetime spots per week to be aired on a Monday, Wednesday, and Friday, over a four-week period, the time they are scheduled will be different each day. Here is a possible rotation set-up:

	MON	WED	FRI
Week I	7:15	6:25	9:10
Week II	8:22	7:36	8:05
Week III	6:11	9:12	7:46
Week IV	9:20	8:34	6:52

Rather than purchase a consecutive week schedule, advertisers may choose to purchase time in flights, an alternating pattern of being on one week and off the next. For instance, a client with a seasonal business or one that is geared toward holiday sales may set up a plan in which spots are scheduled at specific times throughout the year. Thus, an annual flight schedule may look something like this:

Feb. 13–19 Washington's Birthday Sale
    10 A 60s
Mar. 14–17 St. Patrick's Day Celebration
    8 ROS 30s
Apr. 16–21 Easter Parade Days
    20 TAP 30s
May 7–12 Mother's Day Sale
    6 AAA and 6 AA 30s
June 1–15 Summer Sale Days
    30 ROS 60s
Aug. 20–30 Back-to-School Sale
    15 A 60s
Sep. 24–Oct. 6 Fall Sale Bonanza
    25 ROS 60s
Nov. 25–Dec. 19 Christmas Sale
    25 AAA 60s and 20 A 30s

Let's take a look at the wisdom behind a few of the preceding flights. The client purchases 10 spots in A time during the week that precedes Washington's Birthday to reach the home female audience. The A time on this station is 10:00 a.m. to 3:00 p.m., so a schedule of spots here does a good job of targeting women who work at home. The client uses a TAP plan to move Easter inventory. This will get the client's spot in all dayparts to help her reach as many dif-

ferent people as possible at the best unit price. During the back-to-school days of late August, the client once again targets the strongest female daypart on the station, and around Christmas time the client purchases the heaviest flight because this is the so-called do-or-die period (the time when business potential reaches its peak). The heavier spot purchase will help ensure success during this crucial time. Selling in flights makes a lot of sense to many advertisers because of its calendar relevance.

Salespeople use rate cards to plan and compute buys. It is generally perceived as a poor idea to simply leave it with a prospective client to figure out, even if such a request is made. First, few laypersons are really adept at reading rate cards and, second, a station does not like to publicize its rates to its competition, which is what happens when too many station rate cards are in circulation. Granted, it is quite easy for any station to obtain a competitor's sales portfolio, but stations prefer to keep a low

FIGURE 4.8
Some stations use a rate card that reflects demographic variations of their audience. This particular card also provides salespeople a negotiating range for selling airtime. A "low" and "high" rate are indicated.

Demographic Rate Card Monday–Sunday 6 A.M.–Midnight			
Demographic	Low	High	Rating
Teens	$230	$500	5.0
12–24 Persons	$235	$400	5.2
12–24 Males	$210	$350	4.8
12–24 Females	$240	$500	5.5
18–24 Persons	$215	$350	3.6
18–24 Males	$200	$330	3.4
18–24 Females	$215	$350	3.6
18–34 Persons	$180	$250	3.0
18–34 Males	$180	$250	2.9
18–34 Females	$180	$250	3.0
18–49 Persons	$170	$225	2.4
18–49 Males	$165	$225	2.2
18–49 Females	$175	$225	2.6
25–34 Persons	$180	$250	2.7
25–34 Males	$180	$250	2.6
25–34 Females	$180	$250	3.0
25–49 Persons	$150	$200	1.9
25–49 Males	$140	$200	1.7
25–49 Females	$150	$200	1.9
25–54 Persons	$130	$190	1.2
25–54 Males	$130	$190	1.1
25–54 Females	$130	$190	1.2

profile as a means of retaining a competitive edge.

Radio marketing expert Jay Williams, Jr., contends that the station rate card is on its way to obsolescence. "Most radio stations have gotten away or are getting away from using rate cards as much of the business is driven by supply and demand. Jennifer McCann, GM of Burlington Broadcasters, told me recently that 'While many small market stations still print and rely on rate cards, stations in major markets do not.' Using systems similar to 'yield management' systems first introduced by the airline industry, medium and larger stations often use programs such as Maxigrid to manage and price their spot inventory to ensure their sales goals. A radio station is usually faced with uneven and ever-changing demands on a limited amount of commercial time. Certain dayparts near the end of the week, special programming, and drive times near holidays might be easily sold out, yet other time periods might have plenty of 'avails.' Using an inventory management system enables stations to continuously price their inventory by day, daypart, and even by the hour well in advance. This knowledge gives the sales department the up-to-the minute pricing and 'avail' information it needs to serve the client and allows the station to maintain the maximum control of its inventory. Even in smaller markets, rate cards are not used much except as a point for negotiating. Rate cards are often confusing and focus attention on the individual spot cost rather than the total cost of an advertising campaign. To compete against other media, radio has realized the value of creating customized presentations and programs for clients to respond to their specific needs and goals. Clients and agencies sometimes do ask to see a rate card, but they are rapidly becoming extinct."

FIGURE 4.9
Stations sell features to motivate advertisers. Courtesy WIZN.

Points of the Pitch

Not all sales are made on the first call; nonetheless, the salesperson does go in with the hopes of closing an account. The first call generally is designed to introduce the station to the prospective sponsor and to determine the sponsor's needs. However, the salesperson should always be prepared to propose a buy that is suitable for the account. This means that some homework must be done relative to the business before an approach is made. "First determine the client's needs, as best as possible. Then address those needs with a schedule built to reach the client's customers. Don't walk into a business cold or without some sense of what the place is about," advises Friedman.

Should all go smoothly during the initial call, the salesperson may opt to go for an order there and then. If the account obliges, fine. In the event that the prospective advertiser is not prepared to make an immediate decision, a follow-up appointment must be made. The callback should be accomplished as close to the initial presentation as possible to prevent the impression made then from fading or growing cold. The primary objective of the return call is to close the deal and get the order. To strengthen the odds, the salesperson must review and assess any objections or reservations that may have arisen during the first call and devise a plan to overcome them. Meanwhile, the initial proposal may be beefed up to appear even more attractive to the client, and a "spec" tape (see the later section "Spec Spots") for the business can be prepared as further enticement.

Should the salesperson's efforts fail the second time out, a third and even fourth call are made. Perseverance does pay off, and many salespeople admit that just when they figured a situation was hopeless, an account said yes. "Of course, beating your head against the wall accomplishes nothing. You have to know when your time is being wasted. Never give up entirely on an account; just approach it more sensibly. A phone call or a drop-in every so often keeps you in their thoughts," says general sales manager Ron Piro.

What follows are two checklists. The Do list contains some suggestions conducive to a positive sales experience, and the Don't list contains things that will have a negative or counterproductive effect.

Do

- Research the advertiser; be prepared; have a relevant plan in mind.
- Be enthusiastic; think positive.
- Display self-confidence; believe in yourself and the product.
- Smile; exude friendliness, warmth, and sincerity.

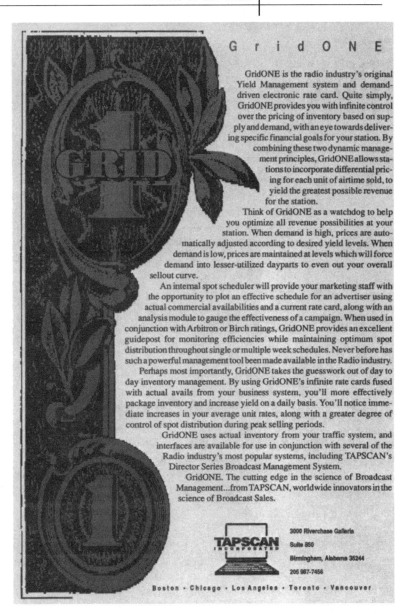

- Listen; be polite, sympathetic, and interested.
- Tell of the station's successes; provide testimonial material.
- Think creatively.
- Know your competition.
- Maintain integrity and poise.
- Look your best; check your appearance.
- Be objective and keep proper perspective.
- Pitch the decision maker.
- Ask for the order that will do the job.
- Service the account after the sale.

FIGURE 4.10
Electronic rate cards employ a grid approach for inventory control. Courtesy TAPSCAN.

Don't

- Pitch without a plan.
- Criticize or demean the client's previous advertising efforts.
- Argue with the client. This just creates greater resistance.
- Badmouth the competition.
- Talk too much.
- Brag or be overly aggressive.
- Lie, exaggerate, or make unrealistic promises.
- Smoke or chew gum in front of the client.
- Procrastinate or put things off.
- Be intimidated or kept waiting an unreasonable amount of time.
- Make a presentation unless you have the client's undivided attention.
- Lose your temper.
- Ask for too little; never undersell a client.
- Fail to follow up.
- Accept a "no" as final.

FIGURE 4.11
A cluster breakdown highlighting sales organization. Courtesy Citadel.

Checklists like the preceding ones can serve only as basic guidelines. Anyone who has spent time on the street as a station account executive can expand on this or any other such checklist. For the positive-thinking radio salesperson, every call gives something back, whether a sale is made or not.

Overcoming common objections is a necessary step toward achieving the sale. Here are some typical "put-offs" presented to radio sales reps:

1. Nobody listens to radio commercials.
2. Newspaper ads are more effective.
3. Radio costs too much.
4. Nobody listens to your station.
5. We tried radio, and it didn't work.
6. We don't need any more business.
7. We've already allocated our advertising budget.
8. We can get another station for less.
9. Business is off, and we haven't got the money.
10. My partner doesn't like radio.

And so on. There are countless rebuttals for each of these statements, and a knowledgeable and skilled radio salesperson can turn such objections into positives.

Levels of Sales

There are three levels from which the medium draws its sales: retail, local, and national. Retail accounts for the biggest percentage of the industry's income, over 70 percent. Retail, also referred to as *direct*, sales involve the radio station on a one-to-one basis with advertisers within its signal area.

In this case, a station's account executive works directly with the client and earns a commission of approximately 15 percent on the airtime he or she sells. An advertiser who spends $1,000 would benefit the salesperson to the tune of $150. A newly hired salesperson without previous experience generally will work on a direct retail basis and will not be assigned advertising agencies until he or she has become more seasoned and has displayed some ability. Generally speaking, the smaller

A medium market Cluster structure
Citadel Broadcasting, Worcester, MA
Information from Mary Ann Bolger, NSM, Citadel Broadcasting, Worcester

This group has 3 stations in a market with very few "home" stations (because of the proximity to Boston, Providence, Manchester & Springfield/Hartford).
Stations are WXLO, 104.5, WWFX, 100.1 & WORC, 98.9

They have a VP/GM for all 3 stations

They have one Sales Manager for WXLO
    They have six sellers for WXLO who only sell WXLO

They have a second Sales Manager for The Fox and WORC (oldies)
    They have a separate team for The Fox with 3 sellers
    And another team to sell WORC Oldies 98.9 with three sellers

They have a National Sales Manager for all stations

They have one Traffic Manager for WXLO & The Fox
They have another Traffic Manager for WORC and The Cat (a station in Athol that they own—bought it to move shortspaced WWFX closer to Worcester).

the radio station, the more dependent it is on retail sales, although most medium- and metro market stations would be in trouble without strong business on this level.

All stations, regardless of size, have some contact with advertising agencies. Here again, however, the larger a market, the more a station will derive its business from ad agencies. This level of station sales generally is classified as local. The number of advertising agencies in a market will vary depending on its size. A sales manager will

HOWARD STERN _speaks out_ _on Advertising!_

FIGURE 4.12
The self-proclaimed "king of all media" pitches for radio. Courtesy 97.1 FM Talk.

I said to many people that, when I envisioned being on the radio, I didn't envision being just a disc jockey. I'm a salesman. There are certainly lots of mediums out there that one can advertise in, but I always envisioned a very aggressive medium. I envisioned a guy coming to me and saying, "Look, I gotta sell product. And I don't have the budget of Proctor & Gamble." I have found that we have the kind of medium, where somebody puts some kind of pre-recorded spot on our show and people sit through those commercials, because they're waiting to hear what we're going to do next! Especially live commercials, I want them to be entertaining, so no one's going to tune out and I'm going to sell a lot of product. I take it as a personal mission to sell a product for people. You know, I've had companies come to me, who were doing about a million dollars in business, and after a couple of weeks on the air with me, they are doing 13 million dollars of business. That's tremendous impact. That's what we're really all about anyway. Keeping people tuned in during the commercials. I've had sponsors who for years avoided my radio program, saying, "I don't know if it's the right environment." And then when times got a little tough, they said, "..., I gotta sell some product or I'm going to be out of business." Boom. They're there now. And they sell product. We have very effective advertising. We're the people who smack you in the face and say, "Oops. Here's a great sponsor. Here's why we think that they are good. Here's how they can save you money. Here's their basic pitch. Give them a chance. Give them a call." And we are very, very aggressive in that.

I've heard disc jockeys say that they don't want to read live commercials, they don't want to record a commercial with their voice on it. Hey, you know, we're all working together. It's one giant effort, and I'm not going to get paid if I don't have advertisers, and I recognize that. I also think that I have an obligation to an advertiser. I don't want a guy comin' on to my show and not getting results. I want them getting results through the roof.

An excerpt from a 4 page interview with Howard Stern discussing advertisers seeking an aggressive medium. Taken from FMQB, July 12, 1991 divide the market's agencies among his reps as equitably as possible, sometimes using a merit system. In this way, an account executive who has worked hard and produced results will be rewarded for his efforts by being given an agency to work. The top billers, that is, those salespeople who bring in the most business, often possess the greatest number of agencies, or at least the most active. Although the percentage of commission a salesperson is accorded, typically 6 to 8 percent, is less than that derived from retail sales, the size of the agency buys usually is far more substantial.

FIGURE 4.13
Courtesy WIZN-FM.

The third category of station sales comes from the national level. In most cases, it is the general sales manager who works with the station's rep company to secure buys from advertising agencies that handle national accounts. Again, national business is greater for the metro station than it is for the rural. Agencies justify a buy on numbers and little else, although it is not uncommon for small market stations, which do not even appear in ratings surveys, to be bought by major accounts interested in maintaining a strong local or community image.

Producer Ty Ford observes that agency involvement has decreased in recent years because of intensified competition among the different media and the unpredictable national economy. "Increased competition from cable, television, radio, and print has forced many ad agencies out of business. Stations now frequently offer 'agency discounts' to direct-retail clients just to close the sale. Also, more retail companies are forming their own in-house agencies." Although this may be true, the ad agency is still an important factor in station revenues.

Each level of sales—retail, local, or national—must be sufficiently cultivated if a station is to enjoy maximum prosperity. To neglect any one of these levels would result in a loss of station revenue.

The Wizard of Rock
106.7 WIZN   the Buzz 99.9

Nine Reasons to Advertise

1. **Advertising Creates Store Traffic**. Continuous store traffic is the first step toward increasing sales and expanding your base of shoppers. The more people who come into your store, the more opportunities you have to make sales.

2. **Advertising Attracts New Customers**. Your market changes constantly. Newcomers to your area mean new customers to reach. People earn more money. The shopper who wouldn't consider your business a few years ago may be a prime customer now.

3. **Advertising Encourages Repeat Business**. Shoppers don't have the store loyalty they once did. They have mobility and freedom of choice. You must advertise to keep up with your competition.

4. **Advertising Generates Continuous Business**. Your doors are open. Employees are on the payroll. As long as you're in business, you've got over head to meet, and new people to reach.

5. **Advertising is an Investment in Success**. A survey of 3,000 companies found that advertisers who maintained or expanded advertising over 5 years saw sales increase an average of 100%, while those who cut advertising grew at less than half the rate of those advertising steadily.

6. **Advertising Keeps You in the Competitive Race**. There are only so many customers in the market ready to buy at any one time. You have to advertise to keep regular customers, and to counter-balance the advertising of your competition.

7. **Advertising Keeps Your Business Top-of-Mind with Shoppers**. Many people go from store to store comparing prices, quality and service. Your name must be fresh in their minds when they decide to buy.

8. **Advertising Gives Your Business a Successful Image**. It tells your customers that your doors are open and you're ready for business. Advertising that is vigorous and positive can bring shoppers into the marketplace, regardless of the economy.

9. **Advertising Brings In Big Bucks for Your Business**. Advertising works. Businesses that succeed are usually strong, steady advertisers. Look around. You'll find the most aggressive and consistent advertisers are almost invariably the most successful. Join their ranks by advertising, and watch your business grow!

Spec Spots

One of the most effective ways to convince an advertiser to use a station is to provide a fully produced sample commercial, or "spec spot." If prepared properly and imaginatively, a client will find it difficult to deny its potential. Spec tapes often are used in callbacks when a salesperson needs to break down a client's resistance. More than once, a clever spec spot has converted an adamant "no" into an "okay, let's give it a shot." Spec spots also are used to reactivate the interest of former accounts who may not have spent money on the station for a while and who need some justification to do so.

Ralph Guild

On the Future Market for Radio

The radio industry has undergone radical but positive change in recent years and will continue to experience significant evolutionary changes between now and the end of the decade. Ironically, these changes are, in many ways, the result of a constant that we have witnessed throughout the history of the medium. Radio consistently has demonstrated a tremendous ability to adapt to a variety of market conditions, whether they be economic or competitive in nature. It is this flexibility, a by-product of intelligent industry leadership, that has fueled radio's growth in the past and will continue to elevate the industry to new heights in the years to come.

FIGURE 4.14
Ralph Guild.

Specs also are effective tools for motivating clients to "heavy-up" or increase their current spot schedules. A good idea can move a mountain, and salespeople are encouraged by the sales manager to develop spec tape ideas. Many sales managers require that account executives make at least one spec tape presentation each week. The sales manager may even choose to critique spec spots during regularly scheduled meetings.

The information needed to prepare a spec spot is acquired in several ways. If a salesperson already has called on a prospective client, he should have a very good idea of what the business is about as well as the attitude of the retailer toward the enterprise. The station sales rep is then in a very good position to prepare a spot that directly appeals to the needs and perceptions of the would-be advertiser. If a salesperson decides that the first call on a client warrants preparing a spec tape, then he or she may collect information on the business by actually browsing through the store as a customer might. This gives the salesperson an accurate, firsthand impression of the store's environment and merchandise. An idea of how the store perceives itself, and specific information such as address and hours, can be derived by checking its display ad in the Yellow Pages if it has one, or by examining any ads it may have run in the local newspaper. Flyers that the business may have distributed also provide useful information for the formulation of the copy used in the spec spot. Listening to commercials the advertiser may be running on another station also gives the salesperson an idea of the direction in which to move.

Again, the primary purpose of a spec spot is to motivate a possible advertiser to buy time. A spec that fails to capture the interest and appreciation of the individual for which it has been prepared may be lacking in the necessary ingredients. It is generally a good rule of thumb to avoid humor in a spec, unless the salesperson has had some firsthand experience with the advertiser. Nothing fails as abysmally as a commercial that attempts to be funny and does not come across as such to the client—thus, the saying "What is funny to one person may be silly or offensive to another."

Although spec spots are, to some extent, a gamble, they should be prepared in such a way that the odds are not too great. Of course, a salesperson who believes in an idea must have the gumption to go with it. Great sales are often inspired by unconventional concepts.

Objectives of the Buy

A single spot on a radio station seldom brings instant riches to an advertiser. However, a thoughtfully devised plan based on a formula of frequency and consistency will achieve impressive results, contends general manager John Gregory. "It has to be made clear from the start what a client hopes to accomplish by advertising on your station. Then a schedule that realistically corresponds with the client's goals must be put together. This means selling the advertiser a sufficient number of commercials spread over a specific period of time. An occasional spot here and there doesn't do much in this medium. There's a right way to sell radio, and that isn't it."

Our lists of dos and don'ts of selling suggested that the salesperson "ask for the order that will do the job." It also said not to undersell an account. Implicit in the first point is the idea that the salesperson has determined what kind of schedule the advertiser should buy to get the results expected. Too often salespeople fail to ask for what they need for fear the client will balk. Thus, they settle for what they can get

without much resistance. This, in fact, may be doing the advertiser a disservice, since the buy that the salesperson settles for may not fulfill declared objectives. "It takes a little courage to persist until you get what you think will do the job. There is the temptation just to take what the client hands you and run, but that technique usually backfires when the client doesn't get what he expected. As a radio sales rep, you should know how best to sell the medium. Don't be apologetic or easily compromised. Sell the medium the way it should be sold. Write enough of an order to get the job done," says sales manager Ron Piro.

Inflated claims and unrealistic promises should never be a part of a sales presentation. Avoid "If you buy spots on my station, you'll have to hire additional salespeople to handle the huge crowds." Salespeople must be honest in their projections and in what a client may expect from the spot schedule he or she purchases. "You will notice a gradual increase in store traffic over the next few weeks as the audience is exposed to your commercial over WXXX" is the better approach. Unfulfilled promises ruin any chances of future buys. Too often salespeople, caught up in the enthusiasm of the pitch, make claims that cannot be achieved. Radio is a phenomenally effective advertising medium. This is a proven fact. Those who have successfully used the medium can attest to the importance of placing an adequate order. "An advertiser has to buy a decent schedule to get strong results. Frequency is essential in radio," notes Piro. A radio sales axiom says it best: "The more spots aired, the more impressions made, and the more impressions made, the more impressed the client."

Prospecting and List Building

When a salesperson is hired by a radio station, he or she is customarily provided with a list of accounts to which airtime may be sold. For an inexperienced salesperson, this list may consist of essentially inactive or dormant accounts, that is, businesses that either have been on the air in the past or those that have never purchased airtime on the station. The new sales rep is expected to breathe life into the list by selling spot schedules to those accounts listed, as well as by adding to the list by bringing in new business. This is called *list building*, and it is the primary challenge facing the new account executive.

A more active list, one that generates commissions, will be given to the more experienced radio salesperson. A salesperson may be persuaded to leave one station in favor of another based on the contents of a list, which may include large accounts and prominent advertising agencies. Lists held by a station's top billers invariably contain the most enthusiastic radio users. Salespeople cultivate their lists as a farmer does his fields. The more the account list yields, the more commissions in the salesperson's pocket.

New accounts are added to a sales rep's list in several ways. Once the status of the list's existing accounts is determined, which is accomplished through a series of in-person calls and presentations, a salesperson must begin prospecting for additional business. Area newspapers are a common source. When a salesperson finds an account that he wishes to add to his or her list, the account must be "declared." This involves consulting the sales manager for approval to add the account to the salesperson's existing list. In some cases the account declared may already belong to another salesperson. If it is an open account, the individual who comes forward first usually is allowed to add it to his or her list.

Other sources for new accounts include the Yellow Pages, television stations, and competing radio outlets, and today, station salespeople are also tapping the Internet and using e-mail to enhance their search for clients. Every business in the area is listed

in the Yellow Pages, which contains many display ads that provide useful information. Local television stations are viewed with an eye toward their advertisers. Television can be an expensive proposition, even in smaller markets, and businesses that spend money on it may find radio's rates more palatable. On the other hand, if a business can afford to buy television, it often can afford to embellish its advertising campaign with radio spots. Many advertisers place money in several media—newspaper, radio, television—simultaneously. This is called a *mixed media* buy and is a proven advertising formula for the obvious reason that the client is reaching all possible audiences.

FIGURE 4.15
Stations sell sponsored programs, often at a premium rate.
Courtesy WIZN and WHKL.

Finally, accounts currently on other stations constitute good prospects since they obviously already have been sold on the medium.

In the course of an average workday, a salesperson will pass hundreds of businesses, some of which may have just opened their doors, or are about to do so. Sales reps must keep their eyes open and be prepared to make an impromptu call. The old saying "the early bird gets the worm" is particularly relevant in radio sales. The first account executive into a newly launched business often is the one who gets the buy.

A list containing dozens of accounts does not necessarily ensure a good income. If those businesses listed are small spenders or inactive, little in the way of commissions will be generated and billing will be low. The objective of list building is not merely to increase the number of accounts, but rather to raise the level of commissions it produces. In other words, a list that contains 30 accounts, of which 22 are active, is preferable to one with 50 accounts containing only 12 that are doing business with the station. A salesperson does not get points for having a lot of names on his list.

It is the sales manager's prerogative to shift an account from one salesperson's list to another's if he or she believes the account is being neglected or handled incorrectly. At the same time, certain in-house accounts, those handled by the sales manager, may be added to a sales rep's list as a reward for performing well. A salesperson's account list also may be pared down if the sales manager concludes that it is disproportional with the others at the station. The attempt to more equitably distribute the wealth may cause a brouhaha with the account person whose list is being trimmed. The sales manager attempting this feat may lose a top biller; thus, he or she must consider the ramifications of such a move and proceed accordingly. This may even mean letting things remain as they are. The top biller often is responsible for as much as 30 to 40 percent of the station's earnings.

Planning the Sales Day

A radio salesperson makes between 75 and 100 in-person calls a week, or on the average of 15 to 20 each day. This requires careful planning and organization. Ron Piro advises preparing a day's itinerary the night before. "There's nothing worse than facing the day without an idea of where to go. A salesperson can spare himself that dreaded sensation and a lot of lost time by preparing a complete schedule of calls the night before."

When preparing a daily call sheet, a salesperson, especially one whose station covers a vast area, attempts to centralize, as much as possible, the businesses to be contacted. Time, energy, and gas are needlessly expended through poor planning. A sales rep who is traveling 10 miles between each presentation can get to only half as many clients as the person with a consolidated call sheet. Of course, there are days when a salesperson must spend more time traveling. Not every day can be ideally plotted. It may be necessary to make a call in one part of the city at 9 a.m. and be in another part at 10 a.m. A salesperson must be where he or she feels the buys are going to be made. "Go first to those businesses likeliest to buy. The tone of the day will be sweetened by an early sale," contends Piro.

Sales managers advise their reps to list more prospects than they expect to contact. In so doing, they are not likely to run out of places to go should those prospects they had planned to see be unavailable. "You have to make the calls to make the sales. The more calls you make, the more the odds favor a sale," points out Gene Etheridge.

Itineraries should be adhered to regardless of whether a sale is made early in the day, says WNRI's John Gregory. "You can't pack it in at ten in the morning because you've closed an account. A salesperson who is easily satisfied is one who will never make much money. You must stay true to your day's game plan and follow through. No all-day coffee klatch at the local Ho-Jo's or movie matinee because you nailed an order after two calls."

The telephone is one of the salesperson's best tools. Although it is true that a client cannot sign a contract over the phone, much time and energy can be saved through its effective use. Appointments can be made and a client can be qualified via the telephone. That is to say, a salesperson can ascertain when the decision maker will be available. "Rather than travel twenty miles without knowing if the person who has the authority to make a buy will be around, take a couple of minutes and make a phone call. As they say, 'time is money.' In the time spent finding out that the store manager or owner is not on the premises when you get there, other, more productive calls can be made," says Charles Friedman.

If a client is not available when the salesperson appears, a callback should be arranged for either later the same day or soon thereafter. The prospective advertiser should never be forgotten or relegated to a call three months hence. The sales rep should try to rearrange his or her schedule to accommodate a return visit the same day, given that the person to see is available. However, it is futile to make a presentation to someone who cannot give full attention. The sales rep who arrives at a business only to find the decision maker overwhelmed by distractions is wise to ask for another appointment. In fact, the client will perceive this as an act of kindness and consideration. Timing is important.

A record of each call should be kept for follow-up purposes. When calling on a myriad of accounts, it is easy to lose track of what transpired during a particular call. Maintaining a record of a call requires little more than a brief notation after it is made. Notes may then be periodically reviewed to help determine what action should be taken on the account. Follow-ups are crucial. There is nothing more embarrassing and disheartening than to discover a client, who was pitched and then forgotten, advertising on another station. Sales managers usually require that salespeople turn in copies of their call sheets on a daily or weekly basis for review purposes.

Selling With and Without Numbers

Not all stations can claim to be number one or two in the ratings. In fact, not all stations appear in any formal ratings survey. Very small markets are not visited by Arbitron or other rating services for the simple reason that there may be only one station broadcasting in the area. An outlet in a nonsurvey area relies on its good reputation in the community to attract advertisers. In small markets, salespeople do not work out of a ratings book, and clients are not concerned with cumes and shares. In the truest sense of the word, an account person must sell the station. Local businesses often account for more than 95 percent of a small market station's revenue. Thus, the stronger the ties with the community, the better. Broadcasters in rural markets must foster an image of good citizenship in order to make a living.

Civic mindedness is not as marketable a commodity in the larger markets as are ratings points. In the sophisticated multistation urban market, the ratings book is the bible. A station without numbers in the highly competitive environment finds the task of earning an income a difficult one, although there are numerous examples of low-rated stations that do very well. However, "no numbers" pretty much puts a metro area station out of the running for agency business. Agencies almost invariably "buy by the book." A station without numbers "works the street," to use the popular phrase, focusing its sales efforts on direct business.

An obvious difference in approaches exists between selling the station with ratings and the one without. In the first case, a station centers its entire presentation around its high ratings. "According to the latest Arbitron, WXXX-FM is number one with adults 24 to 39." Never out of the conversation for very long are the station's numbers, and at advertising agencies the station's standing speaks for itself. "We'll buy WXXX because the book shows that they have the largest audience in the demos we're after."

The station without ratings numbers sells itself on a more personal level, perhaps focusing on its unique features and special blend of music and personalities, and so forth. In an effort to attract advertisers, non-rated outlets often develop programs with a targeted retail market in mind; for example, a home "how-to" show designed to interest

hardware and interior decor stores, or a cooking feature aimed at food and appliance stores.

The salesperson working for the station with the cherished "good book" must be especially adept at talking numbers, since they are the key subject of the presentation in most situations. "Selling a top-rated metro station requires more than a pedestrian knowledge of numbers, especially when dealing with agencies. In big cities, retailers have plenty of book savvy, too," contends Piro.

Selling without numbers demands its own unique set of skills, notes WNRI's Gregory. "There are really two different types of radio selling—with numbers and without. In the former instance, you'd better know your math, whereas in the latter, you've got to be really effective at molding your station to suit the desires of the individual advertiser. Without the numbers to speak for you, you have to do all the selling yourself. Flexibility and ingenuity are the keys to the sale."

FIGURE 4.16
A radio sales contract written by an account executive. Courtesy WXLO-FM.

Advertising Agencies

Advertising agencies came into existence more than a century ago and have played an integral role in broadcasting since its inception. During radio's famed heyday, advertising agencies were omnipotent. Not only did they handle the advertising budgets of some of the nation's largest businesses, but they also provided the networks with fully produced programs. The programs were designed by the agencies for the specific satisfaction of their clients. If the networks and certain independent stations wanted a company's business, they had little choice but to air the agency's program. This practice in the 1920s and 1930s gave ad agencies unprecedented power. At one point, advertising agencies were the biggest supplier of network radio programming. By the 1940s, agencies were forced to abandon their direct programming involvement, and the industry was left to its own devices, or almost. Agencies continued to influence the content of what was aired. Their presence continues to be felt today, but not to the extent that it was prior to the advent of television.

Agencies annually account for hundreds of millions in radio ad dollars. The long, and at times turbulent, marriage of radio and advertising agencies was, and continues to be, based on the need of national companies to convey their messages on the local level and the need of the local broadcaster for national business. It is a two-way street.

Today hundreds of advertising agencies use the radio medium. They range in size from mammoth to minute. Agencies such as Young and Rubicam, J. Walter Thompson, Dancer Fitzgerald Sample, and Leo Burnett bill in the hundreds of millions annually and employ hundreds. More typical, however, are the agencies scattered throughout the country that bill between one-half and two-and-a-half million dollars each year and employ anywhere from a half dozen to 20 people. Agencies come in all shapes and sizes and provide various services, depending on their scope and dimensions.

The process of getting national business onto a local station is an involved one. The major agencies must compete against dozens of others to win the right to handle the advertising of large companies. This usually involves elaborate presentations and substantial investments by agencies. When and if the account is secured, the agency must then prepare the materials–audio, video, print–for the campaign and see to it that the advertiser's money is spent in the most effective way possible. Little is done without extensive marketing research and planning. The agency's media buyer oversees the placement of dollars in the various media. Media buyers at national agencies deal with station and network reps rather than directly with the stations themselves. It would be impossible for an agency placing

FIGURE 4.17
Courtesy RAB.

YOU have to maximize your advertising investment by reaching your best prospects...

RADIO reaches the big spenders!

Upscale individuals with above-average incomes and affluent lifestyles spend more of their disposable income on "big-ticket" items—and spend more of their time with Radio.

Household Income $50,000+

	Weekly Reach	Average Daily Time Spent Listening
Adults 18+	96.9%	2:53
Men 18+	97.6%	2:57
Women 18+	96.1%	2:47

Want professionals and managers? Radio delivers! These decision-makers have money to spend ... and Radio is the best marketing medium to reach these influential men and women.

Professional/Managerial, $50,000+Household Income

	Weekly Reach	Average Daily Time Spent Listening
Adults 18+	97.5%	2:37
Men 18+	98.1%	2:44
Women 18+	98.0%	2:30

Source: RADAR ® 50, Fall 1994, © Copyright Statistical Research, Inc.

a buy on 400 stations to personally transact with each.

There basically are three types of agencies: *full-service agencies*, which provide clients with a complete range of services, including research, marketing, and production; *modular agencies*, which provide specific services to advertisers; and *in-house agencies*, which handle the advertising needs of their own business.

The standard commission that an agency receives for its service is 15 percent on billing. For example, if an agency places $100,000 on radio, it earns $15,000 for its efforts. Agencies often charge clients additional fees to cover production costs, and some agencies receive a retainer from clients.

The business generated by agencies constitutes an important percentage of radio's revenues, especially for medium- and large

FIGURE 4.18
A rep company
explains itself.
Courtesy Katz.

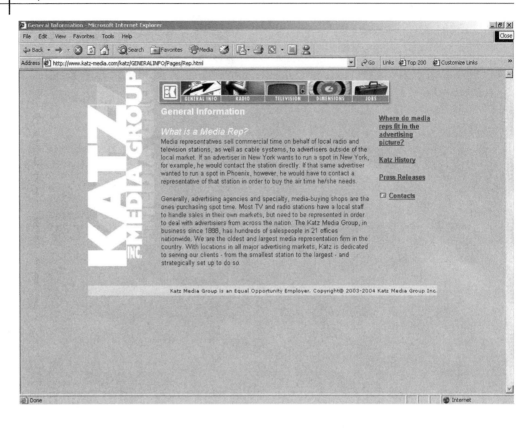

market stations. However, compared to other media, such as television for example, radio's allocation is diminutive. The nation's top three agencies invest over 80 percent of their broadcast budgets in television. Nonetheless, hundreds of millions of dollars are channeled into radio by agencies that recognize the effectiveness of the medium.

Rep Companies

Rep companies are the industry's middlemen (see figure 4.18). Rep companies are given the task of convincing national agency media buyers to place money on the stations they represent. Without their existence, radio stations would have to find a way to reach the myriad of agencies on their own — an impossible feat.

With few exceptions, radio outlets contract the services of a station rep company.

Even the smallest station wants to be included in buys at the national level. The rep company basically is an extension of a station's sales department. The rep and the station's sales manager work together closely. Information about a station and its market are crucial to the rep. The burden of keeping the rep fully aware of what is happening back at the station rests on the sales manager's shoulders. Since a rep company based in New York or Chicago would have no way of knowing that its client-station in Arkansas has decided to carry the local college's basketball games, it is the station's responsibility to make the information available. A rep cannot sell what it does not know exists. Of course, a good rep will keep in contact with a station on a regular basis simply to keep up on station changes.

There are far fewer radio station reps than there are ad agencies, and with the clustering of stations by radio corporations, the number of rep companies has dwindled dra-

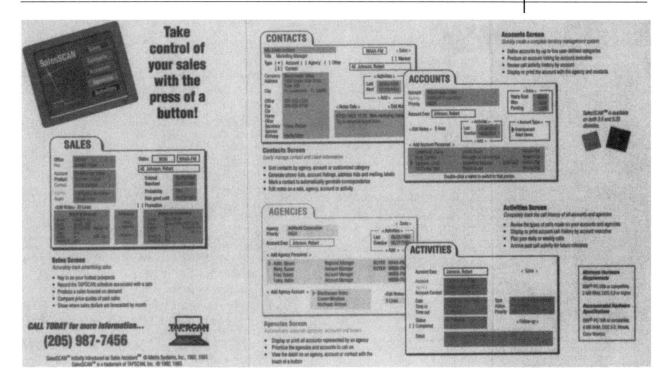

FIGURE 4.19
The computer is an integral part of most sales departments. Courtesy TAPSCAN.

matically as broadcasters assume the burden of representing themselves. Today there are just a handful of major rep companies handling the 9,000-plus commercial stations around the country because the huge radio companies assume this function in-house. "In their heyday in the 70s, many national and regional rep firms served individual stations and group radio owners, but because of pressures from increased costs, pressure from client stations on commission rates, and the creation of unwired network radio, an attempt to compete with the lower rates of traditional radio networks that lowered radio rates, many were forced to close or merge through the 80s and 90s. With consolidation, where one, two, or three groups now control most radio stations in a given market, the need for multiple reps evaporated," says Williams.

Major rep firms, such as Katz (owned by Clear Channel) and Interep, pitch agencies on behalf of hundreds of client stations. The large and very successful reps often refuse to act as the envoy for small market stations because of their lack of earning potential.

A rep company typically receives a commission of between 5 and 12 percent on the spot buys made by agencies, and since the national advertising money usually is directed first to the medium and large markets, the bigger commissions are not to be made from handling small market outlets. Many rep companies specialize in small-market stations, however, especially in the age of consolidation.

Although a small rep company may work the agencies on behalf of numerous stations, it will seldom handle two radio outlets in the same market. Doing so could result in a rep company being placed in the untenable position of competing with itself for a buy, thus creating an obvious conflict of interest. In the past few years, many larger rep firms have taken on multiple stations in the same market due to the clustering approach of their clients.

The majority of station reps provide additional services. In recent years many have expanded into the areas of programming and management consultancy, and almost all offer clients audience research data, as well as aid in developing station promotions and designing sales materials such as rate cards.

Nontraditional Revenue

It is estimated that over $600 million in radio revenue comes from co-op advertising—no small piece of change, indeed. As a consequence of a negative economy, however, the co-op market went a bit flat in the first half of the 1990s, says broadcaster Peter Drew. "Actually there is less co-op nowadays. Things are tight on every level, of course. It is more difficult today to qualify and collect. This is the result of higher accruals and inventory requirements. Still,

FIGURE 4.20
Station trade agreement form. Courtesy WXLO-FM.

WXLO
104.5FM

FORM OF TRADE AGREEMENT

Today's Date:
Client Name:
Address:

Account Executive:
Contact:
Title:
Telephone # :

Dear :

This letter, when signed by you and by us, will constitute our agreement relating to an exchange of goods and services for advertising time on the above named radio station.

A.   ADVERTISING TIME PROVIDED BY STATION
1.   We will furnish you with advertising time on our station having an aggregate *net value* at the time the ads run, of_____.   All trades are at a 1-to-1 ratio.
2.   Restrictions apply as to when advertising can run and are subject to availability. Your account executive has worked out the details and your trade can run as follows (or per attached sales order):

Trade Expiration date:
3.   All advertising copy submitted to us hereunder shall be subject to our advertising and broadcast standards at the station's sole discretion.
4.   In the event that such advertising incurs any talent, announcer or production charges, you will be responsible for paying the same upon receipt of our invoice, and such charges are not to be included in the value of the advertising time provided to you hereunder. Further, *there is no agency commission payable on such advertising.*

B.   GOODS AND SERVICES PROVIDED TO THE STATION
1.   In consideration of the advertising time provided to you hereunder, you will furnish and make available to us, within the period stated in section A.2, the following goods or services (if hotel trade, are conference rooms included?):

These goods and services have a net fair market value of :
2.   If goods are provided hereunder, you hereby warrant that the same shall be delivered new and in perfect condition.

co-op money is worth pursuing. A little more effort is required to acquire it." Co-op advertising involves the cooperation of three parties: the retailer whose business is being promoted, the manufacturer whose product is being promoted, and the medium used for the promotion. In other words, a retailer and manufacturer get together to share advertising expenses. For example, Smith's Sporting Goods is informed by the Converse Running Shoes representative that the company will match, dollar for dollar up to $5,000, the money that the retailer invests in radio advertising. The only stipulation of the deal is that Converse be promoted in the commercials on which the money is spent. This means that no competitive product can be mentioned. Converse demands exclusivity for its contribution.

Manufacturers of practically every conceivable type of product, from lawn mowers to mobile homes, establish co-op advertising budgets. A radio salesperson can use co-op to great advantage. First the station account executive must determine the extent of co-op subsidy a client is entitled to receive. Most of the time the retailer knows the answer to this. Frequently, however, retailers do not take full advantage of the co-op funds that manufacturers make available. In some instances, retailers are not aware that a particular manufacturer will share radio advertising expenses. Many potential advertisers have been motivated to go on the air after discovering the existence of co-op dollars. Mid-sized retailers account for the biggest chunk of the industry's co-op revenues. However, even the smallest retailer likely is eligible for some subsidy, and a salesperson can make this fact known for everyone's mutual advantage.

The sales manager generally directs a station's co-op efforts. Large stations often employ a full-time co-op specialist. The individual responsible for stimulating co-op revenue will survey retail trade journals for pertinent information about available dollars. Retail associations also are a good source of information, since they generally possess manufacturer co-op advertising lists. The importance of taking advantage of co-op opportunities cannot be overstressed. Some stations, especially metro market outlets, earn hundreds of thousands of dollars in additional ad revenue through their co-op efforts.

From the retailer's perspective, co-op advertising is not always a great bargain. This usually stems from copy constraints imposed by certain manufacturers, which give the retailer a 10-second tag-out in a 30- or 60-second commercial. Obviously, this does not please the retailer who has split the cost of advertising 50/50. In recent years, this type of copy domination by the manufacturer has decreased somewhat, and a more equitable approach, whereby both parties share evenly the exposure and the expense, is more commonplace.

Co-op also is appealing to radio stations since they do not have to modify their billing practices to accommodate the third party. Stations simply bill the retailer and provide an affidavit attesting to the time commercials aired. The retailer, in turn, bills the manufacturer for its share of the airtime. For its part, the manufacturer requires receipt of an affidavit before making payment. In certain cases, the station is asked to mail affidavits directly to the manufacturer. Some manufacturers stipulate that bills be sent to audit houses, which inspect the materials before authorizing payment.

Event marketing is another key form of nontraditional revenue generation. This involves the creation of a popular event, such as a food or arts festival, wherein merchants pay to be associated with it. This has become a very common and successful way for stations to make income without adding to their on-air spot loads. Says Jay Williams, Jr., "Stations are going outside the traditional spot load box and engaging in different ways to generate income for their stations."

3. You shall pay sales and/or use tax on goods and services provided, as well as all shipping, delivery or handling charges associated with such goods or services.

4. Please list any restrictions as to the use of these goods or services:

_____
_____
_____

5. Please list any directions as to how these goods or services will be used:

_____
_____
_____

C. MISCELLANEOUS PROVISIONS

1. In the event you in any breach your obligations under this agreement, we have the right to immediately cease airing any advertising or time provided hereunder.

2. We will furnish you with monthly invoices and statements setting forth the advertising time furnished hereunder, and you will furnish us with monthly invoices and statements setting forth the goods or services delivered to us each month. Such invoices and statements must be marked as "trade" and sent directly to our accounting department.

3. In the event any of the goods or services specified in B.1 are not provided to us within the period specified in A.2, you shall be obligated to pay to us immediately upon demand and in cash an amount equal to the value of such goods or services remaining to be provided by you.

4. Unless otherwise specifically agreed, we and you shall each have the right to terminate this agreement by giving not less than fourteen (14) days prior notice of termination to the other.

5. This contract is subject to the terms and conditions of all licenses issued to us for the station, to all Federal, State and municipal laws and regulations, and to all rules and regulations, orders and decisions of the Federal Communications Commission nor or hereafter in effect.

6. Each of us warrants to the other that it has the full legal power, authority, and right to enter into this agreement and perform our respective obligations hereunder.

7. If this agreement is signed by an advertising agency, the agency and the ultimate sponsor will be jointly and severally responsible for the performance of the advertiser's obligations hereunder.

8. You may not assign your rights and duties under this agreement to any either party without prior written consent.

Please indicate your agreement to the foregoing by signing under the words "Agreed to and Accepted."

Very truly yours,

WXLO RADIO   **AGREED TO AND ACCEPTED:**

_____   _____
General Manager   **Authorized Signature**

_____   _____
General Sales Manager   **Name**

_____   _____
Controller   **Title**

Trade-Outs

Stations commonly exchange airtime for goods, although top-rated outlets, whose time is sold at a premium, are less likely to swap spots for anything other than cash. Rather than pay for needed items, such as office supplies and furnishings, studio equipment, meals for clients and listeners, new cars, and so forth, a station may choose to strike a deal with merchants in which airtime is traded for merchandise. There are advertisers who use radio only on a trade basis. A station may start out in an exclusively trade relationship with a client in the hope of eventually converting him to cash. Split contracts also are written when a client agrees to provide both money and mer-

FIGURE 4.20
continued

chandise. For example, WXXX-FM needs two new office desks. The total cost of the desks is $800. An agreement is made whereby the client receives a $1,400 ROS spot schedule and $600 cash in exchange for the desks. Trade-outs are not always this equitable. Stations often provide trade clients with airtime worth two or three times the merchandise value in order to get what is needed. Thus, the saying "need inspires deals."

Many sales managers also feel that it makes good business sense to write radio trade contracts to fill available and unsold airtime, rather than let it pass unused. Once airtime is gone, it cannot be retrieved, and yesterday's unfilled availability is a lost opportunity.

CHAPTER HIGHLIGHTS

1. Selling commercials keeps most radio stations on the air. Between 1920 and today, advertising revenues and forms reflected the ebb and flow of radio's popularity. Today, advertising dollars are selectively spent on spots aired during times of the day and on stations that attract the type of audience the advertiser wants to reach.

FIGURE 4.21
A call for sales interns. Courtesy WPLJ-FM.

2. An effective radio commercial makes a strong and lasting impression on the mind of the listener.

3. A successful account executive needs an understanding of research methods, marketing, finance; some form of sales experience; and such personal traits as ambition, confidence, honesty, energy, determination, intelligence, and good grooming.

4. Since the 1970s, programming people have made successful job transitions to sales because they have a practical understanding of the product they are selling.

5. Although an increasing number of station managers are being drawn from programming people, a sales background is still preferred.

6. The sales manager, who reports directly to the station or cluster's general manager, oversees the account executives, establishes departmental policies, develops sales plans and materials, conceives campaigns and promotions, sets quotas, works closely with the program director to develop salable features, and sometimes sells.

7. Rates for selling airtime vary according to listenership and are published on the station's rate card. The card lists terms of payment and commission, nature of copy and due dates, station's approach to discounting, rate protection policy, as well as feature and spot rates. Rate cards are beginning to fade from the scene as new approaches to selling airtime evolve.

8. Station listenership varies according to time of day, so rate card daypart classifica-

The ABC Radio Station Group
New York City
SALES INTERNSHIPS WITH WPLJ-FM

WPLJ-FM is a high profile, hit-driven personality radio station with lots of listener involvement, big contests and great promotions. WPLJ plays artists like Goo Goo Dolls, Sugar Ray, Alanis Morissette, Creed, Pink, Shakira, Matchbox 20, and Dave Matthews Band combined with older hits from artists like REM, Sting, Sheryl Crow and U2 to create our signature sound. WPLJ is located in Midtown Manhattan, the capitol of the entertainment and advertising industries.

The WPLJ Sales Department is looking for bright, energetic and outgoing undergraduate and graduate students who are interested in pursuing a career in radio sales or advertising. If you are team-oriented and thrive in a fast-paced environment, we want to hear from you! There is no better way to jumpstart a career in radio, communications or advertising / marketing. You will work directly with one of the top radio sales teams in New York City gaining hands-on, practical experience. College credit must be earned for the internship. Students must be enrolled in a degree program in a communications or business-related field. Hours are flexible to fit your schedule. Internships are available in all semesters. For Summer 2002, apply by April 15th.

Interested students should send their resume and a cover letter telling us a little bit about themselves and why they want to participate in our sales internship program. Email your resume and cover letter to nyradioresumes@abc.com. The subject header must read "WPLJ SALES INTERNSHIP PROGRAM". You can also send it by regular mail to Linda Wnek, Diversity Recruitment Coordinator, WPLJ-FM Sales Internship Program, Two Penn Plaza - 17th Floor, New York, NY 10121.

tions range from the highest costing AAA (typically 6 to 10 a.m. weekdays) to C (usually midnight to 6 a.m.). Fixed-position drivetime spots are usually among the most expensive to purchase.

9. Many stations use a grid structure because it allows for considerable rate flexibility. Grids are inventory sensitive, and they let a station remain viable when business is slow.

10. For advertisers with limited funds, run-of-station (ROS), best-time-available (BTA), or total-audience-plan (TAP) are cost-effective alternatives.

11. Because few accounts are closed on the first call, it is used to introduce the station to the client and to determine its needs. Follow-up calls are made to offset reservations and, if necessary, to improve the proposal. Perseverance is essential.

12. Radio sales are drawn from three levels: retail, local, and national. Retail sales are direct sales to advertisers within the station's signal area. Local sales are obtained from advertising agencies representing businesses in the market area. National sales are obtained by the station's rep company from agencies representing national accounts.

13. A fully produced sample commercial (spec spot) is an effective selling tool. It is used to break down client resistance on call-backs, to interest former clients who have not bought time recently, and to encourage clients to increase their schedules.

14. The salesperson should commit the advertiser to sufficient commercials, placed properly, to ensure that the advertiser achieves his or her objectives. Underselling is as self-defeating as overselling.

15. New accounts are added to a salesperson's list by "prospecting": searching newspapers, Yellow Pages, television ads, competing radio station ads, and new store openings. Only open accounts may be added (those not already declared by another salesperson at the same station).

FIGURE 4.22
Sales reps at their computers. Courtesy WIZN-FM.

16. Because a salesperson must average 15 to 20 in-person calls each day, when preparing a daily call sheet it is important to logically sequence and centralize the businesses to be contacted. Also, advance telephone contacts can eliminate much wasted time.

17. The Internet and e-mail are useful sales and prospecting tools for account executives.

18. A salesperson at a station with a high rating has a decided advantage when contacting advertisers. Stations with low or no numbers must focus on retail sales (work the street), developing programs and programming to attract targeted clients. Stations in nonsurvey areas must rely on their image of good citizenship and strong community ties.

19. Ad agencies annually supply hundreds of millions of dollars in advertising revenue to stations with good ratings. Media buyers at the agencies deal directly with station and network reps.

20. A station's rep company must convince national agency media buyers to select their station as their advertising outlet for the area. Therefore, the station's sales manager and the rep must work together closely.

21. Among nontraditional revenue (NTR) sources are co-op advertising, which involves the sharing of advertising expenses by the retailer of the business being promoted and the manufacturer of the product being promoted, and events marketing, wherein stations create events in which merchants invest their promotional dollars.

22. Rather than pay for needed items or to obtain something of value for unsold time, a station may trade (trade-out) advertising airtime with a merchant in exchange for specific merchandise.

APPENDIX: A Station Owner Conveys His Sales Philosophy to His Manager

To: Rich KREZWICK
Fr: Jay Williams, Jr.
Re: sales.

FIGURE 4.23
RAB's co-op material provides pertinent facts. Courtesy RAB.

The Advertiser's Guide To Using Radio Co-op

Discover how co-operative advertising on Radio builds traffic and sales for your business, without breaking your budget.

Radio Advertising Bureau, Inc. • 304 Park Avenue South, New York, NY 10010
1 (800) 252-RADIO • **FAX** (212) 254-8713
New York, Atlanta, Chicago, Detroit, Houston, Los Angeles

Although I am not familiar with what happens every day, I do think I have a general idea of the sales philosophy and structure that has gotten us where we are, both positively and negatively. As I see the declining sales as a percentage of goal in a marketplace that is hotter now than at any time in the past four years, I think it's time we continue our discussion on a more specific level. To that end, I thought I would outline what I see from here (to see where you agree/disagree or can supply additional information) and suggest some solutions (as I have certainly seen similar trends many times before). First my suggestions.

1. Let's get Casey out of the station for a few days (your suggestion, actually). I think he needs some perspective, and there's nothing like seeing another problem to see your own better.

2. Let's give Casey a sales call quota. Sales managers learn both real problems (not self-manufactured) on the street, and they learn solutions. More importantly, they're on the front lines with their salespeople and can better relate to them and teach them. He needs to be more of a player-coach. Perhaps a minimum of 20 calls a week.

3. Let's do real meetings that teach the "consultant sell." This, in my opinion, is the philosophy that has always been missing (in the past year or so) that (a) makes us look as if we don't care about the client's problems and (b) puts downward pressure on rates. The consultant sell, which I do every day for DMR and frequently for WLKZ, talks about clients' needs and revolves around solutions. I never, as a result, and I do mean *never*, get into a rate discussion. Conversely, WXLO is now selling spots and inventory. We're like a beer distributor, competing against other beers. It's totally the wrong way to sell.

4. Let's figure out a way to hire someone to really handle vendor, interactive phones, and other nonspot revenues that you and I both know can be sold at a premium instead of the despicable "value added." Perhaps you should be the sales manager of this special sales branch, starting with one or two people. The two-check philoso-

phy in action. Get us in the direction you and I have talked about—as a marketing group instead of spot salespeople (or really, spot whores as I see it).

5. Let's put a stop to any sales criticism of programming, even if it's warranted. At Fairbanks broadcasting, I learned how little criticisms can become a culture if unchecked. In reality, they are more than critiquing the product they must turn around and sell, they (salespeople) are giving themselves an excuse for poor sales, low rates, and giveaways to clients. I was brought up with the philosophy that only the best could sell for station XXXX; if you can't, get the hell out of the way and we'll hire someone who can. It changed the paradigm–and the success of the stations I worked with.

6. Let's hire at least one more, maybe two more, salespeople and specifically target Metrowest and southern New Hampshire. I know people like Peter's Auto Sales in Nashua, and other major advertisers, that need business from south and west of Nashua. We can help, but we don't have the horses to develop that business. With not enough salespeople competing for the available spots, it also lessens demand and that, in WXLO's "beer distributor" mentality, lowers rates.

As we've talked about much of this, I'm sure you will agree with much of it, but I think we must now act quickly. Fourth-quarter buys and rates are being set; too much later and the die will be cast and we won't be hitting the cash flow numbers you want and the station needs. I offer these as my first steps to changing the structure. (I'm referring to a $4,000/person seminar taught by a consultant to the Motorola management last week. In shorthand, most manage events. Some manage the patterns caused by the events, yet these both yield poor results as they are reactions to past

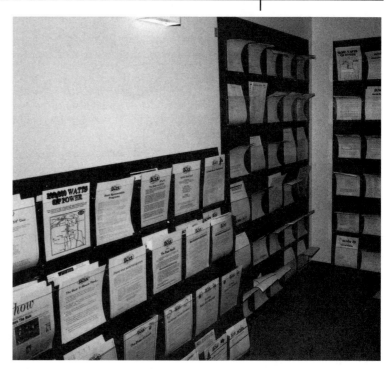

FIGURE 4.24
Walls of sales materials for use by reps and clients. Courtesy WIZN-FM.

events. Smart managers manage structure.) Our structure, and the philosophy you generated and that I generated in programming, is being changed in sales. This change in structure (because of the coterminous change in philosophy) is changing our patterns (sales curves) and events (individual sales, rates, complaints, bonuses to clients, low-rate packages, etc.). That's why I have proposed these solutions versus mere package or rate changes, etc. Let me know what you think.

SUGGESTED FURTHER READING

Aaker, David A., and Myers, John G. *Advertising Management*, 2nd ed. Englewood Cliffs, N.J.: Prentice Hall, 1982.

Barnouw, Erik. *The Sponsor: Notes on a Modern Potentate.* New York: Oxford University Press, 1978.

Bergendort, Fred. *Broadcast Advertising.* New York: Hastings House, 1983.

Bouvard, Pierre, and Marx, Steve. *Radio Advertising's Missing Ingredient: The Optimum Effective Scheduling System.* Washington, D.C.: NAB, 1991.

Bovee, Courtland, and Arena, William F. *Contemporary Advertising.* Homewood, Ill.: Irwin, 1982.

Broadcast Marketing Company. *Building Store Traffic with Broadcast Advertising.* San Francisco: Broadcast Marketing Company, 1978.

Burton, Philip Ward, and Sandhusen, Richard. *Cases in Advertising.* Columbus, Ohio: Grid Publishing, 1981.

Culligan, Matthew J. *Getting Back to the Basics of Selling.* New York: Crown, 1981.

Cundiff, Edward W., Still, Richard R., and Govoni, Norman A.P. *Fundamentals of Modern Marketing,* 3rd ed. Englewood Cliffs, N.J.: Prentice Hall,1980.

Delmar, Ken. *Winning Moves: The Body Language of Selling.* New York: Warner, 1984.

Dunn, W. Watson, and Barban, Arnold M. *Advertising: Its Role in Modern Marketing,* 4th ed. Hinsdale, Ill.: Dryden Press, 1978.

Gardner, Herbert S., Jr. *The Advertising Agency Business.* Chicago: Crain Books, 1976.

Gilson, Christopher, and Berkman, Harold W. *Advertising Concepts and Strategies.* New York: Random House, 1980.

Heighton, Elizabeth J., and Cunningham, Don R. *Advertising in the Broadcast and Cable Media,* 2nd ed. Belmont, Calif.: Wadsworth Publishing, 1984.

Herweg, Godfrey W., and Herweg, Ashley Page. *Making More Money Selling Radio Advertising without Numbers.* Washington, D.C.: NAB, 1995.

Hoffer, Jay, and McRae, John. *The Complete Broadcast Sales Guide for Stations, Reps, and Ad Agencies.* Blue Ridge Summit, Pa.: Tab Books, 1981.

Johnson, J. Douglas. *Advertising Today.* Chicago: SRA, 1978.

Jugenheimer, Donald W., and Turk, Peter B. *Advertising Media.* Columbus, Ohio: Grid Publishing, 1980.

Keith, Michael C. *Selling Radio Direct.* Boston: Focal Press, 1992.

Kleppner, Otto. *Advertising Procedure,* 7th ed. Englewood Cliffs, N.J.: Prentice Hall, 1979.

McGee, William L. *Broadcast Co-Op, the Untapped Goldmine.* San Francisco: Broadcast Marketing Company, 1975.

Montgomery, Robert Leo. *How to Sell in the 1980s.* Englewood Cliffs, N.J.: Prentice Hall, 1980.

Murphy, Jonne. *Handbook of Radio Advertising.* Radnor, Pa.: Chilton Books, 1980.

National Association of Broadcasters. *Think Big: Event Marketing for Radio.* Washington, D.C.: NAB, 1994.

Rhoads, B. Eric, et al., eds. *Sales and Marketing.* West Palm Beach, Fla.: Streamline Press, 1995.

Shane, Ed. *Selling Electronic Media.* Boston: Focal Press, 1999.

Shaver, Mary Alice. *Make the Sale: How to Sell Media with Marketing.* New York: Copy Workshop, 1995.

Sissors, Jack Z., and Surmanek, Jim. *Advertising Media Planning,* 2nd ed. Chicago: Crain Books, 1982.

Standard Rate and Data Service: Spot Radio. Skokie, Ill.: SRDS, annual.

Warner, Charles, and Buchman, Joseph. *Broadcasting and Cable Selling,* 2nd ed. Belmont, CA.: Wadsworth Publishing, 1993.

Willing, Si. *How to Sell Radio Advertising.* Blue Ridge Summit, Pa.: Tab Books, 1977.

News from the Start

The medium of radio was used to convey news before news of the medium had reached the majority of the general public. Ironically, it was the sinking of the *Titanic* in 1912 and the subsequent rebroadcast of the ship's coded distress message that helped launch a wider awareness and appreciation of the newfangled gadget called the *wireless telegraph*. It was not until the early 1920s, when the "wireless" had become known as the "radio," that broadcast journalism actually began to evolve.

A historical benchmark in radio news is the broadcast of the Harding–Cox election results in 1920 by stations WWJ in Detroit and KDKA in Pittsburgh, although the first actual newscast is reported to have occurred in California a decade earlier. Despite these early ventures, news programming progressed slowly until the late 1920s. By then, two networks, NBC and CBS, were providing national audiences with certain news and information features.

Until 1932, radio depended on newspapers for its stories. That year newspapers officially perceived the electronic medium as a competitive threat. Fearing a decline in readership, they imposed a blackout. Radio was left to its own resources. The networks put forth substantial efforts to gather news and did very well without the wire services on which they had come to rely. Late in 1934, United Press (UP), International News Services (INS), and Associated Press (AP) agreed to sell their news services to radio, thus ending the boycott. However, by then the medium had demonstrated its ability to fend for itself.

Radio has served as a vital source of news and information throughout the most significant historical events. When the nation was gripped by economic turmoil in the 1930s, the incumbent head-of-state, Franklin D. Roosevelt, demonstrated the tremendous reach of the medium by using it to address the people. The majority of Americans heard and responded to the president's talks.

Radio's status as a news source reached its apex during World War II. On-the-spot reports and interviews, as well as commentaries, brought the war into the nation's living rooms. In contrast to World War I, when the fledgling wireless was exclusively used for military purposes, during World War II radio served as the primary link between those at home and the foreign battlefronts around the globe. News programming during this troubled period matured, while the public adjusted its perception of the medium, casting it in a more austere light. Radio journalism became a more credible profession.

The effects of television on radio news were wide ranging. While the medium in general reeled from the blow dealt it by the *enfant terrible*, in the late 1940s and early 1950s news programming underwent a sort of metamorphosis. Faced with drastically reduced network schedules, radio stations began to localize their news efforts. Attention was focused on area news events rather

FIGURE 5.1
News is a prominent
feature on most radio
stations. Courtesy
RAB.

Radio Is The First Morning News Source

Morning(6 AM-10 AM)	Radio	TV	News-papers	Other/None
Persons 12+	49%	29%	15%	7%
Teens 12-17	60	21	12	7
Adults 18+	48	30	16	6
Adults 18-34	53	28	13	6
Adults 25-54	50	29	16	5
College Grads.	46	27	22	5
Prof./Mgr. Males	55	19	20	6
F/T Working Women	56	27	11	6
$50K+ Income	49	28	18	5

Radio Is The First News Source At Midday

Midday(10 AM-3 PM)	Radio	TV	News-papers	Other/None
Persons 12+	36%	24%	14%	26%
Teens 12-17	30	24	17	29
Adults 18+	37	24	14	25
Adults 18-34	43	19	18	20
Adults 25-54	41	18	15	26
College Grads.	36	17	15	32
Prof./Mgr. Males	36	9	23	32
F/T Working Women	48	9	12	31
$50K+ Income	44	10	17	29

Radio Is The Major Source of News

Morning (6AM-10 AM)	Radio	TV	News-papers	Other/None
Persons 12+	42%	31%	18%	9%
Teens 12-17	54	29	9	8
Adults 18+	41	31	19	9
Adults 18-34	45	28	20	7
Adults 25-54	43	29	20	8
College Grads.	38	24	30	8
Prof./Mgr. Males	48	16	27	9
Working Women	49	28	15	8
$50K+ Income	45	21	27	7

Radio Is The First Source For Local Emergency News

	Radio	TV	Other/None
Persons 12+	50%	48%	2%
Teens 12-17	50	49	1
Adults 18+	50	48	2
Adults 18-34	50	49	1
Adults 25-54	54	44	2
College Grads.	56	42	2
Prof./Mgr. Males	57	40	3
F/T Working Women	51	47	2

than national and international. Stations that had relied almost exclusively on network news began to hire newspeople and broadcast a regular schedule of local newscasts. By the mid-1950s the transformation was nearly complete, and radio news had become a local programming matter. Radio news had undergone a 180-degree turn, even before the medium gave up trying to directly compete on a program-for-program basis with television. By the time radio set a new and revivifying course for itself by programming for specific segments of the listening audience, local newscasts were the norm.

Since its period of reconstruction in the 1950s, radio has proven time and time again to be the nation's first source of information about major news events. The majority of Americans first heard of the assassination of President Kennedy, and the subsequent shootings of Martin Luther King, Jr., and Senator Robert Kennedy over radio. In 1965 when most of the northeast was crippled by a power blackout, battery-powered radios literally became a lifeline for millions of people by providing continuous news and information until power was restored.

During the 1970s and 1980s, news on both the world and local levels reached radio listeners first. Today the public knows that radio is the first place to turn for up-to-the-minute news about occurrences halfway around the world, as well as in its own backyard.

News and Today's Radio

More people claim to listen to radio for music than for any other reason. Somewhat surprising, however, is that many of these same people admit to relying on the medium for the news they receive. Recent studies have found that although most of those surveyed tuned in to radio for entertainment, three-quarters considered news programming important. These surveys also ascertained that radio is the first morning news source for two-thirds of all full-time working women.

According to the Radio Advertising Bureau (RAB), over 50 percent of young adults get their first news of the day from radio. In comparison, only 16 percent of adults rely on newspapers as the first source of daily news. Practically all of the nation's 9,000 commercial stations program news to some extent. Radio's tremendous mobility and pervasiveness has made it an instant and reliable news source for over 170 million Americans.

Despite all of this, however, consultant Ed Shane argues that, "Radio news is in a sad state." The deregulation of the medium since the 1980s has inspired a decline in local radio news service, according to many sources. "Listen to the news on many local stations and you're hearing announcers from Metro Network's MetroSource, a linkup of Metro's local traffic services into a combination newswire and network. Because Metro has operations in 81 markets, covering 2,000 radio and TV stations, the system creates a formidable presence. To its credit, Metro covers news pretty well. Presentation is not its forte. Outsourcing one of radio's essential services is a cost-cutting measure, and does not enhance quality. After the devastating Oklahoma City tornadoes in May 1999, the National Association of Broadcasters placed an ad in USA Today and other publications congratulating 'local broadcasters' for their fine job of informing the public about the impending storms and then covering the damage that ensued. Most of the quotations in the ad were from TV stations or about TV stations. Radio complained, of course, but a local official was quoted as saying 'radio just simulcasts TV audio.'"

Says WBZ GM Ted Jordon, "In one sense we suffered from the same market compression as everyone else. But in other ways, it's easier today as there was more AM competition. All things considered, the news quality is as good, but now the systems in place are better, the networks we use (ABC & CBS) are better and more responsive, and the stringers are better. We used to have our own Washington, DC bureau because we didn't trust the networks to deliver the story. Now we can. They have really become responsive to the needs of the local stations. There is now a greater sharing of resources at our operations. We have a dotted line relationship with WBZ TV. Their newspeople give updates on our air and our anchors appear on television. We are able to co-brand the stations and get a larger share of mind."

Adds Jay Williams, "They have been able to cut costs by reallocating resources, working with their TV affiliate, using better systems, working more closely with the networks, and the like. As to the talk that there are fewer real news sources today, I know Ted believes that not to be the case. Just the opposite, in fact."

The Newsroom

The number of individuals working in a radio station newsroom will vary depending on the size of a station, whether it is part of a cluster operation or a single outlet, and its format. On the average, a station in a small market employs one or two full-time newspeople. Of course, some outlets find it financially unfeasible to hire newspeople. These stations do not necessarily ignore news, rather they delegate responsibilities to their deejays to deliver brief newscasts at specified times, often at the top of the hour. Stations approaching news in this manner make it necessary for the on-air person to collect news from the wire service during

FIGURE 5.2
Newsroom in a cluster
operation. Courtesy
Clear Channel.

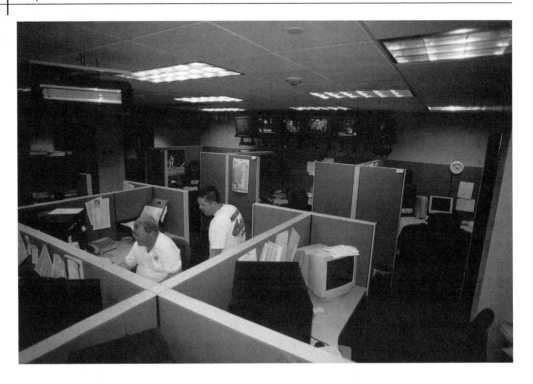

FIGURE 5.2
Newsroom in a cluster
operation. Courtesy
Clear Channel.

record cuts and broadcast it nearly verbatim. Little, if any, rewrite is done, because the deejay simply does not have the time to do it. About the only thing that persons at "rip 'n' read" outlets can and must do is examine wire copy before going on the air. This eliminates the likelihood of mistakes. Again, all of this is accomplished while the records are spinning.

NPR reporter Corey Flintoff warns against neglecting to examine wire copy before airtime. "We've all been caught with stuff that appears to scan at first sight but turns out to be incomprehensible when you read it."

Music-oriented stations in larger markets rarely allow their deejays to do news. Occasionally the person jockeying the overnight shift will be expected to give a brief newscast every hour or two, but in metro markets this is fairly uncommon. There is generally a newsperson on duty around the clock. A top-rated station in a medium market typically employs four full-time newspeople; again, this varies depending on the status of the outlet (one of a cluster of stations)

and the type of programming it airs. For example, Easy Listening stations that stress music and de-emphasize talk may employ only one or two newspeople. Meanwhile, an AC station in the same market may have five people on its news staff in an attempt to promote itself as a heavy news and information outlet, even though its primary product is music. Certain music stations in major markets hire as many as a dozen news employees. This figure may include not only on-air newscasters, but writers, street reporters, and technical people as well. Stringers and interns also swell the figure.

During the prime listening periods when a station's audience is at its maximum, newscasts are programmed with greater frequency, sometimes twice as often as during other dayparts. The newsroom is a hub of activity as newspeople prepare for newscasts scheduled every 20 to 30 minutes. Half a dozen people may be involved in assembling news, but only two may actually enter the broadcast booth. A primetime newscast schedule may look something like this:

A.M. Drive Coverage	P.M. Drive Coverage
Smith 6:25 a.m.	Lopez 3:25 p.m.
Bernard 7:00 a.m.	Gardner 4:00 p.m.
Smith 7:25 a.m.	Lopez 4:25 p.m.
Bernard 8:00 a.m.	Gardner 5:00 p.m.
Smith 8:25 a.m.	Lopez 5:25 p.m.
Bernard 9:00 a.m.	Gardner 6:00 p.m.
Smith 9:25 a.m.	Lopez 6:25 p.m.

Midday and evening are far less frenetic in the newsroom, and one person per shift may be considered sufficient.

A standard-size newsroom in a medium market will contain several pieces of audio equipment, not to mention office furniture such as desks, computers, typewriters, file cabinets, and so on. Reel-to-reel recorders and cassette and cartridge machines are important tools for the newsperson. The newsroom also will be equipped with various monitors to keep newspeople on top of what is happening at the local police and fire departments and weather bureau. Various wire service machines provide the latest news, sports, stock, and weather information, as well as a host of other data. Depending on the station's budget, two or more news services may be used. Stations with a genuine commitment to news create work areas that are designed for maximum efficiency and productivity.

In situations where newsrooms have been combined and consolidated due to LMAs and the relaxation of duopoly rules, more personnel, equipment, and space may be in evidence, since the plant itself may be serving myriad signals.

The All-News Station

Stations devoted entirely to news programming arrived on the scene in the mid-1960s. Program innovator Gordon McLendon, who had been a key figure in the development of two music formats, Beautiful Music and Top 40, implemented All-News at WNUS-AM ("NEWS") in Chicago. In 1965, Group W, Westinghouse Broadcasting, changed WINS-AM in New York to All-News, and soon did the same at more of its metro outlets: KYW-AM, Philadelphia, and KFWB-AM, Los Angeles. While Group W was converting several of its outlets to non-music programming, CBS decided that All-News was the way to go at WCBS-AM, New York; KCBS-AM, San Francisco; and KNX-AM, Los Angeles.

Not long after KCBS in San Francisco began its All-News programming, another Bay City station, KGO-AM, introduced the hybrid News/Talk format in which news shares the microphone with conversation and interview features. Over the years, the hybrid approach has caught on and leads the pure All-News format in popularity.

Because of the exorbitant cost of running a news-only operation, it has remained primarily a metro market endeavor. It often costs several times as much to run an effective All-News station as it does to run one broadcasting music. This usually keeps small market outlets out of the business. Staff size in All-News stations far exceeds that of formats that primarily serve up music. Whereas a lone deejay is needed at an Adult Contemporary or Top 40 station, All-News requires the involvement of several people to keep the air sound credible.

Even though the cost of running a news station is high, the payback can more than justify expenditures. However, this is one format that requires a sizable initial investment, as well as the financial wherewithal and patience to last until it becomes an established and viable entity. Considerable planning takes place before a station decides to convert to All-News, since it is not simply a matter of hiring new jocks and updating the music library. Switching from a music format to All-News is dramatic and anything but cosmetic.

AM has always been the home of the All-News station. There are only a handful of FM News outlets. The format's prevalence

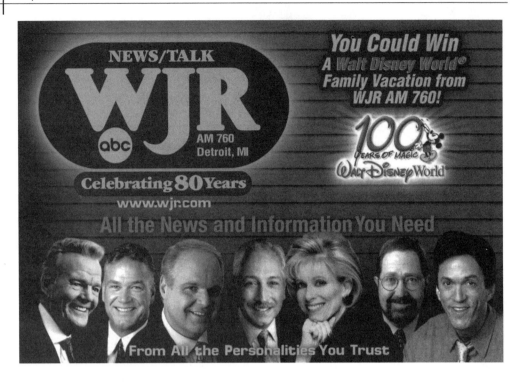

on AM has grown considerably since the late 1970s, when FM took the lead in listeners. The percentage of All-News and News/Talk formats on AM continued to increase in the 1980s as the band lost more and more of its music listeners to FM. However, All-News stations in many metro markets keep AM at the top of the ratings charts. In the early 1990s, it was common to find one AM outlet among the leaders, and almost invariably it programmed nonmusic. Some media observers predict that All-News will make significant inroads into FM.

The Electronic Newsroom

The use of computers (and online resources) in the radio newsroom has increased significantly since their introduction in December 1980 at KCBS in San Francisco. Computers linked to the various wire and information services are used to access primary and background data on fast-breaking stories and features. Many stations

have installed video display terminals (VDTs) in on-air studios. Instead of hand-held copy, newscasters simply broadcast off the screens. Desktop computers have replaced typewriters in the newsrooms at larger stations as well as at the smaller stations. The speed and agility with which copy can be produced and edited makes a computer the perfect tool for broadcast journalists.

In 1986 Boston All-News station WEEI-AM installed Media Touch's Touchstone system, thus converting their entire operation to computer. Newspeople access and store data and even activate equipment simply by touching a computer screen.

Computers have become the norm even in nonmetro market outlets. "There's not much resistance remaining against computers in the newsroom, especially since the advent of cheaper PCs and the improvement of programs like Newspro, which is the system we use here at NPR. It allows us to access and manipulate about a half-dozen wire services. We can split screen and write stories while searching the wires, and so on.

FIGURE 5.4
Computerized news assignments file. Computers have transformed the radio newsroom. Courtesy Jefferson Pilot Data Systems.

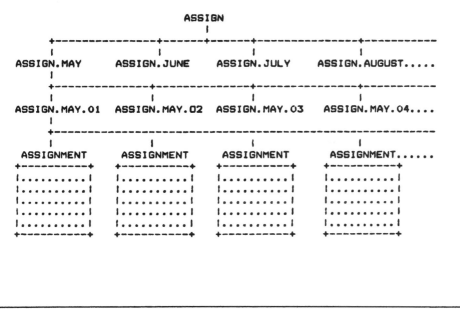

```
FILE CABINET ORGANIZATION:

Each of the "file cabinets" named above are organized just like
the file cabinets you use in your newsroom today.  For example,
let's look at how you might arrange the ASSIGN file cabinet.

The main file cabinet is named ASSIGN.  Inside are file drawers
for each month.  Therefore, you have one drawer named ASSIGN.MAY,
another named ASSIGN.JUNE, another named ASSIGN.JULY and so on.
Inside of each file drawer are the file folders.  Using
ASSIGN.MAY for example, there's a file folder for assignments for
each day of the month -- ASSIGN.MAY.01, ASSIGN.MAY.02,
ASSIGN.MAY.03 and so on.  Finally inside of each file folder are
the individual sheets of paper that hold the assignment
information for each day.  You can have as many of these as you
need -- there's no limit.

The diagram below shows how this organization might appear if
charted.
                              ASSIGN
                                 |
     +-------------------+------------+--------------------+------------
     |                   |            |                    |
ASSIGN.MAY        ASSIGN.JUNE   ASSIGN.JULY        ASSIGN.AUGUST.....
     |
     +-------------------+------------+--------------------+----------
     |                   |            |                    |
ASSIGN.MAY.01    ASSIGN.MAY.02  ASSIGN.MAY.03      ASSIGN.MAY.04....
     |
     +-------------------+------------+--------------------+----------
     |                   |            |                    |
 ASSIGNMENT         ASSIGNMENT    ASSIGNMENT          ASSIGNMENT......
 +----------+       +----------+  +----------+        +----------+
 |..........|       |..........|  |..........|        |..........|
 |..........|       |..........|  |..........|        |..........|
 |..........|       |..........|  |..........|        |..........|
 |..........|       |..........|  |..........|        |..........|
 |..........|       |..........|  |..........|        |..........|
 +----------+       +----------+  +----------+        +----------+
```

There are many more sophisticated systems too. We're considering buying the D-CART system that is used by the Australian Broadcasting Corporation. This system incorporates digital audio right onto the screen," comments Cory Flintoff.

Producer Ty Ford observes, "Computers are an integral part of radio newsrooms now, and on the increase is auto-download of wire copy to word processing terminals, as well as search-by-word or topic search, auto-word count and digital archiving of sound bites with a computer database for retrieval. To put it in the contemporary lexicon, radio news is 'online.'"

More and more newsrooms utilize the Internet and e-mail. It makes sense that the information highway be accessed by a medium determined to keep its listening public informed and up-to-date. The Internet has become the best resource for information on every conceivable topic. As a search medium there is none better. Data of every variety are at the fingertips of all newspeople today. The world of cyberspace has revolutionized news gathering. Says broadcaster and academic Larry Miller, "The evolution has been from old-fashioned teletype 'wire' by landlines, to satellites, to computers and the Internet. Even audio is accessed on-line."

Although some news directors initially resisted the idea of a computerized newsroom for various reasons, most now regard it as the standard in even the tiniest radio station newsroom. News director Larry Jewett suggests that today's newspeople, and individuals anticipating careers in radio news, become computer and Internet savvy. "Computers are a fact of life now. They cannot be ignored. Newspeople, and would-be newspeople, should learn all they can about computer technology because it is fast becoming an integral part of the profession."

The News Director

News directors, like other department heads, are responsible for developing and implementing policies pertaining to their area, supervising staff members, and handling budgetary concerns. These are basic to any managerial position. However, the news department poses its own unique challenges to the individual who oversees its operation. These challenges must be met with a considerable degree of skill and know-how. Education and training are important. Surveys have concluded that station managers look for college degrees when hiring news directors. In addition, most news directors have, on the average, five years of experience in radio news before advancement to the managerial level.

The news director and program director work together closely. At most stations, the PD has authority over the news department, since everything going over the air or affecting the air product is his or her direct

concern and responsibility. Any changes in the format of the news or in the scheduling of newscasts or newscasters may, in fact, have to be approved by the station's programmer. For example, if the PD is opposed to the news director's plans to include two or more taped reports (actualities) per newscast, he may withhold approval. Although the news director may feel that the reports enhance the newscasts, the PD may argue that they create congestion and clutter. In terms of establishing the on-air news schedule, the PD works with the news director to ensure that the sound of a given newsperson is suitably matched with the time slot he or she is assigned.

Getting the news out rapidly and accurately is a top priority of the news director. "People tune radio news to find out what is happening right now. That's what makes the medium such a key source for most people. While it is important to get news on the air as fast as possible, it is more important that the stories broadcast be factual and correct. You can't sacrifice accuracy for the sake of speed. As a radio news director my first responsibility is to inform our audience about breaking events on the local level. That's what our listeners want to hear," says Judy Smith, who functions as a one-person newsroom at the San Antonio station. "Because I'm the only newsperson on duty, I have to spend a lot of time verifying facts on the phone and recording actualities. I don't have the luxury of assigning that work to someone else, but it has to be done."

Larry Jewett perceives his responsibilities similarly. "First and foremost, the news director's job is to keep the listener informed of what is happening in the world around him. A newsperson is a gatherer and conveyor of information. News is a serious business. A jock can be wacky and outrageous on the air and be a great success. On the other hand, a newsperson must communicate credibility or find another occupation."

Gathering local news is the most time-consuming task facing a radio news director, according to news director Cecilia Mason.

"To do the job well you have to keep moving. All kinds of meetings—governmental, civic, business—have to be covered if you intend being a primary source of local news. A station with a news commitment must have the resources to be where the stories are, too. A news director has to be a logistical engineer at times. You have to be good at prioritizing and making the most out of what you have at hand. All too often there are just too many events unfolding for a news department to effectively cover, so you call the shots the best way that you can. If you know your business, your best shot is usually more than adequate."

In addition to the gathering and reporting of news, public affairs programming often is the responsibility of the news director. This generally includes the planning and preparation of local information features, such as interviews, debates, and even documentaries.

What Makes a Newsperson?

College training is an important criterion to the radio news director planning to hire personnel. It is not impossible to land a news job without a degree, but formal education is a definite asset. An individual planning to enter the radio news profession should consider pursuing a broadcasting, journalism, or liberal arts degree. Courses in political science, history, economics, and literature give the aspiring newsperson the kind of well-rounded background that is most useful. "Coming into this field today, a college degree is an attractive, if not essential, credential. There's so much that a newsperson has to know. I think an education makes the kind of difference you can hear, and that's what our business is about. It's a fact that most people are more cognizant of the world and write better after attending college. Credibility is crucial in this business, and college training provides some of that. A degree is something that I

FIGURE 5.5 Small market newsrooms are becoming scarce as the result of deregulation and consolidation.

would look for in prospective newspeople," says Cecilia Mason.

Even though education ranks high, most news directors still look for experience first. "As far as I'm concerned, experience counts the most. I'm not suggesting that education isn't important. It is. Most news directors want the person that they are hiring to have a college background, but experience impresses them more. I believe a person should have a good understanding of the basics before attempting to make a living at something. Whereas a college education is useful, a person should not lean back and point to a degree. Mine hasn't gotten me a job yet, though I wouldn't trade it for the world," notes Jewett. Newsman Smith agrees, "The first thing I think most news directors really look for is experience. Although I have a bachelor of arts degree myself, I wouldn't hold out for a person with a college diploma. I think if it came down to hiring a person with a degree versus someone with solid experience, I'd go for the latter."

Gaining news experience can be somewhat difficult, at least more so than acquiring deejay experience. Small stations, where the beginner is most likely to break

There's a Radio Format for Everyone

Read: The News/Talk format captures a 20.5% share of Radio listening among persons 45-54.

Format	45-54 Share	Format	55-64 Share
News/Talk/Information	20.5%	News/Talk/Information	28.1%
Adult Contemporary (AC)	17.5%	Adult Contemporary (AC)	15.2%
Oldies	13.7%	Country	12.6%
Country	9.2%	Oldies	12.3%
Alternative	7.2%	Hispanic	5.9%
Urban	6.0%	Urban	5.7%
Hispanic	5.6%	NAC/Smooth Jazz	4.5%
Classic Rock	5.6%	Adult Standards	3.9%
NAC/Smooth Jazz	5.1%	Classical	3.2%
Contemporary Hits Radio (CHR)	4.4%	Religious	3.1%
Religious	2.9%	Contemporary Hits Radio (CHR)	1.9%
Album Rock (AOR)	1.9%	Classic Rock	1.7%
Classical	1.6%	Alternative	0.8%
Adult Standards	1.0%	Album Rock (AOR)	0.6%
Remaining Formats	3.4%	Remaining Formats	0.5%

Format	65+ Share
News/Talk/Information	41.5%
Adult Standards	12.4%
Country	9.7%
Adult Contemporary (AC)	9.3%
Oldies	5.1%
Classical	4.7%
Hispanic	4.7%
Religious	3.8%
NAC/Smooth Jazz	3.4%
Urban	2.8%
Contemporary Hits Radio (CHR)	1.1%
Classic Rock	0.5%
Album Rock	0.2%
Alternative	0.2%
Remaining Formats	0.6%

Source: Arbitron American Radio Trends — Fall 2001; 94 Continuous Measurement Markets; Monday-Sunday 6 a.m.-midnight average quarter-hour share.

FIGURE 5.6
The news/talk/ information format is a ratings topper. Courtesy RAB.

into the business, have slots for several deejays but seldom more than one for a newsperson. It becomes even more problematic when employers at small stations want the one person that they hire for news to bring some experience to the job. Larger stations place even greater emphasis on experience. Thus, the aspiring newsperson is faced with a sort of Catch 22 situation, in which a job cannot be acquired without experience and experience cannot be acquired without a job.

News director Frank Titus says that there are ways of gaining experience that will lead to a news job. "Working in news at high school and college stations is very valid

experience. That's how Dan Rather and a hundred other newsmen got started. Also working as an intern at a commercial radio station fattens out the resume. If someone comes to me with this kind of background and a strong desire to do news, I'm interested."

Among the personal qualities that most appeal to news directors are enthusiasm, aggressiveness, energy, and inquisitiveness. "I want someone with a strong news sense and unflagging desire to get a story and get it right. A person either wants to do news or doesn't. Someone with a pedestrian interest in radio journalism is more of a hindrance to an operation than a help," contends Mason. Titus wants someone who is totally devoted to the profession. "When you get right down to it, I want someone on my staff who eats, drinks, and sleeps news."

On the practical side of the ledger, newsman Sherman Whitman says typing or keyboard skills are essential. "If you can't type, you can't work in a newsroom. It's an essential ability, and the more accuracy and speed the better. It's one of those skills basic to the job. A candidate for a news job can come in here with two degrees, but if that person can't type, that person won't be hired. Broadcast students should learn to type." Meanwhile, Jewett stresses the value of possessing a firm command of the English language. "Proper punctuation, spelling, and syntax make a news story intelligible. A newsperson doesn't have to be a grammarian, but he or she had better know where to put a comma and a period and how to compose a good clean sentence. A copy of Strunk and White's *Elements of Style* is good to have around."

An individual who is knowledgeable about the area in which a station is located has a major advantage over those who are not, says Whitman. "A newsperson has to know the town or city inside out. I'd advise anybody about to be interviewed for a news position to find out as much as possible about the station's coverage area. Read back issues of newspapers, get socioeconomic

FIGURE 5.7
A press release explains the service of AP's All-News Radio. Courtesy Associated Press.

stats from the library or chamber of commerce, and study street directories and maps of the town or city in which the station is located. Go into the job interview well informed, and you'll make a strong impression."

Unlike a print journalist, a radio newsperson also must be a performer. In addition to good writing and news-gathering skills, the newsperson in radio must have announcing abilities. Again, training is usually essential. "Not only must a radio newsperson be able to write a story, but he or she has to be able to present it on the air. You have to be an announcer, too. It takes both training and experience to become a really effective newscaster. Voice performance courses can provide a foundation," says Smith. Most colleges with broadcasting programs offer announcing and newscasting instruction.

Entry-level news positions pay modestly, whereas newspeople at metro market stations earn impressive incomes. With experience come the better paying jobs. Finding that first full-time news position often takes patience and determination. Several industry trade journals, such as *Broadcasting*, the Radio-Television News Directors Association's (RTNDA) *Communicator*, *Radio and Records*, and others, list news openings.

Preparing the News Story

Clean copy is imperative. News stories must be legible and intelligible and designed for effortless reading by the newscaster, or several different newscasters. Typos, mispunctuation, awkward phrasing, and incorrect spelling are anathema to the person at the microphone. Try reading the following news story aloud and imagine yourself in a studio broadcasting to thousands of perplexed listeners:

THEPRESIDENT   STATD   TODXAY
THAT HE
WILL   SEED   RELECTION   TO   A
SECOND
TURMIN OFFICE, DEPICE ROOMERS
THAT HE WILT LEAVE WASHINDON
TO
PURDUE A QUEER IN HOLLYWOOD.

Going on the air with copy riddled with errors is inviting disaster. About the only things right about the preceding news copy are that it is typed in uppercase and double-spaced. Here are a few suggestions to keep in mind when preparing a radio news story:

1. Type neatly. Avoid typos and cross-outs. Eliminate a typing error completely. If it is left on the page, it could trip you up during a broadcast.
2. Use uppercase throughout the story. It is easier to read. Don't forget, the story you are writing is going to be read on the air.
3. Double-space between lines for the same reason uppercase is used—copy is easier to read. Space between lines of copy keeps them from merging when read aloud.
4. Use one-inch margins. Don't run the copy off the page. Uniformity eliminates errors. At the same time, try not to break up words.
5. Avoid abbreviations, except for those meant to be read as such: YMCA, U.S.A., NAACP, AFL/CIO.
6. Write out numbers under ten, and use numerals for figures between 10 and 999. Spell out thousand, million, and so forth. For example, 21 million people, instead of 21,000,000 people. Numbers can be tricky, but a consistent approach prevents problems.
7. Use the phonetic spelling for words that may cause pronunciation difficulties, and underline the stressed syllable: Monsignor (Mon-seen-yor).
8. Punctuate properly. A comma out of place can change the meaning of a sentence.
9. When in doubt, consult a standard style guide. In addition, both AP and UPI publish handbooks on newswriting.

Notice how much easier it is to read a news story that is correctly prepared:

THE   PRESIDENT   STATED   TODAY
THAT HE
WILL   SEEK   REELECTION   TO   A
SECOND
TERM IN OFFICE, DESPITE RUMORS
THAT HE WILL LEAVE WASHINGTON
TO
PURSUE A CAREER IN HOLLYWOOD.

Since radio news copy is written for the ear and not for the eye, its style must reflect that fact. In contrast to writing done for the printed page, radio writing is more conversational and informal. Necessity dictates this. Elaborately constructed sentences containing highly sophisticated language may effectively communicate to the reader but create serious problems for the listener, who must digest the text while it is being spoken. Whereas the reader has the luxury to move along at his or her own pace, the radio listener must keep pace with the newscaster or miss out on information. Radio writing must be accessible and immediately comprehensible. The most widely accepted and used words must be chosen so as to prevent confusion on the part of the listener, who usually does not have the time or opportunity to consult the dictionary. "Keep it simple and direct. No compound-complex sentences with dozens of esoteric phrases and terms. Try to picture the listener in your mind. He is probably driving a car or doing any number of things. Because of the nature of the medium, writing must be concise and conversational," contends Judy Smith.

Corey Flintoff agrees. "Copy should be adapted to a conversational style. Titles should be simplified and numbers rounded off."

News stories must be well structured and organized. This adds to their level of understanding. The journalist's five W's—who, what, when, where, and why—should be incorporated into each story. If a story fails to provide adequate details, the listener may tune in elsewhere to get what radio commentator Paul Harvey calls "the rest of the story."

When quoting a source in a news story, proper attribution must be made. This increases credibility while placing the burden of responsibility for a statement on the shoulders of the person who actually made it:

THE DRIVER OF THE CAR THAT STRUCK
THE BUILDING APPEARED INTOXI-CATED, ACCORDING TO LISA BARNES,
WHO VIEWED THE INCIDENT.

Observes Flintoff on the matter of attribution, "I prefer to identify a source at the beginning of the sentence on the theory that its more conversational. Thus, 'Lisa Barnes, a witness, said the driver . . .' or 'Lisa Barnes saw the car crash into the building. She said the driver. . . .' Incidentally, I think there's a danger of legal problems using a witness's speculation that someone is drunk. I've had similar problems in the past, and I never use anything about potential intoxication unless there's a police test for drugs or alcohol."

Uncorroborated statements can make a station vulnerable to legal actions. The reliability of news sources must be established. When there are doubts concerning the facts, the newsperson has a responsibility to seek verification.

Organizing the Newscast

News on music-oriented radio stations commonly is presented in five-minute blocks and aired at the top or bottom of the hour, During drivetime periods stations often increase the length and/or frequency of newscasts. The five minutes allotted news generally is divided into segments to accommodate the presentation of specific information. A station may establish a format that allows for two minutes of local and regional stories, one minute for key national and international stories, one minute for sports, and 15 seconds for weather information. A 30- or 60-second commercial break will be counted as part of the five-minute newscast.

The number of stories in a newscast may be preordained by program management or may vary depending on the significance and scope of the stories being reported. News policy may require that no stories, except in particular cases, exceed 15 seconds. Here the idea is to deliver as many stories as possible in the limited time available, the underlying sentiment being that more is better. In five minutes, 15 to 20 items may be covered. In contrast, other stations prefer that key stories be addressed in greater detail. As few as 5 to 10 news items may be broadcast at stations taking this approach.

Stories are arranged according to their rank of importance, the most significant story of the hour topping the news. An informed newsperson will know what stories deserve the most attention. Wire services weigh each story and position them accordingly in news roundups. The local radio newsperson decides what wire stories will be aired and in what order.

Assembling a five-minute newscast takes skill, speed, and accuracy. Stories must be updated and rewritten to keep news broadcasts from sounding stale.

This often requires that telephone calls be made for late-breaking information. Meanwhile, on-the-scene voicers (actualities) originating from audio news services (UPI, AP) or fed by local reporters must be taped and slotted in the newscast. "Preparing a fresh newscast each hour can put you in mind of what it must have been like to be a contestant on the old game show 'Beat the Clock.' A conscientious newsperson is

FIGURE 5.8
Five-minute newscast
format clock.

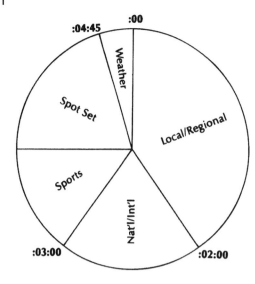

FIGURE 5.9
A top market news
station offers a profile
of itself. Courtesy
Infinity.

a vision of perpetual motion," observes Cecilia Mason.

Finally, most newspeople read their news copy before going on the air. "Reading stories cold is foolhardy and invites trouble. Even the most seasoned newscasters at metro market stations take the time to read over their copy before going on," comments Whitman. Many newspeople read copy aloud in the news studio before airtime. This gives them a chance to get a feel for their copy. Proper preparation prevents unpleasant surprises from occurring while on the air.

The Wire Services

Without the aid of the major broadcast news wire services, radio stations would find it almost impossible to cover news on national and international levels. The wire services are a vital source of news information to nearly all of the nation's commercial radio stations. Both large and small stations rely on the news copy fed them by either the Associated Press or United Press International, the two most prominent news wire services.

Broadcast wire services came into existence in the mid-1930s, when United Press (which became United Press International in 1958 after merging with International News Service) began providing broadcasters with news copy. Today the UPI and AP serve over 7,500 broadcast outlets.

Both news sources supply subscriber stations with around-the-clock coverage of national and world events. Over 100,000 stringers furnish stories from across the globe. The AP and UPI also maintain regional bureaus for the dissemination of local news. Each wire service transmits over 20 complete news summaries daily. In addition, they provide weather, stock market, and sports information, as well as a formidable list of features and data useful to the station's news and programming efforts.

WBZ NEWS RADIO **1030**

1170 SOLDIERS FIELD ROAD BOSTON MASSACHUSETTS 02134 TELEPHONE (617) 787-7000

WBZ NewsRadio 1030

A Brief Description

WBZ NewsRadio, the first commercially licensed station in the country, has been broadcasting to New Englanders for almost 80 years. Our award winning coverage has earned WBZ many honors including 2000's "News Station of the Year," from the Associated Press, and three recent Marconi Awards, "The Most Prestigious Radio Award Available."

 WBZ has close to a million listeners weekly. The exclusive all news format creates a foreground listening environment, that delivers results for our advertisers.

 Our award winning news anchors and reporters have an aggregate experience level of over 100+ years in broadcasting!

 Our combined resources of both radio and television make up the largest news gathering organization in New England. Many of our radio anchors gain exposure daily on WBZ-TV 4 adding to their tremendous popularity.

 WBZ highlights advertisers' messages by airing commercials as islands surrounded by news, traffic, weather or business reports. During our news, your commercial is always the first and only sixty second commercial in a commercial break.

 WBZ's 50,000 watt clear channel signal reaches all of New England, and at night 38 states and six Canadian Providences. Our reach is unparalleled!

 We maintain a 52 week marketing campaign promoting ourselves on TV, print, web, and at countless on-site events throughout New England.

 WBZ is a leader in community involvement spearheading many events including Children's Hospital Telethon and fundraising, Call for Action, Domestic Violence and StormCenter.

 WBZ is the flagship station for the Boston Bruins and the Boston Bruins Radio Network and the only place fans can catch every game every time they play.

Rates for wire service vary depending on the size of the radio market, and audio service is available for an additional fee. Some 1,800 stations use UPI and AP audio news feeds.

Broadcasters are evenly divided over the question as to which is the best wire service. Each news service has about the same number of radio stations under contract.

Both major wire services have kept pace with the new technologies. In the mid-1980s, UPI alone purchased 6,000 Z-15 desktop computers from Zenith Data Systems. Satellites also are utilized by the two news organizations for the transmission of teletype, teletext, and audio. The wire services have become as wireless as the wireless itself.

Radio Network News

During the medium's first three decades, the terms *networks* and *news* were virtually synonymous. Most of the news broadcast over America's radio stations emanated from the networks. The public's dependence on network radio news reached its height during World War II. As television succeeded radio as the mainstay for entertainment programming in the 1950s and 1960s, the networks concentrated their efforts on supplying affiliates with news and information feeds. This approach helped the networks regain their footing in radio after a period of substantial decline. By the mid-1960s, the majority of the nation's stations utilized one of the four major networks for news programming.

In 1968, ABC decided to make available four distinct news formats designed for compatibility with the dominant sounds of the day. American Contemporary Radio Network, American FM Radio Network, American Entertainment Radio Network, and American Information Network each offered a unique style and method of news presentation. ABC's venture proved enormously successful. In the 1970s, over 1,500 stations subscribed to one of ABC's four news networks.

In response to a growing racial and ethnic awareness, the Mutual Broadcasting System (MBS) launched two minority news networks in 1971. Though the network's Black news service proved to be a fruitful venture, its Spanish news service ceased operation within two years of its inception. Mutual discovered that the ethnic group simply was too refracted and diverse to be effectively serviced by one network and that the Latin listeners they did attract did not constitute the numbers necessary to justify operation.

In 1973 the network also went head-to-head with ABC by offering a network news service (Mutual Progressive Network) that catered to rock-oriented stations. Mutual's various efforts paid off by making it second only to ABC in number of affiliates. After years of financial difficulties, MBS went silent in 1999, ending nearly seven decades of radio news service.

The News and Information Service (NIS) was introduced by NBC in 1975 but ended in 1977. NIS offered client stations an All-News format. Fifty minutes of news was fed to stations each hour. The venture was abandoned after only moderate acceptance. CBS, which has offered its member stations World News Roundup since 1938, and NBC have under 300 affiliates apiece.

Several state and regional news networks do well, but the big three, ABC, NBC, and CBS, continue to dominate. Meanwhile, independent satellite news and information networks and the cable news services, such as CNN, have joined the field and more are planned.

The usual length of a network newscast is five minutes, during which time affiliates are afforded an opportunity to insert local sponsor messages at designated times. The networks make their money by selling national advertisers spot availabilities in their widely broadcast news. Stations also pay the networks a fee for the programming they receive.

FIGURE 5.10
Most talk shows focus on discussions of the hot news stories and social issues of the day. Jim Bohannon is among the most popular. Courtesy Westwood One.

According to Metro Network president David Saperstein, today "more and more stations are realizing the benefits that exist in outside news services, which provide the information that listeners would otherwise seek elsewhere. This allows the station to focus its marketing dollars, thus directing resources toward optimizing and maintaining what draws and keeps listeners." Of course, this latter trend has raised additional concerns about the decline in local news coverage as cited in recent RTNDA surveys. Station consolidations have resulted in the erosion of local news operations.

Radio Sportscasts

Sports is most commonly presented as an element within newscasts (refer back to Figure 5.8). Although many stations air sports as programming features unto themselves, most stations insert information, such as scores and schedules of upcoming games, at a designated point in a newscast and call it sports. Whether a station emphasizes sports largely depends on its audience. Stations gearing their format for youngsters or women often all but ignore sports. Adult-oriented stations, such as Middle-of-the-Road, will frequently offer a greater abundance of sports information, especially when the station is located in an area that has a major league team.

Stations that hire individuals to do sports, and invariably these are larger outlets since few small stations can afford a full-time sportsperson, look for someone who is well versed in athletics. "To be good at radio sports, you have to have been involved as a participant somewhere along the line. That's for starters, in my opinion. This doesn't mean that you have to be a former major leaguer before doing radio sports, but to have a feel for what you're talking about, it certainly helps to have been on the field or court yourself. A good sportscaster must have the ability to accurately analyze a sport through the eyes and body of the athlete," contends John Colletto, sports director, WPRO-AM, Providence, Rhode Island.

Unlike news that requires an impartial and somewhat austere presentation, sportscasts frequently are delivered in a casual and even opinionated manner. "Let's face it, there's a big difference between nuclear arms talks between the United States and the Soviets and last night's Red Sox/Yankees score. I don't think sports reports should be treated in a style that's too solemn. It's entertainment, and sportscasters should exercise their license to comment and analyze," says Colletto.

Although sports is presented in a less heavy-handed way than news, credibility is an important factor, contends Colletto. "There is a need for radio sportscasters to establish credibility just as there is for newspeople to do so. If you're not believable, you're not listened to. The best way to win the respect of your audience is by demonstrating a thorough knowledge of the game and by sounding like an insider, not just a guy reading the wire copy. Remember, sports fans can be as loyal to a sportscaster as they are to their favorite team. They want to hear the stories and scores from a person they feel comfortable with."

The style of a news story and a sports story may differ considerably. Although news is written in a no-frills, straightforward way, sports stories often contain colorful collo-quialisms and even popular slang. Here is an example by radio sportswriter Roger Crosley:

THE DEAN COLLEGE RED DEMON FOOTBALL TEAM RODE THE STRONG RUNNING OF FULLBACK BILL PALAZOLLO YESTERDAY TO AN 18–16 COME FROM BEHIND VICTORY OVER THE AMERICAN INTERNATIONAL COLLEGE JUNIOR VARSITY YELLOW JACKETS. PALAZOLLO CHURNED OUT A TEAM HIGH 93 YARDS ON TWENTY-FIVE CARRIES AND SCORED ALL THREE TOUCHDOWNS ON BLASTS OF 7, 2, AND 6 YARDS. THE DEMONS TRAILED THE HARD-HITTING CONTEST 16–6 ENTERING THE FINAL QUARTER. PALA-ZOLLO CAPPED A TWELVE-PLAY 81-YARD DRIVE WITH HIS SECOND SIX-POINTER EARLY IN THE STANZA AND SCORED THE CLINCHER WITH 4:34 REMAINING. THE DEMONS WILL PUT THEIR 1 AND 0 RECORD ON THE LINE NEXT SUNDAY AT 1:30 AGAINST THE ALWAYS TOUGH HOLY CROSS JAYVEES IN WORCESTER.

Sportscasters are personalities, says WPRO's Colletto, and as such must be able to communicate on a different level than newscasters. "You're expected to have a sense of humor. Most successful sportscast-ers can make an audience smile or laugh. You have to be able to ad-lib, also."

The wire services and networks are the primary source for sports news at local sta-tions. On the other hand, information about the outcome of local games, such as high school football and so forth, must be acquired firsthand. This usually entails a call to the team's coach or a direct report from a stringer or reporter.

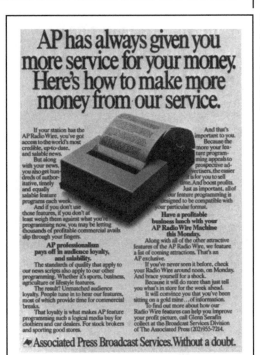

FIGURE 5.11
Associated Press promotional piece. AP claims more subscribers than any other wire service. Courtesy AP.

FIGURE 5.12
Network-affiliated All-News stations, such as WCBS, invest heavily in promotion in efforts to establish a strong image in their markets. Courtesy of WCBS.

In August 1967, WCBS Radio became WCBS NEWSRADIO. During those 15 years, WCBS has become the station millions of people rely on for radio news. And today, WCBS is listened to by more adults than any other radio station in the country.

For radio news, the biggest...and.... the best in the business.

WCBS NEWSRADIO
New York

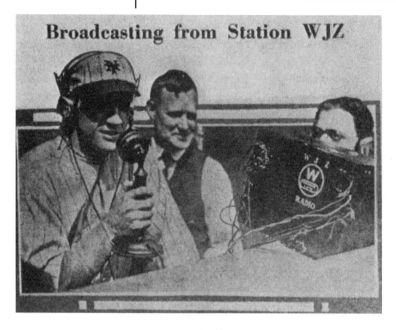

Broadcasting from Station WJZ

Radio News and The FCC

The government takes a greater role in regulating broadcast journalism than it does print. Whereas it usually maintains a hands-off position when it comes to newspapers, the government keeps a watchful eye on radio to ensure that it meets certain operating criteria. Since the FCC perceives the airways as public domain, it expects broadcasters to operate in the public's interest.

The FCC requires that radio reporters present news factually and in good faith. Stories that defame citizens through reckless or false statements may not only bring a libel suit from the injured party but action from the FCC, which views such behavior on the part of broadcasters as contrary to the public's interest. Broadcasters are protected under the First Amendment and therefore have certain rights, but as public trustees they are charged with the additional responsibility of acting in a manner that benefits rather than harms members of society.

Broadcasters are free to express opinions and sentiments on issues through editorials. However, to avoid controversy, many radio stations choose not to editorialize even though the FCC encourages them to do so.

News Ethics

The highly competitive nature of radio places unusual pressure on newspeople. In a business where being first with the story is often equated with being the best, certain dangers exist. Being first at all costs can be costly, indeed, if information and facts are not adequately verified. As previously mentioned, it is the radio journalist's obligation to get the story straight and accurate before putting it on the air. Anything short of this is unprofessional.

The pressures of the clock, if allowed, can result in haphazard reporting. If a story cannot be sufficiently prepared in time for the upcoming news broadcast, it should be withheld. Getting it on-air is not as important as getting it on-air right. Accuracy is the newsperson's first criterion. News accounts should never be fudged. It is tantamount to deceiving and misleading the public.

News reporters must exhibit discretion not only in the newsroom but also when on the scene of a story. It is commendable to assiduously pursue the facts and details of a story, but it is inconsiderate and insensitive to ignore the suffering and pain of those involved. For example, to press for comments from a grief-stricken parent whose child has just been seriously injured in an accident is callous and cruel and a disservice to all concerned, including the station the newsperson represents. Of course, a newsperson wants as much information as possible about an incident, but the public's right to privacy must be respected.

Objectivity is the cornerstone of good reporting. A newsperson who has lost his or her capacity to see the whole picture is handicapped. At the same time, the newsperson's job is to report the news and not create it. The mere presence of a member of the media can inspire a disturbance or agitate a volatile situation. Staging an event for the sake of increasing the newsiness of a story is not only unprofessional, but illegal. Groups have been known to await the arrival of reporters before initiating a disturbance for the sake of gaining publicity. It is the duty of reporters to remain as innocuous and uninvolved as possible when on an assignment.

Several industry associations, such as RTNDA and Society of Professional Journalists, have established codes pertaining to the ethics and conduct of broadcast reporters.

Traffic Reports

Traffic reports are an integral part of drive-time news programming at many metropolitan radio stations. Although providing listeners with traffic condition updates can be costly, especially air-to-ground reports that require the use of a helicopter or small plane, they can help strengthen a station's community service image and also generate substantial revenue. To avoid the cost involved in airborne observation, stations sometimes employ the services of local auto clubs or put their own mobile units out on the roads. A station in Providence, Rhode Island, broadcasts traffic conditions from atop a 20-story hotel that overlooks the city's key arteries.

Says David Saperstein, "Companies like Metro Network provide stations with outside traffic reporting services in a manner that is more cost- and quality-effective than a station handling it themselves."

Traffic reports are scheduled several times an hour throughout the prime commuter periods on stations primarily catering to adults, and they range in length from 30 to 90 seconds. The actual reports may be done by a station employee who works in other areas of programming when not surveying the roads, or a member of the local police department or auto club may be

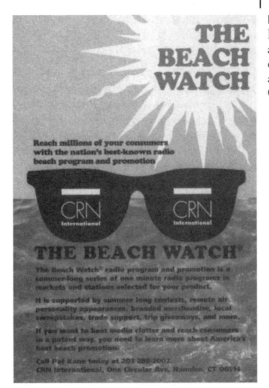

FIGURE 5.14
Information features are popular elements of news and public affairs programming. Courtesy CRN.

FIGURE 5.15
Traffic reports are often a central element of news broadcasts. Courtesy Metro Traffic.

hired for the job. Obviously, the prime criterion for such a position is a thorough knowledge of the streets and highways of the area being reported.

News in Music Radio

In the 1980s, the FCC saw fit to eliminate the requirement that all radio stations devote a percentage of their broadcast day to news and public affairs programming. Opponents of the decision argued that such a move would mark the decline of news on radio. In contrast, proponents of the deregulation commended the FCC's actions that allow for the marketplace to determine the extent to which nonentertainment features are broadcast. In the late 1980s, RTNDA expressed the concern that local news coverage had declined. This, they said, had resulted in a decrease in the number of news positions around the country. Supporting their contention they pointed out that several major stations, such as KDKA, WOWO, and WIND, had cut back their news budgets.

At that time, RTNDA's Bob Priddy noted, "There has been a perceived decline in the amount of news broadcast. I don't see this as a cold-hearted act on the part of station managers, but rather one frequently inspired by economics. The decline in news programming is particularly alarming when you realize that it is at a time when a number of new stations are entering the airwaves."

In 1992, RTNDA's president, Dave Bartlett, declared, "Deregulation really hasn't taken news off radio. News is far from dead on the medium. The vast majority do news. All deregulation did was allow the marketplace to adjust at will. A lot of shifting has occurred, but the aggregate is the same." A couple of years later, a survey published in the association's newsletter, *Communicator*, told a different story. The report revealed that hundreds of radio newsrooms had, in fact, closed down, and it suggested many more would likely occur. In 1994, *Radio World* reported that over 1,100 radio news operations had closed since the deregulation of the medium.

News director Sherman Whitman believes that the radio audience wants news even when a station's primary product is music. "The public has come to depend on the medium to keep it informed. It's a volatile world and certain events affect us all. Stations that aim to be full-service cannot do so without a solid news schedule."

Cecilia Mason says that economics alone will help keep news a viable entity at many radio stations. "While a lot of stations consider news departments expense centers, news is a money maker. This is especially true during drivetime periods when practically everyone tuned wants information, be it weather, sports, or news headlines. I don't see a growing movement to eliminate news. However, I do see a movement to soften things up, that is, to hire voices instead of radio journalists. In the long run, this means fewer news jobs, I suppose. Economics again. While stations, for the most part, are not appreciably reducing the amount of time devoted to airing news, I suspect that some may be thinning out their news departments. Hopefully, this is not a prelude to a measurable cutback. News is still big business, though."

"Responsible broadcasters know that it is the inherent duty of the medium to keep the public apprised of what is going on," claims Larry Jewett. "While radio is primarily an entertainment medium, it is still one of the country's foremost sources of information. Responsible broadcasters—and most of us are—realize that we have a special obligation to fulfill. The tremendous reach and immediacy that is unique to radio forces the medium to be something more than just a jukebox."

News director Frank Titus believes that stations will continue to broadcast news in the future. "There might be a tendency to invest less in news operations, especially at more music-oriented outlets, as the result of the regulation change and rampant consolidations, but news is as much a part of what radio is as are the deejays and songs. What it comes right down to is people want news broadcasts, so they're going to get them.

FIGURE 5.16
Global news has become local news. Courtesy Global Radio News.

That's the whole idea behind the commission's FCC's actions. There's no doubt in my mind that the marketplace will continue to dictate the programming of radio news."

News director Roger Nadel concurs. "As the age of the average listener increases, even people tuning in 'music' stations find themselves in need of at least minimal doses of news. So long as those stations are doing well financially, owners can be content to maintain some kind of a news operation. News is not likely to disappear; not even at music stations."

In recent years, this optimism has significantly diminished as a result of station clustering, consolidation, and downsizing and the continued elimination of radio news requirements.

CHAPTER HIGHLIGHTS

1. Although the first newscast occurred in 1910, broadcast journalism did not evolve until the early 1920s. The broadcast of the Harding–Cox election results in 1920 was a historical benchmark.

2. Because newspapers perceived radio as a competitive threat, United Press (UP), International News Service (INS), and Associated Press (AP) refused to sell to radio outlets from 1932 until 1934. Radio, however, proved it could provide its own news sources.

3. The advent of television led radio outlets to localize their news content, which meant less reliance on news networks and the creation of a station news department.

4. Surveys by the National Association of Broadcasters and the Radio Advertising Bureau found that more people tune in to radio news for their first daily source of information than turn to television or newspapers.

5. The size of a station's news staff depends on the degree to which the station's format emphasizes news, the station's market size, the emphasis of its competition, and station consolidations. Small stations often have no newspeople and require deejays to "rip 'n' read" wire service copy.

6. Large news staffs may consist of newscasters, writers, street reporters, and tech people, as well as stringers and interns.

7. Computers in radio newsrooms are used as links to the various wire, news, and database services, as display terminals for reading news copy on the air, and as word processors for writing and storing news.

8. The news director, who works with and for the program director, supervises news staff, develops and implements policy, handles the budget, ensures the gathering of local news, is responsible for getting out breaking news stories rapidly and accurately, and plans public affairs programming.

9. News directors seek personnel with both college education and experience. However, finding a news slot at a small station is difficult, since its news staffs are small, so internships and experience at high school and college stations are important. Additionally, such personal qualities as enthusiasm, aggressiveness, energy, inquisitiveness, keyboarding skills, a knowledge of the area where the station is located, announcing abilities, and a command of the English language are assets.

10. News stories must be legible, intelligible, and designed for effortless reading. They should sound conversational, informal, simple, direct, concise, and organized.

11. Actualities (on-the-scene voicers) are taped from news service feeds or recorded by station personnel at the scene.

12. Wire services are the primary, and often only, sources of national and international news for most stations. Associated Press and United Press International are the largest.

13. The FCC expects broadcasters to report the news in a balanced and impartial manner. Although protected under the First Amendment, broadcasters making reckless or false statements are subject to both civil and FCC charges.

14. Ethically, newspersons must maintain objectivity, discretion, and sensitivity.

15. The FCC's deregulation of news and public affairs programming in the 1980s and widespread station clustering in recent years has prompted concern by industry officials and others that radio news service is on the decline, if not on the cusp of extinction.

SUGGESTED FURTHER READING

Bartlett, Jonathan, ed. *The First Amendment in a Free Society.* New York: H. W. Wilson, 1979.

Bittner, John R., and Bittner, Denise A. *Radio Journalism.* Englewood Cliffs, N.J.: Prentice Hall, 1977.

Bliss, Edward J. *Now the News.* New York: Oxford Press, 1991.

—, and Patterson, John M. *Writing News for Broadcast*, 2nd ed. New York: Columbia University Press, 1978.

Block, Mervin. Writing Broadcast News. San Francisco: Bonus Books, 1997.

Boyd, Andrew. *Broadcast Journalism*, 5th ed. Boston: Focal Press, 2001.

Boyer, Peter J. *Who Killed CBS?* New York: Random House, 1988.

Charnley, Mitchell. *News by Radio*. New York: Macmillan, 1948.

Culbert, David Holbrook. *News for Every man: Radio and Foreign Affairs in Thirties America*. Westport, Conn.: Greenwood Press, 1976.

Day, Louis A. *Ethics in Media Communications*. Belmont, Calif.: Wadsworth Publishing, 1991.

Fang, Irving. *Radio News/Television News*, 2nd ed. St. Paul, Minn.: Rada Press, 1985.

—. *Those Radio Commentators*. Ames: Iowa State University Press, 1977.

Friendly, Fred W. *The Good Guys, The Bad Guys, and the First Amendment: Free Speech vs. Fairness in Broadcasting*. New York: Random House, 1976.

Frost, Chris. *Reporting for Journalists*. New York: Routledge, 2002.

Garvey, Daniel E. *News Writing for the Electronic Media*. Belmont, Calif.: Wadsworth Publishing, 1982.

Gibson, Roy. *Radio and Television Reporting*. Boston: Allyn & Bacon, 1991.

Gilbert, Bob. *Perry's Broadcast News Handbook*. Knoxville, Tenn.: Perry Publishing, 1982.

Hall, Mark W. *Broadcast Journalism: An Introduction to News Writing*. New York: Hastings House, 1978.

Hitchcock, John R. *Sportscasting*. Boston: Focal Press, 1991.

Hood, James R., and Kalbfeld, Brad, eds. *The Associated Press Handbook*. New York: Associated Press, 1982.

Hunter, Julius K. *Broadcast News*. St. Louis: C. V. Mosby Company, 1980.

Johnston, Carla. *Election Coverage: Blueprint for Broadcasters*. Boston: Focal Press, 1991.

Kalbfeld, Brad. *Broadcast News Handbook*. New York: McGraw Hill, 2000.

Keirstead, Phillip A. *All-News Radio*. Blue Ridge Summit, Pa.: Tab Books, 1980.

Mayeux, Peter. *Broadcast News Writing and Reporting*. Chicago: Waveland Press, 2000.

Nelson, Harold L. *Laws of Mass Communication*. Mineola, N.Y.: The Foundation Press, 1982.

Simmons, Steven J. *The Fairness Doctrine and the Media*. Berkeley: University of California Press, 1978.

Stephens, Mitchell. *Broadcast News: Radio Journalism and an Introduction to Television*. New York: Holt, Rinehart and Winston, 1980.

UPI Stylebook: A Handbook for Writing and Preparing Broadcast News. New York: United Press International, 1979.

White, Ted. *Broadcast News Writing*. New York: Macmillan, 1984.

Wulfemeyer, K. Tim. *Broadcast News-Writing*. Ames: Iowa State University Press, 1995.

Research

Who Is Listening?

As early as 1929, the question of listenership was of interest to broadcasters and advertisers alike. That year Cooperative Analysis of Broadcasting (CAB), headed by Archibald M. Crossley, undertook a study to determine how many people were tuned to certain network radio programs. Information was gathered by phoning a preselected sample of homes. One of the things the survey found was that the majority of listening occurred evenings between 7 and 11 p.m. This became known as radio's "prime time" until the 1950s.

On the local station level, various methods were employed to collect audience data, including telephone interviews and mail-out questionnaires. However, only a nominal amount of actual audience research was attempted during the late 1920s and early 1930s. For the most part, just who was listening remained somewhat of a mystery until the late 1930s.

In 1938 C. E. Hooper, Inc. began the most formidable attempt up to that time to provide radio broadcasters with audience information. Like Crossley's service, Hooper also utilized the telephone to accumulate listener data. CAB relied on listener recall; Hooper, however, required that interviewers make calls until they reached someone who was actually listening to the radio. This approach became known as the "coincidental" telephone method. Both survey services found their efforts limited by the fact that 40 percent of the radio listening homes in the 1930s were without a telephone.

As World War II approached, another major ratings service, known as the Pulse, began to measure radio audience size. Unlike its competitors, Pulse collected information by conducting face-to-face interviews. Interest in audience research grew steadily throughout the 1930s and culminated in the establishment of the Office of Radio Research (ORR) in 1937. Funded by a Rockefeller Foundation grant, the ORR was headed by Paul F. Lazarsfeld, who was assisted by Hadley Cantril and Frank Stanton. The latter would go on to assume the presidency of CBS in 1946 and would serve in that capacity into the 1970s. Over a 10-year period, the ORR published several texts dealing with audience research findings and methodology. Among them were Lazarsfeld and Stanton's multivolume *Radio Research*, which covered the periods of 1941–1943 and 1948–1949. During the same decade, Lazarsfeld also published book-length reports on the public's attitude toward radio: *The People Look at Radio* (1946) and *Radio Listening in America* (1948). Both works cast radio in a favorable light by concluding that most listeners felt the medium did an exemplary job. The Pulse and Hooper were the prevailing radio station rating services in the 1950s as the medium worked at regaining its footing following the meteoric rise of television. In 1965 Arbitron Ratings began measuring radio audience size through the use of a diary, which required respondents to document their listening habits over a seven-day period. By the 1970s Arbitron reigned as the leading radio measurement company, while Hooper and Pulse faded from the scene. To provide the radio networks and their affiliates and advertisers with much-needed ratings information, Statistical Research, Inc., of New Jersey, introduced Radio's All Dimension Audience Research (RADAR) in 1968. The company gathers its information through telephone interviews to more than 6,000 households. In the 1990s, Arbitron retained its hold on first place among services measuring radio audiences, especially since the demise of Birch/ Scarborough, which gained considerable acceptance following its debut in the late 1970s. In 1991, this audience measurement company became yet another victim of the economic malaise.

Ratings companies must be reliable, and credibility is crucial to success. Therefore, measurement techniques must be tried and true. Information must be accurate, since millions of dollars are at stake. In 1963 the Broadcast Rating Council was established to monitor, audit, and accredit the various ratings companies. The council created performance standards to which rating services are expected to adhere. Those that fail to meet the council's operating criteria are not accredited. A nonaccredited ratings service will seldom succeed. In 1982 the Broadcast Rating Council was renamed the Electronic Media Planning Council to reflect a connection with the ratings services dealing with the cable television industry.

The Ratings and Survey Services

The extreme fragmentation of today's listening audience, created by the almost inestimable number of stations and formats, makes the job of research a complex but necessary one. All stations, regardless of size, must put forth an effort to acquaint themselves with the characteristics of the audience, says Edward J. Noonan, codirector, Survey Research Associates. "A station cannot operate in a vacuum. It has to know who is listening and why before making any serious programming changes." Today this information is made available through several ratings services and research companies. More stations depend on Arbitron audience surveys than any other.

Since the collapse of Birch/Scarborough, broadcasters have had little choice but to subscribe to Arbitron—that or go without the listening estimates on which so many agencies and advertisers rely. However, the radio audience survey industry has begun to expand, if only slowly. For example, in recent years, additional listener/ratings services have begun to emerge. AccuRatings is one example. It began to measure audiences in major metropolitan areas in the mid-1990s. Troy research is another. It relies on Internet-based research that involves online surveys pertaining to stations' music playlists. Similar companies were beginning to surface to the relief of many broadcasters concerned with Arbitron's hold. Arbitron's dominance has indeed caused anxiety in the radio community. Many managers and programmers were more than disturbed by the failure of the alternative measurement service. Arbitron covers over 250 markets ranging in size from large to small. Arbitron claims over 2,700 radio clients and a staff of 3,000 interviewers who collect listening information from 2 million households across the country. All markets are measured at least once a year during the spring; however, larger markets are measured on an ongoing basis year round. Until the early 1980s, metro markets traditionally were rated in the spring and fall. However, six months between surveys was considered too long in light of the volatile nature of the radio marketplace.

To determine a station's ranking, Arbitron follows an elaborate procedure. First the parameters of the area to be surveyed are established. Arbitron sees fit to measure

FIGURE 6.1
Trade associations like
RAB offer broadcasters
detailed data on
which to base their
efforts. Courtesy RAB.

CONSUMER PROFILE
Adults 18-34

Gender

51 %
Men

49 %
Women

Income

Over $50,000	32%
$25,000-$50,000	40%
Under $25,000	28%

Occupation

Professional/Managerial	18%
Technical, Sales, and Administrative Support	20%
Service	11%
Precision Production and Craft & Farming, Forestry and Fishing	8%
Operators, Fabricators and Laborers	9%

Education

15%
High School
or Less

29%
Completed
High School

29%
Some College/
Trade School

27%
Completed
College
or More

Sociographic Shoppers Profile

Brand Loyal	27%
Cautious	49%
Venturesome	24%

Own Home   **58%**

Households with Children   **49%**

Average Weekday Non-Newspaper Readers   **48%**

Demographic Breakout

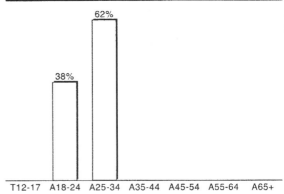

62%

38%

T12-17   A18-24   A25-34   A35-44   A45-54   A55-64   A65+

Lifestyle Profile by PRIZM® Groups

GROUP	DESCRIPTION	
S2	The Affluentials	10.7%
S3	Inner Suburbs	10.4%
S1	Elite Suburbs	9.8%
T3	Working Towns	8.6%
C2	2nd City Centers	7.9%
C3	2nd City Blues	7.5%
R3	Rustic Living	7.4%
T1	Landed Gentry	6.9%
U2	Urban Midscale	5.6%
T2	Exurban Blues	5.5%
R2	Heartlanders	4.9%
U3	Urban Cores	4.5%
R1	Country Families	3.9%
U1	Urban Uptown	3.8%
C1	2nd City Society	2.6%

Adults 18-34 Consumer Profile   *Media Targeting 2000 — conducted by The Arbitron Company in cooperation with the Radio Advertising Bureau*   3-A

FIGURE 6.1
continued

MEDIA HABITS
Adults 18-34

Average Weekday Share of Time Spent with Each Medium

6AM-6PM

Radio	48%
Television	39%
Newspapers	7%
Magazines	6%

Average time spent with all media: 4hrs., 49mins.

6AM-Mid

Radio	38%
Television	52%
Newspapers	5%
Magazines	5%

Average time spent with all media: 7hrs., 36mins.

Competitive Weekly Reach
(percent exposed to medium)

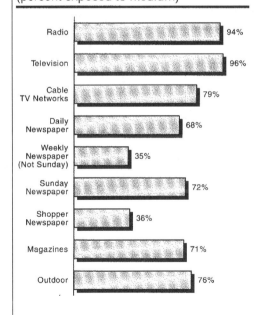

Radio	94%
Television	96%
Cable TV Networks	79%
Daily Newspaper	68%
Weekly Newspaper (Not Sunday)	35%
Sunday Newspaper	72%
Shopper Newspaper	36%
Magazines	71%
Outdoor	76%

Media Exposure Prior to Purchasing

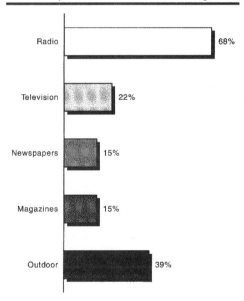

Radio	68%
Television	22%
Newspapers	15%
Magazines	15%
Outdoor	39%

**Percent of Shoppers Reached by Medium
Within 1 Hour of Largest Purchase**
*(Respondents reporting any purchase
within 24 hours prior to contact)*

3-B

*Media Targeting 2000 — conducted by
The Arbitron Company in cooperation with
the Radio Advertising Bureau*

Adults 18-34 Media Habits

FIGURE 6.1
continued

MEDIA HABITS
Adults 18-34

Shopping and Radio

96 %	Use Car When Shopping
92 %	Listen to Radio When Driving to Shop
32 MINUTES	Average Time Car Radio Is On When Driving to Shop

Eating Out and Radio

94 %	Use Car When Eating Out
90 %	Listen to Radio When Driving to Eat Out
26 MINUTES	Average Time Car Radio Is On When Driving to Eat Out

Radio Usage of Working Commuters

89 %	Commute by Car to Work
90 %	Listen to Radio While Car Commuting
46 MINUTES	Average Time Listening to Radio While Car Commuting

Availability of Radio at Work

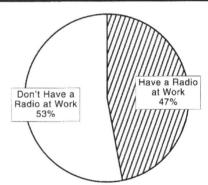

Don't Have a Radio at Work 53%

Have a Radio at Work 47%

Adults 18-34 Media Habits

Media Targeting 2000 — conducted by The Arbitron Company in cooperation with the Radio Advertising Bureau

3-C

REPORT CONTENTS AND MAP PAGE

This is the first page of an Arbitron Radio Market Report. This page, in addition to showing a map of the Radio Market survey area and table of Report contents, contains a basic introduction to the Report, restrictions on the use of the Report, a copyright infringement warning, the survey time period, frequency of measurement and Arbitron's schedule of radio surveys for the year.

1 ▶ The map shows the survey area(s) included in a market definition and for which audience estimates are reported. Areas in grey are not included in a market definition (unless it is a part of an ADI to be reported for that particular market) and will have no audience estimates included in the Report.

2 ▶ The Metro Survey Area (MSA) of the reported market is shown by horizontal hatching.

3 ▶ The Total Survey Area (TSA) of the reported market is shown in white.

4 ▶ The Areas of Dominant Influence (ADI) of the reported market, if applicable, is shown by diagonal hatching.

FIGURE 6.2
First page of an Arbitron Radio Market Report containing an explanation of what constitutes the survey area. Courtesy Arbitron.

FIGURE 6.3
Arbitron sample
explanation. Courtesy
Arbitron.

POPULATION ESTIMATES AND SAMPLE DISTRIBUTION BY AGE/SEX GROUP

1 ▶ The estimated populations of reported demographic categories within survey area(s) are reported for the Metro Survey Area, Area of Dominant Influence (where applicable), and the Total Survey Area.

2 ▶ The ratio (expressed as a percentage) of each reported demographic's estimated population to the estimated population of all persons age 12 or older within the relevant survey area.

3 ▶ The number of unweighted diaries in-tab, from persons in reported demographics, expressed as a percentage of the total number of unweighted in-tab diaries from all persons age 12 or older.

4 ▶ The distribution of in-tab diaries after weighting for reported demographics expressed as a percentage of the total number of tabulated diaries from all persons age 12 or older.

5 ▶ The total persons age 12 or older in the Metro and the percent of those persons living in military housing, college dormitories and other group quarters.

6 ▶ The number of estimated residences in the predesignated sample, number of homes contacted, number of homes in which diaries were placed, number of persons with whom diaries were placed and the number of persons who returned usable diaries (see The Sample, Section II, for further definition of these terms) are reported for Metro, ADI (if applicable), and TSA. Standard and ESF sample statistics are reported separately along with a total sample.

Total Survey Area

	1 Estimated Population	**2** Estimated Population as Percent of Tot. Persons 12 +	**3** Percent of Unweighted In-Tab Sample	**4** Percent of Weighted In-Tab Sample
Men 18-24	115,900	7.2	6.4	7.2
Men 25-34	139,900	8.7	8.5	8.7
Men 35-44	107,300	6.6	6.7	6.6
Men 45-49	49,400	3.1	2.5	3.1
Men 50-54	54,600	3.4	2.9	3.4
Men 55-64	96,300	6.0	7.0	6.0
Men 65 +	94,700	5.9	4.2	5.9

Area of Dominant Influence

Men 18-24	104,200	7.2	6.3	7.2
Men 25-34	124,900	8.6	8.1	8.6
Men 35-44	96,500	6.6	7.1	6.6
Men 45-49	44,800	3.1	2.3	3.1
Men 50-54	49,300	3.4	2.7	3.4
Men 55-64	86,300	5.9	7.0	5.9
Men 65 +	84,000	5.8	4.1	5.8

Metro Survey Area

Men 18-24	74,800	7.2	6.8	7.1
Men 25-34	90,900	8.6	8.5	8.6
Men 35-44	71,500	6.8	7.3	6.8
Men 45-49	33,500	3.2	2.4	3.2
Men 50-54	36,800	3.5	2.5	3.5
Men 55-64	62,300	5.9	6.7	5.9
Men 65 +	57,600	5.4	3.8	5.4

Metro Persons Living in Group Quarters

5 ▲

	% Military	% College	% Other Group Quarters
Total Persons 12 + 13,476,300	.1	.4	1.7

Diary Placement and Return Information

	Metro	ADI	TSA
Standard Residential Listings in Designated Sample	751	1,033	1,185
ESF Residential Listings in Designated Sample	359	380	383
Total Residential Listings in Designated Sample	1,110	1,413	1,568
Standard Contacts (homes in which telephone was answered)	740	1,023	1,568
ESF Contacts (homes in which telephone was answered)	353	359	374
Total Contacts (homes in which telephone was answered)	1,093	1,382	11,514
Standard Homes in Which Diaries Were Placed	657	920	1,037
ESF Homes in Which Diaries Were Placed	253	257	283
Total Homes in Which Diaries Were Placed	910	1,177	1,320
Standard Individuals Who Were Sent a Diary	1,562	2,210	2,487
ESF Individuals Who Were Sent a Diary	588	600	625
Total Individuals Who Were Sent a Diary	2,150	2,810	3,112
Standard Individuals Who Returned a Usable Diary (In-Tab)	1,031	1,421	1,610
ESF Individuals Who Returned a Usable Diary (In-Tab)	360	374	398
Total Individuals Who Returned a Usable Diary (In-Tab)	1,391	1,795	2,008

listening both in the city or urban center, which it refers to as the Metro Survey Area (MSA), and in the surrounding communities or suburbs, which it classifies Total Survey Area (TSA). Arbitron classifies a station's primary listening locations as its Areas of Dominant Influence (ADI).

Once the areas to be measured have been ascertained, the next thing Arbitron does is select a sample base composed of individuals to be queried regarding their listening habits. Metro-mail provides Arbitron with computer tapes that contain telephone and mailing lists from which the rating company derives its randomly selected sample. Arbitron conducts its surveys over a three- to four-week period, during which time new samples are selected weekly.

When the sample has been established, a letter is sent to each targeted household. The replacement letter informs members of the sample that they have been selected to participate in a radio listening survey and

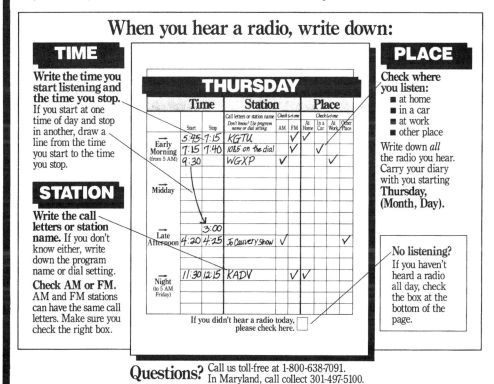

FIGURE 6.4
Instructions for filling out a diary. Accuracy is important. Courtesy Arbitron.

asks their cooperation. Within a couple of days after the letter has been received, an Arbitron interviewer calls to describe the purpose of the survey as well as to determine how many individuals aged 12 or older reside in the household. Upon receiving the go-ahead, Arbitron mails its seven-day survey diary, which requires respondees to log their listening habits. An incentive stipend of a dollar or two accompanies the document. The diary is simple to deal with, and the information it requests is quite basic: time (day/part) tuned to a station, station call letters or program name, whether AM or FM, and where listening occurred–car, home, elsewhere. Although the diary asks for information pertaining to age, sex, and residence, the actual identity or name of those participating is not requested.

FIGURE 6.5
Diary log sheet. This current sheet includes a checkmark box for "at work," a feature not found in earlier sheets. Courtesy Arbitron.

Prior to the start of the survey, a representative of Arbitron makes a presurvey follow-up call to those who have agreed to participate. This is done to make certain that the diary has been received and that everyone involved understands how to maintain it. Another follow-up call is made during the middle of the survey week to ascertain if the diary is being kept and to remind each participant to return it promptly on completion of the survey. Outside the metro area, follow-ups take the form of a letter. The diaries are mailed to Beltsville, Maryland, for processing and computation.

Arbitron claims that 65 out of every 100 diaries it receives are usable. Diaries that are inadequately or inaccurately filled out are not used. Upon arriving at Arbitron headquarters, diaries are examined by editors and rejected if they fail to meet criteria. Any diary received before the conclusion of the survey period is immediately voided, as are those that arrive more than 12 days after the end of the survey period. Diaries with blank or ambiguous entries also are rejected. Those diaries that survive the editors' scrutiny are then processed through the computer, and their information is tabulated. Computer printouts showing audience estimates are sent to subscribers. Stations receive the "book" within a few weeks after the last day of the survey.

The most recent research tool made available by Arbitron to its subscribers is a telephone-delivered radio market service called Arbitrends, which utilizes the IBM-Xr microcomputer to feed data to stations similarly equipped. Information regarding a station's past and current performances and those of competitors is available at the touch of a finger. Breakouts and tailor-made reports are provided on an ongoing basis by Arbitrends to assist stations in the planning of sales and marketing strategies. The survey company has over 13 billion characters reserved on computer disk packs. Arbitron also makes available its Arbitrends Rolling Average Printed Reports to those stations

without computers. To date, Arbitron has prepared over 380,000 radio market reports.

Arbitron's most formidable rival in recent years was Birch/Scarborough, headquartered in New Jersey. As a radio audience measurement service, Birch provided clients with both quantitative and qualitative data on local listening patterns, audience size, and demographics. Birch interviewers telephoned a prebalanced sample of households during the evening hours, seven days a week, to acquire the information they needed. "Respondents aged twelve or older were randomly selected from both listed and nonlisted telephone households. These calls were made from highly supervised company WATTS facilities," notes Phil Beswick, vice president of the defunct Birch/Scarborough broadcast services. The sample sizes varied depending on the size of the market being surveyed. For example, Birch/Scarborough contacted approximately 1,100 households in a medium market and between 2,000 and 8,000 in major metro markets.

A wide range of reports were available to clients, including the *Quarterly Summary Report* estimates of listening by location, county by county, and other detailed audience information; *Standard Market Report*, audience analysis especially designed for small market broadcasters; *Capsule Market Report*, listening estimates in the nation's smallest radio markets; *Condensed Market Report*, designed specifically for radio outlets in markets not provided with regular syndicated measurements and where cost was a key consideration; *Monthly Trend Report*, an ongoing picture of the listening audience so that clients might benefit from current shifts in the marketplace; *Prizm*, lifestyle-oriented radio ratings book that defined radio audiences by lifestyle characteristics in more than 85 markets; and BirchPlus, a microcomputerized system (IBM-PC) ratings retrieval and analysis. Fees for Birch/ Scarborough services were based on market size. Birch provided subscribers with general product consumption and media usage data. In late 1994, Arbitron purchased 50 percent of the Scarborough Research Corporation, with plans to offer stations expanded data about their listeners.

Dozens of other research companies throughout the country (among them Coleman Research, Bolton Research Corporation, Mark Kassof and Company, Spectrum Research, Frank N. Magid Associates, DIR, Star, Paragon Research, Shane Media, Hagan Media Research, Gallup Services, Mediabase, TAPSCAN, Rantel Research, and others cited herein) provide broadcasters with a broad range of useful audience information. Many utilize approaches similar to Arbitron (and formerly Birch) to collect data; still others use different methods. "Southeast Media Research offers four research methods: focus groups, telephone studies, mail intercepts, and music tests," explains Don Hagen, the company's president. Christopher Porter, associate director of Surrey Research, says that his company uses similar techniques.

Meanwhile, audience researcher Dick Warner claims that the telephone recall method is the most commonly used and effective approach to radio audience surveying. "The twenty-four-hour telephone recall interview, in my estimation, yields the most reliable information. Not only that, it is quick and current—important factors in a rapidly moving and hyperdynamic radio marketplace."

In her book *Listening In*, scholar Susan Douglas notes that new technologies have been developed to more effectively track listening. For instance, she cites databases such as MapMAKER that "can map the geography of a radio station's listeners and correlate their location with retailer trading areas." Says Douglas, "The company is developing a pocket people meter, based on the 'latest military technology,' designed to track radio listening electronically no matter where the person is and to eliminate the [Arbitron] diary altogether."

On the subject of music testing, Coleman Research's Rebecca Reising notes that her company's approach is unique. "We developed F.A.C.T., short for Fit Acceptance and Compatibility Test. F.A.C.T.'s proprietary research methods and sophisticated databases make it much more powerful, reliable, and useful than old-fashioned music testing methods. As quick and efficient as old tests, F.A.C.T. provides a sophistication of interpretation of music tests not offered by any other research company."

In the hyperactive radio industry arena, both traditional and novel audience survey techniques must ultimately prove themselves by assisting stations in their unrelenting quest for stronger ratings numbers.

Qualitative and Quantitative Data

Since their inception in the 1930s, ratings services primarily have provided broadcasters with information pertaining to the number of listeners of a certain age and gender tuned to a station at a given time. It was on the basis of these quantitative data that stations chose a format and advertisers made a buy.

Due to the explosive growth of the electronic media in recent years, the audience is presented with many more options, and the radio broadcaster, especially in larger markets, must know more about his intended listeners in order to attract and retain them. Subsequently, the need for more detailed information arose. In the 1990s, in-depth research is available to broadcasters from numerous sources. In this age of highly fragmented audiences, advertisers and agencies alike have become less comfortable with buying just numbers and look for audience qualities, notes Surrey's Christopher Porter. "The proliferation of stations has resulted in tremendous audience fragmentation. There are so many specialized formats out there, and many target the same piece of demographic pie. This predicament, if it can be called that, has made amply clear the need for qualitative, as well as quantitative, research. With so many stations doing approximately the same thing, differentiation is of paramount importance."

Today a station shooting for a top spot in the ratings surveys must be concerned with more than simply the age and sex of its target audience. Competitive programming strategies are built around an understanding and appreciation of the lifestyles, values, and behavior of those listeners sought by a station.

In-House Research Techniques

Research data provided by the major survey companies can be costly. For this reason and others, stations frequently conduct their own audience studies. Although stations seldom have the professional wherewithal and expertise of the research companies, they can derive useful information through do-it-yourself, in-house telephone, face-to-face, and mail surveys.

Telephone surveying is the most commonly used method of deriving audience data on the station level. It generally is less costly than the other forms of in-house research, and sample selection is less complicated and not as prone to bias. It also is the most expedient method. There are, however, a few things that must be kept in mind when conducting call-out surveys. One, not everyone has a phone and many numbers are unlisted. People also are wary of phone interviews for fear that the ultimate objective of the caller is to sell something. The public is inundated by phone solicitors (both human and computerized). Finally, extensive interviews are difficult to obtain over the phone. Five to 10 minutes usually is the extent to which an interviewee will submit to questioning. Call-out inter-

view seminars and instructional materials are available from a variety of sources, including the telephone company itself.

Internet and e-mail services provide another valuable means for those radio stations that survey their audiences. Many stations employ computers for call-out research purposes. There are many obvious benefits, interactivity and archiving foremost among them. The face-to-face or personal interview also is a popular research approach at stations, although the cost can be higher than call-out, especially if a vast number of individuals are being surveyed in an auditorium setting. The primary advan-

Quick questions

1 What is your age?
___ years

2 Are you male or female?
☐ Male ☐ Female
　1　　　2

3 Where do you live?
City _____
County _____
State _____
Zip _____

4 Do you work away from home?

☐ Yes ☐ No
　1　　2

If yes: How many hours per week do you usually work away from home? Check (✓) one.

Less than 20　20-29　30 or more
☐　　☐　　☐
1　　2　　3

Your opinion counts

Use this space to tell us how you feel about radio. Make any comments you like about stations, announcers or programs.

FIGURE 6.6
Diary holder demographic information page and further instructions. Courtesy Arbitron.

FIGURE 6.7
Arbitron estimates
show where a station
stands in its market.
Courtesy Arbitron.

AVERAGE SHARE TRENDS

The Trends section provides an indication of individual station performance and the relative standing among stations for periods prior to the most recent survey. The duration reported in this section may include as many as five discrete Arbitron survey rating periods, always including the most recent. Trends may not always reflect actual changes over time due to changes in methodology, station operations, etc.

1 ▶ The estimates reported are average persons shares in the Metro Survey Area, by individual stations, on the basis of broad demographics in specific dayparts. A share is the percent of all listeners in a demographic group that are listening to a specific station. This percent is calculated by dividing the Average Quarter-Hour Persons to a station by the Average Quarter-Hour Persons to all stations.

2 ▶ Total listening (Metro Totals) in the market, expressed as a rating, is also reported. This is the sum of all reported stations' Average Quarter-Hour estimates plus those for stations not meeting Minimum Reporting Standards and unidentified listening.

3 ▶ Reported dayparts are as follows:
Monday-Sunday 6AM-Midnight
Monday-Friday 6AM-10AM
Monday-Friday 10AM-3PM
Monday-Friday 3PM-7PM
Monday-Friday 7PM-Midnight

4 ▶ Reported demographics are as follows:
Total Persons 12+
Men 18+
Women 18+
Teens 12-17

5 ▶ A " + " indicates station changed call letters.

6 ▶ A "**" indicates station not reported for that survey.

Figure 6.7 (continued)

tages of the in-person interview are that questions can be more substantive and greater time can be spent with the respondees. Of course, more detailed interviews are time consuming and usually require refined interviewing skills, both of which can be cost factors.

Mail surveys can be useful for a host of reasons. To begin with, they eliminate the need to hire and train interviewers. This alone can mean a great deal in terms of money and time. Because no interviewers are involved, one source of potential bias also is eliminated. Perhaps most important is that individuals questioned through the mail are somewhat more inclined toward candor since they enjoy greater anonymity. The major problem with the mail survey approach stems from the usual low rate of response. One in every five questionnaires mailed may actually find its way back to the station. The length of the questionnaire must be kept relatively short, and the questions succinct and direct. Complex questions create resistance and may result in the survey being ignored or discarded.

Large and major market outlets usually employ someone to direct research and

FIGURE 6.8

Sample page from an Arbitron *Radio Report.* Courtesy Arbitron.

Average Quarter-Hour Listening Estimates

PHILADELPHIA — SUNDAY 3:00PM-7:00PM

AVERAGE PERSONS—TOTAL SURVEY AREA, IN HUNDREDS

TOT. PERS. 12+	MEN 18-24	25-34	35-44	45-54	55-64	WOMEN 18-24	25-34	35-44	45-54	55-64	TNS 12-17	STATION CALL LETTERS
392		13	27	27	27	3	6	30	21	65	6	KYW
-1												WBCB
625	15	38	42	59	106	3	31	47	23	66	9	WCAU
562	59	16	41	5	26	65	78	53	8		178	WCAU FM
100		23				4	8	8	9			WDAS
437	107	38	7	25	13	48	107	11	13	15	53	WDAS FM
358		7	19	41	28	3	28	4	58	47		WEAZ
108	11	6	4	35		5	20	8	12			WFIL
12				3								WFLN
166			13	12	14	3	18	10	28	9		WFLN FM
178			13	15	14	3	18	10	28	9		TOTAL
109		10			8		5	14	33	26	13	WHAT
52		1				18					33	WIFI
269	14	99	31			28	74	1	6		16	WIOQ
172		4	12	4	20		15	24	16	40	27	WIP
96		2	5	19		13	10	30	17			WKSZ
427	18	94	11	34		29	100	33	38	14	30	WMGK
423	95	93	3	2	6	73	75	15			61	WMMR
551		15	13	70	65	16	28	39	73	41		WPEN
3			1								2	WSNI
146		28	21			23	49				25	WSNI FM
149		28	22			23	49				27	TOTAL
32	11					9	4				3	WSSJ
585	116	116	31		12	69	79	43	5	7	107	WUSL
19									19			WVCH
270	15			26		5	28	27	13	55	1	WWDB
97	10	4	8	11		2	15	14	20	4	2	WWSH
432	88	86		2	10	124	40	3	9	5	65	WYSP
40			17				17				4	WZZD
122				40	30			2			32	WJBR FM
113	12	20				54					27	WPST
52	12	11		2		16			8		3	WSTW
24			18		6							WTTM
55								17	13			WOR

AVERAGE PERSONS—METRO SURVEY AREA, IN HUNDREDS

TOT. PERS. 12+	MEN 18-24	25-34	35-44	45-54	55-64	WOMEN 18-24	25-34	35-44	45-54	55-64	TNS 12-17	STATION CALL LETTERS
350		13	22	14	24	3	6	26	11	62	6	KYW
-1												WBCB
570	15	38	42	50	86	3	31	47	17	46	9	WCAU
420	59	16	27	5	26	59	51	28			126	WCAU FM
91		23				4	8	8				WDAS
343	32	38	7	25	13	48	88	11	13	15	53	WDAS FM
239		7	2	5	23	3		4	34	42		WEAZ
100	11	6	4	29		5	18	8	12		3	WFIL
12				3								WFLN
144			13	12	14	3	5	10	28	9		WFLN FM
156			13	15	14	3	5	10	28	9		TOTAL
109		10			8		5	14	33	26	13	WHAT
23		1				14					8	WIFI
263	14	94	31			28	74		6		16	WIOQ
144		4	12	4	20		13	24		30	27	WIP
76		2	5	10		9	10	30	10			WKSZ
374	18	83	11	27		29	70	28	38	14	30	WMGK
352	74	88	3	2	6	71	47	15			46	WMMR
533		15	13	70	47	16	28	39	73	41		WPEN
3			1								2	WSNI
146		28	21			23	49				25	WSNI FM
149		28	22			23	49				27	TOTAL
32	11					9	4				3	WSSJ
466	75	87	31		12	51	79	38	5	7	81	WUSL
-1												WVCH
237	15			26		5	28	27		55	1	WWDB
68	10	4	8	11		2	15	7	5	4	2	WWSH
289	63	52		2	10	75	8	3	9	5	62	WYSP
40			17				17				2	WZZD
18								2			13	WJBR FM
67	12	20				20					15	WPST
18				2		16						WSTW
24			18		6							WTTM
13											13	WOR

SHARES—METRO SURVEY AREA

TOT. PERS. 12+ %	MEN 18-24 %	25-34 %	35-44 %	45-54 %	55-64 %	WOMEN 18-24 %	25-34 %	35-44 %	45-54 %	55-64 %	TNS 12-17 %	STATION CALL LETTERS
5.7		1.9	6.7	3.9	6.5	.6	.8	6.3	3.6	16.2	1.1	KYW
												WBCB
9.3	3.1	5.5	12.8	13.9	23.3	.6	4.4	11.4	5.6	12.0	1.7	WCAU
6.9	12.2	2.3	8.2	1.4	7.0	11.3	7.2	6.8			23.4	WCAU FM
1.5		3.4				.8	1.1	1.9				WDAS
5.6	6.6	5.5	2.1	7.0	3.5	9.2	12.4	2.7	4.2	3.9	9.9	WDAS FM
3.9		1.0	.6	1.4	6.2		1.0	11.1	11.0			WEAZ
1.6	2.3		.9	1.2	8.1		1.0	2.5	1.9	3.9	.6	WFIL
.2					.8							WFLN
2.6			4.0	4.1	3.8	.6	.7	2.4	9.2	2.3		WFLN FM
2.6			4.0	4.1	3.8	.6	.7	2.4	9.2	2.3		TOTAL
1.8		1.5			2.2		.7	3.4	10.8	6.8	2.4	WHAT
.4		.1				2.7					1.5	WIFI
4.3	2.9	13.7	9.4			5.4	10.4		2.0		3.0	WIOQ
2.4		.6	3.6	1.1	5.4		1.8	5.8		7.8	5.0	WIP
1.2		.3	1.5	2.8		1.7	1.4	7.2	3.3			WKSZ
6.1	3.7	12.1	3.3	7.5		5.5	9.9	6.8	12.4	3.7	5.6	WMGK
5.8	15.3	12.8		.9	.6	1.6	13.6	6.6	3.6		8.6	WMMR
8.7		2.2	4.0	19.5	12.7	3.1	3.9	9.4	23.9	10.7		WPEN
.2												WSNI
2.4		4.1	6.4			4.4	6.9				4.6	WSNI FM
2.4		4.1	6.7			4.4	6.9				5.0	TOTAL
.5	2.3					1.7	.6				.6	WSSJ
7.6	15.5	12.7	9.4		3.3	9.8	11.1	9.2	1.6	1.8	15.1	WUSL
												WVCH
3.9	3.1			7.2		1.0	3.9	6.5		14.4	.2	WWDB
1.1	2.1	.6	2.4	3.1		.4	2.1	1.7	1.6	1.0	.4	WWSH
4.7	13.0	7.6			.6	2.7	14.3	1.1	.7	2.9	1.3	WYSP (11.5)
.7				4.7				2.4		1.0	.4	WZZD
.3					3.5			.5		.8		WJBR FM
1.1	2.5	2.9				3.8					2.8	WPST
.3			.6			3.1						WSTW
.3			5.5	1.6								WTTM
.2										3.4		WOR

| | TOTAL LISTENING IN METRO SURVEY AREA | 6102 | 484 | 686 | 329 | 359 | 369 | 523 | 710 | 414 | 306 | 383 | 538 |

Footnote Symbols: (*) means audience estimates adjusted for actual broadcast schedule.

ARBITRON RATINGS

survey efforts. This person works closely with upper management and department heads, especially the program director and sales manager. These two areas require data on which to base programming and marketing decisions. At smaller outlets, area directors generally are responsible for conducting surveys relevant to their department's needs. A case in point would be the PD who plans a phone survey during a special broadcast to help ascertain whether it should become a permanent program offering. To accomplish this task, the programmer enlists the aid of a secretary and two interns from a local college. Calls are made, and data are collected and analyzed.

The objective of a survey must be clear from the start, and the methodology used to acquire data should be as uncomplicated as possible. Do-it-yourself surveys are limited in nature, and overly ambitious goals and expectations are seldom realized. However, in-house research can produce valuable information that can give a station a competitive edge. Today, no radio station can operate in a detached way and expect to prosper.

Every station has numerous sources of information available to it. Directories containing all manner of data, such as population statistics and demographics, manufacturing and retailing trends, and so on, are available at the public library, city hall, chamber of commerce, and various business associations. The American Marketing Association and American Research Foundation also possess information designed to guide stations with their in-house survey efforts.

Research Deficits

Although broadcasters refer deferentially to the ratings surveys as the "book" or "bible," the stats they contain are audience-listening estimates—no more, and, it is hoped, no less. Since their inception, research compa-

nies have been criticized for the methods they employ in collecting audience listening figures. The most prevalent complaint has had to do with the selection of samples. Critics have charged that they invariably are limited and exclusionary. Questions have persisted as to whether those surveyed are truly representative of an area's total listenership. Can 1 percent of the radio universe accurately reflect general listening habits? The research companies defend their tactics and have established a strong case for their methodology.

In the 1970s, ratings companies were criticized for neglecting minorities in their surveys. In efforts to rectify this deficiency, both Arbitron and Birch established special sampling procedures. The incidence of nontelephone households among Blacks and Hispanics tends to be higher. The survey companies also had to deal with the problem of measuring Spanish-speaking people. Arbitron found that using the personal-retrieval technique significantly increased the response rate in the Spanish community, especially when bilingual interviewers were used. The personal-retrieval technique did not work as well with Blacks, since it was difficult to recruit interviewers to work in many of the sample areas. Thus, Arbitron used a telephone retrieval procedure that involved callbacks to selected households over a seven-day period to document listening habits. In essence, the interviewer filled out the diaries for those being surveyed. In 1982, Arbitron implemented Differential Survey Treatment (DST), a technique designed to increase the response rate among Blacks. The survey company provides incentives over the customary 50 cents to $1 to certain Black households. Up to $5 is paid to some respondents. DST employs follow-up calls to retrieve diaries.

During its years of operation Birch/Scarborough Research employed special sampling procedures and bilingual interviewers to collect data from the Hispanic population. According to the company, its samples yielded a high response rate among Blacks. Thus, Birch did not use other special sampling controls. Ethnic listening reports containing average quarter-hour and cume estimates for Hispanics, Blacks, and others were available from the company in a format similar to that of its Capsule Market Report.

Both survey companies employed additional procedures to survey other nontelephone households, especially in markets that have a large student or transient population. In the late 1970s, a Boston station targeting young people complained that Arbitron failed to acknowledge the existence of over 200,000 college students who did not have personal phone listings. The station, which was rated among the top five in the market at the time, contended that a comprehensive survey of the city's listening audience would bear out the fact that they were, in fact, number one.

Similar complaints of skewed or inconclusive surveys persist today, but the procedures and methods used by the major radio audience research companies, although far from perfect, are more effective than ever. Christopher Porter says the greatest misconception about research data is that they are absolutes etched in granite. "The greatest fallacy is that research findings are gospel. This goes not only for the quantitative studies but for focus groups as well. Regardless of the methodology, any findings should be used as a 'gut adjuster,' rather than a 'gut replacer.' Sampling error is often ignored in a quantitative study, even in an Arbitron report. When we report that 25 percent of a sample feels some way about something, or when a station with a 4.1 beats one with a 3.8 in a book, most station managers and PDs take all these statistics at face value."

Rip Ridgeway, former vice president of Arbitron Ratings, believes that stations place too much emphasis on survey results. "I think that station hierarchy puts too much credence on the ratings estimates. They're an indicator, a sort of report card on a

station's performance. They're not the absolute end all. To jump at the next numbers and make sweeping changes based on them generally is a big mistake."

Radio executive Lorna Ozman concurs with both Porter and Ridgeway and warns that research should help direct rather than dictate what a station does. "I use research, rather than letting it use me. The thing to remember is that no methodology is without a significant margin of error. To treat the results of a survey as gospel is dangerous. I rely on research to provide me with the black-and-white answers and depend on

FIGURE 6.9
Radio station promotional pieces often reflect research and survey data provided by Arbitron and other companies. Courtesy WBMX.

THE MARKET

RADIO ADVERTISING VS. OTHER MEDIA

According to figures from Robert Coen, Senior Vice President, Director of Forecasting at McCann Erickson, radio presently accounts for $8.8 billion in annual revenue. Of this $8.8 billion, $2.1 billion is attributed to "national" sales, while $6.7 billion is considered "local" sales. The combined total translates into approximately 7% of the total $130 billion advertising marketplace.

By contrast, television (broadcast and cable) accounts for $28.3 billion in annual revenue, approximately 22% of the total marketplace, print (newspaper and magazine) accounts for $40.5 billion, or 31% of the market, direct mail accounts for $23.2 billion, or 18% of the market, and other media account for $29.6 billion or 23%.

CONSUMER INFLUENCE VS. SHARE OF MARKET

A look at each medium's average consumer influence time versus share of total advertising revenue shows a startling imbalance for radio in the total marketplace. Despite its 36% of consumer influence time, radio only has 7% of total advertising revenue.

The other media consumer influence shares vs. share of total marketplace are significantly more in line. Television has a 49% consumer influence time, controlling 22% of the advertising marketplace, Print (newspapers and magazines) has 15% consumer influence time, controlling 31% of the marketplace.

TOTAL ADVERTISING BY MEDIA
1990 PROJECTIONS BY McCANN-ERICKSON
TOTAL DOLLARS IN MILLIONS

SHARE OF TIME SPENT WITH MEDIA VS.
SHARE OF TOTAL ADVERTISING DOLLARS

FIGURE 6.10
The Interep Radio Store Research Division conducts ongoing research designed to enhance radio's take of the national advertising budget. Courtesy Interep Radio Stores.

myself to make determinations on the gray areas. Research never provided a radio station with the glitter to make it sparkle."

Station general manager Richard Bremkamp also expresses concern over what he perceives as an almost obsessive emphasis on survey statistics. "The concern for numbers gets out of hand. There are some really good-sounding stations out there that don't do good book, but the money is in the numbers. Kurt Vonnegut talks about the 'Universal Will to Become' in his books. In radio that can be expanded to the Universal Will to Become Number One. This is good if it means the best, but that's not always what it means today."

The proliferation of data services has drawn criticism from broadcasters who feel that they are being oversurveyed and over-researched. When Arbitron introduced its computerized monthly ratings service (Arbitrends), the chairman of its own radio advisory council opposed the venture on the grounds that it would cause more confusion and create more work for broadcasters. He further contended that the monthly service would encourage short-term buying by advertisers. Similar criticism was lodged against Birch/Scarborough's own computerized service, BirchPlus. However, both services experienced steady growth.

Compounding the task of audience surveying, says Ed Shane, is the fact that "lower response rates are affecting all research." Continues Shane, "Telephone research operations have the same problem because people are burned out on solicitation by phone. For a recent research project, we made 20,100 phone calls to yield 405 respondents. As already indicated, some researchers suggest turning to the Internet for surveys. It's sure convenient, because the respondents come to the researcher. However, until Internet usage levels are as ubiquitous as the telephone, the sample generated from Internet surveys is not projectable across the population as a whole."

David Pearlman concurs. "Audience research is increasingly hard to acquire. Response rates is the foremost issue facing Arbitron, or any one else measuring listening or consumer habits."

How Agencies Buy Radio

The primacy of numbers perhaps is best illustrated through a discussion of how advertising agencies place money on radio stations. It is the media buyer's job to effectively and efficiently invest the advertiser's money—in other words, to reach the most listeners with the budget allotted for radio use. According to media buyer Lynne Price, the most commonly employed method determines the cost per point (CPP) of a given station. Lynne explains the procedure: "A media buyer is given a budget and a gross rating point (GRP) goal. Our job is to buy to our GRP goal, without going over budget, against a predetermined target audience, i.e., adults 25 to 54, teens, men 18 to 34, etc. Our CPP is derived by taking the total budget and dividing by the GRP goal, or total number of rating points we would like to amass against our target audience. Now, using the CPP as a guideline, we take the cost per spot on a given station, and divide by the rating it has to see how close to the total CPP the station is. This is where

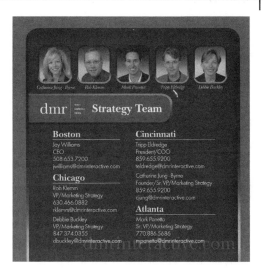

FIGURE 6.11
The more a station knows about its audience, the more effectively it can program itself. Courtesy DMR.

the negotiation comes in. If the station is way off, you can threaten not to place advertising until they come closer to what you want to spend."

The other method used to justify station buys is cost per thousand (CPM). Using this technique, the buyer determines the cost of reaching 1,000 people at a given station. The CPM of one station is then compared with that of another's to ascertain efficiency. To determine a station's CPM, the buyer must know the station's average quarter-hour audience (AQH persons) estimate in the daypart targeted and the cost of a commercial during that time frame. The following computation will provide the station's CPM: by dividing the number of people reached into the cost of the commercial, the cost per thousand is deduced.

$$\frac{\$30 \text{ for } 60 \text{ seconds}}{25 \ (000) \ AQH} = \$1.20 \text{ CPM}$$

Thus, the lower the CPM, the more efficient the buy. Of course, this assumes that the station selected delivers the target audience sought. Again, this is the responsibility of the individual buying media for an agency. It should be apparent by now that many things are taken into consideration before airtime is purchased.

Careers in Research

The number of media research companies grew rapidly since the late 1960s but slowed in the post Telecom Act 1990s as station consolidation became the rule of the land. Today dozens of research houses nationwide offer audience measurement and survey data to the electronic media and allied fields. Job opportunities in research have increased proportionately. Persons wanting to work in the research area need sound educational backgrounds, says Surrey's Porter. "College is essential. An individual attempting to enter the field today without formal training is at a serious disadvantage. In fact, a master's degree is a good idea." Dr. Rob Balon, president of Balon and Associates, agrees with Porter. "Entering the research field today requires substantial preparation. College research courses are where to start."

Researcher Ed Noonan is of the same opinion. "It is a very competitive and demanding profession. Formal training is very important. I'd advise anyone planning a career in broadcast research to get a degree in communications or some related field and heavy-up on courses in research methodology and analysis, statistics, marketing, and computers. Certain business courses are very useful, too."

To Don Hagen of Southeast Media Research, a strong knowledge of media is a key criterion when hiring. "One of the things that I look for in a job candidate is a college background in electronic media. That's the starting point. You have to know more today than ever before. Audience research has become a complex science."

As might be expected, research directors also place considerable value on experience. "The job prospect who offers some

experience in the research area, as well as a diploma, is particularly attractive," notes researcher Dick Warner. Ed Noonan concurs. "Actual experience in the field, even if it is gained in a summer or part-time job, is a big plus." Christopher Porter advises aspiring researchers to work in radio to get a firsthand feel for the medium. "A hands-on knowledge of the broadcast industry is invaluable, if not vital, in this profession."

In the category of personal attributes, Dick Warner puts inquisitiveness at the top of the list. "An inquiring mind is essential. The job of the researcher is to find and collect facts and information. Curiosity is basic to the researcher's personality." Don Hagen adds objectivity and perceptiveness to the list, and Dwight Douglas of Burkhart/Douglas and Associates emphasizes interactive skills. "People skills are essential, since selling and servicing research clients are as important as the research itself."

Although not everyone is suited for a career in audience research, those who are find the work intellectually stimulating and financially rewarding.

The Future of Research in Radio

Most experts agree that the role of research in radio will continue to grow despite the trend toward downsizing and clustering. They base their predictions on the ever-increasing fragmentation and niching of the listening audience, which makes the jobs of targeting and positioning more complex. "The field of broadcast research has grown considerably in the last two decades, and there is every reason to suspect that the growth will continue. As demographic targets and formats splinter, there will be an increasingly greater need to know. Much of the gut feel that has propelled radio programming will give way to objective

Ted Bolton

FIGURE 6.12
Ted Bolton.

Bolton is a quantitative research company—our main objective is to get the opinions of radio listeners on virtually anything having to do with the sound of a given station (or future station). There are several methods we use to get the info:

- **Perceptual studies**. These are in-depth surveys that gather opinions on issues such as music preferences, station personalities, competitors, etc. All respondents are included based on their age, listening habits (e.g., favorite station), favorite music types, ethnicity, county of residence, and anything else of importance to the station (client). These surveys run 15 to 20 minutes.

Respondents are selected at random. We also do tracking studies,

What a Research Company Does

which include respondents from the original survey and which measure changes in opinion (usually six months out from the original survey).

Perceptual studies are the foundation of research, because they provide overall market information: perceptions of the client's station and its competitors, which the station uses to make programming, marketing, and sales decisions. The information gathered also aids us in designing a research program for the station.

- **Music and program testing**.
  There are several commonly used methods for testing music and program elements.

1. *Auditorium testing*. This is the industry standard for testing music that may be aired on the station. Respondents are screened according to station listenership, and paid an incentive between $35 and $50, depending on market size. The typical test involves 100 to 150 respondents; they are usually split into two groups. Each group gathers at a hotel, where they listen on speakers to 350 to 400 hooks (5 to 10 seconds of a song, the most memorable part). In total, 700 to 800 hooks will be tested. The respondents score each hook, using a 1 to 5 (or similar) scale. They also note if they are familiar with the song, and give it a burn score if they're tired of hearing the song.
Bolton does "Personalized Music Tests" (PMT) instead of auditorium tests. Respondents in a PMT come to a facility at a time of their choice, and they test the hooks on

Walkman-style cassette players with headphones. We've found that we have a better turnout than the auditorium tests, and that the results are better because each respondent hears the hooks the same way (in an auditorium, respondents are at different distances from the speakers) without distractions from other listeners. Auditorium tests are still the industry standard, however.

2. *Perceptual analyzer tests*. In both of the previous methods, respondents typically score hooks with paper and pencil. The data then must be coded and tabulated before the client sees the results. A recent development, perceptual analyzer tests, gives a client instant information. Respondents give their scores on dials or keypads, which are hooked into a computer. As the scores are given, the computer produces an instant, continuous EKG-like graph that shows averages for different groups—a station's "core" listeners and its competitors' listeners, for instance. We've found this method (we call the test "BoltScan") to be most useful in testing music in the original order that it actually aired, thereby showing us both popular songs that keep listeners tuned in, and the stuff that causes tune-out. It works the same way for testing morning shows, comedy bits, and so on.

3. *Call-out music research*. This is a staple of radio programming. Respondents of a specific age and listening group–typically core listeners in a tight age range–are

called at home and asked to score 25 to 30 hooks. The test is obviously short, and can be conducted biweekly or even weekly. This information is most useful for trending the familiarity, popularity, and burnout of songs (usually new songs) over time. Call-out is a task often assigned to station interns, but a number of research companies offer the service as well.

4. *Focus groups and listener panels.* Focus groups are, of course, used for all kinds of consumer product testing, and radio is no exception. Again, respondents are screened for age and listenership. Chosen participants are paid a small incentive, and come to a focus group facility or hotel room in groups of 8 to 12. Station staff observe while the moderator asks the respondents about their likes and dislikes of station attributes, including music preferences, personalities, competing stations, etc.

Listener panels are more informal and are usually done in-house by the station. Respondents are recruited on the air or from the station's database. Again, respondents are asked for their opinions about the station.

5. *Statistics.* Although some complicated statistical methods are sometimes used, the vast majority of data analysis involves "descriptive" statistics: frequency and average scores. Frequency is a computation of how many people fit into a category or choose a given response to a question. Averages (mean, median, mode) are measures of average or typical performance. For most research reports, these basic statistics are enough.

Some more sophisticated statistics are used to look for relationships and differences between groups: correlation ANOVA (analysis of variance), t-tests, chi-square, and cluster and factor analysis. For instance, we often use cluster analysis to separate respondents into distinct groups, such as Modern Rock and Classic Rock lovers. This helps a station to determine which artists are unique elements in a specific audience's tastes.

Why do research? Not every radio programmer is a convert to the gospel of research. It is expensive, and stations are always on a tight budget. Many programmers have done just fine using experience and their gut to get them through. Additionally, as people become more guarded with their privacy, both in terms of personal information and home invasion with the telephone, research becomes a more difficult and expensive proposition.

Yet the market intelligence research provides is vital to the stations. As deregulation approaches, and station values skyrocket, gut feelings alone won't be enough to keep a multimillion dollar station on top. Research provides information that can make the gut feeling more of a sure thing, or tell you that your gut is all wrong. But it is a tool, much as a computer or a tape recorder is. Even the best research is useless if it's not studied and properly applied. And shoddy research *can* do a lot more harm than good.

Bolton Research Director Doug Keith assembled the preceding material.

research that is based on a plan," contends Dwight Douglas.

Christopher Porter sees the fragmentation and niching as creating a greater demand for research. "With the inevitability of more competition in already overcrowded markets, the need to stay abreast of market developments is critical. Yes, the role of research will continue to grow."

Although the role of research in the programming of large market stations is significant, the expense involved will continue to limit many smaller stations to in-house methods, claims Ed Noonan. "Professional research services can be very costly. This will keep research to a minimum in lesser markets, although there will be more movement there than in the past. Call-out research will continue to be a mainstay for the small station."

"Cost-effective ways to perform and utilize sophisticated psychographic data have made the computer standard equipment at most stations, small and large alike. Research is becoming a way of life everywhere, and computers are an integral part of the information age. Computers encourage more do-it-yourself research at stations, as well," contends WGAO station manager Vic Michaels.

FIGURE 6.13
Arbitron's Portable People Meter (PPM) was met with opposition. Courtesy Arbitron.

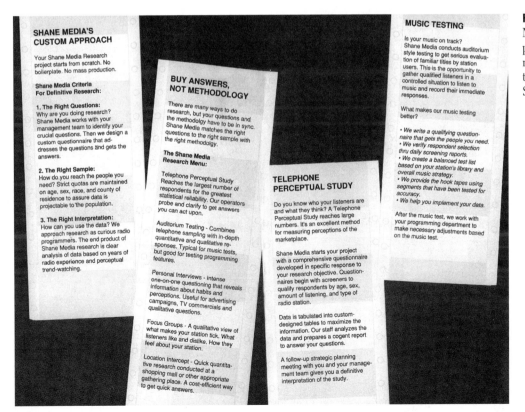

FIGURE 6.14
Many consultants provide a host of research services to their clients. Courtesy Shane Media.

Dick Warner contends that technological advances also will improve the nature and quality of research. "We'll see more improvement in methodology and a greater diversity of applicable data as the result of high-tech innovations. I think the field of research will take a quantum leap in the 1990s. It has in the 1970s and 1980s, but the size of the leap will be greater in the last decade of this century."

Today it is common for stations to budget 5 to 10 percent of their annual income to research, and it is probable that this figure will increase, says Christopher Porter. "As it evolves, it is likely that the marketplace will demand that more funds be allocated for research purposes. Research may not guarantee success, but it's not getting any easier to be successful without it."

Research has been a part of radio broadcasting since its modest beginnings in the 1920s, and it appears that it will play an even greater role in the operations of stations as the new century unfolds.

CHAPTER HIGHLIGHTS

1. Beginning in the late 1920s, surveys were conducted to determine the most popular stations and programs with various audience groupings. Early surveys (and their methods) included C. E. Hooper, Inc. (telephone), Cooperative Analysis of Broadcasting (telephone), and The Pulse (in-person). In 1968 Radio's All Dimension Audience Research (telephone to 6,000 households) began to provide information for networks. The current leader among local market audience surveys is Arbitron (week-long diary).

2. In 1963 the Broadcast Rating Council was established to monitor, audit, and accredit ratings companies. In 1982 it was renamed the Electronic Media Planning Council to reflect its involvement with cable television ratings.

3. Arbitron measures listenership in the Metro Survey Area (MSA); that is, the city or urban center, and the Total Survey Area (TSA), which covers the surrounding communities.

4. A station's primary listening locations are called Areas of Dominant Influence (ADI).

5. The Arbitron daily diary logs time tuned to a station; station call letters or program name; whether AM or FM; where listening occurred; and the listener's age, sex, and area of residence.

6. From the late 1970s to the early 1990s, Birch/Scarborough gathered data by calling equal numbers of male and female listeners aged 12 and over. Clients were offered seven different report formats, including a computerized data retrieval system. The company went out of business on December 31, 1991.

7. With today's highly fragmented audiences, advertisers and agencies are less comfortable buying just ratings numbers and look for audience qualities. Programmers must consider not only the age and sex of the target audience, but also their lifestyles, values, and behavior.

8. Station in-house surveys utilize telephone, computer, face-to-face, and mail methods.

9. In response to complaints about "missed" audiences, the major survey companies adjusted their survey techniques to ensure inclusion of minorities and nontelephone households. Today's survey results are more accurate.

10. Ratings data should only direct, not dictate, what a station does.

11. Media buyers for agencies use station ratings to determine the most cost-effective buy for their clients. Two methods they use are the cost per rating point (CPP) and the cost per thousand (CPM).

FIGURE 6.15
Targeting the right
audience is what it's
all about. Courtesy
Infinity.

FIGURE 6.16
Web sites offer stations
enormous research
opportunities.
Courtesy RRR.

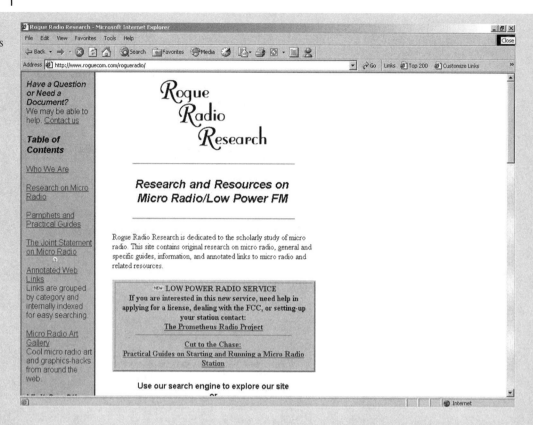

12. Although the significant increase in the number of broadcast research companies (several dozen nation-wide) has created a growing job market, a college education is necessary. Courses in communications, research methods, statistics, marketing, computers, and business are useful. Beneficial personal traits include inquisitiveness, objectivity, perceptiveness, and interpersonal skills.

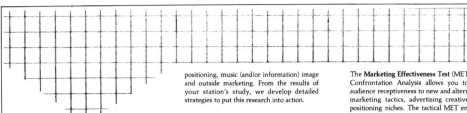

THE BENCHMARK STUDY™ Perceptual/Strategic

The Benchmark Study is a custom telephone perceptual study of your marketplace conducted from our international interviewing center in Austin. This is essential once per year in every competitive market and is recommended at six month intervals for new formats and highly volatile, changing, competitive situations. A benchmark is anything a listener uses to reconstruct radio listening in an unaided recall situation (such as an Arbitron diary or Birch interview). The higher the level of unaided recall, the higher the ratings. You receive detailed descriptions of your station's (and competitors') benchmarks as well as strategic recommendations for maximizing benchmark opportunities. Don't let budget constraints keep you from investing in needed research. Benchmark has devised an innovation which allows these studies to generate direct revenue for your station. This can cover your research investment and even become an additional revenue center.

The **Marketing Effectiveness Test** (MET) is a part of The Benchmark Study. This examines listener understanding of your station's handle, positioning, music (and/or information) image and outside marketing. From the results of your station's study, we develop detailed strategies to put this research into action.

FORMAT PREFERENCE STUDIES

Format Preference Studies actually use a variety of methods depending on the market situation. The goals are to identify a potentially profitable niche in the market, to design a product for that niche that serves the listener's needs and to create a marketing plan that will establish and nurture the new format. In testing for a music niche, we use a system of playing *actual audio music mixes* down the phone line instead of relying on verbal descriptions of the artists.

THE CONFRONTATION ANALYSIS™ Evaluation/Tactical

Confrontation Analysis is an auditorium research technique which has replaced focus groups as the primary method of gathering *evaluative* information. It takes its name from the process in which listeners "confront" taped audio and video segments of programming and advertising. This "confrontation" triggers open-end evaluative responses that would be impossible to obtain in a telephone survey. Yet, unlike focus groups, Confrontation Analysis eliminates bias of group interaction, moderator bias and solves the problem of small sample size. You receive reliable evaluations on the effectiveness of various tactical approaches.

The **Marketing Effectiveness Test** (MET) in a Confrontation Analysis allows you to test audience receptiveness to new and alternative marketing tactics, advertising creative and positioning niches. The tactical MET ensures that you are effectively communicating with the diarykeeper.

FREQUENCY BASED MUSIC TEST™ Cluster Analysis

Available in the form of call-out research and *auditorium* testing, the Frequency Based Music Test is a proven technique which effectively measures burnout as well as answering the question of how often listeners *really* want to hear a record. As with all Benchmark research services, all the work is done in-house with no "farming out." From recruiting to data processing, we deliver you a professional, high quality music report.

CUSTOM RESEARCH AND CONSULTATION

With over ten years of radio research experience, The Benchmark Company will design custom research to fit your exact needs. From agency/advertiser studies to vulnerability testing and advertising pre-tests, The Benchmark Company has the experience to help you solve problems and take advantage of opportunities.

FIGURE 6.17
Services available from one research company. Courtesy The Benchmark Company.

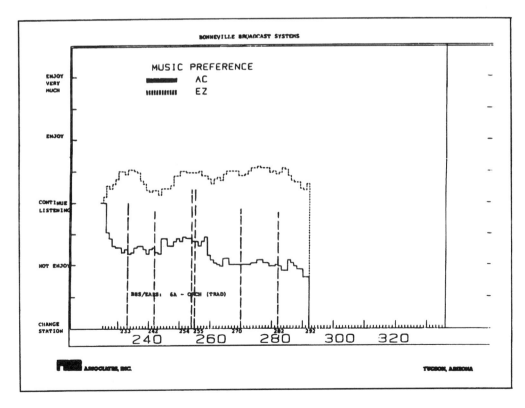

FIGURE 6.18
The electronic music testing graph shows where listening drops off. In this test the preferences of Adult Contemporary and Easy Listening listeners were gauged as certain tunes were played. Courtesy FMR Associates.

FIGURE 6.19
The electronic music testing graph shows audience reaction to specific songs. Even the ID is tested. Courtesy FMR Associates.

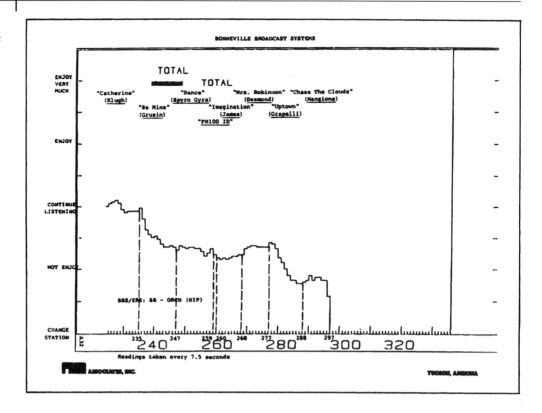

FIGURE 6.20
Demographic information is still the coin of the realm in audience research despite a much more qualitative orientation by advertisers. Courtesy Arbitron.

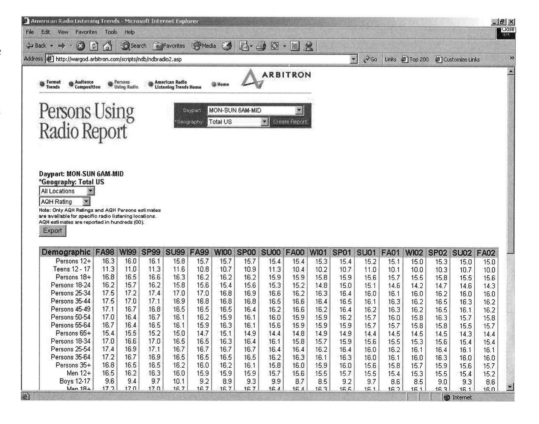

Radio
RESEARCH REPORT
From Robert E. Galen, Senior Vice President, Research

AVOID RADIO PLANNING ERRORS BEWARE OF:

- ## THE GRP TRAP
- ## THE CPP MYTH

FIGURE 6.21
Some broadcasters contend that there are inherent failures in across-the-board GRP/CPP buying by agencies. RAB publishes this report to caution against the pitfalls of buying formulas. Courtesy RAB.

FIGURE 6.22
APPENDIX 6A: RAB'S Radio Research Glossary.

RADIO RESEARCH GLOSSARY

RAB Guide To Key Terms And Formulas

A wealth of terminology has come to describe the many dimensions of Radio audience research. As new buying and planning techniques are developed, new terms are added to the vocabulary and even established terms take on new meanings. To help you understand and use today's language of Radio audience research, RAB has prepared this brief guide.

FIGURE 6.22
continued

AUDIENCE RESEARCH TERMS

AVERAGE QUARTER-HOUR AUDIENCE (AQH PERSONS)

An average of the number of people listening for at least five minutes in each quarter-hour over a specified period of time. In modern Radio average quarter-hour measurement should be considered a measure of Total Time Spent Listening (see below).

AVERAGE QUARTER-HOUR RATING (AQH RATING)

Average Quarter-Hour Audience expressed as a percentage of the population being measured. *

$$\text{AQH PERSONS} \div \text{POPULATION} = \text{AQH RATING}$$

SHARE OF AUDIENCE (SHARE)

The percentage of those listening to Radio in the AQH that are listening to a particular station.

$$\text{AQH PERSONS} / \text{ONE STATION} \div \text{AQH PERSONS} / \text{RADIO} = \text{SHARE}$$

Because the AQH actually reflects Total Time Spent Listening, Share Of Audience is the share of Total Time Spent Listening to Radio.

CUMULATIVE AUDIENCE (CUME PERSONS)

Also called Unduplicated Audience, it is the number of different people listening for at least five minutes during a specified period of time. Cume Audience is the potential group that can be exposed to advertising on a radio station, just as readership is the potential exposure group for a magazine or newspaper.

CUMULATIVE RATING (CUME RATING)

Cumulative Audience expressed as a percentage of the population being measured. *

$$\text{CUME PERSONS} \div \text{POPULATION} = \text{CUME RATING}$$

TOTAL TIME SPENT LISTENING (TTSL)

The number of quarter-hours of listening to Radio or to a station by the population group being measured. *

$$\text{AQH PERSONS} \times \text{QUARTER-HOURS IN TIME PERIOD} = \text{TTSL} \text{(IN QUARTER HOURS)}$$

AVERAGE TIME SPENT LISTENING (TSL)

The time spent listening by the average person who listens to Radio or to a station.

$$\text{TTSL} \div \text{CUME PERSONS} = \text{TSL}$$

Average Time Spent Listening is an indicator of audience availability to advertising messages. The more time spent listening, the greater opportunity for exposure and ability to develop frequency.

AUDIENCE TURNOVER (T/O)

The number of times the Average Quarter-Hour Audience is replaced by new listeners in a specified period of time. Audience Turnover is also the number of announcements required to reach approximately 50% of the station's Cumulative Audience in the time period.

$$\text{CUME PERSONS} \div \text{AQH PERSONS} = \text{T/O}$$

The population being measured can be all people or any demographic group.

FIGURE 6.22
continued

SCHEDULE MEASUREMENT TERMS

REACH

The number of different people who are exposed to a schedule of announcements, i.e., those listening during a quarter-hour when announcements are aired.

Reach can also be expressed as a Rating (percentage of the population being measured):

PERSONS REACHED ÷ POPULATION = REACH RATING

GROSS IMPRESSIONS

The total number of exposures to a schedule of announcements. Not a measure of the number of different people exposed to a commercial.

AQH PERSONS × NUMBER OF ANNOUNCEMENTS = GROSS IMPRESSIONS

FREQUENCY

The average number of times the audience reached by an advertising schedule (those listening during a quarter-hour when an announcement is aired) is exposed to a commercial.

GROSS IMPRESSIONS ÷ REACH = FREQUENCY

GROSS RATING POINTS (GRPs)

Gross Impressions expressed as a percentage of the population being measured. * One Rating Point equals one percent of the population.

GROSS IMPRESSIONS ÷ POPULATION = GRPs

It can also be derived by combining AQH Ratings:

AQH RATING × NUMBER OF ANNOUNCEMENTS = GRPs

COST PER THOUSAND (CPM)

The basic term to express Radio's unit cost. It establishes 1000 as the basic unit for comparing Radio values. Most frequently used to compare the cost of 1000 Gross Impressions on different stations, it can also be used to compare the cost of reaching 1000 people.

$$\frac{\text{SCHEDULE COST}}{\text{GROSS IMPRESSIONS (IN THOUSANDS)}} = \text{CPM}$$

COST PER RATING POINT (CPP)

An expression of Radio's unit cost using a Rating Point, which is one percent of the population being measured *. Cost Per Rating Point is often used for planning Radio in conjunction with GRPs.

$$\frac{\text{SCHEDULE COST}}{\text{GROSS RATING POINTS}} = \text{CPP}$$

* The population being measured can be all people or any demographic group.

FIGURE 6.22
continued

REACH / FREQUENCY EVALUATIONS

REACH / FREQUENCY FORMULAS

There are three factors in any Reach / Frequency formula: 1) Reach, 2) Frequency and 3) GRPs. Their relationship is expressed in these formulas, with any two factors predicting the third:

$$REACH \times FREQUENCY = GRPs$$
$$GRPs \div FREQUENCY = REACH$$
$$GRPs \div REACH = FREQUENCY$$

For example, if 100 GRPs are purchased and the advertiser has determined a 4 Frequency is necessary, the Reach will be 25. These formulas make Radio planning extremely flexible.

EFFECTIVE FREQUENCY

The minimum level of frequency—number of exposures—determined to be effective in achieving the goals of an advertising campaign (e.g., awareness, recall, sales, etc.). This level will vary with individual products or services and the marketing objectives of the campaign.

FREQUENCY DISTRIBUTION

A tabulation separating those reached by a schedule, according to their minimum levels of exposure: 2 or more times, 3 or more times, 4 or more times, etc.

EFFECTIVE REACH

The number of people reached by a schedule at the pre-determined level of Effective Frequency.

EFFECTIVE RATING POINTS (ERPs)

Effective Reach expressed as a percentage of the population being measured. *

$$EFFECTIVE\ REACH \div POPULATION = ERPs$$

* The population being measured can be all people or any demographic group.

For further information please contact RAB Research.

RAB

Radio Advertising Bureau, Inc.
485 Lexington Avenue, New York, N.Y. 10017 • (212) 599-6666

XII. GLOSSARY OF TERMS

FIGURE 6.23
APPENDIX 6B:
Arbitron's Glossary of
Terms.

ADVANCE RATINGS/An Arbitron Ratings Radio Special Service's service that provides a client, via telephone, with selected estimates which will appear in his market report (RMR) as soon as the report has been approved for printing.

AGE/SEX POPULATIONS/Estimates of population, broken out by various age/sex groups within a county.

AM-FM TOTAL/A figure shown in market reports for AM-FM affiliates in time periods when they are simulcast.

ARBITRENDS/An Arbitron Ratings service, introduced in 1984 and available through Radio Special Services. Delivers averages of tabulated Radio audience listening estimates directly to clients' microcomputers in two types of reports: (1) Rolling Average Report, containing averages of listening estimates from three consecutive Arbitron Radio survey months; and (2) Quarterly Report, containing estimates from a three-month Arbitron survey.

ARBITRON INFORMATION ON DEMAND (AID)/An Arbitron Ratings Radio Special Services information service for direct access clients (via terminals) and indirect access clients (via AID division of Radio Special Services Department). Provides audience estimates and Reach and Frequency information, based on the same diaries that are used in the processing of the Radio Market Reports (RMRs).

ARBITRON SURVEY WEEK NUMBER/All fifty-two weeks in a year are assigned a number from 01-53 consecutively, beginning with the week in which January 1 falls. Appears on the diary label and serves as a quality check to ensure that a diary is placed in the correct week of a survey.

AREA OF DOMINANT INFLUENCE (ADI)/An exclusive geographic area, defined by Arbitron Television, consisting of sampling units in which the home-market television stations receive a preponderance of viewing. Every county in the United States (excluding Alaska and Hawaii) is allocated exclusively to one ADI.

A-SALE TAPE/An Arbitron Ratings Radio Special Services data tape of ADI estimates for one or more of the top fifty ADI markets available to agency and station clients that subscribe to the RMRs. Also known as "ASL" or "ADI" tape.

ASCRIPTION/A statistical technique that allocates radio listening proportionate to each conflicting station's diaries as calculated on a county basis using up to four surveys' TALO from the previous year, excluding the most recently completed survey for those markets with back-to-back surveys. Diary credit is randomly assigned automatically to a station based on its share of total diaries in the county.

AUDIENCE/A group of households, or a group of individuals, that are counted in a radio audience according to any one of several alternative criteria.

AVERAGE QUARTER-HOUR PERSONS/The estimated number of persons who listened at home and away to a station for a minimum of five minutes within a given quarter-hour. The estimate is based on the average of the reported listening in the total number of quarter-hours the station was on the air during a reported time period. This estimate is shown for the MSA, TSA and, where applicable, the ADI.

AVERAGE QUARTER-HOUR RATING/The Average Quarter-Hour Persons estimate expressed as a percentage of the universe. This estimate is shown in the MSA and, where applicable, the ADI.

AVERAGE QUARTER-HOUR SHARE/The Average Quarter-Hour estimate for a given station expressed as a percentage of the Average Quarter-Hour Persons estimate for the total listening in the MSA within a given time period. This estimate is shown only in the MSA.

AWAY FROM HOME LISTENING/Estimates of listening for which the diarykeeper indicated listening was done away from home, either "in a car" or "some other place."

CLIENT TAPE/A magnetic tape containing the same data as the Arbitron Ratings reports, sent to clients who subscribe to the printed report.

CONDENSED RADIO MARKET/Generally a small to middle-sized radio market; most are surveyed only once, in the Spring. The Metro and TSA sample objectives are considerably less than those for Standard Radio Markets and an abbreviated version of the Standard Radio Market Report is produced.

CONFLICT/Two or more stations using the same or similar slogan/program/personality/sports identification in the same county and qualifying under Arbitron's "One Percent TALO" criteria.

CONSOLIDATED METROPOLITAN STATISTICAL AREA (CMSA)/As defined by the U. S. Government's Office of Management and Budget; a grouping of closely related Primary Metropolitan Statistical Areas.

COUNTY SLOGAN EDIT FILE/A county-by-county listing of stations whose signals penetrate a county. Denotes all One Percent TALO qualifying stations. Includes each station's call letters, slogan ID, city and county of license, exact frequency and network affiliation(s). An internal document used to process diary entries.

FIGURE 6.23
continued

CUME PERSONS/The estimated number of different persons who listened at home and away to a station for a minimum of five minutes within a given daypart. (Cume estimates may also be referred to as "cumulative," "unduplicated," or "reach" estimates.) This estimate is shown in the MSA, TSA and ADI.

CUME RATING/The estimated number of Cume Persons expressed as a percentage of the universe. This estimate is shown for the MSA only.

DAYPART/The days of a week and the portion of those days for which listening estimates are calculated (e.g., Monday-Sunday 6AM-Midnight, Monday-Friday 6AM-10AM).

DEMOGRAPHICS/Statistical identification of human populations according to sex, age, race, income, etc.

DISCRETE DEMOGRAPHICS/Uncombined or non-overlapping sex/age groupings for listening estimates (e.g., men and/or women 18-24, 25-34, 35-44, etc.) as opposed to "target" group demographics (e.g., men and/or women 18 + , 18-34, 18-49, 25-49).

DUAL CITY OF IDENTIFICATION/A multi-city identification, with the city of license required to be named first in all multi-city identification announcements, according to FCC guidelines (see section 73.1201 (B) (2), amended October 19, 1983). Also known as Home Market Guidelines, at Arbitron.

EFFECTIVE SAMPLE BASE (ESB)/An estimate of the size of simple random samples (in which all diaries have equal values) that would be required to provide the same degree of statistical reliability as the sample actually used to produce the estimates in a report.

ELECTRONIC MEDIA RATING COUNCIL (EMRC)/An organization that accredits broadcast ratings services; performs annual audits of the compliance of a service with certain minimum standards.

ETHNIC CONTROLS/Arbitron Ratings placement and weighting techniques used in certain sampling units to establish proper representation of the black and/or Hispanic populations in the Metros of qualifying Arbitron Radio Markets.

EXCLUSIVE CUME LISTENING/The estimated number of Cume Persons who listened to one and only one station within a given daypart.

EXPANDED SAMPLE FRAME (ESF)/A universe that consists of unlisted telephone households — households which do not appear in the current or available telephone directories because either (a) they have requested their telephone number not to be listed or (b) they are households where the assigned telephone number is not listed in the directory because of the date of installation and the date of telephone directory publication.

FACILITY FORM/(See Station Information Form.)

FLIP/A computerized edit procedure that assigns aberrated call letters to legal call letters, or the AM designation of a set of call letters may be changed to an FM designation, e.g., WODC-AM flips to WOBC-AM and WOBC-FM flips to WOBC-AM.

GROUP QUARTERS/Residences of all persons not living in nuclear households. The population in group quarters includes, for example, persons living in college dormitories, homes for the aged, military barracks, rooming houses, hospitals and institutions.

HOME MARKET GUIDELINES/The criteria by which a radio station with multi-city identification can be reported Home to an Arbitron Radio Metro Area. Also known as Dual City of Identification.

HOME NUMBER/A unique four-digit number assigned to each household within a county being sampled.

IN-TAB/The number of usable diaries actually tabulated in producing an Arbitron Ratings report.

LISTED SAMPLE/Names, addresses, and telephone numbers of selected potential diary-keepers derived from telephone directories.

LOCAL MARKET REPORT (LMR)/A syndicated report for a designated market; also known as SRMR (Standard Radio Market Report) and RMR (Radio Market Report).

MARKET TOTALS/The estimated number of persons in the market who listened to reported stations, as well as to stations that did not meet the Minimum Reporting Standards, and/or to unidentified stations.

MENTION/The number of different diaries in which a station is mentioned once with at least five minutes of listening, in a quarter-hour, (does not indicate all the entries to a station in one diary); appears in county and station TALO.

METROPOLITAN STATISTICAL AREA (MSA)/As defined by the U.S. Government's Office of Management and Budget; a free-standing metropolitan area, surrounded by nonmetropolitan counties and not closely associated with other metropolitan areas.

METRO TOTALS AND ADI TOTALS (Total Listening in Metro Survey Area or Total Listening in the ADI)/The Metro and ADI total estimates include estimates of listening to reported stations as well as to stations that did not meet the Minimum Reporting Standards plus estimates of listening to unidentified stations.

NETWORK AFFILIATE/A broadcasting station, usually independently owned, in contractual agreement with a network in which the station grants the network an option on specific time periods for the broadcast of network-originated programs.

FIGURE 6.23
continued

NEW ENGLAND COUNTY METROPOLITAN AREA (NECMA)/As defined by the U.S. Government's Office of Management and Budget; New England MSA or PMSA definition adjusted to a whole county definition.

ONE PERCENT (1%) TALO RULE/An Arbitron radio procedure that establishes a cutoff point for resolving conflicts. The cutoff is one percent of the *previous year's* TALO by county, by station. All "potential" conflicting stations are analyzed to determine whether they qualify for conflict resolution. If only one of the two or more stations "potentially" in conflict receives one percent or more of the mentions in that county, then that station will receive credit for the contested entries in that county. However, if two or more of the stations "potentially" in conflict receive one percent or more of the total mentions in that county, each is considered in conflict. Ascription procedures are then instituted to determine proper listening credit.

PREMIUM/A token cash payment most often mailed with the diaries; serves as an inducement for a diarykeeper to participate in the survey and to return the diary to Arbitron. A premium is sent for each person twelve years of age and older in a household. The amount of the premium may vary.

PRIMARY METROPOLITAN STATISTICAL AREA (PMSA)/As defined by the U. S. Government's Office of Management and Budget; a metropolitan area that is closely related to another.

RATING/(See Average Quarter-Hour Rating and Cume Rating.)

REACH (Station)/Each county in which it has been determined by Arbitron Ratings that the signal for a specific radio station may be received.

R-SALE TAPE/An Arbitron Radio Special Services data tape of Metro and TSA estimates from one or more of the RMRs; available to clients who subscribe to the RMRs; also known as "RSL" or "Market Report data tape."

SHARE/The percentage of individuals listening to radio, who are listening to a specific station at a particular time.

SLOGAN/An on-air identifier used in place of or in conjunction with a station's call letters or exact frequency.

STATION INFORMATION FORM/A computer-generated form that lists essential station information including: power (day and night), frequency, sign-on/sign-off times, simulcasting (if any), slogan ID, network affiliates and national representative (if applicable). The Station Information Form is forwarded for verification to the applicable station prior to the survey period.

STATION INFORMATION PACKET/A set of forms mailed by Arbitron Ratings to a radio station approximately fifty days prior to each survey; allows station to change its slogan ID, sign-on/sign-off times, and make routine programming changes; included are forms for: Station Information, Programming Schedule Information, and Sports Programming.

STATION REACH FILE/A county-by-county file of stations that can be received in a county. This file is based on previous diary history and is updated with recent diary information as well as changes in power/antenna height; replaces the subjective review of all diary mentions within a county each survey to determine whether or not the mentions are "logical." Also, a station-by-station file of total counties reached.

TARGET DEMOGRAPHICS/Audience groupings containing multiple discrete demographics (e.g., men and/or women 18+, 18-34, 18-49, 25-49, etc.) as opposed to discrete demographics (e.g., men and/or women 18-24, 25-34, 35-44, etc.).

TECHNICAL DIFFICULTIES (TD)/Time period(s) of five or more consecutive minutes, in a quarter-hour, during the survey period in which a station listed in an Arbitron Ratings market report notified Arbitron Ratings in writing of technical difficulties including, but not limited to, times it was off the air or operating at reduced power.

TIME SPENT LISTENING (TSL)/An estimate of the amount of time the average person spends listening to a radio or to a station during a specified time period.

$$\frac{\text{Quarter-Hours in Time Period} \quad \mathbf{X} \quad \text{Average Quarter-Hours Persons Audience}}{\text{Cume Audience}} = \text{TSL}$$

TOTAL AUDIENCE LISTENING OUTPUT (TALO)/ The number of diaries in which a station is "mentioned" in (a) a market, (b) a county, or (c) another designated geographic area; a county-by-county printout showing the stations that are mentioned in the in-tab diaries and the number of mentions for each station; can be used to rank stations, to calculate weekly cumes and raw bases.

UNCOMBINED LISTENING ESTIMATES/ (See Discrete Demographics.)

UNIVERSE/The estimated total number of persons in the sex/age group and geographic area being reported.

UNLISTED SAMPLE/(See Expanded Sample Frame.)

FIGURE 6.23
continued

UNUSABLE DIARIES/Returned diaries determined to be unusable according to established Arbitron Ratings Radio Edit procedures.

UUUU/Unidentified; listening that could not be interpreted as belonging to a specific station.

FREQUENTLY USED ABBREVIATIONS

ADI	Area of Dominant Influence
AID	Arbitron Information on Demand
AQH	Average Quarter-Hour
CMSA	Consolidated Metropolitan Statistical Area
CRMR	Condensed Radio Market Report
CSB	Client Service Bulletin
DST	Differential Survey Treatment
EMRC	Electronic Media Rating Council
ESB	Effective Sample Base
ESF	Expanded Sample Frame
HDBA	High Density Black Area
HDHA	High Density Hispanic Area
LMR	Local Market Report
MMAC	MetroMail Advertising Company
MRS	Minimum Reporting Standards
MSA	Metro Survey Area
	Metropolitan Statistical Area
MSI	Market Statistics, Inc.
NECMA	New England County Metropolitan Area
PMSA	Primary Metropolitan Statistical Area
PPDV	Persons Per Diary Value
PPH	Persons Per Household
PSA	Primary Signal Area
PUR	Persons Using Radio
QM	Quarterly Measurement
RMR	Radio Market Report
SRDS	Standard Rate and Data Service, Inc.
SRMR	Standard Radio Market Report
SU	Sampling Unit
TALO	Total Audience Listening Output
TAR	Trading Area Report
TD	Technical Difficulty
TSA	Total Survey Area
TSL	Time Spent Listening

By Tripp Eldredge, President
Ami Davidson, Project Management
Direct Marketing Results
November 2002

FIGURE 6.24
Direct Marketing
Results relies on
research data to
present its marketing
goals. Courtesy DMR.

MARKETING GOALS

There are several objectives stations strive to reach when executing a marketing campaign. For example:

◆ Increase Top of Mind awareness and cume.
◆ Increase P1 listening.
◆ Increase P1 conversion.
◆ Develop new cume and TSL for WXXX.
◆ Develop new cume and TSL, particularly in workplace settings where high Time Spent Listening (TSL) can be achieved.
◆ Maintain and protect current P1 listeners.
◆ Continue to build a fortress of at-work listeners.
◆ Increase involvement and use of WXXX in workplace settings where high TSL can be achieved.
◆ Convert WXXX P2's and P3's (currently P1 to WAAA, WBBB, and WCCC) into P1's.
◆ Build a database of core listeners.
◆ Continue to build a database of core listeners.

STRATEGY

The average person listens to 3–5 radio stations per week. They listen for about 3 hours a day (21 hours/week). They are a P1 to the station that they listen to the most, a P2 to the second most listened to station, and so on. Heavy users (i.e., P1's) drive radio listening. In most stations, 75–90% of their listening is driven by their P1's. In terms of TSL, P1's are 22 times more valuable than P3's. Like many products and services, loyalty (i.e., P1's) comes from regular, frequent, and repeated contact to the most appropriate people with a benefit-driven message. Marketing campaigns that build loyalty and get ratings are:

◆ Highly targeted to high-potential P1's
◆ Focused, with a clear, benefit-driven message and call-to-action
◆ Reinforced through frequent, repeated and varied contact vehicles

1. The success of every marketing campaign is driven by its ability to:
2. Target the appropriate and likely type of listeners
3. Present them with a message that provides a salient benefit to the listener
4. Delivered using a multi-layered, multi-contact approach in a short period of time
5. Consistently followed up with messages that reinforce and remind.

TARGETING IS KEY

The key to any marketing program is reaching the right audience. No matter what combination of elements you use, if you're hitting the wrong people (those that will never

FIGURE 6.24
continued

be P1's) you're wasting your money. In radio, there are several sophisticated tools that help to precision-target the right people by their actual listening levels (behaviors) over a defined physical area (geography) and by a psychographical model. Unfortunately, few stations take the time to use one of the most important tools available to them, PD-Advantage. Using a combination of these tools, and Prizm-coding, we can now geo-behaviorally target those most likely to become P1's to the station.

Targeting Goals

The targeting goal is three-fold; 1) reach the best prospects for WXXX to produce new cume (particularly in the targeted households); 2) maintain the current level of P1's; and 3) cultivate new core listeners to WXXX, that is, convert P2's and P3's (P1's of your competitors) to WXXX P1's.

Before we talk about the steps in the targeting analysis, let's first review the value of WXXX's and the competitors' heavy users. The concept of heavy users applies across many different consumer categories. In his book, The End of Marketing as We Know It, Coca-Cola Chief Marketing Officer, Sergio Zyman, said that much of the 50% increase in Coca-Cola sales in just five years was driven by their strategy to gain and maintain heavy users of soft drinks (not just Coke P1's). Zyman writes, "heavy users are obviously more profitable than light users. So once you recognize them as a specific segment, you can tailor your marketing to maintain and increase the usage of your heavy consumers and to win your competitors' heavy consumers . . . develop programs that address heavy users."

In radio, we have two types of "heavy users." The first type is the ARBITRON DIARY KEEPER. These are the only ones that matter. Everything we do must be directed and filtered to get through to those DIARY KEEPERS. Given that perspective, we want to focus on those diary keepers who are HEAVY USERS of the station and the format (i.e., the competitors'). In radio, heavy users typically account for a large majority of the listening to a station. In fact, on average, you need 22 P3's to equal the listening of just one P1! This is a key factor in our targeting for WXXX's marketing and promotional plans.

WXXX P2's and P3's are your best target. They're already familiar with the station so you won't need to start from zero awareness. And they're already sampling the station (albeit for a short time). Finally, you know who and where they are. They're your competitors' P1's.

The Message

Consumers receive, on average, more than 3,000 commercial messages per day. In order to break through, your message needs to be clear, benefit-driven, and have a compelling call-to-action. The more personalized the message, the higher the likelihood it will be read. And the more integrated it is with our on-air elements and your supporting marketing components, the greater the impact on potential listeners.

FIGURE 6.24
continued

THE PLAN

Too often, we fail to create a marketing communication plan. Instead, we focus on choosing just a tool (i.e., direct mail, telemarketing, billboards, etc.). In order to break through to the consumer, your plan must have frequency, which reinforces the message you're communicating. Varying the delivery of the message (i.e., through a combination of vehicles) helps to break through. Multiple component campaigns have a much-increased likelihood of success. For example, think of Arbitron: they start with a postcard, follow up with a phone call, send you a direct mail piece in the form of a diary, followed by a letter, and so on. An effective plan employs multiple elements to ensure the message breaks through and uses the most appropriate sequence to achieve the marketing objectives.

TELEMARKETING

Telemarketing is an efficient and *cost-effective* way of targeting, finding, and converting P1 listeners. It's the only way to achieve all three steps quickly.

Telemarketing generates 1) impressions, 2) awareness, 3) recall and 4) sampling among those most likely to become real P1 or P2 listeners. Telemarketing programs designed to build P1 cume and increase TSL can also capture new information about listeners' music preferences, opinions, listening habits, purchase habits and lifestyles. Once a station commits to obtaining this information, it will have initiated a viable, usable database of confirmed, loyal listeners—the foundation for an on-going, permission-based, listener communication plan. Unlike mass media with its shotgun approach, telemarketing is more effective because it concentrates on finding, communicating with and then personally involving only those most likely to listen-Arbitron diary keepers. Considering the fact that 10% of a station's cume accounts for 45% of total listening on average, the reason for this focused approach becomes clear.

You can also collect verbatim comments about your via the telemarketing call! This process, gives you virtually real time information on your station, except with a much large sample. With telemarketing, you can jump-start the development of a *dialogue* with your listeners.

DIRECT MAIL

Direct Mail is a personal, specific and targeted vehicle that reinforces a radio station's marketing position and image with a strong visual message. Direct Mail enables you to cross-promote with your other media: print, billboard, on-air promotions, etc. Types of Direct Mail can include, but are not limited to, personalized laser-printed letters with enclosures such as magnets, coupon packets, reply cards, etc., personal billboards, videos, CD's, CD-ROM's, cassettes, newsletters, calendars, birthday and greeting cards.

FIGURE 6.24
continued

E-MAIL MARKETING

By using an e-mail marketing system you can send individualized focused messages instantly, with powerful, attention-getting graphics to your audience database. Some systems even feature built-in bounce and reply management to make the job of managing your e-mail campaigns simple. You can track click-through and response with the trackable URL system, send HTML, Rich Media, text or AOL mail, and create filters to segment audience members.

WEBFORM

This is Permission marketing at its best. By creating an enrollment Webform you allow your listeners the opportunity to register on line. The Webform will capture the listener's e-mail address (along with permission to use it), home address and other data. This information is invaluable when trying to build a database of core listeners. You can also incorporate a link from the station's website to this Webform to optimize the effectiveness.

THE INTERNET

The Internet enables delivery of personalized messages with targeted content and real-time interaction and can be integrated into traditional target-marketing programs or used on its own. The Internet can deliver trackable URL's and track click-throughs on links and banners, filter and sort the list using any characteristic and collect opt-in demographic data. Online promotions drive listening back to the station with a reinforcement of the on-air message and creates word-of-mouth and pass-along listenership.

FAX REMINDER

Another point of contact from WXXX could be delivered as fax. This fax will be sent to reinforce both the new listener's commitment to listen and your marketing message. Because of its At-Work delivery it drives listening in the workplace where longer TSL can occur.

SUGGESTED FURTHER READING

Arbitron Company. *Research Guidelines for Programming Decision Makers.* Beltsville, Md.: Arbitron Company, 1977.

Balon, Robert E. *Radio In the '90's.* Washington, D.C.: NAB Publishing, 1990.

Bartos, Rena. *The Moving Target, What Every Marketer Should Know about Women.* New York: The Free Press, 1982.

Berger, Arthor Asa. *Media and Communication Research.* London: Altamira Press, 2000.

Broadcast Advertising Reports. New York: Broadcast Advertising Research, periodically.

Broadcasting Yearbook. Washington, D.C.: Broadcasting Publishing, 1935 to date, annually.

Browne, Bortz, and Coddington (consultants). *Radio Today—And Tomorrow.* Washington, D.C.: NAB, 1982.

Buzzard, Karen. *Electronic Media Ratings.* Boston: Focal Press, 1992.

Chappell, Matthew N., and Hooper, C. E. *Radio Audience Measurement.* New York: Stephen Day Press, 1944.

Compaine, Benjamin, et al. *Who Owns the Media? Confrontation of Ownership in the Mass Communication Industry,* 2nd ed. White Plains, N.Y.: Knowledge Industry Publications, 1982.

Duncan, James. *American Radio.* Kalamazoo, Mich.: Author, twice yearly.

—. *Radio in the United States: 1976–82. A Statistical History.* Kalamazoo, Mich.: Author, 1983.

Electronic Industries Association. *Electronic MarketData Book.* Washington, D.C.: EIA, annually.

Eastman, Susan Tyler. *Research in Media Promotion.* Mahwah, N.J.: LEA, 2000.

Fletcher, James E., ed. *Handbook of Radio and Television Broadcasting: Research Procedures in Audience, Programming, and Revenues.* New York: Van Nostrand Reinhold, 1981.

Jamieson, Kathleen Hall, and Campbell, Karlyn Kohrs. *The Interplay of Influence: Mass Media and Their Publics in News, Advertising, and Politics.* Belmont, Calif.: Wadsworth Publishing, 1983.

Jensen, Klaus Bruhn. *Handbook of Media and Communications Research.* New York: Routledge, 2002.

Lazarsfeld, Paul F., and Kendall, Patrick. *Radio Listening in America.* Englewood Cliffs, N.J.: Prentice Hall, 1948.

McDowell, Walter. *Troubleshooting Audience Research.* Washington, D.C.: NAB, 2000.

National Association of Broadcasters. *Audience Research Sourcebook.* Washington, D.C.: NAB Publishing, 1991.

National Association of Broadcasters. *Radio Financial Report.* Washington, D.C.: NAB, 1955 to date, annually.

Radio Facts. New York: Radio Advertising Bureau, published annually.

Shane, Ed. *Selling Electronic Media.* Boston: Focal Press, 1999.

Webster, James G., Phelan, Patricia, and Lichty, Lawrence W. *Ratings Analysis: Theory and Practice,* 2nd ed. Hillsdale, N.J.: Lawrence Erlbaum Associates, 2000.

Wimmer, Roger D., and Dominick, Joseph. *Mass Media Research: An Introduction,* 4th ed. Belmont, Calif.: Wadsworth Publishing, 1994.

7 Promotion

Past and Purpose

Of necessity, radio stations are shameless self-promoters. "WXXX—the station without equal," "For the best in music and news tune WXXX," or "You're tuned to the music giant—WXXX" certainly illustrate this point. Why must stations practice self-glorification? The answer is simple: to keep the listener interested and tuned. The highly fragmented radio marketplace has made promotion a basic component of station operations. Five times as many stations vie for the listening audience today as did when television arrived on the scene. It is competition that makes promotion necessary.

Small stations as well as large promote and market themselves. In the single station market, stations promote to counter the effects of other media, especially the local newspaper, which often is the archrival of small town outlets. Since there is only one station to tune to, promotion serves to maintain listener interest in the medium. In large markets, where three stations may be offering the same format, promotion helps a station differentiate itself from the rest. In this case, the station with the best promotion often wins the ratings war.

Radio recognized the value of promotion early. In the 1920s and 1930s, stations used newspapers and other print media to inform the public of their existence. Remote broadcasts from hotels, theaters, and stores also attracted attention for stations and were a popular form of promotion during the medium's golden age. Promotion-conscious broadcasters of the pretelevision era were just as determined to get the audience to take notice as they are today. From the start, stations used whatever was at hand to capture the public's attention. Call letters were configured in such a way as to convey a particular sentiment or meaning: WEAF/New York, Water, Earth, Air, Fire; WOW/Omaha, Woodmen Of the World; and WIOD/ Miami, Wonderful Isle Of Dreams. In addition, placards were affixed to vehicles, buildings, and even blimps as a means of heightening the public's awareness.

As ratings assumed greater prominence in the age of specialization, stations became even more cognizant of the need to promote. The relationship between good ratings and effective promotion became more apparent. In the 1950s and 1960s, programming innovators such as Todd Storz and Gordon McLendon used promotions and contests with daring and skill, even a bit of lunacy, to win the attention of listeners.

The growth of radio promotion has paralleled the proliferation of frequencies. "The more stations you have out there, the greater the necessity to promote. Let's face it, a lot of stations are doing about the same thing. A good promotion sets you apart. It gives you greater identity, which means everything when a survey company asks a listener what station he or she tunes. Radio is an advertising medium in and of itself. Promotion makes a station salable. You sell yourself so that you have something to sell advertisers," observes Las Vegas radio station promotion director (also called promotion manager) Charlie Morriss. Stations that once confined the bulk of their promotional effort to spring and fall to coincide with rating periods now find it necessary to engage in promotional campaigns on an ongoing basis throughout the year, notes Morriss. "More competition and monthly audience surveys mean that stations have to keep the promotion fire burning continually, the analogy being that if the flame goes out you're likely to go cool in the ratings. So you really have to hype your outlet every opportunity you get. The significance of the role of promotion in contemporary radio cannot be overstated."

The vital role that promotion plays in radio is not likely to diminish as hundreds of more stations enter the airways by the turn of the century.

"Promotion has become as much a part of radio as the records and the deejays who spin them, and that's not about to change," contends promotion director John Grube.

Promotions—Practical and Bizarre

The idea behind any promotion is to win listeners. Over the years, stations have used a variety of methods, ranging from the conventional to the outlandish, to accomplish this goal. "If a promotion achieves top-of-the-mind awareness in the listener, it's a winner. Granted, some strange things have been done to accomplish this," admits Mississippi broadcaster Bob Lima.

Promotions designed to captivate the interest of the radio audience have inspired some pretty bizarre schemes. In the 1950s, Dallas station KLIF placed overturned cars on freeways with a sign on their undersides announcing the arrival of a new deejay, Johnny Rabbitt. It would be hard to calculate the number of deejays who have lived

atop flagpoles or in elevators for the sake of a rating point.

In the 1980s the shenanigans continued. To gain the listening public's attention, a California deejay set a world record by sitting in every seat of a major league ballpark that held 65,000 spectators. In the process of the stunt, the publicity-hungry deejay injured his leg. However, he went on to accomplish his goal by garnering national attention for himself and his station. Another station offered to give away a mobile home to contestants who camped out the longest on a platform at the base of a billboard. The challenge turned into a battle of wills as three contestants spent

FIGURE 7.1
Courtesy
Communications
Graphics, Inc.

FIGURE 7.2
Stations promote their superstars. Courtesy KPWR and KDKA.

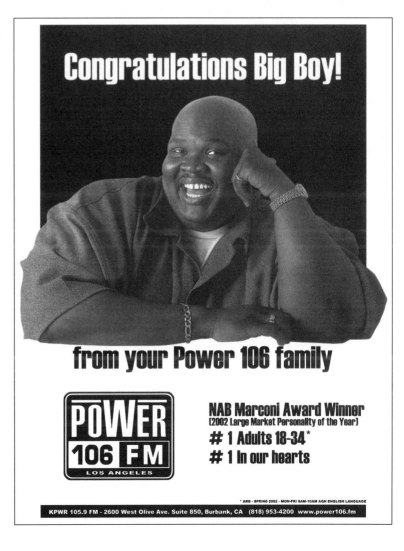

"Thanks, we appreciate it..."

JOHN CIGNA
AND THE K-TEAM
WEEKDAYS 5~9AM

If it's important to you, you know it's on the K-Team with John Cigna. He gives listeners a wake-up call with informative interviews, trivia challenges and fun features to get people going.

Pittsburgh's most comprehensive morning program keeps listeners informed with Bob Kopler's news every half hour plus breaking stories. Goose Goslin has sports on the quarter-hours. There's also AAA's Rita Maloney in the Traffic Tower and Accu-Weather four times an hour.

John joined KDKA Radio in 1973 as an overnight talk show host, serving for ten years before taking the reins of the K-Team in 1983. Whether he's conducting a K-Team poll or discussing the day's issues with callers, John Cigna remains an important voice in Pittsburgh.

KDKA AM 1020 ◉
One Gateway Center Pittsburgh Pennsylvania 15222 (412) 575-2525

FIGURE 7.2
continued

months trying to outlast each other. In the end, one of the three was disqualified and the station, in an effort to cease what had become more of an embarrassment than anything else, awarded the two holdouts recreational vehicles.

Today, promotions have gotten edgier, especially on those stations featuring shock jock shows. Things can and do get out of hand when personalities go to the extreme to draw listeners' attention with on-air pranks and giveaways. Howard Stern has held all manner of scatological promotions and contests, many centered around women removing their clothes, and Opie and Anthony asked listeners to have sex in public places. This ultimately got them removed from the air thus indicating that there are limits to what a station can do to get audience notice. The tone and tenor of station promotions have certainly changed over the decades, notes Larry Miller. "Although occurring in what now seems a gentler and kinder world, my personal favorite is the one about a station in LA in the early 1950s that sent out a 'free Valhalla Oil credit card' to listeners. Well, there was no such oil company, but loyal listeners nevertheless spent a good deal of time searching for a Valhalla gas station. Everybody had a laugh."

Reporter Peg Harney offers testimony that the bizarre still occurs in radio promotions. "As a publicity stunt and also to get people to use the local public library, a station in Ft. Worth, Texas, a couple years back announced it had hidden cash in small denominations in the fiction section. Approximately 800 people descended on the library and proceeded to pull books off the shelves looking for the money. The library had not been notified that the station was going to make the announcement, and it was totally taken by surprise. The librarian said that approximately 4,000 books were pulled from the shelves—some of them had pages torn out—and that people were climbing on the bookcases and making a tremendous mess. The station was forced to make a public apology, and it promised full financial restitution."

One of the most infamous examples of a promotion gone bad occurred when a station decided to air-drop dozens of turkeys to a waiting crowd of listeners in a neighborhood shopping center parking lot. Unfortunately, the station discovered too late that turkeys are not adept at flying at heights above 30 feet. Consequently, several cars were damaged and witnesses traumatized as turkeys plunged to the ground. This promotion-turned-nightmare was depicted in an episode of the television sitcom *WKRP in Cincinnati*.

The list of glitches is seemingly endless. In the late 1960s a station in central Massachusetts asked listeners to predict how long its air personality could ride a carousel at a local fair. The hardy airman's effort was cut short on day three when motion sickness got the best of him and he vomited on a crowd of spectators and newspaper photographers. A station in California came close to disaster when a promotion that challenged listeners to find a buried treasure resulted in half the community being dug up by overzealous contestants.

These promotions did indeed capture the attention of the public, but in each case the station's image was somewhat tarnished. The axiom that any publicity, good or bad, is better than none at all can get a station into hot water, contends station promotion director Chuck Davis. "It's great to get lots of exposure for the station, but if it makes the station look foolish, it can work against you."

The vast majority of radio contests and promotions are of a more practical nature and run without too many complications. Big prizes, rather than stunts, tend to draw the most interest and thus are offered by stations able to afford them. In the mid-1980s, WASH-AM, Washington, D.C., and KSSK-AM, Honolulu, both gave a lucky listener a million dollars. Cash prizes always have attracted tremendous response. Valuable prizes other than cash also can boost ratings. For example, Los Angeles station KHTZ-AM experienced a sizable jump in its ratings when it offered listeners a chance to win a $122,000 house (this was a decade ago). Increased ratings also resulted when KHJ-AM, Los Angeles, gave away a car every day during the month of May.

Promotions that involve prizes, both large and small, spark audience interest, says Rick Peters, vice president of programming, Sconnix Broadcasting. "People love to win something or, at least, feel that they have a shot at winning a prize. That's basic to human nature, I believe. You really don't have to give away two city blocks, either. A listener usually is thrilled and delighted to win a pair of concert tickets."

Although there are numerous examples to support the view that big prizes get big audiences, there is an ample amount to support the contention that low-budget giveaways, involving T-shirts, albums, tickets, posters, dinners, and so forth are very useful in building and maintaining audience interest. In fact, some surveys have revealed that smaller, more personalized prizes may work better for a station than the high-priced items. CDs, concert tickets, and dinners-for-two rank among the most popular contest prizes, according to surveys. Cheaper items usually also mean more numerous or frequent giveaways.

The Promotion Director's/ Manager's Job

Not all stations employ a full-time promotion director. But most stations designate someone to handle promotional responsibilities. At small outlets, the program director or even the general manager assume promotional chores. Larger stations and

FIGURE 7.3
Station promotion in the early 1920s with an airborne antenna. Courtesy Westinghouse Electric.

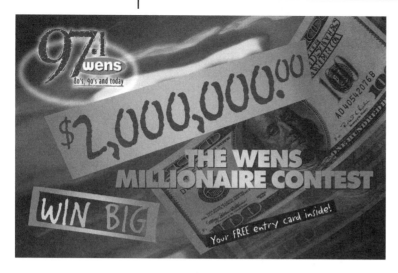

FIGURE 7.4
Stations use point of purchase posters to promote their contests. Courtesy WENS-FM.

FIGURE 7.5
Giving away "hot" items generates audience interest Courtesy KNEW-AM.

station clusters with bigger operating budgets typically hire an individual or individuals to work exclusively in the area of promotion. "At major market stations, you'll find a promotion department that includes a director and possibly assistants. In middle-sized markets, such as ours, the promotion responsibility is often designated to someone already involved in programming," says Bob Lima.

Observes Ed Shane, "Some promotion managers consider themselves 'marketing directors.' There are two levels of job responsibility for promotion people. Some are glorified 'banner hangers,' who make sure the grunt work is done at a station promotion or a live broadcast. Others are true department heads who exhibit leadership and vision within their operations."

Indeed the promotion director's responsibilities are manifold. Essential to the position are a knowledge and understanding of the station's audience. A background in research is important, contends Grube. "Before you can initiate any kind of promotion you must know something about who you're trying to reach. This requires an ability to interpret various research data that you gather through in-house survey efforts or from outside audience research companies, like Birch and Arbitron. You don't give away beach balls to 50-year-old men. Ideas must be confined to the cell group you're

trying to attract."

Writing and conceptual skills are vital to the job of promotion director, says Morriss. "You prepare an awful lot of copy of all types. One moment you're composing press releases about programming changes, and the next you're writing a 30-second promo about the station's expanded news coverage or upcoming remote broadcast from a local mall. Knowledge of English grammar is a must. Bad writing reflects negatively on the station. The job also demands imagination and creativity. You have to be able to come up with an idea and bring it to fruition."

Chuck Davis agrees with Morriss and adds that although the promotion person should be able to originate concepts, a certain number of ideas come from the trades and other stations. "When this is the case, and it often is, you have to know how to adapt an idea to suit your own station. Of course, the promotion must reflect your location. Lifestyles vary almost by region. A promotion that's successful at a station in Louisiana may bear no relevance to a station with a similar format in Michigan. On the other hand, with some adjustments, it may work as effectively there. The creativity in this example exists in the adaptation."

Promotion directors must be versatile. A familiarity with graphic art generally is necessary, since the promotion director will be involved in developing station logos and image IDs for advertising in the print media and billboards. The promotion department also participates in the design and preparation of visuals for the sales area.

The acquisition of prize materials through direct purchase and trades is another duty of the promotion person, who also may be called on to help coordinate sales co-op arrangements. "You work closely with the sales manager to arrange tie-ins with sponsors and station promotions," contends Morriss.

Like other radio station department heads, it is the promotion director's responsibility to ensure that the rules and regulations established by the FCC, relevant to the promotions area, are observed. This will be discussed further later in the chapter, in the section, "Promotions and the FCC."

Of course, it is important that a promotion director maintain a high level of communication with other station personnel, particularly the program director and sales manager, who are almost always an integral part of a promotion's execution and implementation. Everyone should be in the know about contests and promotions.

On a final note (corroborating Ed Shane's preceding contention), Lynn Christian observes that, "The word *marketing* has become the rallying cry today. At a BPME meeting the question was raised as to whether a promotion director should be designated 'marketing director,' and given upgraded status in a station—that is, parity with the program director and sales manager. In the light of the horrendous competition and the need to survive in what has been a very soft market, it makes sense to acknowledge the value and importance of an effective promotion (marketing) director."

Whom Promotion Directors Hire

In each section devoted to hiring in preceding and subsequent chapters, college training is listed as a desirable, if not necessary, attribute. This is no less true in the area of radio station promotion. "My advice to an individual interested in becoming a promotion person would be to get as much formal training as possible in marketing, research, graphics, writing, public relations, and, of course, broadcasting. The duties of the promotion director, especially at a large station, are diverse," notes Rick Peters of TK Communications.

Charlie Morriss agrees with Peters and adds, "A manager reviewing the credentials of candidates for a promotion position will expect to find a statement about formal training, that is, college. Of course, nothing is a substitute for a solid track record. Experience is golden. This is a very hands-on field. My advice today is to get a good education and along the way pick up a little experience, too."

Familiarity with programming is important, contends Lima, who suggests that prospective promotion people spend some time on the air. "Part-timing it on mike at a station, be it a small commercial outlet or a college facility, gives a person special insight into the nature of the medium that he or she is promoting. Working in sales also is valuable. In the specific skills department, I'd say the promotion job candidate should have an eye for detail, be well organized, and possess exemplary writing skills. It goes without saying that a positive attitude and genuine appreciation of radio are important as well."

Both John Grube and Chuck Davis cite wit and imagination as criteria for the job of promotion. "It helps to be a little wacky and crazy. By that I mean able to conceive of entertaining, fun concepts," says Grube. Davis concurs, "This is a convivial medium. The idea behind any promotion or contest is to attract and amuse the listener. A zany, off-the-wall idea is good, as long as it is based in sound reasoning. Calculated craziness requires common sense and creativity, and both are qualities you need in order to succeed in promotion."

The increasing competition in the radio marketplace has bolstered job opportunities in promotion. Thus, the future appears bright for individuals planning careers in this facet of the medium.

Types of Promotion

There are two primary categories of station promotion: on-air and off-air. The former will be examined first since it is the most prevalent form of radio promotion. Broadcasters already possess the best possible vehicle to reach listeners, so it should come as no surprise that on-air promotion is the most common means of getting word out on a station. The challenge confronting the promotion director is how to most effectively market the station so as to expand and retain listenership. To this end, a number of promotional devices are employed, beginning with the most obvious—station call letters. "The value of a good set of call letters is inestimable," says KGLD's Bremkamp. "A good example is the call letters of a station I once managed which have long been associated with the term *rich* and all that it implies: 'Hartford's Rich Music Station—WRCH.'"

Call letters convey the personality of a station. For instance, try connecting these call letters with a format: WHOG, WNWS, WEZI, WODS, WJZZ, WIND, WHTS. If you guessed Country, News, Easy Listening, Oldies, Jazz, Talk, and Hits you were correct. The preceding call letters not only identify their radio stations, but they literally convey the nature or content of the programming offered.

Larry Miller adds, "Anything that can be made to spell 'KISS' is always a favorite with listeners, starting with a KISS station in the Northwest back in the 1950s. Other similar calls include 'Magic' for a soft AC, 'Zoo' for a wild and crazy CHR or Hot AC, or 'Rock' as in K-Rock. In Hawaii, calls that spell Hawaiian words have always been popular, such as K-POI. In the early 1970s, the ABC group of O&O FMs changed call letters to reflect 'hip' or local culture with calls like KLOS in LA or KSFX in San Francisco or WRIF in Detroit or WPLJ (white port and lemon juice) in New York."

When stations do not possess call letters that create instant recognition, they often couple their frequency with a call letter or two, such as JB-105 (WPJB-FM 105) or KISS-108 (WXKS-FM 108). This also improves the retention factor. Slogans frequently are a part of the on-air ID. "Music Country—WSOC-FM, Charlotte";

"A Touch of Class—WTEB-FM, New Bern"; "Texas Best Rock—KTXQ-FM, Fort Worth" are some examples. Slogans exemplify a station's image. When effective, they capture the mood and flavor of the station and leave a strong impression in the listener's mind. It is standard programming policy at many stations to announce the station's call letters and even its slogan each time a deejay opens the microphone. This is especially true during ratings sweeps when survey companies ask listeners to identify the stations they tune in to. "If your calls stick in the mind of your audience, you've hit a home run. If they don't, you'll go scoreless in the book. You've got to carve them into the listener's gray matter and you start by making IDs and signatures that are as memorable as possible," observes Rick Peters.

Jay Williams, Jr., observes that call letters are being used less and less in the digital age. "Stations identify themselves using their frequencies (92.5) today more than their call letters. This has become the case since the radio dial became digitized. The emphasis is now more numerical than alphabetical. Even the alpha-numeric approach (Magic 92) has faded in favor of simply stating the station's frequency."

It is a common practice for stations to "bookend"—place call letters and/or frequencies before and after all breaks between music. For example, "WHJJ. Stay tuned for a complete look at local and national news at the top of the hour on WHJJ." Deejays also are told to graft the station call letters onto all bits of information: "92.9 Time," "102.5 Temperature" "102.5 Weather," and so on. There is a rule in radio that call letters can never be overannounced. The logic behind this is clear. The more a station tells its audience what it is tuned to, the more apt it is to remember, especially during rating periods.

On-air contests are another way to capture and hold the listener's attention. Contests must be easy to understand (are the rules and requirements of the contest easily understood by the listener?) and possess entertainment value (will nonparticipants be amused even though they are not actually involved?). A contest should engage the interest of all listeners, players and nonplayers alike.

A contest must be designed to enhance a station's overall sound or format. It must fit in, be compatible. Obviously, a mystery sound contest requiring the broadcast of loud or shrill noises would disrupt the tranquility and continuity of an Easy Listening station and result in tune-out.

Successful contests are timely and relevant to the lifestyle of the station's target audience, says Bob Lima. "A contest should offer prizes that truly connect with the listener. An awareness of the needs, desires, and fantasies of the listener will help guide a station. For example, giving away a refrigerator on a hot hit station would not really captivate the 16-year-old tuned. This is obvious, of course. But the point I'm making is that the prizes that are up for grabs should be something the listener really wants to win, or you have apathy."

The importance of creativity already has been stated. Contests that attract the most attention often are the ones that challenge the listener's imagination, contends Morriss. "A contest should have style, should attempt to be different. You can give away what is perfectly suitable for your audience, but you can do it in a way that creates excitement and adds zest to the programming. The goal of any promotion is to set you apart from the other guy. Be daring within reason, but be daring."

On-air promotion is used to inform the audience of what a station has to offer: station personalities, programs, and special features and events. Rarely does a quarter-hour pass on any station that does not include a promo that highlights some aspect of programming:

"Tune in WXXX's News at Noon each weekday for a full hour of . . ."
"Irv McKenna keeps 'Nightalk' in the air

FIGURE 7.6
Station folders and packets are designed to correspond with a station's brand ID. Courtesy Infinity.

midnight to six on the voice of the valley–WXXX. Yes, there's never a dull moment . . ."
"Every Saturday night WXXX turns the clock back to the fifties and sixties to bring you the best of the golden oldies . . ."
"Hear the complete weather forecast on the hour and half hour throughout the day and night on your total service station–WXXX . . ."

On-air promotion is a cost-efficient and effective means of building an audience when done correctly, says John Grube. "There are good on-air promotions and weak or ineffective on-air promotions.

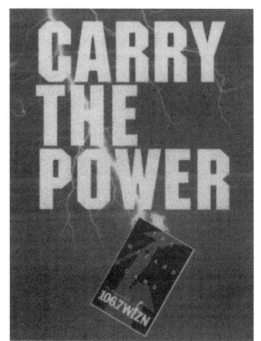

FIGURE 7.7
Dramatic station promotion poster. Courtesy WIZN.

The latter can inflict a deep wound, but the former can put a station on the map. As broadcasters, the airtime is there at our disposal, but we sometimes forget just how potent an advertising tool we have."

Radio stations employ off-air promotional techniques to reach people not tuned. Billboards are a popular form of outside promotion. To be effective they must be both eye-catching and simple. Only so much can be stated on a billboard, since people generally are in a moving vehicle and have only a limited amount of time to absorb a message. Placement of the billboard also is a key factor. To be effective, billboards must be located where they will reach a station's intended audience. Whereas an All-News station would avoid the use of a billboard facing a high school, a rock music outlet may prefer the location.

Bus cards are a good way to reach the public. Cities often have hundreds of buses on the streets each day. Billboard companies also use benches and transit shelters to get their client's message across to the population. Outside advertising is an effective and fairly cost-efficient way to promote a radio station, although certain billboards at heavy traffic locations can be extremely expensive to lease.

Newspapers are the most frequent means of off-air promotion. Stations like the reach and targeting that newspapers can provide. In large metro areas, alternative newspapers, such as the *Boston Phoenix*, are very effective in delivering certain listening cells. The *Phoenix* enjoys one of the largest readerships of any independent press in the country. Its huge college-age and young professional audience makes it an ideal promotional medium for stations after those particular demographics. Whereas the readership of the more conventional newspapers traditionally is low among young people, it is high in older adults, making the mainstream publications useful to stations targeting the over-40 crowd.

Newspapers with large circulations provide a great way to reach the population at large, but they also can be very costly, although some stations are able to trade airtime for print space. Newspaper ads must be large enough to stand out and overcome the sea of advertisements that often share the same page. Despite some drawbacks, newspapers usually are the first place radio broadcasters consider when planning an off-air promotion.

Television is a costly but effective promotional tool for radio. A primary advantage that television offers is the chance to target the audience that the station is after. An enormous amount of information is available pertaining to television viewership. Thus, a station that wants to reach the 18- to 24-year-olds is able to ascertain the programs and features that best draw that particular cell.

The costs of producing or acquiring ready-made promos for television can run high, but most radio broadcasters value the opportunity to actually show the public what they can hear when they tune to their station. WBZ-AM in Boston used local television extensively to promote its former morning personality, Dave Maynard, and its current sunrise news team. Ratings for the Westinghouse-owned station have been consistently high, and management points to their television promotion as a contributing factor.

Bumper stickers are manufactured by the millions for distribution by practically every commercial radio station in the country. The primary purpose of stickers is to increase call letter awareness. Over the years, bumper stickers have developed into a unique pop-art form, and hundreds of people actually collect station decals as a hobby. Some station bumper stickers are particularly prized for the lifestyle or image they portray. Youths, in particular, are fond of displaying their favorite station's call letters. Stations appealing to older demographics find that their audiences are somewhat less enthusiastic about bumper stickers.

Stations motivate listeners to display bumper stickers by tying them in with on-air promotions:

FIGURE 7.8
Newspapers are popular radio promotion vehicles. Courtesy WBCN, WFNX, WAAF, and WHK.

WXXX WANTS TO GIVE YOU A THOUSAND DOLLARS. ALL YOU HAVE TO DO IS PUT AN X-100 BUMPER STICKER ON YOUR CAR TO BE ELIGIBLE. IT'S THAT SIMPLE. WHEN YOUR CAR IS SPOTTED BY THE X-100 ROVING EYE, YOUR LICENSE NUMBER WILL BE ANNOUNCED OVER THE AIR. YOU WILL THEN HAVE THIRTY MINUTES TO CALL THE STATION TO CLAIM YOUR ONE THOUSAND DOLLARS....

Hundreds of ways have been invented to entice people to display station call letters. The idea is to get the station's name out to the public, and 10,000 cars exhibiting a station's bumper sticker is an effective way to do that. Says Ed Shane, "Visibility is part of the answer. Station promotion has reached new levels of creativity and intrusion—skateboard jumpers, rolling

FIGURE 7.9
Bumper stickers
visually convey a
station's sound and
image. Courtesy Mo
Money Associates.

radios, inflatables in the boots, guitars, frogs."

Stations give away thousands of items displaying station call letters and logos annually. Among the most common promotional items handed out by stations are posters, T-shirts, calendars, key chains, coffee mugs, music hit lists, book covers, pens, and car litter bags. The list is vast.

Plastic card promotions have done well for many stations. Holders are entitled to a variety of benefits, including discounts at various stores and valuable prizes. The bearer is told to listen to the station for information as to where to use the card. In addition, holders are eligible for special on-air drawings.

Another particularly effective way to increase a station's visibility is to sponsor special activities, such as fairs, sporting events, theme dances, and concerts. Hartford's Big Band station, WRCQ-AM, has received significant attention by presenting an annual music festival that has attracted over 25,000 spectators each year, plus the notice of other media, including television and newspapers.

Personal appearances by station personalities are one of the oldest forms of off-air promotion, but still a very effective one. Remote broadcasts from malls, beaches, and the like also aid in getting the word of the station out to the public.

One last means of marketing a station is offered by Jay Williams, Jr., CEO, Direct Marketing Results: "Promotion and marketing have never been more critical. In the current economy, stations have to do everything they can to draw and hold an audience. Direct marketing through mail and/or by telephone is a very cost-effective way to target an audience and to keep a station in front of radio listeners, especially during rating periods. Telepromoting is becoming more prevalent. Directed or targeted marketing makes sense because stations must be more effective with what they have. The business of radio is changing. Audiences are fragmenting, brand loyalties are eroding. Mass marketing is losing its impact. Person-to-person or individualized marketing delivers tangible results."

Ed Shane concurs with Williams, adding, "Direct marketing is the wave of the one-to-one future. More direct mail, telemarketing, database management, and computer interaction."

Sales Promotion

Promoting a station can be very costly, as much as half a million dollars annually in some metro markets. To help defray the cost of station promotion, advertisers are often recruited. This way both the station and the sponsor stand to benefit. The station gains the financial wherewithal to execute certain promotions that it could not do on its own, and the participating advertiser gains valuable exposure by tying in with special station events. Stations actually can make money and promote themselves simultaneously if a client purchases a substantial spot schedule as part of a promotional package. Says Larry Miller, "An effective promotional campaign should try to include a sales component, in part to help allay the costs of advertising. If it's done right, it will bring in new business for the station."

There are abundant ways to involve advertisers in station promotion efforts. They run the gamut from placing advertisements and coupons on the back of bumper stickers to joining the circus for the day; for example, "WXXX brings the 'Greatest Show on Earth' to town this Friday night, and you go for half price just by mentioning the name of your favorite radio station— WXXX." The ultimate objective of a station/sponsor collaborative is to generate attention in a cost-efficient manner. If a few dollars are made for the station along the way, all the better.

As stated previously, the promotion director also works closely with the station's sales department in the preparation and design of sales promotion materials, which include items such as posters, coverage maps, ratings breakouts, flyers, station profiles, rate cards, and much more.

Research and Planning

To effectively promote a station, the individual charged with the task must possess a thorough knowledge of the station and its audience. This person must then ascertain the objective of the promotion. Is it the aim of the promotion to increase call letter awareness, introduce a new format/feature/personality or bolster the station's

FIGURE 7.10
Whatever graphic it takes to get the attention of the audience. Courtesy Froggy FM.

community service image? Of course, the ultimate goal of any promotion is to enhance listenership.

Effective promotions take into account both internal and external factors. An understanding of the product, consumer, and competition is essential to any marketing effort, including radio. Each of these three areas presents the promotion director with questions that must be addressed before launching a campaign. As stated earlier in this chapter, it is imperative that the promotion or contest fit the station's sound; in other words, be compatible with the format. This accomplished, the next consideration is the relevancy of the promotion to the station's audience. For example, does it fit the listener's lifestyle? Third, is the idea fresh enough in the market to attract and sustain interest?

Observes programming executive Corinne Baldassano, "You must institute ongoing research to make sure your target audience is happy with what it's hearing. You can make adjustments depending on the feedback you get from the research. Those stations that have succeeded have been single-minded in their desire to achieve their goals. They establish a market position and do everything they can to fulfill audience expectations. The other major ingredient for success with promotions is fun. You have to have fun with the promotion while you're doing all the work. If you and your staff have a good time, it is conveyed to the listeners and potential advertisers. It makes a station hard to beat."

Concerning the basic mechanics of the contest, the general rule is that if it takes a long time to explain, it is not appropriate for radio. "Contests that require too much explanation don't work well in our medium. That is not to say that they have to be thin and one-dimensional. On the contrary, radio contests can be imaginative and captivating without being complicated or complex," notes John Grube.

FIGURE 7.11
Direct marketing helps increase audience awareness of a radio station. Courtesy DMR.

The planning and implementation of certain promotions may require the involvement of consultants who possess the expertise to ensure smooth sailing. Contests can turn into bad dreams if potential problems are not anticipated. Rick Sklar, who served as program director for WABC in New York for nearly 20 years, was responsible for some of the most successful radio promotions ever devised, but not all went without a hitch. In his autobiographical book, *Rocking America* (St. Martin's Press, 1984), Sklar told of the time that he was forced to hire, at great expense, 60 office temporaries for a period of one month to count the more than 170 million ballots received in response to the station's "Principal of the Year" contest. The previous year the station had received a paltry 6 million ballots.

On another occasion, Sklar had over 4 million WABC buttons manufactured as part of a promotion that awarded up to $25,000 in cash to listeners spotted wearing one. What Sklar did not anticipate was the huge cost involved in shipping several million metal buttons from various points around the country. The station had to come up with thousands of unbudgeted dollars to cover air freight. Of course, both miscalculations were mitigated by the tremendous success of the promotions, which significantly boosted WABC's ratings.

An even more bizarre experience befell Dallas deejay Ron Chapman when he jokingly asked listeners to send $20 without explaining why. The listening faithful, assuming Chapman's request to be a part of a legitimate station promotion, mailed in nearly a quarter of a million dollars. This left the station (KVIL-FM) with the interesting problem of what to do with the money. "We're flabbergasted," exclaimed Chapman. "We never expected this to happen." The moral to this tale is never underestimate the power of the medium. Plan before implementing.

Careful planning during the developmental phase of a promotion generally will prevent any unpleasant surprises, says Bob

SHANE MEDIA PROGRAM DIRECTOR'S CHECKLIST

We all know what it takes to be a good program director — develop and direct your station's on-air sound, conduct or oversee research, develop and reinforce a positive station image in the community, accept responsibility for air staff ... the list goes on and on. The difficulty, however, is getting it all done. We've broken the program director's many jobs into daily, weekly, bi-weekly and monthly increments. It's a checklist that'll help you get things done.

DAILY
A. Direction of on-air sound
❑ Morning Show Meeting
- ○ Review day's high and low points
- ○ Evaluate talent plans for next day
- ○ Plan next day's benchmarks
- ○ Brainstorm ideas for topicality

❑ Casual feedback to each air talent in other dayparts

❑ Check at least one daypart at competitor

❑ Listen to your station 15 minutes outside drive times

❑ Check announcer activity schedule
- ○ Shifts
- ○ Promotions

❑ Give assignments to
- ○ Music director
- ○ Production director
- ○ Promotion director

❑ Music logs for next day
- ○ Create
- ○ Review

❑ Review commercial discrepancy report

B. Liaison with Sales Department
❑ Provide creative copy and scheduling input

❑ Make decisions on new promotional opportunities

❑ Talk to a client to see how the station is working

WEEKLY
A. Direction of on-air sound
❑ Listen to one hour of your station *uninterrupted*
- ○ Rotate times until you've heard every daypart
- ○ Check positioning, call letter delivery, contest play and enthusiasm, relatability
- ○ Check music flow

❑ Monitor competition for an hour *uninterrupted*
- ○ Know key positioning
- ○ Review contesting
- ○ Track promotions
- ○ Evaluate music
- ○ Review findings with GM and/or GSM

❑ Music meeting
- ○ Discuss adds and moves with MD
  - △ Do adds and moves reflect station mission and music research?
- ○ Have MD circulate an internal list and provide new records for jocks to audition

○ Check music software system

○ Check turnovers of all rotations

○ Check histories on selected songs

○ Review Selector's "Most Frequently Played Analysis" or Powergold's "History"

❑ Promotion meeting
- ○ Brief post-mortem on last week's promotions
- ○ Review calendar for this weekend, next week
- ○ Be sure all promotions fit station image and accomplish cume or TSL goals
- ○ Ask promotion director for follow-up summary (or circulate one you create)
- ○ Make sure assignments are clear

❑ Production meeting
- ○ Discuss needs for coming promotions
- ○ Evaluate image promos & schedule new ones
- ○ Review announcer scheduling
- ○ Brainstorm ideas

❑ Engineering meeting
- ○ Review previous week's discrepancy reports
- ○ Advise chief of anything that needs repair
- ○ Review technical side of remotes
- ○ Discuss costs & savings ideas

EVERY TWO WEEKS
A. Direction of on-air sound
❑ Aircheck session with talent other than morning
- ○ Recap in writing

❑ Be sure you've listened to every announcer in every daypart at direct competitor

---

Lima. "Practical and hypothetical projections should be made. Radio can fool you by its pulling power. If a promotion catches on, it can exceed all expectations. You've got to be prepared for all contingencies. These are nice problems to have, but you can get egg on your face. Take a good look at the long and short of things before you bolt from the starting gate. Don't be too hasty or quick to execute. Consider all the variables, then proceed with care."

Lima tells of a successful promotion at WVMI that required considerable organization and planning. "We called it 'The Great Easter Egg Hunt.' What was basically an Easter egg hunt at a local park here in Biloxi attracted over 11,000 people. A local bottler co-sponsored the event and provided many of the thousands of dollars in prizes. The station hyped the event for several weeks over the air, and a little off-air promotion was done. The reason the promotion worked so well is that there actually was a need for a large, well-organized Easter

event. We did our homework in selecting and executing this promotion, which turned out to be a big winner."

Charlie Morriss shares an account of a successful promotion at radio station KOMP. "Jocks flew around the Las Vegas skies in several World War II fighter planes owned by Miller Beer while our call letters were written by a skywriter. The effect was stunning. This promotion worked because skywriting is so rare these days and not many people have seen a squadron of vintage warplanes. It also worked because it didn't cost us a penny. It was a trade agreement with Miller. We gave them the exposure, and they gave us the air show. Of course, a lot of details had to be worked out in advance."

The most effective promotion in recent years at New London's WSUB involved awarding contestants an elaborate night out on the town. Chuck Davis relates: "Our 'Night Out' promotion has been popular for some time. The station gets premium

FIGURE 7.12
A checklist designed to keep a station in the hearts and minds of its audience. Courtesy Shane Media.

FIGURE 7.13
The prize van is on the prowl. Courtesy Infinity.

mix 98-5   mix 98-5   mix 98-5   mix 98-5   mix 98-5

 Van Appearance

The MIX 98-5 Expedition can be spotted throughout New England at MIX 98-5 station appearance! At every appearance, the **MIX WHEEL OF PRIZES CLOSET** is on-site for contestants to win great prizes. Lucky winners get to choose a gift off the shelf that corresponds with the color on the wheel.

During each appearance, the MIX 98-5 promotion coordinators arrive in the MIX Expedition ready to give away great station premium and create excitement while supporting your marketing message to your target consumers.

Sponsor receives:

1. 2 hour station appearance with Wheel of Prizes, Sound System, Station Van, and giveaways.

2. On-air promotional announcements to run prior to the appearance.

3. Inclusion on MIX 98-5 Web Site - www.mix985.com

Source: Arbitron Spring 2002/Scarborough 2002

concert tickets through a close alliance with a New York concert promoter. It then finds a sponsor to participate in the giveaway and provides him with counter signs and an entry box so that people may register in his store. The sponsor then becomes part of the promotion and in return purchases an air schedule. Contestants are told to go to the store to register for the 'Night Out,' thus increasing store traffic even more. In addition, the sponsor agrees to absorb the expense of a limousine to transport the winners, who also are treated to a preconcert dinner at a local restaurant that provides the meals in exchange for promotional consideration—a mention on the air in our 'Night Out' promos. In the end, the station's cost amounts to a couple of phone calls, a cardboard sign, and a box. Reaction has always been great from all parties. The sponsor likes the tie-in with the promotion. The restaurant is very satisfied with the attention it receives for providing a few dinners, and the concert promoter gets a lot of exposure for the acts that he books simply by giving the station some tickets. It works like a charm. We please our audience and also put a few greenbacks in the till."

In the end, making certain that everything is kosher with the execution of a promotion or contest is absolutely crucial, notes Larry Miller. "Another perhaps apocryphal tale of things going amiss is the San Francisco Top 40 station that did a Lucky License Plate contest during morning drive. Everybody listening stopped and got out of their car to check their license plate to see it they had won. This caused a monumental traffic jam, and the authorities were not pleased."

The point already has been made that a station can ill afford not to promote itself in today's highly competitive marketplace. Promotions are an integral part of contemporary station operations, and research and planning are what make a promotion a winner.

Budgeting Promotions

Included in the planning of a promotion are cost projections. The promotion director's budget may be substantial or all but nonexistent. Stations in small markets often have minuscule budgets compared to their giant metro market counterparts. But then again, the need to promote in a one or two-station market generally is not as great as it is in multistation markets. To a degree, the promotion a station does is commensurate with the level of competition.

A typical promotion at an average-size station may involve the use of newspapers, plus additional hand-out materials, such as stickers, posters, buttons, and an assortment of other items depending on the nature of the promotion. Television and billboards may also be utilized. Each of these items will require an expenditure unless some other provision has been made, such as a trade agreement in which airtime is swapped for goods or ad space.

The cost involved in promoting a contest often constitutes the primary expense. When WASH-FM in Washington, D.C., gave away a million dollars, it spent $200,000 to purchase an annuity designed to pay the prize recipient $20,000 a year for 50 years. The station spent nearly an equal

FIGURE 7.14
Promoting a station using web sites. Courtesy Shane Media.

amount to promote the big giveaway. Most of the promotional cost resulted from a heavy use of local television.

Almost a decade ago KHTZ-FM in Los Angeles spent over $300,000 on billboards and television to advertise its dreamhouse giveaway. The total cost of the promotion approached a half million dollars. The price tag of the house was $122,000. Both of these high-priced contests accomplished their goals—increased ratings. In a metro market, one rating point can mean a million dollars in ad revenue. "A promotion that contributes to a two- or three-point jump in the ratings is well worth the money spent on it," observes Rick Peters.

FIGURE 7.15
Bus boards (this one in Canada) get the word out about stations. Courtesy DMR.

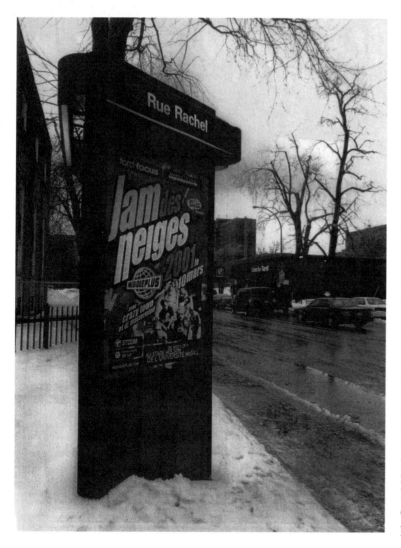

The promotion director works with the station manager in establishing the promotion budget. From there, it is the promotion director's job to allocate funds for the various contests and promotions that are run throughout the station's fiscal period. Just as in every other area of a station, computers are becoming a prominent fixture in the promotion department. "If you have a large budget, a computer certainly makes life a lot easier. The idea is to control the budget and not let it control you. Obviously computers have been a big help in this respect," states Marlin R. Taylor, who also contends that large sums of money need not be poured into promotions if a station is on target with its programming. "In 1983, the Malrite organization came to New York and launched Z-100, a contemporary hit-formatted outlet, moving it from 'worst to first' in a matter of months. They did a little advertising and gave away some money. I estimate that their giveaways totaled less dollars than some of their competitors spent on straight advertising. But the station's success was built on three key factors: product, service, and employee incentives. Indeed, they do have a quality product. Second, they are providing a service to their customers or listeners, and, third, the care and feeding of the air staff and support team are obvious at all times. You don't necessarily have to spend a fortune on promotion." Larry Miller agrees, "A really good promotion director can do effective promotions without spending a lot of money. First, utilize 'on air' promotions; second, trade out for stuff like contest prizes and newspaper advertising. You can do much for very little through a combined effort with programming."

Since promotion directors frequently are expected to arrange trade agreements with merchants as a way to defray costs, a familiarity with and understanding of the station's rate structure is necessary. Trading airtime for use in promotions is less popular at highly rated stations that can demand top dollars for spots. Most stations, however, prefer to exchange available airtime for goods and services needed in a promotion, rather than pay cash.

Promotions and the FCC

Although the FCC has dropped most of its rules pertaining to contests and promotions, it does expect that they be conducted with propriety and good judgment. The basic obligation of broadcasters to operate in the public interest remains the primary consideration. Section 73.1216 of the FCC's rules and regulations (as printed in the *Code of Federal Regulations*) outlines the do's and don'ts of contest presentations.

Stations are prohibited from running a contest in which contestants are required to pay in order to play. The FCC regards as lottery any contest in which the elements of prize, chance, and consideration exist. In other words, contestants must not have to risk something in order to win.

Contests must not place participants in any danger or jeopardize property. Awarding prizes to the first five people who successfully scale a treacherous mountain or swim a channel filled with alligators certainly would be construed by the FCC as endangering the lives of those involved. Contestants have been injured and stations held liable more than once. In the case of the station in California that ran a treasure hunt resulting in considerable property damage, it incurred the wrath of the public, town officials, and the FCC. In a more tragic example of poor planning a listener was killed during a "find the disk jockey" contest. The station was charged with negligence and sustained a substantial fine.

Stations are expected to disclose the material terms of all contests and promotions conducted. These include the following:

- Entering procedures
- Eligibility requirements
- Deadlines

- When or if prizes can be won
- Value of prizes
- Procedure for awarding prizes
- Tie-breaking procedures

The public must not be misled concerning the nature of prizes. Specifics must be stated. Implying that a large boat is to be awarded when, in fact, a canoe is the actual prize would constitute misrepresentation, as would suggesting that an evening in the Kon Tiki Room of the local Holiday Inn is a great escape weekend to the exotic South Seas.

The FCC also stipulates that any changes in contest rules must be promptly conveyed to the public. It makes clear, too, that any rigging of contests, such as determining winners in advance, is a direct violation of the law and can result in a substantial penalty, or even license revocation.

Although the FCC does not require that a station keep a contest file, most do. Maintaining all pertinent contest information, including signed prize receipts and releases by winners, can prevent problems should questions or a conflict arise later.

Stations that award prizes valued at $600 or more are expected by law to file a 1099-MISC form with the IRS. This is done strictly for reporting purposes, and stations incur no tax liability. However, failure to do so puts a station in conflict with the law.

Broadcast Promotion and Marketing Executives

The Broadcasters Promotion Association (BPA) was founded in 1956 as a nonprofit organization expressly designed to provide information and services to station promotion directors around the world. In the late 1980s its name was changed to Broadcast Promotion and Marketing Executives (BPME). In the 1990s, the organization became Promax International. Its objectives are as follows:

- Increase the effectiveness of broadcast promotion personnel
- Improve broadcast promotion methods, research principles, and techniques
- Enhance the image and professional status of its members and members of the broadcast promotion profession
- Facilitate liaison with allied organizations in broadcasting, promotion, and government
- Increase awareness and understanding of broadcast promotion at stations, in the community, and at colleges and universities

Promax conducts national seminars and workshops on promotion-related subjects. Further information about the organization may be obtained on its web site: www.promax.org.

CHAPTER HIGHLIGHTS

1. To keep listeners interested and tuned, stations actively promote their image and call letters. Small market stations promote themselves to compete for audience with other forms of media. Major market stations use promotion to differentiate themselves from competing stations.

2. Radio recognized the value of promotion early and used print media, remote broadcasts, and billboards to inform the public. Later, ratings surveys proved the importance of effective promotions.

3. Greater competition because of the increasing number of stations and monthly audience surveys means today's stations must promote themselves continually.

4. The most successful (attracting listenership loyalty) promotions involve large cash or merchandise prizes.

5. A successful promotion director possesses knowledge and understanding of the station's audience; a background in research and marketing, writing, and conceptual skills; the ability to adapt existing concepts to a particular station; and a familiarity with graphic art. The promotion director is responsible for acquiring prizes through trade or purchase and for compliance with FCC regulations covering promotions.

6. On-air promotions are the most common method used to retain and expand listenership. Such devices as slogans linked to the call letters and contests are common.

7. To "bookend" call letters means to place them at the beginning and conclusion of each break. To "graft" call letters means to include them with all informational announcements.

8. Contests must have clear rules and must provide entertainment for players and nonplayers alike. Successful contests are compatible with the station's sound, offer prizes attractive to the target audience, and challenge the listener's imagination.

9. Off-air promotions are intended to attract new listeners. Popular approaches include billboards, bus cards, newspapers, television, bumper stickers, discount cards, giveaway items embossed with call letters or logo, deejay personal appearances, special activity sponsorship, remote broadcasts,

direct mail, faxing, and telemarketing. Station web sites are promotional tools.

10. To offset the sometimes substantial cost of an off-air promotion, stations often collaborate with sponsors to share both the expenses and the attention gained.

11. FCC regulations governing promotions are contained in Section 73.12116. Basically, stations may not operate lotteries, endanger contestants, rig contests, or mislead listeners as to the nature of the prize.

12. Promax International provides information and services to station promotion directors.

SUGGESTED FURTHER READING

Aaker, David A., and Myers, John G. *Advertising Management*, 2nd ed. Englewood Cliffs, N.J.: Prentice Hall, 1982.

Bergendorff, Fred L. *Broadcast Advertising and Promotion: A Handbook for Students and Professionals.* New York: Hastings House, 1983.

Dickey, Lew. *The Franchise: Building Radio Brands.* Washington, D.C.: NAB Publications, 1994.

Donnelly, William J. *Planning Media: Strategy and Imagination.* New York: Pearson Education, 1995.

Eastman, Susan Tyler, Klein, Robert A., and Ferguson, Douglas. *Promotion and Marketing for Broadcasting, Cable, and the Web.* 4th ed. Boston: Focal Press, 2001.

Gompertz, Rolf. *Promotion and Publicity Handbook for Broadcasters.* Blue Ridge Summit, Pa.: Tab Books, 1977.

Macdonald, Jack. *The Handbook of Radio Publicity and Promotion.* Blue Ridge Summit, Pa.: Tab Books, 1970.

Matelsi, Marilyn. *Broadcast Programming and Promotion Work Text.* Boston: Focal Press, 1989.

National Association of Broadcasters. *Best of the Best Promotions*, III. Washington, D.C.: NAB Publications, 1994.

Nickels, William. *Marketing Communications and Promotion*, 3rd ed. New York: John Wiley & Sons, 1984.

Peck, William A. *Radio Promotion Handbook.* Blue Ridge Summit, Pa.: Tab Books, 1968.

Rhoads, B. Eric, et al., eds. *Programming and Promotions.* West Palm Beach, Fla.: Streamline Press, 1995.

Roberts, Ted E.F. *Practical Radio Promotions.* Boston: Focal Press, 1992.

Savage, Bob. *Perry's Broadcast Promotion Sourcebook.* Oak Ridge, Tenn.: Perry Publications, 1982.

Shane, Ed. *Selling Electronic Media.* Boston: Focal Press, 1999.

Stanley, Richard E. *Promotions*, 2nd ed. Englewood Cliffs, N.J.: Prentice Hall, 1982.

Traffic and Billing

The Air Supply

A station sells airtime. That is its inventory. The volume or size of a given station's inventory depends chiefly on the amount of time it allocates for commercial matter. For example, some stations with Easy Listening and Adult Contemporary formats deliberately restrict or limit commercial loads as a method of enhancing overall sound and fostering a "more music–less talk" image. Other outlets simply abide by commercial load stipulations as outlined in their license renewal applications.

A full-time station has over 10,000 minutes to fill each week. This computes to approximately 3,000 minutes for commercials, based on an 18-minute commercial load ceiling per hour. In the eyes of the sales manager, this means anywhere from 3,000 to 6,000 availabilities or slots—assuming that a station sells 60- and 30-second spot units—in which to insert commercial announcements.

From the discussion until now, it should be apparent that inventory control and accountability at a radio station are no small job. They are, in fact, the primary duty of the person called the traffic manager.

The Traffic Manager

A daily log is prepared by the traffic manager (also referred to as the traffic director). This document is at once a schedule of programming elements (commercials, features, public service announcements) to be aired and a record of what was actually aired. It serves to inform the on-air operator of what to broadcast and at what time, and it provides a record for, among other things, billing purposes.

Let us examine the process involved in logging a commercial for broadcast beginning at the point at which the salesperson writes an order for a spot schedule.

1. The salesperson writes an order and returns it to the station.
2. The sales manager then checks and approves the order.
3. The sales secretary types the order.
4. Copies of the formalized order are distributed to the traffic manager, sales manager, billing, salesperson, and client.
5. The order is placed in the traffic scheduling book or entered into the computer for posting to the log by the traffic manager.
6. The order is logged, commencing on the start date according to the stipulations of the buy.

Although the preceding is both a simplification and generalization of the actual process, it does convey the basic idea. Keep in mind that not all stations operate in exactly the same manner. The actual method for preparing a log will differ, too, from station to station depending on whether it is done manually or by computer. Those outlets using the manual system (very

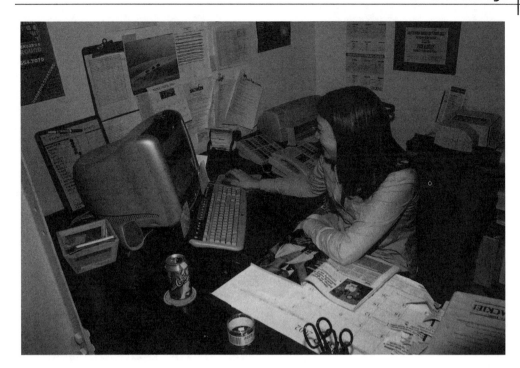

few remain) often simplify the process by preparing a master or semipermanent log containing fixed program elements and even long-term advertisers. Short-term sponsors and other changes will be entered on an ongoing basis. This method significantly reduces typing. The master may be imprinted on plastic or Mylar, and entries can be made and erased according to need. Once the log is prepared, it is then copied and distributed.

It is the traffic manager's responsibility to see that an order is logged as specified and that each client is treated fairly and equitably. A sponsor who purchases two spots, five days a week during morning drive, can expect to receive good rotation for maximum reach. It is up to the traffic manager to schedule the client's commercials in as many quarter-hour segments of the daypart as possible. The effectiveness of a spot schedule is reduced if the spots are logged in the same quarter-hour each day. If a spot is logged at 6:45 daily, it is only reaching those people tuned at that hour each day. However, if on one day it is logged at 7:15 and then at 8:45 on another, and so

on, it is reaching a different audience each day. It also would be unfair to the advertiser who purchased drivetime to have spots logged only prior to 7:00 a.m., the beginning of the prime audience period.

The traffic manager maintains a record of when a client's spots are aired to help ensure effective rotation. Another concern of the traffic manager is to keep adequate space between accounts of a competitive nature. Running two restaurants back-to-back or within the same spot set likely would result in having to reschedule both at different times at no cost to the client.

It also falls within the traffic manager's purview to make sure copy and production tapes are in on time. Most stations have a policy, often stated in their rate card, requiring that commercial material be on hand at least 48 hours before it is scheduled for broadcast. Traffic manager Carol Bates of Providence, Rhode Island, says that getting copy before the air date can be a problem. "It is not unusual to get a tape or copy a half-hour before it is due to air. We ask that copy be in well in advance, but sometimes it's a matter of minutes. No station is unfamiliar

```
                        WXLO-FM UNIT AVAILS REPORT
 Date: 8/6/99                    Time: 12:09p                        Page 1
              ROS - Probable distribution of schedules not using standard dayparts
```

	Allowed	Exclusive Daypart Sold	Remain	%Sold	ROS	w/Multiple Dayparts Sold	Remain	%Sold	Exclusive Amount	Multiple Amount
Monday 8/2/99										
12a-5a	50	11	39	22%	4	15	35	30%	118	133
5a-10a	66	35	31	53%	20	55	11	83%	3,547	4,645
10a-3p	55	23	32	41%	22	45	10	81%	2,534	3,650
3p-8p	55	15	40	27%	25	40	15	72%	1,467	2,521
8p-12a	45	5	40	11%	23	28	17	62%	212	1,033
TOTAL	271	89	182	32%	94	183	88	67%	7,879	11,983
Tuesday 8/3/99										
12a-5a	50	16	34	32%	4	20	30	40%	205	220
5a-10a	66	34	32	51%	22	56	10	84%	3,097	4,274
10a-3p	55	26	29	47%	22	48	7	87%	2,986	4,192
3p-8p	55	22	33	40%	24	46	9	83%	2,199	3,265
8p-12a	45	4	41	8%	28	32	13	71%	164	1,120
TOTAL	271	102	169	37%	100	202	69	74%	8,652	13,073
Wednesday 8/4/99										
12a-5a	50	17	33	34%	4	21	29	42%	257	274
5a-10a	66	50	16	75%	10	60	6	90%	4,569	4,995
10a-3p	55	21	34	38%	25	46	9	83%	2,359	3,567
3p-8p	55	39	16	70%	12	51	4	92%	3,924	4,466
8p-12a	45	3	42	6%	30	33	12	73%	136	1,289
TOTAL	271	130	141	47%	81	211	60	77%	11,246	14,593
Thursday 8/5/99										
12a-5a	50	21	29	42%	3	24	26	48%	163	177
5a-10a	66	40	26	60%	19	59	7	89%	3,732	4,497
10a-3p	55	32	23	58%	19	51	4	92%	3,569	4,480
3p-8p	55	38	17	69%	15	53	2	96%	3,895	4,533
8p-12a	45	3	42	6%	35	38	7	84%	90	1,288
TOTAL	271	134	137	49%	91	225	46	83%	11,450	14,977
Friday 8/6/99										
12a-5a	50	21	29	42%	3	24	26	48%	172	186
5a-10a	66	46	20	69%	14	60	6	90%	4,096	4,689
10a-3p	55	30	25	54%	20	50	5	90%	3,426	4,416
3p-8p	55	32	23	58%	19	51	4	92%	3,220	4,076
8p-12a	45	6	39	13%	30	36	9	80%	223	1,282
TOTAL	271	135	136	49%	86	221	50	81%	11,139	14,651
Saturday 8/7/99										
12a-5a	50	18	32	36%	4	22	28	44%	124	135
5a-10a	63	11	52	17%	42	53	10	84%	393	2,259
10a-3p	55	13	42	23%	39	52	3	94%	1,119	3,039
3p-8p	55	12	43	21%	36	48	7	87%	582	2,188
8p-12a	45	3	42	6%	29	32	13	71%	130	1,122
TOTAL	268	57	211	21%	150	207	61	77%	2,349	8,744
Sunday 8/8/99										
12a-5a	50	13	37	26%	3	16	34	32%	0	1
5a-10a	32	5	27	15%	21	26	6	81%	185	936
10a-3p	50	15	35	30%	31	46	4	92%	1,002	2,215
3p-8p	55	9	46	16%	36	45	10	81%	489	1,921
8p-12a	45	0	45	0%	22	22	23	48%	0	680
TOTAL	232	42	190	18%	113	155	77	66%	1,676	5,755
Total 8/2/99-8/8/99										
12a-5a	350	117	233	33%	25	142	208	40%	1,041	1,129
5a-10a	425	221	204	52%	148	369	56	86%	19,621	26,297
10a-3p	380	160	220	42%	178	338	42	88%	16,996	25,562
3p-8p	385	167	218	43%	167	334	51	86%	15,778	22,973
8p-12a	315	24	291	7%	197	221	94	70%	957	7,817
TOTAL	1855	689	1166	37%	715	1404	451	75%	54,395	83,780

FIGURE 8.2

An availability report for a one-week period. Courtesy WXLO-FM.

with having to make up spots due to late copy. It's irritating but a reality that you have to deal with."

Station traffic manager Jan Hildreth says that holiday and political campaign periods can place added pressure on the traffic person. "The fourth quarter is the big money time in radio. The logs usually are jammed, and availabilities are in short supply. The workload in the traffic department doubles. Things also get pretty chaotic around elections. It can become a real test for the nerves. Of course, there's always the late order that arrives at 5 p.m. on Friday that gets the adrenaline going."

There are few station relationships closer than that of the traffic department with pro-gramming and sales. Programming relies on the traffic manager for the logs that function as scheduling guides for on-air personnel. Sales depends on the traffic department to inform it of existing availabilities and to process orders onto the air. "It is crucial to the operation that traffic have a good relationship with sales and programming. When it doesn't, things begin to happen. The PD has to let traffic know when something changes; if not, the system breaks down. This is equally true of sales. Traffic is kind of the heart of things. Everything passes through the traffic department. Cooperation is very important," observes radio station traffic manager Barbara Kalulas.

The Traffic Manager's Credentials

A college degree usually is not a criterion for the job of traffic manager. This is not to imply that skill and training are not necessary. Obviously the demands placed on the traffic manager are formidable, and not everyone is qualified to fill the position. "It takes a special kind of person to effectively handle the job of traffic. Patience, an eye for detail, plus the ability to work under pressure and with other people are just some of the qualities the position requires," notes radio executive Bill Campbell.

Typing or keyboard skills are vital to the job. A familiarity with computers and word processing has become necessary, because most stations have given up the manual system of preparing logs in favor of the computerized method.

Many traffic people are trained in-house and come from the administrative or clerical ranks. It is a position that traditionally has been filled by women. Even though traffic salaries generally exceed that of purely secretarial positions, this is not an area noted for its high pay. Although the traffic manager is expected to handle many responsibilities, the position generally is perceived as more clerical in nature than managerial.

Traffic managers frequently make the transition into sales or programming. The considerable exposure to those particular areas provides a solid foundation and good springboard for those desiring to make the change.

Directing Traffic

Computers vastly enhance the speed and efficiency of the traffic process. Computers store copious amounts of data, retrieve information faster than humanly possible, and schedule and rotate commercials with precision and equanimity, to mention only a few of the features that make the new technology especially adaptive for use in the traffic area (see figures 8.2, 8.3, and 8.4).

Computers are an excellent tool for inventory control, contends former broadcast computer consultant Vicki Cliff. "Radio is a commodity not unlike a train carload of perishables, such as tomatoes. Radio sells time, which is progressively spoiling. The economic laws of supply and demand are classically applied to radio. Computers can assist in plotting that supply and demand curve in determining rates to be charged for various dayparts at any given moment.

"Inventory control is vital to any business. Radio is limited in its availabilities and seasonal in its desirability to the client. In a sold-out state, client value priorities must be weighted to optimize the station's billing. All things being equal, the credit rating of the client should be the deciding factor. Computers can eliminate the human subjectivity in formulating the daily log."

The cost of computerizing traffic has kept a small percentage of stations from converting from the manual system, notes Cliff. "Purchasing a personal computer for the traffic function is okay, but if a station

```
WXLO-FM  Fitchburg, MA                    Saturday, August 7, 1999      3 =25
                          TOTALS  PAGE


        Time totals are shown in HH:MM:SS format    * = hour changed by log editing

        HOURLY   SPOT   TOTALS:
           Hour        Units    Commercial      Political      Total Time
        12:00a- 1:00a *    6       :05:00          :00:00        :05:00
         1:00a- 2:00a *    4       :04:00          :00:00        :04:00
         2:00a- 3:00a      4       :04:00          :00:00        :04:00
         3:00a- 4:00a      4       :04:00          :00:00        :04:00
         4:00a- 5:00a      3       :03:00          :00:00        :03:00
         5:00a- 6:00a *    4       :01:00          :00:00        :01:00
         6:00a- 7:00a *   14       :14:00          :00:00        :14:00
         7:00a- 8:00a *   14       :13:00          :00:00        :13:00
         8:00a- 9:00a *   14       :14:00          :00:00        :14:00
         9:00a-10:00a *   11       :11:00          :00:00        :11:00
        10:00a-11:00a *   11       :11:00          :00:00        :11:00
        11:00a-12:00p *   11       :11:00          :00:00        :11:00
        12:00p- 1:00p *   11       :11:00          :00:00        :11:00
         1:00p- 2:00p *   11       :11:00          :00:00        :11:00
         2:00p- 3:00p *   11       :11:00          :00:00        :11:00
         3:00p- 4:00p *   11       :10:00          :00:00        :10:00
         4:00p- 5:00p *   10       :10:00          :00:00        :10:00
         5:00p- 6:00p *   10       :09:00          :00:00        :09:00
         6:00p- 7:00p *    9       :08:00          :00:00        :08:00
         7:00p- 8:00p *    8       :04:30          :00:00        :04:30
         8:00p- 9:00p *    7       :06:00          :00:00        :06:00
         9:00p-10:00p *    6       :04:00          :00:00        :04:00
        10:00p-11:00p *    6       :04:00          :00:00        :04:00
        11:00p-12:00a *    4       :02:30          :00:00        :02:30


        SPOT   TOTALS   BY   TYPE:
        Type      Number    Total Time
        CM         140      2:20:00
        PSA          2        :02:00
        PRO         10        :10:00
        POL          0        :00:00
        TRD         27        :26:00
        HOZ         20        :20:00
        SPO          5        :00:00
        N/C          0        :00:00
        BON          0        :00:00
        OTH          0        :00:00
        TOTALS     204      3:18:00


        TOTAL   PROGRAM   TIME   BY   TYPE:
        Type     Total Time
         N         :04:00
         A         :00:00
         PA        :00:00
         R         :00:00
         S         :00:00
         O         :00:00
        Edit       :00:00
        Pol        :00:00
        Ed         :00:00
```

desires to perform several functions, it may find itself out of luck. There are limits as to what can be done with a personal computer. On the other hand, a larger capacity, mainframe computer can be a major expense, although the functions it can perform are extraordinary. An online, real-time system can be costly also. Line expenses can really add up. Those station managers considering computerizing must gather all possible data to determine if the system they're considering will cost justify itself."

In an interview in *Radio Ink*, WPOC-FM's Jim Dolan observed that "The move right now is toward putting your sales force in the field armed with laptops and instantaneous online access to inventory, availability, and contract information. And the PC-based systems seem to be evolving faster

FIGURE 8.3
A breakout of hourly spot totals. Courtesy WXLO-FM.

```
WXLO-FM  Fitchburg, MA              Saturday, August 7, 1999
                   ANNOUNCER'S PAGE


                     M I S S E D   S P O T S :
Len      Advertiser           Reason    1  2  3  4  5  6  7  8  9  10
```

FIGURE 8.4
The form used by on-air people to cite missed commercials. Courtesy WXLO-FM.

than the minicomputer systems in this regard."

Various types of traffic and billing software are available. Dozens of companies, most notably Marketron, Columbine, Bias Radio, Custom Business Systems, Jefferson Pilot, and The Management, specialize in providing broadcasters with software packages. Prices for computer software vary depending on the nature and content of the program.

Compatible hardware is specified by the software manufacturer. Most software is IBM-PC compatible, however. Companies and consultants specializing in broadcast computerization are listed in *Broadcasting Yearbook*.

According to the NAB, the majority of stations were utilizing computers, especially in the area of traffic, in the 1990s. Notes Jay Williams, Jr., "Traffic and accounting for many affiliated stations are now being done by modem from corporate offices. Even

sales is becoming more computer-powered. It won't be long before avails and pricing will be offered to stations, acceptance of an order will be confirmed by a keystroke, and the commercial downloaded on command."

In the age of widespread station clustering, it is common for a centralized traffic (and billing) department to handle the work of several outlets that are owned by the same company or group. In this case, the staff of the "hub" department (the one handling all of the work) may be enlarged to accommodate the increased demands. Obviously this also means that the traffic departments at the various stations in the cluster are no longer necessary and therefore are typically eliminated.

Adds Williams, "Consolidation and technology have provided opportunities for savings in traffic, bookkeeping, engineering, and other internal operations. Formerly every station had its own traffic manager or traffic person managing two stations, but technology has allowed radio companies to think outside of the building. Tele-Media Corporation operates several stations at one location. At pre-set times, each of the stations faxes broadcast orders to Tele-Media's facility in Albany, New York, where the commercials are entered into a master computer system. Completed logs are then emailed to each station where they are printed out and used for broadcast. In the near future, Tele-Media's stations will email the orders, rather than fax them, making the process that much more efficient. This centralized traffic system has worked so well, that Tele-Media has established its traffic center as a separate business unit and offers services to other non-owned stations."

Billing

At most stations, advertisers are billed for the airtime they have purchased after a portion or all of it has run. Few stations require that sponsors pay in advance. It is the job of the billing department to notify the advertiser when payment is due. Al Rozanski, former business manager of WMJX-FM, Boston, explains the process involved once a contract has been logged by the traffic department. "We send invoices out twice monthly. Many stations bill weekly, but we find doing it every two weeks cuts down on the paperwork considerably. The first thing my billing person does is check the logs to verify that the client's spots ran. We don't bill them for something that wasn't aired. Occasionally a spot will be missed for one reason or another, say a technical problem. This will be reflected on the log because the on-air person will indicate this fact. Invoices are then generated in triplicate by our computer. We use an IBM System 34 computer and Columbine software. This combination is extremely versatile and efficient. The station retains a copy of the invoice and mails two to the client, who then returns one with the payment. The client also receives an affidavit detailing when spots were aired. If the client requests, we will notarize the invoice. This is generally necessary for clients involved in co-op contracts." The billing procedure at WMJX-FM is representative of that at many stations.

Not all radio stations have a full-time business manager on the payroll. Thus, the person who handles billing commonly is responsible for maintaining the station's financial records or books as well. In this case, the services of a professional accountant may be contracted on a regular periodic basis to perform the more complex bookkeeping tasks and provide consultation on other financial matters.

Accounts that fail to pay when due are turned over to the appropriate salesperson for collections. If this does not result in payment, a station may use the services of a collection agency. Should its attempt also fail, the station likely would write the business off as a loss at tax time.

The FCC and Traffic

Program log requirements were eliminated by the FCC in the early 1980s as part of the era's formidable deregulation movement. Before then the FCC expected radio stations to maintain a formal log, which—in addition to program titles, sponsor names, and length of elements—reflected information pertaining to the nature of announcements (commercial material, public service

FIGURE 8.5
Integrated traffic/accounting systems are much in vogue at radio stations.

RADIO TRAC

"The Traffic and Accounting Software of the 90's"

RADIO TRAC is one of the most comprehensive traffic and accounting software packages available. It is a completely integrated system, rich in flexibility and user-friendliness.

RADIO TRAC was designed and developed with the benefits of 17 years background in radio traffic management, 25 years in accounting/controller functions, and over 20 years experience in the development of computer software applications.

RADIO TRAC's customizing features allow each station a perfect fit for its particular needs and changing situations without costly additional software programming.

The TRAFFIC module, from initial order entry to the finished program log, is designed for speed, ease of data entry, immediate log format changes, and printed or on-line display of pertinent information.

The ACCOUNTS RECEIVABLE module provides a complete billing process including preparation of the sales journal, invoices, statements and accounts receivable; it also provides advertiser information, a cash receipts entry process, sales projections, a myriad of information screens and reports on all accounts receivable-related functions, and posting to the General Ledger.

The ACCOUNTS PAYABLE module processes and reports accounts payable data including accounts payable invoices, check preparation vendor information, activity reports, and posting to the General Ledger.

The GENERAL LEDGER module gathers posted entries from the Accounts Payable, Accounts Receivable and from the General Ledger systems and ultimately produces an easy to read customized financial statement.

The SALES module provides useful information on screen and in report form on salesperson performance, bulk contract status and advertiser activity.

The MANAGEMENT module supplies useful administrative and personnel information.

FIGURE 8.6
Spot schedule order
form. Courtesy
WMJX-FM.

Traffic Order   Date _____

CODE GROUP							BUYER INFORMATION		CREDIT INFORMATION
Station		Product No.			Agency Estimate No.		Name		Name
Agency Number		Category			Rate Card		Telephone		Telephone
Advertiser Number		Billing Period			Co-Op Invoice		Account Type		Credit Check
Contract Number		Invoice Times			Dealer Invoice		X		Credit Limit
Salesman Number		Agency Commission		%	Discount	%	Z		Contract Year
Salesman Name					Annct. Type		Special Instructions:		
Advertiser					Advertiser Avail Code				
To Be Logged As					Contract Avail Code				

Option	Line No.	Group	Type	Minum. Separ.		Broadcast Dates		Flight	Section	Class	Spots/Pgm Duration	Annct. Length	Time Schedule		Spots Per Week	Broadcast Pattern							Control	Rate	Plan	Unit	Music/Comedies	Live	Video	Audio	Agency Copy Number	Rack Number	Cr. Code M/G For
				Prd	Adv	Start	End						Start	End		Mon	Tue	Wed	Thur	Fri	Sat	Sun											

Agency Name and Address _____ Zip/PC. _____

	PACKAGE									
	PLAN	FREQ.	RATE	B'casts	Rate	Totals By Rate	B'casts	Rate	Totals By Rate

Billing Name and Address _____ Zip/PC. _____

Contract Totals → Gross
Agency Comm.
Net

X To Cancel Order Before Start

PRINTED IN U.S.A.

FIGURE 8.7
Traffic managers
check logs before
placing them in the
control room.
Courtesy WHJJ-AM.

announcement), source of origination (live, recorded, network), and the type of program (entertainment, news, political, religious, other). Failing to include this information on the log could have resulted in punitive actions against the station by the FCC.

Although stations no longer must keep a program log under existing rules, some sort of document is still necessary to inform programming personnel of what is scheduled for broadcast and to provide information for both the traffic and billing departments pertaining to their particular functions. A log creates accountability. It is both a programming guide and a document of verification.

Stations are now at liberty to design logs that serve their needs most effectively and efficiently. The WMJX log form shown in figure 8.11 is an example of a log that has been designed to meet all of its station's needs in the most economical and uncomplicated way.

There are no stipulations regarding the length of time that logs must be retained. Before the elimination of the FCC program log regulations, stations were required to retain logs for a minimum of two years. Today most stations still hold onto logs for that amount of time for the sake of accountability.

CHAPTER HIGHLIGHTS

1. Each commercial slot on a station is called an *availability*. Availabilities constitute a station's salable inventory.

2. The traffic manager (or traffic director) controls and is accountable for the broadcast time inventory.

3. The traffic manager prepares a log to inform the deejays of what to broadcast and at what time.

4. The traffic manager is also responsible for ensuring that an ad order is logged as specified, that a record of when each client's spots are aired is maintained, and that copy and production tapes are in on time.

5. Programming relies on the traffic manager for the logs that function as scheduling guides for on-air personnel; the sales department depends on the traffic manager to inform them of existing availabilities and to process orders onto the air.

6. Although most traffic people are trained in-house and are drawn from the administrative or clerical ranks, they must possess patience, an eye for detail, the ability to work under pressure, and keyboarding skills.

7. Most traffic departments have been computerized to enhance speed and efficiency. Therefore, traffic managers must be computer knowledgeable.

8. In many instances, consolidation (clustering) has eliminated individual station traffic and billing departments and outside companies have assumed the task.

9. Based on the spots aired, as recorded and verified by the traffic department, the billing department sends invoices weekly or biweekly to each client. Invoices are notarized for clients with co-op contracts.

10. Since the FCC eliminated program log requirements in the early 1980s, stations have been able to design logs that inform programming personnel of what is scheduled for broadcast and that provide necessary information for the traffic and billing departments.

FIGURE 8.8
Terms and conditions of an advertising buy. Courtesy WXLO-FM.

STANDARD TERMS AND CONDITIONS

1 Approvals. Station reserves the right to approve all advertising, which approval shall not be unreasonably withheld. Advertiser agrees that advertisements and promotions which it runs in accordance with this Agreement shall be in accordance with applicable rules and policies established from time to time by Station.

2. Commercial Content. Station assumes no responsibility, obligation or liability with respect to the content or style of the advertising provided by the Advertiser and Advertiser agrees to indemnify Station for any liability which may result from broadcasting said commercial. In an effort to provide the community with wholesome entertainment, Station reviews all programming and commercials which it places for broadcast, and reserves the right to reject any particular advertisement provided by Advertiser. See station's production guidelines for a thorough detail of stations commercial policies.

3. Additional Requested Broadcasts. Except as otherwise agreed to in writing, if Advertiser continues to request that Station broadcast advertising beyond that specified herein, additional broadcasts shall be considered a part of this contract, at the rate established by the Station from time to time, and otherwise subject to these terms and conditions, until otherwise agreed to in writing.

4. Confirmations and Cancellations. All contracts and revisions are scrutinized for accuracy prior to mailing. Upon receipt of station contracts by Advertiser, it is Advertiser's responsibility to notify Station of any possible discrepancy. If Station receives no notice within seven (7) days of issue, the contract or revision will be considered correct and Advertiser will be responsible for payment. Station requires two (2) weeks notice of cancellation.

5. Trademarks and Non-Exclusivity. This Agreement does not grant Advertiser the rights to use tradenames, trademarks or service marks of Station. No merchandising, promotional or other special consideration, nor any product category exclusivity or other protection regarding any broadcast, will be provided by Station in connection with the scheduled advertising unless specifically set forth in this Agreement.

6. Failure to Broadcast Commercials. Advertiser acknowledges that commercials occasionally may not be broadcast when scheduled due to events beyond the reasonable control of Station. In the event scheduled advertising is not broadcast when scheduled. Station shall be entitled to place advertising on a subsequent, comparable broadcast, on a "make good" basis. In no event shall Station be liable for any consequential or incidental damages relating to its failure to air scheduled advertising.

7. Execution by Agency. If this Agreement is entered into by an Advertising Agency on behalf of an Advertiser, said Agency jointly and severally undertakes the obligations of Advertiser hereunder.

8. Massachusetts Law. This Agreement is made and entered into in Massachusetts and shall be interpreted, construed and enforced in accordance with the laws of the Commonwealth of Massachusetts.

CREDIT POLICY

1. Extension of Credit. Standard Station credit policy is cash in advance for Advertiser's first order, pending approval of credit, and said credit will not be extended without a completed and signed credit application from Advertiser on file.

2. Credit limits. Individual credit limits are established at the sole discretion of Station and are subject to review from time to time.

COMMISSIONS AND DISCOUNTS

1. Agency Commissions. Commissions will be paid by Station only to established Advertising Agencies in good standing.

PAYMENTS

1. Payments. Standard Station payment policy is that all invoices are due and payable net thirty (30) days from receipt of invoice.

2. Late Charges. Any amounts due Station from Advertiser not paid within (30) days of receipt of invoice are subject to a five percent (5%) late payment charge.

3. Collections. In the event of any collection action or litigation to collect amounts due from Advertiser, Station shall be entitled to reasonable cost of collection and attorneys fees as determined by the Court.

FIGURE 8.9
The traffic department provides key information to salespeople through special computer programs that manage inventory. Courtesy Marketron.

Traffic

Accurate Demand Pricing

The Marketron Act II and IV radio traffic systems supply spot data to a program called FirstRate. This program analyzes and categorizes this data in a completely different way than anything before. The goal is to present a picture of information that will offer greater assistance in manipulating inventory and controlling price. The end objective of FirstRate is to provide the sales staff with the ability to produce a schedule that reflects pricing based upon demand. The computer uses (3) elements to do this. First, it knows how much inventory is sold out into the future. Secondly, it knows what the sales managers

CONTRACT

106.7 WIZN   the Buzz 99.3

WIZN ☐   WBTZ ☐

PO Box 1067 ■ Burlington, VT 05402-1067
(802) 860-2440 ■ Fax (802) 860-1818

☐ NEW ORDER
☐ SUPERSEDES PREVIOUS
☐ ADD TO
☐ CANCEL

DATE _____
CONTRACT # _____
ACCOUNT # _____
PO # / EST # _____

☐ DIRECT   ☐ AGENCY
☐ LOCAL   ☐ NATIONAL   ☐ REGIONAL
☐ CASH   ☐ TRADE   ☐ POLITICAL ☐ CO-OP
☐ BROADCAST   ☐ CALENDAR
☐ NET   ☐ GROSS

ADVERTISER _____
ADDRESS _____
CITY/STATE/ZIP _____
CONTACT _____
PHONE# _____
FAX # _____
AGENCY _____
ADDRESS _____
CITY/STATE/ZIP _____
BUYER _____
LOG AS _____
COMPETING PRODUCTS _____
PACKAGE/PROGRAM _____
SALESPERSON _____

AUTHORIZED BY _____

NOTES _____

LINE	DAYPART START	DAYPART END	BROADCAST PATTERN M	T	W	T	F	S	S	# SPOTS WEEK	FLIGHT	DATES START	DATES END	LENGTH	RATE	CART #	PRODUCT	EXTRA COMMENT

						# OF BROADCASTS	RATE	TOTAL

JANUARY	FEBRUARY	MARCH	APRIL	MAY	JUNE	JULY	AUGUST	SEPTEMBER	OCTOBER	NOVEMBER	DECEMBER	CONTRACT TOTAL

SIGNATURE _____   DATE _____

SERIES 563
73113 4/00

FIGURE 8.10
Traffic and billing receive copies of orders written by sales reps. Courtesy WIZN-FM.

FIGURE 8.11
A station log
indicating when
program elements and
commercials are aired.
Courtesy WXLO-FM.

WDIS AM1170 Norfold, MA 02056

DATE: 10/28/02   HOUR: 0700–0800   PROGRAM: TALK AMERICA

Time	Element		
:00:00	NETWORK NEWS		
:05:00	LOCAL AVAIL (1: 30)		
	AOL BB/LOCAL NEWS		
:06:30	**TALK AMERICA RESUMES**		
:21:00	LOCAL AVAIL (2: 00)		
:23:00	Talk America Resumes		
:30:00	**Local Avail (3: 00)**		
:33:00	TALK AMERICA RESUMES		
:51:00	LOCAL AVAIL (2:00)		
	ENTERTAINMENT BOOK	TR	60 TAPE
	SEVEN-ELEVEN	TR	30 TAPE
:53:00	TALK AMERICA RESUMES		
:58:50	LOCAL AVAIL (1:00)		
	IKON	TR	60 TAPE
:59:50	LEGAL ID		

OPERATOR SIGNATURE_____

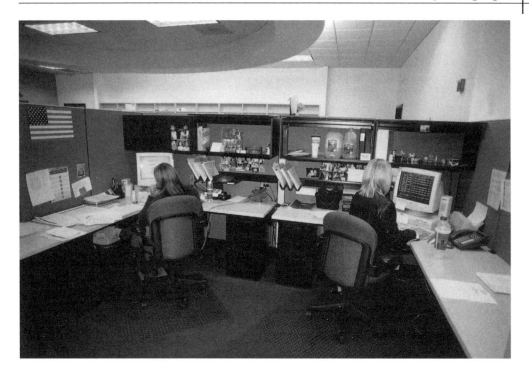

FIGURE 8.12
Traffic department in cluster operation. Courtesy Clear Channel.

FIGURE 8.13
When spots are to appear in a log after it has been printed, they are hand-entered. Courtesy WXLO-FM.

FIGURE 8.14
Standard form used
for clients involved in
co-op agreements.
Courtesy WMJX-FM.

ANA/RAB FORM FOR SCRIPT (IF TAPE IS USED, PREPARE SCRIPT FROM TAPE)

wmjx 106 fm
The _magic_ is the music. ®

ANA/RAB RADIO "TEAR-SHEET"
FORM AT BOTTOM OF SCRIPT PERMITS KNOWING
HOW MANY TIMES THIS SCRIPT RAN, AT WHAT
COST.

Client: For:

        Begin: End: Date:

STATION DOCUMENTATION STATEMENT APPROVED BY THE CO-OPERATIVE ADVERTISING
COMMITTEE OF THE ASSOCIATION OF NATIONAL ADVERTISERS

This announcement was broadcast_____times, as entered in the station's program log. The times this
announcement was broadcast were billed to this station's client at our invoice(s) number/dated
_____at his earned rate of:

$_____each for_____announcements, for a total of $_____
$_____each for_____announcements , for a total of $_____
$_____each for_____announcements, for a total of $_____

Signature of station official

(Notarize above)   Typed name and title   Station

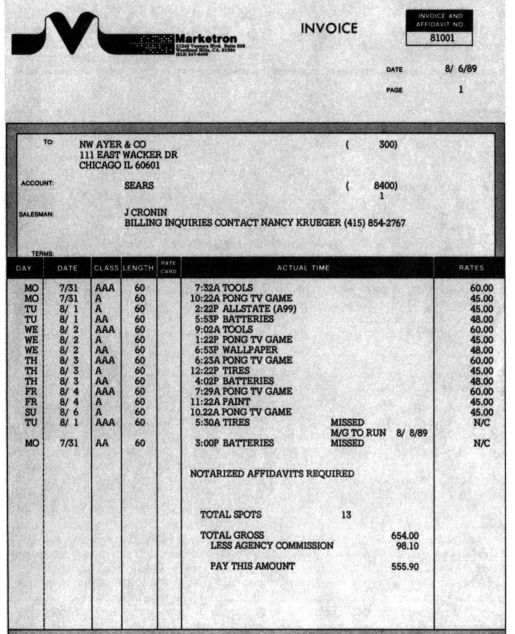

FIGURE 8.15
Example of station invoice sent to an ad agency. Notice that the commission is deducted from the total gross. Courtesy Marketron.

FIGURE 8.16
A traffic manager
explains her job.
Courtesy
WIZN/WBTZ.

A Traffic Manager's Account

Every radio station has a person who manages "traffic". Traffic management is the scheduling of commercials. Client orders are entered into the traffic software specifying the dates, times, length, and rate of the requested commercials.

Once the order is entered, the questions "Who wants to advertise?" and "When do they want to be on the air?" are answered. Clients can choose to run a certain number of commercials over a period of days or they can opt for a specific number of commercials on specific days. In general, the more detailed the client specifications for placement, the greater the cost of the commercial.

After deciding when they want to run and how much flexibility they have in day placement, the client must choose the scheduling plan. Every radio station has a "run of station" plan that means the client's commercials will be placed randomly by the computer in whatever openings are available. This is generally called ROS or BTA (best times available), and is the least expensive placement option. A client may want to ensure that his commercials will run throughout the day. A plan that guarantees an even distribution throughout the dayparts is the next step up from an ROS schedule. Clients who specifically want a certain number of commercials in a particular daypart on a chosen day will pay the highest rate for the individual commercial unit. The customary dayparts are 6AM–10AM, 10AM–3PM, 3PM–7PM, 7PM–Mid.

The next question after "Who" wants to advertise and "When" is "What do they want to advertise?" The two most common reasons for advertising are "image" and "event". A client may want to advertise on a consistent basis to have their name and message in the public awareness or they may want to hype a particular event or sale.

Commercials may be produced by the radio station production department from a script or copy points provided by the client. Finished commercials can be sent in the form of reel, over the internet (MP3), or through commercial delivery systems. However the commercial arrives, the information about how to run that commercial must go to the traffic manager. The acceptable dates and times for each commercial are entered into the computer as well as rotation instructions if there are multiple commercials running for a client. Code numbers or information about the commercials that must be provided on the invoice are also entered.

Once all the contracts and traffic instructions are input, the traffic manager assembles and arranges a daily log. A multi-level priority system is used to ensure that the clients specifying the most detailed placement are scheduled first. If the traffic and in-studio computers are linked, the commercial log is immediately in place and ready to be merged with the music log. Any additions, deletions, or adjustments are registered as they occur. If the traffic and in-studio computer systems are not linked, the completed commercial log is transferred by disk and changes are entered manually into the traffic software.

Invoices specifying the date and time that each commercial aired are generated from the finalized log information.

SUGGESTED FURTHER READING

Diamond, Susan Z. *Records Management: A Practical Guide*. New York: AMACOM, 1983.

Doyle, Dennis M. *Efficient Accounting and Record Keeping*. New York: David McKay and Company, 1977.

Heighton, Elizabeth J., and Cunningham, Don R. *Advertising in the Broadcast and Cable Media*, 2nd ed. Belmont, Calif.: Wadsworth Publishing, 1984.

Keith, Michael C. *Selling Radio Direct*. Boston: Focal Press, 1992.

Murphy, Jonne. *Handbook of Radio Advertising*. Radnor, Pa.: Chilton, 1980.

Shane, Ed. *Selling Electronic Media*. Boston: Focal Press, 1999.

Slater, Jeffrey. *Simplifying Accounting Language*. Dubuque, Iowa: Kendall-Hall Publishing, 1975.

Warner, Charles, and Buchman, Joseph. *Broadcasting and Cable Selling*, 2nd ed. Belmont, Calif.: Wadsworth Publishing, 1993.

Wild, Tony. *Best Practice in Inventory Management*. New York: John Wiley & Sans, 1998.

Zeigler, Sherilyn K., and Howard, Herbert H. *Broadcast Advertising: A Comprehensive Working Textbook*, 2nd ed. Columbus, Ohio: Grid Publishing, 1984.

9 Production

A Spot Retrospective

A typical radio station will produce thousands of commercials, public service announcements, and promos annually. Initially, commercials were broadcast live, due to a lack of recording technology. In the 1920s, most paid announcements consisted of lengthy speeches on the virtues of a particular product or service. Perhaps the most representative of the commercials of the period was one of the first ever to be broadcast, which lasted over 10 minutes and was announced by a representative of a Queens, New York, real estate firm. Aired live over WEAF in 1922, by today's standards the message would sound more like a classroom lecture than a broadcast advertisement. Certainly no snappy jingle or ear-catching sound effects accompanied the episodic announcement.

Most commercial messages resembled the first until 1926. On Christmas Eve of that year the radio jingle was introduced, when four singers gathered for a musical tribute to Wheaties cereal. It was not for several years, however, that singing commercials were commonplace. For the most part, commercial production during the medium's first decade was relatively mundane. The reason was twofold: The government had resisted the idea of blatant or direct commercialism from the start, which fostered a low-key approach to advertising, and the medium was just in the process of evolving and therefore lacked the technical and creative wherewithal to present a more sophisticated spot.

Things changed by 1930, however. The austere, no-frills pitch, occasionally accompanied by a piano but more often done a cappella, was gradually replaced by the dialogue spot that used drama or comedy to sell its product. A great deal of imagination and creativity went into the writing and production of commercials, which were presented live throughout the 1930s. The production demands of some commercials equaled and even exceeded those of the programs they interrupted. Orchestras, actors, and lavishly constructed sound effects commonly were required to sell a chocolate-flavored syrup or a muscle liniment. By the late 1930s, certain commercials had become as famous as the favorite programs of the day. Commercials had achieved the status of pop art.

Still, the early radio station production room was primitive by today's standards. Sound effects were mostly improvised show by show, commercial by commercial, in some cases using the actual objects with which sounds were identified. Glass was shattered, guns fired, and furniture overturned as the studio's on-air light flashed. Before World War II, few sound effects were available on records. It was just as rare for a station to broadcast prerecorded commercials, although 78 rpm and wire recordings were used by certain major advertisers. The creation of vinyl discs in the 1940s inspired more widespread use of electrical transcriptions for radio advertising purposes. Today sound effects are taken from specially designed cassettes and CDs.

The live spot was the mainstay at most stations into the 1950s, when two innovations brought about a greater reliance on the prerecorded message. Magnetic recording tape and 33 LPs revolutionized radio production methods. Recording tape brought about the greatest transformation and, ironically, was the product of Nazi scientists who developed acetate recorders and tape for espionage purposes. The adoption of magnetic tape by radio stations was costlier and thus occurred at a slower pace than 33 rpm, which essentially required a turntable modification.

Throughout the 1950s, advertising agencies grew to rely on LPs. By 1960, magnetic tape recorders were a familiar piece of studio equipment. More and more commercials were prerecorded. Some stations, especially those automated, did away with live announcements entirely, preferring to tape everything to avoid on-air mistakes.

Commercials themselves became more sophisticated sounding since practically anything could be accomplished on tape. Perhaps no individual in the 1960s more effectively demonstrated the unique nature

FIGURE 9.1
A 1926 Western Electric microphone. Courtesy Jim Steele.

of radio as an advertising medium than did Stan Freberg. Through skillful writing and the clever use of sound effects, Freberg transformed Lake Michigan into a basin of

FIGURE 9.2
Today mixing is done in the digital box. Courtesy WIZN.

hot chocolate crowned by a 700-foot-high mountain of whipped cream, and no one doubted the feat.

Today the sounds of millions of skillfully prepared commercials trek through the ether and into the minds of practically every man, woman, and child in America. Good writing and production are what make the medium so successful.

Formatted Spots

In the 1950s the medium took to *formatting* in order to survive and prosper. Today listeners are offered myriad sounds from which to choose. There is something for practically every taste. Stations concentrate their efforts on delivering a specific format, which may be defined as Adult Contemporary, Country, Easy Listening, or any one of a dozen others. As you will recall from the discussion in Chapter 3, each format has its own distinctive sound, which is accomplished through a careful selection and arrangement of compatible program elements. To this end, commercials attempt to reflect a station's format. In the age of consolidation, says Larry Miller, "There is a tendency to do one size fits all at the agency level. In-house local retail may be more customized to fit the format. We used to make a point of avoiding loud rock 'n' roll spots at the classical station I worked for, but I'm not sure if that's still a consideration."

The Production Room

Generally speaking, metro market stations and clusters employ a full-time production person (known variously as production director, production manager, or production chief). This individual's primary duties are to record voice-tracks and mix commercials and PSAs (public service announcements). Other duties involve the maintenance of the bed and sound effects library and the mixdown of promotional material and special programs, such as public affairs features, interviews, and documentaries.

Stations that do not have a slot for a full-time production person divide work among the on-air staff. In this case, the program director often oversees production responsibilities, or a deejay may be assigned several hours of production duties each day and be called the production director.

At most medium and small outlets, on-air personnel take part in the production process. Production may include the simple transfer of an agency spot into the computer system, a mixdown that requires a single bed (background music) under a 30-second voicer, or a multi-element mixdown of a 60-second two-voicer with sound effects and several bed transitions. Station production can run from the mundane and to the exciting and challenging (mixing a commercial without words conveyed through a confluence of sounds).

Most production directors, in this digital age often called imaging directors, are recruited from the on-air ranks, having acquired the necessary studio dexterity and know-how to meet the demands of the position. In addition to the broad range of mixdown skills required by the job, a solid knowledge of editing is essential. The production director routinely is called on to make rudimentary splices or perform more complex editing chores, such as the rearrangement of elements in a 60-second concert promo. Editing is covered in more detail later in this chapter.

The production director/imaging director works closely with many people, but perhaps most closely with the program director. The person responsible for production is expected to have a complete understanding of the station's programming philosophy and objective. This is necessary since commercials constitute an element of programming and therefore must fit in. A production person must be able to determine when an incoming commercial clashes with the station's image. When a question exists as to the spot's appropriateness, the program director will be called on to make the final judgment, since it is he or she who is ultimately responsible for what gets on the air. In the final analysis, station production is a product of programming. In most broadcast organizations, the production director answers to the program director. It is a logical arrangement given the relationship of the two areas.

The production director also works closely with the station copywriter. Their combined efforts make or break a commercial. The copywriter conceives of the concept, and the producer brings it to fruition. The traffic department also is in close and constant contact with production, because one of its primary responsibilities is to see that copy gets processed and placed in the on-air studio where it is scheduled for broadcast.

Once again the extensive clustering of station facilities in the age of consolidation finds many production responsibilities centralized. By now many radio groups have established one production hub to mix the spots of their other outlets, especially when in the same market. Typically this has resulted in the downsizing of individual station production staffs and the elimination of comprehensive mixdown studios at these sites.

The Studios

A radio station has two kinds of studios: on-air and production. Both share basic design features and have comparable equipment. In cluster operations where stations are co-located, there is often a single primary production facility. For ease of movement and accessibility, audio equipment commonly is set up in a U-shape within which the operator or producer is seated.

The standard equipment found in radio studios includes an audio console (com-

FIGURE 9.3
This cutting-edge multitrack digital studio is in contrast with the analog studio in Figure 9.4. Courtesy Wheatstone.

FIGURE 9.4
Although each production studio is unique, the basics of layout are fairly consistent from station to station. For the sake of ease and accessibility, most studios are developed in a U-shape or a variation thereof. However, computer workstations have had an effect on equipment layout, since most work is done on the mouse and keyboard. Courtesy Clear Channel.

monly referred to as the "board"), computer workstation, reel-to-reel tape decks (less and less), cartridge (cart) machines (less and less), cassette decks, compact disc machines, mini-disc machines, digital effects boxes, and a patch panel. (See figure 9.4)

Audio Console

The audio console is the centerpiece, the very heart of the radio station. Dozens of manufacturers produce audio consoles, and although design characteristics vary, the

TYPICAL AUDIO PRODUCTION CHAIN

basic components remain relatively constant. Consoles come in all different sizes and shapes and may be monaural, stereo, or multitrack, but all contain inputs that permit audio energy to enter the console, outputs through which audio energy is fed to other locations, VU meters that measure the amount or level of sound, pots (faders) that control gain or the quantity of sound, monitor gains that control in-studio volume, and master gains for the purpose of controlling general output levels. (See figure 9.6, 9.7, and 9.8)

Since the late 1960s, the manufacture of consoles equipped with linear faders has surpassed those with rotary faders. *Slide* (another term used) faders perform the same function as the more traditional pots, and they are easier to read and handle.

Cue Mode. A low-power amplifier is built into the console so that the operator may hear audio from various sources without it actually being distributed to other points. The purpose of this is to facilitate the setup of certain sound elements, such as records and tapes, for eventual introduction into the mixdown sequence. (See figure 9.9)

Reel-to-Reel Tape Machines

The reel-to-reel machine is becoming less prominent in studios due to digitization. These machines have three magnetic heads whose purpose it is to record sound (convert electrical energy into magnetic energy), play back sound (convert magnetic energy into electrical energy), and erase magnetic impressions from recording tape. (See figure 9.12)

Most reel-to-reel machines are capable of recording at two speeds, although some models offer three. The tape speeds most commonly available on broadcast quality, state-of-the-art reel-to-reel machines are 3 3/4, 7 1/2, and 15 IPS (inches per second). The middle speed, 7 1/2, is used most frequently by broadcasters. The reason is a practical one: although some stations may possess machines with 3 3/4 or 15 IPS tape speeds, all have reel-to-reels with 7 1/2 IPS.

FIGURE 9.5
Transduction points in a typical audio chain.

FIGURE 9.6
Multichannel board. Courtesy Auditronics.

FIGURE 9.7
Audio console with
linear faders, popularly
referred to as a "slide"
board. Courtesy
Auditronics.

FIGURE 9.8
Eight-mixer ("pot")
monaural console.
Courtesy Broadcast
Electronics.

Therefore, stations and agencies making
dubs for distribution do so at 7 1/2 IPS.
In-house recording often is accomplished at
high speed (15 IPS) because the sound
quality is better and editing is easier.

Reel-to-reel tape machines are available
in monaural, stereo, and multitrack. The
last allows for overdubbing or sound-on-
sound recording, which gives the producer
greater control over the mix of sound elements. Multitrack recorders come in 4-, 8-,
16-, 24-, and 36-channel formats. They have
become increasingly popular since the
1970s, although they can be extremely

costly—prohibitively so for many small
market stations.

Cart Machines

Cartridge tape machines came into use in
the late 1950s and drastically simplified
the recording and playback process. Today
cart machines are becoming rare objects in
studios because of the introduction of digital
mixing equipment. A continuous loop of
quarter-inch magnetic tape within a plastic
container (cart) is used to record everything
from commercials and promos to music and

short public affairs features. (See figure 9.16)

A magnetic pulse is impressed against the tape surface during the recording process, which permits the cart to recue on its own. Carts come in various lengths—10, 40, 70 seconds—depending on need. They consist of a hub (around which tape is loosely wound), guides, and pressure pads, which keep the tape against the heads of the machine. When the cart machine is activated, a pinch roller presses against a capstan to move the tape.

Mini-Disc Machines

At many stations, analog cart machines are being replaced by random-access mini-disc (record/playback) technology. These new-age cart machines allow producers to digitally archive up to 74 minutes of audio on 2.5-inch reusable discs. Says station manager Vic Michaels, "It's a great replacement for carts, because it's faster, programmable, visual, and competitively priced." Companies like Sony, Harris, Denon, and Otari report heavy sales of the mini-disc machine, which would suggest that the days of the old analog cart deck may be numbered—another victim of the computer age. (See figure 9.17)

Among other things, mini-disc machines offer instant start (there is none of the hesitation or drag common in its analog predecessor), back cueing, track selection, endmarking, automatic fade-in, visual ID and cueing, digital editing, and so forth.

Cassette Tape Machines

Cassette machines, like their analog counterparts, are becoming less apparent in studios. The small tape cassettes can be inserted and removed from the machines without the customary rethreading and rewinding that is required by reel-to-reel machines. Adopted by broadcasters in the mid-1960s, cassette recorders employ 1/8-inch tape that is moved at 1 7/8 IPS. Cas-

sette tapes can hold up to three hours of material. Though not as integral to the production mixdown as mini-disc and CD machines, cassettes are nonetheless a useful piece of studio equipment. On-air cassette machines generally are used to play music, features, and actualities, as well as for aircheck purposes.

Cassette tape recorders come in stereo and monaural and are available in everything from pocket-sized portables to permanent rack-mounted models.

FIGURE 9.9
Cue speaker within console permits producer to set up elements for audio processing. Courtesy LPB.

FIGURE 9.10
Pot in cue mode. Courtesy Broadcast Electronics.

FIGURE 9.11
Magnetic head configuration–erase, record, and playback.

FIGURE 9.12
Multitrack reel-to-reel recording is widespread. This is a 32-track recorder, using 2-inch audio tape. Courtesy Otari.

Audio Tape

In the age of the tapeless studio, magnetic tape is still around enough to require a level of knowledge about it. Magnetic tape is chemically treated with either polyester or acetate, primarily for the sake of preservation. Polyester-backed tape generally is preferred because of its greater durability. It is less affected by extreme temperatures and humidity. Audio tape is produced in varying thicknesses: 0.5, 1.0, and 1.5 millimeters (mm). The thinner the tape, the more that can be contained on a reel. For instance, a

7-inch reel of 0.5-mm tape holds 2,400 feet of tape, whereas the same size reel of 1.5-mm tape holds only half as much, 1,200 feet. The industry standard is 1.5-mm tape because it is stronger and more dependable.

The width of audio tape also varies. The most common tape found in a production studio is 1/4 inch in width. This tape is used on standard mono and stereo reel-to-reel and cartridge machines. Multitrack recorders use anywhere from $1/2$- to 2-inch-wide tape, depending on the number of tracks a machine possesses.

Head Cleaning. The oxide particles from the magnetic tape leave a residue on tape heads. Dust and dirt also accumulate on heads. This can result in a deterioration of sound quality. Therefore, it is necessary to clean a tape machine's heads frequently. This generally is accomplished with cotton swabs and a liquid head cleaner. Many stations use isopropyl alcohol because it is effective and inexpensive.

The procedure for cleaning heads is simple. Moisten the cotton swab with the head cleaner and run it across each head. When the swab becomes slightly discolored, use a fresh one. It is best to use a new swab for each head. Light pressure may be applied to the heads to ensure that surface particles are removed. (See figure 9.19)

Compact Discs

Compact disc players entered the radio production studio in the 1980s. Although CD players are a more integral part of the on-air studio, their value as a piece of production equipment increases daily because of their recording (writing/burning) capabilities. Observes Skip Pizzi: "By far the largest acceptance of digital audio to date has been CD hardware, to the point where it is estimated that over half of the radio stations in the USA use CD to some extent. In major markets, this figure rises steeply. Many of these stations program music exclusively from CD, or nearly so. The practice of pro-

FIGURE 9.13
A typical on-air and production combination. Courtesy WIZN.

FIGURE 9.14
Monitoring the sound wave on the screen. Courtesy WIZN.

viding promotional copies of new releases on CD by record companies (following an earlier period of general reluctance to do so) has fueled a recent surge here. Second- and third-generation professional CD players are also aiding in the process of acceptance, which shows no signs of abating." (See figure 9.20)

Unlike analog discs, which require actual physical contact with a recording, CD

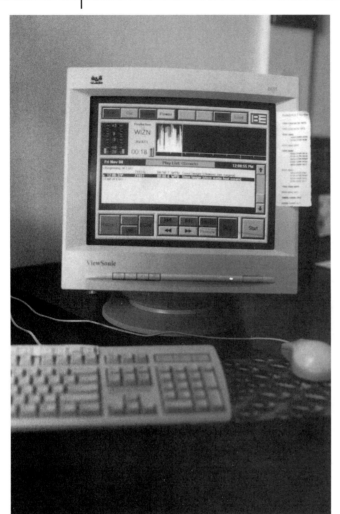

FIGURE 9.15
Production elements
and their mixing are
centered in the
workstation. Courtesy
WIZN.

FIGURE 9.16
Becoming rare is the
cart machine.
Courtesy Broadcast
Electronics.

players employ a laser beam to read encoded data at a rate of 4.3218 million bits per second.

A compact disc is 4.7 inches wide and 1.2 mm thick, and players are quite light and compact as well. This feature alone makes them attractive to broadcasters. But what makes a CD player most appealing to broadcasters is its superior sound. Compact disc players offer, among other features, far greater dynamic range than standard turntables and a lower signal-to-noise ratio. They also eliminate the need for physical contact during cueing, and wowing and distortion are virtually gone.

Because digital discs are specially coated, they are much more resistant to damage than are analog discs. This is not to suggest that CDs are impervious. They are not. In fact, the majority of CD-related problems stem from the discs themselves and not the players. Despite initial claims of the invincibility of the digital disc, experience has shown that mishandling of discs is courting disaster. CDs cannot be mistreated—that is, used as Frisbees or placemats for peanut butter sandwiches—and still be expected to work like new. The simple fact is that although compact discs are more resistant to damage than analog discs, they can be harmed.

Whereas the old turntable tone arm moved from the outside of a disc inward as the plate revolves in a clockwise direction at 33 or 45 rpm, a CD reads a disc from its core outward, moving from 500 rpm on the inside to 200 rpm on the outer edge of the disc.

Most CD players feature a variety of effect options, which can be of particular use to a production mix. Accessing cuts on a CD player is quick and simple, though excerpting segments from a track for inclusion in a mixdown can be somewhat less expedient than doing so on a conventional analog machine. Nonetheless, CD players are a major addition to the production studio. Compact discs are a wonderful source for bed music and sound effects.

Working with a CD unit is anything but complicated. Press a button and a tray ejects (on top-loaded models a door pops open). A disc is placed into the tray, and the press of the same button returns the tray and disc into the player. The operator then selects the track to be played and presses the appropriately numbered button. The audio rolls.

Burnable CD units (CD-R & CD-RW) are prominent in the production room. CD-Rs Allow one time burning, whereas CD-RWs allow multiple burnings.

Digital Audio Tape (DAT)

Digital audio technology was first introduced in the 1970s, and 20 years later it is having a substantial impact on the radio industry, although DAT recording has begun to decline as studios favor other digital recording formats—namely burnable CDs, mini-discs, and workstations. A total departure from analog recording, digital involves the conversion of audio signals into coded pulses—numbers—that are read by a computer sound processor. Digital recording formats quantify numeric values rather than replicate waves. Simply put, in digital, sounds are quantified.

Digital recording is very appealing to broadcasters because it offers a greater dynamic range than analog, and it is nearly noise free; the flutter (caused by variation in speed of tape transport) and wow common to analog are gone, and there is virtually no loss in quality during dubbing. In addition to improved audio quality, digital audio systems can provide several other enhancements that are of specific value to the radio broadcaster. These include playback speed accuracy, stereo phase stability, fast random access, high storage densities, improved portability, and great cost effectiveness relative to broadcast-quality analog systems, observes audio expert Skip Pizzi.

During recording, data are conveyed diagonally (helically) from the machine's head to the magnetic tape surface rather than horizontally—as is the case in analog recording.

Digital audio tape differs from analog tape in a number of ways. It is much thinner—0.5 mm is the qualitative equivalent of the 1.5-mm tape used with analog machines. More tracks may be written on a smaller surface using digital open-reel tape.

FIGURE 9.17
Mini-disc machines are making inroads into studios. Courtesy Denon.

FIGURE 9.18
Production studio equipment rack. Courtesy WIZN.

FIGURE 9.19
When using magnetic
tape, dirty heads can
create numerous
problems, not the least
of which is a
deterioration of sound
quality.

For instance, on a 1/4-inch digital tape up
to 12 tracks may be recorded, and 1/2-inch
supports 28 tracks. Forty tracks may be
recorded onto 1-inch-wide digital tape.

Again, other digital recording technology
has caused DAT to begin a slow fade from
the studio. "DATs are nice but not in wide
use anymore. The appeal of DATs has given
way to the expanded use of computers (with
enormous amounts of hard drive memory)
and CD technology," says Miller.

Turntables

Even today some audio studios possess a
turntable (see figure 9.21). This is especially
true of the production room, even though
stations have long since phased out regular
on-air use of turntables in favor of tape and
compact disks. Nonetheless, turntables may
be present in the control room for special
features that use LPs.

FIGURE 9.20
CD cart players are
popular in both the
on-air studio and the
mixing room. Courtesy
Denon.

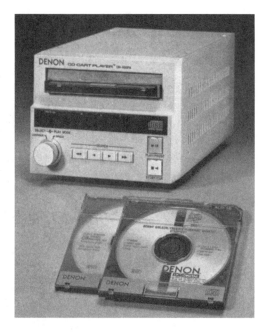

Broadcast turntables are designed for
cueing purposes. Turntables are covered
with felt to allow records to move freely
when being cued, and the tone arm is carefully balanced to prevent record and stylus
damage during this process.

Two methods of record cueing are used.
One involves a technique called *dead-
rolling*, in which an LP is cued and then
activated from the turntable's stop position.
The other, known as *slip-cueing*, requires
that the record be held in place and released

FIGURE 9.21
Although nearly
extinct, turntables can
still be useful to the
producer.

as the turntable rotates. Using the former technique, an LP must be backtracked approximately one-eighth of a turn from the start of the audio and a 45 rpm one-fourth of a turn. This permits the turntable to achieve its proper speed before the sound is reached. When a turntable does not achieve its proper speed before engaging the recording, distortion will occur in the form of a "wow."

Compressors, Equalizers, and Audio Processing

"There are three domains of audio," says producer Ty Ford. "They are amplitude, frequency, and time." Some stations alter amplitude to create the illusion of being louder without actually changing level. This is called *compressing the signal*. Production people use compressors to enhance loudness as well as to eliminate or cut out ambient noise, thus focusing on specifics of mix. Compression often is used as a method of getting listeners to take greater notice of a piece of production and as a remedy to certain problems.

Equalizers (EQs) work the frequency domain of audio by boosting and/or cutting lows (hertz\obHz\cb range) and highs (kilohertz\obkHz\cb range). Equalizers allow producers to correct problems as well as to create parity between different elements of production. They are also useful in creating special effects. EQs are available inboard (part of the audio console) and out-of-board (stand-alone unit) and as part of certain integrated audio effects processors.

Most audio processors (also called *effects processors* or simply *boxes*) are time-domain devices. Stations use these digital boxes to create a wide range of effects such as reverb, echo, flange, and so on.

In the last few years, radio stations have become increasingly interested in what audio processors have to offer their mixes. Today these boxes are a familiar, often integral, item in production rooms at the majority of stations. Their value in the creation of commercials, PSAs, promos, and features is inestimable. The use of samplers and synthesizers is common in radio production rooms too. Samplers let a production person load a studio audio source (recorder, live mike) into its built-in microprocessor and then manipulate the digitized data with the aid of a musical keyboard to create a multitude of effects. Samplers employ magnetic microfloppies and are wired to an audio console so that the sounds they produce may be integrated into mixdown. Samplers are also found in certain audio effects processors with MIDI (Musical Instrument Digital Interface). A sample is a digital recording of a small bit of sound.

"A lot of musical instrument (MI) gear is being introduced into the radio production studio. Synths, samplers, and sequencers are pretty commonplace today," notes Ty Ford.

Many software applications, such as Cool Edit Pro and Pro Tools, have these and other signal processing built in.

Patch Panels and ISDNs

A patch panel consists of rows of inputs and outputs connected to various external sources—studios, equipment, remote locations, network lines, and so forth. Patch panels essentially are routing devices that allow for items not directly wired into an audio console to become a part of a broadcast or production mixdown. (See figure 9.23)

ISDNs are digital phone lines that bring voices and other audio to studios with near perfect sound quality. Since voice tracking has become the means by which so many

FIGURE 9.22
Lexicon multi-effects processor with MIDI function. Courtesy Lexicon.

FIGURE 9.23
The station's patch panel extends the reach and capacity of the control and production room consoles. New generation patch panels have eliminated the plug-in cord as pictured here.

stations fill their airwaves, ISDN connections have become invaluable.

Observes, production director Matt Grasso, "The day of the scratchy cell phone or muddy dedicated line is over. Your talent sounds like they are right in the studio. If they are at a club, not only can they talk, but they can broadcast the music they are playing there right over the air with the same quality you would get from a CD player in the main studio. ISDN means no reel to reels or DATS coming to a station via snailmail either."

Microphones

Microphones are designed with different pickup patterns. Omnidirectional micro-phones are sensitive to sound from all directions (360 degrees), whereas bidirectional microphones pick up sound from two directions (180 degrees). The unidirectional microphone draws sound from only one path (90 degrees), and, because of its highly directed field of receptivity, extraneous sounds are not amplified. This feature has made the unidirectional microphone popular in both the control and production studios, where generally one person is at work at a time. Most studio consoles possess two or more microphone inputs so that additional voices can be accommodated when the need arises. (See figure 9.25)

Omnidirectional and bidirectional microphones often are used when more than one voice is involved. For instance, an omnidirectional may be used for the broadcast or recording of a round-table discussion, and the bidirectional during a one-on-one interview.

Announcers must be aware of a microphone's directional features. Proper positioning in relation to a microphone is important. Being outside the path of a microphone's pickup (off-mike) affects sound quality. At the same time, being too close to a microphone can result in distortion, known as popping and blasting. Keeping a hand's length away from a microphone will usually prevent this from occurring. Windscreens and blast filters may be attached to a microphone to help reduce distortion.

FIGURE 9.24
The look of microphones in the 1920s. Courtesy Jim Steele.

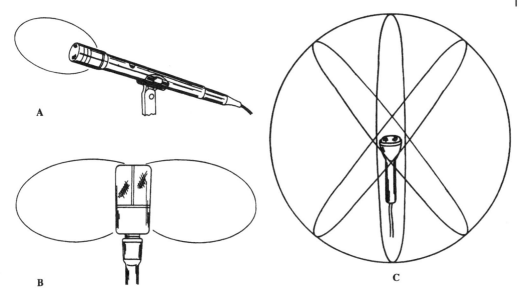

FIGURE 9.25
Microphone pickup patterns: (A) unidirectional, (B) bidirectional, (C) omnidirectional.

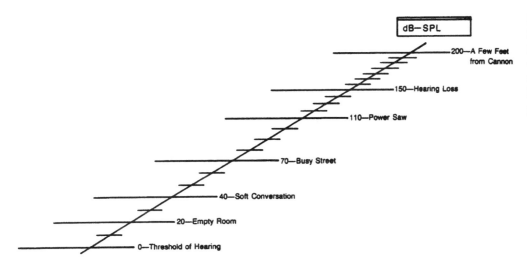

dB—SPL

200—A Few Feet from Cannon

150—Hearing Loss

110—Power Saw

70—Busy Street

40—Soft Conversation

20—Empty Room

0—Threshold of Hearing

FIGURE 9.26
Sound pressure level (SPL) chart depicting volume of different sounds in relation to human aural perception.

Editing

Tape editing can range from a simple repair to a complicated rearrangement of sound elements. Today the old razor approach to editing tape is all but ancient history having lost ground to "nondestructive" tapeless digital and multitrack methods.

Digital audio workstations, which rely on computer technology, are currently used in a vast number of radio production studios. This tapeless approach involves loading audio into a RAM or hard disc and making edits via a monitor (with the aid of a mouse, a keyboard, or a console). Although this technology has been costly in the past, today prices are quite affordable and this has motivated more and more stations to convert to the tapeless studio. Workstations are the studio of the future.

Multitrack editing is another form of razorless or electronic editing. In multitrack editing, a production ingredient is added to (or eliminated from) a separate track. Minidisc machines, as previously stated, provide the producer with another tapeless and nondestructive method for editing sound ingredients.

FIGURE 9.27
Digital audio puts the next-generation studio in a box. A world of production sound at your fingertips. Courtesy Scott.

FIGURE 9.28
A digital mixing board. Courtesy Orban.

About the age-old razor edit approach, Ed Shane comments, "Razor blades are about as useful in the production room as they are for shaving in this Norelco age. I recently reviewed software that turns a computer into a digital workstation for just a few hundred dollars." (See figures 9.29, 9.30, and 9.31.)

Copywriting

Poet Stephen Vincent Benet, who wrote for radio during its heyday, called the medium *the theater of the mind*. Indeed, the person who tunes into radio gets no visual aids but must manufacture images on his or her own to accompany the words and sounds broadcast. The station employee who prepares written material is called a copywriter. A copywriter job consists primarily of writing commercials, promos, and PSAs, with the emphasis on the first of the three.

Not all stations employ a full-time copywriter. This is especially true in small markets where economics dictate that the salesperson write for his or her own account. Deejays also are called on to pen commercials. At stations with bigger operating budgets, a full-time copywriter often will handle the bulk of the writing chores.

Copywriters must possess a complete understanding of the unique nature of the medium, a familiarity with the audience for which the commercial message is intended, and knowledge of the product being promoted. A station's format will influence the style of writing in a commercial; thus, the copywriter also must be thoroughly acquainted with the station's particular programming approach. Commercials must be compatible with the station's sound. For instance, copy written for Lite AC usually is more conservative in tone than that written for Modern Rock stations, and so on.

WXXX

"Home of the Hits" (SFX: Bed in)
TJ'S ROCKHOUSE, MARK STREET, DOWNTOWN BOISE, PRESENTS CLEO AND THE GANG ROCKING OUT EVERY FRIDAY AND SATURDAY NIGHT. AT TJ'S THERE'S NEVER A COVER OR MINIMUM, JUST A GOOD TIME. SUNDAY IDAHO'S MONARCHS OF ROCKABILLY, JOBEE LANE, RAISE THE ROOF AT TJ'S. YOU BETTER BE READY TO SHAKE IT, BECAUSE NOBODY STANDS STILL WHEN JOBEE LANE ROCKS. THURSDAY IS HALF-PRICE NIGHT, AND LADIES ALWAYS GET THEIR FIRST DRINK FREE AT BOISE'S NUMBER ONE CLUB FOR FUN AND MUSIC. TAKE MAIN TO MARK STREET, AND LOOK FOR THE HOUSE THAT ROCKS, TJ'S ROCKHOUSE. (SFX: Stinger out)

WYYY

"Soothing Sounds"

ELEGANT DINING IS JUST A SCENIC RIDE AWAY. (SFX: Bed in and under) THE CRITICALLY ACCLAIMED VISCOUNT (VY-COUNT) INN IN CEDAR GLENN OFFERS PATRONS AN EXQUISITE MENU IN A SETTING WITHOUT EQUAL. THE VISCOUNT'S 18TH CENTURY CHARM WILL MAKE YOUR EVENING OUT ONE TO REMEMBER. JAMISON LONGLEY OF THE WISCONSIN REGISTER GIVES THE VISCOUNT A FOUR-STAR RATING FOR SERVICE, CUISINE, AND ATMOSPHERE. THE VISCOUNT (SFX: Royal fanfare) WILL SATISFY YOUR

FIGURE 9.29
Today most audio editing is done on the screen. Waveforms are altered and manipulated to create the sound sought. Reprinted with permission from Goldwave.

FIGURE 9.30
Editing a multitrack involves adding or deleting tracks. Here BED 2 is replaced by SFX 2 on track 4.

Track 1	VOICE	
Track 2	BED #1	
Track 3	SFX	Before
Track 4	BED #2	

Track 1	VOICE	
Track 2	BED #1	
Track 3	SFX #1	After
Track 4	SFX #2	

ROYAL TASTES. CALL 675-2180 FOR
RESERVATIONS. TAKE ROUTE 17
NORTH TO THE VISCOUNT INN, 31
STONY LANE, CEDAR GLENN.

Some basic rules pertain to the mechanics of copy preparation that should be observed. First, copy is typed in uppercase and is double-spaced for ease of reading. Next, left and right margins are set at one inch. Sound effects are noted in parentheses at that point in the copy where they are to occur. Proper punctuation and grammar are vital, too. A comma in the wrong place can throw off the meaning of an entire sentence. Be mindful, also, that commercials are designed to be heard and not read. Keep sentence structure as uncomplicated as possible. Maintaining a conversational style will make the client's message more accessible.

Timing a piece of copy is relatively simple. There are a couple of methods: One involves counting words, and the other counting lines. Using the first approach, 25 words would constitute 10 seconds, 65 words, 30 seconds, and 125 words, one minute. Counting lines is an easier and quicker way of timing copy. This method is based on the assumption that it takes, on average, 3 seconds to read one line of copy from margin to margin. Therefore, 9 to 10 lines of copy would time out to 30 seconds, and 18 to 20 lines to one minute. Of course, production elements such as sound effects and beds must be included as part of the count and deducted accordingly. For example, 6 seconds' worth of sound effects in a 30-second commercial would shorten the amount of actual copy by two lines.

Since everything written in radio is intended to be read aloud, it is important that words with unusual or uncommon pronunciations be given special attention. Phonetic spelling is used to convey the way a word is pronounced. For instance: "DINNER AT THE FO'C'SLE (FOKE-SIL) RESTAURANT IN LAITONE (LAY-TON) SHORES IS A SEA ADVENTURE." Incorrect pronunciation

has resulted in more than one canceled account. The copywriter must make certain that the announcer assigned to voice-track a commercial is fully aware of any particulars in the copy. In other words, when in doubt spell it out.

Excessive numbers and complex directions are to be avoided in radio copy. Numbers, such as an address or telephone number, should be repeated and directions should be as simple as possible. The use of landmarks ("ACROSS FROM CITY HALL . . .") can reduce confusion. Listeners are seldom in a position to write down something at the exact moment they hear it. Copy should communicate, not confuse or frustrate.

Of course, the purpose of any piece of copy is to sell the client's product. Creativity plays an important role. The radio writer has the world of the imagination to work with and is only limited by the boundaries of his own.

Announcing Tips

Thousands of men and women in this country make their living as radio announcers—this number has dwindled as radio companies consolidate and downsize their staffs and employ voice-tracking to serve multiple stations. In few other professions is the salary range so broad. A beginning announcer may make little more than minimum wage, whereas a seasoned professional in a major market may earn a salary in the six-figure range.

Although announcer salaries can be very good in smaller markets, the financial rewards tend to be far greater at metro market stations, which can afford to pay more. Of course, competition for positions is keener and expectations are higher. "You have to pay your dues in this profession. No one walks out of a classroom and into WNBC. It's usually a long and winding road. It takes time to develop the on-air skills that the big stations want. It's hard work to become really good, but you can make an enormous amount of money, or at least a very comfortable income, when you do," says radio personality Mike Morin.

The duties of an announcer vary depending on the size or ranking of a station. In the small station, announcers generally fill news and/or production shifts as well. For example, a midday announcer at WXXX, who is on the air from 10 a.m. until 3 p.m., may be held responsible for the 4 and 5 p.m. newscasts, plus any production that arises during that same period. Meanwhile, the larger station may require nothing more of its announcers than the taping of voiceovers. Of course, the preparation for an airshift at a major market station can be very time consuming.

An announcer must, above all else, possess the ability to effectively read copy aloud. Among other things, this involves proper enunciation and inflection, which are improved through practice. Programmer Bill Towery contends that the more a person reads for personal enjoyment or enrichment, the easier it is to communicate orally. "I'd advise anyone who aspires to the microphone to read, read, read. The more the better. Announcing is oral interpretation of the printed page. You must first understand what is on the page before you can communicate it aloud. Bottom line here is that if you want to become an announcer, first become a reader."

Having a naturally resonant and pleasant-sounding voice certainly is an advantage. Voice quality still is very important in radio. There is an inclination toward the voice with a deeper register. This is true for female announcers as well as male. However, most voices possess considerable range and with training, practice, and experience even a person with a high-pitched voice can develop an appealing on-air sound. Forcing the voice into a lower register to achieve a deeper sound can result in injury to the vocal chords. "Making the most of what you already have is a lot better than trying to be something you're not. Perfect yourself and be natural," advises Morin.

Relaxation is important. The voice simply is at its best when it is not strained. Moreover, announcing is enhanced by proper breathing, which is only possible when free of stress. Initially, being "on-mike" can be an intimidating experience, resulting in nervousness that can be debilitating. Here are some things that announcers do to achieve a state of relaxation:

1. Read copy aloud before going on the air. Get the feel of it. This will automatically increase confidence, thus aiding in relaxation.
2. Take several deep breaths and slowly exhale while keeping your eyes closed.
3. Sit still for a couple of moments with your arms limp at your sides. Tune out. Let the dust settle. Conjure pleasant images. Allow yourself to drift a bit, and then slowly return to the job at hand.
4. Stand and slowly move your upper torso in a circular motion for a minute or so. Flex your shoulders and arms. Stretch luxuriously.
5. When seated, check your posture. Do not slump over as you announce. A curved diaphragm impedes breathing. Sit erect, but not stiffly.
6. Hum a few bars of your favorite song. The vibration helps relax the throat muscles and vocal chords.
7. Give yourself ample time to settle in before going on. Dashing into the studio at the last second will jar your focus and shake your composure.

In most situations, an accent—regional or otherwise—is a handicap and should be eliminated. Most radio announcers in the south do not have a drawl, and the majority of announcers in Boston put the "r" in the word *car*. A noticeable or pronounced accent will almost always put the candidate for an announcer's job out of the running. Accents are not easy to eliminate, but with practice they can be overcome.

Voice-Tracking

In the age of station consolidation and clusters, radio corporations are finding it cost efficient to feed their stations prerecorded voices. In other words, these days station announcing takes place away from the station as much as it does at the station. Radio companies hire announcers to provide their stations with their voicing needs, so there is less and less on-sight voice origination. One announcer may be the voice of a hundred stations. Through satellite feeds and ISDN lines, local station airwaves are filled with out-of-town voices. When voice-tracking is done at the station level, it is to allow more multitasking opportunities for the announcer. Says Ed Shane, "Voice-tracking is an ideal productivity tool, allowing air talent to pre-record their air shifts in order to use their work time producing commercials, appearing live at sponsor locations, or doing a variety of jobs other than waiting for songs to end in order to deliver a 10 second talkover."

Voice-tracking has generated concern because the ranks of announcers is being thinned down. Jackie O'Brien, Metro Networks director of operations, observes, "The field of radio broadcasting has changed tremendously over the past few years. Many positions have been lost due to the innovation of voice-tracking. While this may be a cost-efficient way to run a radio group, it has taken away the personality of the service. When I started in broadcasting, I felt the position was more than the sound of my own voice. There was a commitment made to service the public with news, information, and a little entertainment. This meant staying on through a snowstorm or covering local elections. It also meant talking the occasional lonely heart out of suicide. I've been at Metro Networks for four years. In that time, I've watched old positions I held in radio disappear to voice-tracking."

Despite concern for the impact voice-tracking has on the announcing profession, more and more stations are using it, and the future would suggest that this practice will grow.

FIGURE 9.31
Digital audio workstations mark a new era in radio production mixing, editing, and storage. Courtesy AKG.

The Sound Library

Music is used to enhance an advertiser's message—to make it more appealing, more listenable. The music used in a radio commercial is called a *bed* simply because it backs the voice. It is the platform on which the voice is set. A station may bed thousands of commercials over the course of a year. Music is an integral component of the production mixdown.

Bed music is derived from a couple of sources. Demonstration CDs (demos) sent by recording companies to radio stations are a primary source, since few actually make it onto playlists and into on-air rotations. These CDs are particularly useful because the music is unfamiliar to the listening audience. Known tunes generally are avoided in the mixdown of spots because they tend to distract the listener from the copy. However, there are times when familiar tunes are used to back spots. Nightclubs often request that popular music be used in their commercials to convey a certain mood and ambiance.

Movie soundtrack CDs are another good place to find beds because they often contain a variety of music, ranging from the bizarre to the conventional. They also are an excellent source for special audio effects, which can be used to great advantage in the right commercial.

On-air CDs are screened for potential production use as well. Although several cuts on an album may be placed in on-air rotation and thereby eliminated for use in the mixdown of commercials, there will be cuts not programmed and therefore available for production purposes.

Syndicated or canned bed music libraries are available at a price and are widely used at larger stations. *Broadcasting Yearbook* contains a complete listing of production companies offering bed music libraries. The majority of stations choose to lift beds from in-house CDs.

Music used for production purposes is catalogued so that it can be located and reused. A system once widely employed used index cards, which could be stored for easy access in a container or on a rotating drum. At most stations today, computers are used to store production library information. Using the manual system, when an account is assigned a certain bed, a card is made and all pertinent data are included on it.

If a card exists for a bed not in current use, and the bed is appropriate for a new account, then either a fresh card will be prepared or the new information penciled onto the existing card.

No production studio is complete without a commercial sound effects library, but in the digital age, many effects are made in-house. Sound effects libraries can be purchased for as little as $100 or they can cost thousands. The quality and selection of effects vary accordingly. Specially tailored audio effects also can run into the thousands but can add a unique touch to a station's sound.

FIGURE 9.32
Production order. Courtesy WBTZ.

CHAPTER HIGHLIGHTS

1. The first radio commercials aired in 1922.

2. Early commercials were live readings: no music, sound effects, or singing.

3. Dialogue spots, using drama and comedy to sell the product, became prominent in the 1930s. Elaborate sound effects, actors, and orchestras were employed.

4. With the introduction of magnetic recording tape and 33 LPs in the 1950s, live commercial announcements were replaced by prerecorded messages.

5. The copy, delivery, and mixdown of commercials must be adapted to match the station's format to avoid audience tune-out.

6. The production director (production manager, production chief) records voice tracks, mixes commercials and PSAs, maintains the bed music and special effects libraries, mixes promotional material and special programs, and performs basic editing chores.

7. At smaller stations the production responsibilities are assigned part-time to on-air personnel or the program director.

8. The production director (increasingly referred to as the imaging director at stations mixing with computers), who usually answers to the program director, also works closely with the copywriter and the traffic manager.

9. For ease of movement and accessibility, both on-air and production studio equipment are arranged in a U shape.

10. The audio console (board) is the central piece of equipment. It consists of inputs, which permit audio energy to enter the console; outputs through which audio energy is fed to other locations; VU meters, which measure the level of sound; pots (faders), which control the quantity (gain) of sound; monitor gains, which control in-studio volume; and master gains, which control general output levels.

FIGURE 9.33
CD library in studio.
Courtesy WIZN.

11. When operating the console in cue mode, the operator can listen to various audio sources without channeling them through an output.

12. Reel-to-reel tape machines are useful for recording at a variety of speeds and are handy for editing.

13. Cartridge tape machines (cart machines), though vanishing from the studio scene, are used for recording and playback at many stations. They employ carts (plastic containers with continuous loops of magnetic tape), which are more compact and convenient than reels of tape.

14. Mini-disc machines are gradually replacing the standard analog cart deck. They let producers digitally mix and archive up to 74 minutes of audio on 2.5-inch reusable discs.

15. Cassette tape machines, although not as integral to the mixdown process, are easy to handle and use convenient tape cassettes. They are often used for airchecks and actualities.

16. Like cartridges, audio tape (magnetic tape), is a vanishing medium. Tape comes in a variety of thicknesses and widths. Acetate and polyester backings provide greater durability.

17. Because oxide particles from the magnetic tape and dust and dirt accumulate on the heads of all tapes of tape machines, the heads should be cleaned regularly with a cotton swab and liquid head cleaner.

18. Compact disc players use a laser beam to decode the disc's surface, which eliminates stylus and turntable noises, distortion, and record damage. Recordable CDs are now in use.

19. Some stations still retain turntables. Once the staple of control rooms, they have been replaced by compact discs and cassettes. Turntables allow a record to be cued, a process that allows the record to reach proper speed before the sound portion is engaged.

WRITE GREAT COPY

Good copy is essential for successful advertising. To make certain the ad will attract customers for your client, remember these points:

1) Make your first sentence count. Does it provoke interest? Does it demand attention? Does it create a mood? If your first sentence doesn't have it, you've lost your best chance at getting the listeners' attention.

2) Keep your copy simple. The most eloquent thoughts are expressed in few words. If good writers can express complex emotions such as "love" simply, why are convoluted sentences needed to sell a leather coat? Cogent copy takes time and effort. The results are worth it.

3) Write for one person. Don't use words like "many of you" that refer to a lot of people listening. Radio isn't TV; people listen and respond to radio as individuals. Make your copy personal.

4) Eliminate the details. Store hours, telephone numbers, the credit cards they accept are useful in newspaper ads, not on radio. People don't listen to radio with a scratch pad handy. These details take up space and won't motivate anyone to buy anything.

5) Use a "locator." Store addresses are hard to remember, harder to visualize where they might be. Listeners relate better to "locators"— places they know or can easily find. "Across from the fairgrounds" will be remembered, "1365 N. King Street" likely won't be.

6) Focus on one thought or idea. What is the single most important thing you want the listener to know? Make it personal, make it entertaining, make it exciting—but concentrate on one theme idea. Never resort to a laundry list of services or use cliches.

7) Create and consistently use a phrase that "positions" the business or product. This will help the listener recall the business and why he/she should go there. Examples: Chevy Trucks: "Like a Rock"; Fox News Channel, "Fair and Balanced"; "Dude, you're gettin' a Dell."

8) After you've written the copy, read it aloud to someone else. Find out what they remembered. You may need to revise it.

BROADCAST MARKETING CONSULTANTS • 35 Main Street, Wayland, Massachusetts 01778 • 508/653-7200 • Fax 508/653-4088

20. Digital audio tape (DAT) offers improved sound reproduction with rerecording capability. Half the size of conventional analog tape cassettes, DAT made inroads into the radio studio environment in the 1990s.

21. Audio processors, samplers, and MIDI enhance a radio production studio's product. Software such as Cool Edit Pro and Pro Tools have these features built in.

22. A patch panel is a routing device, consisting of inputs and outputs, connecting the audio console with various external sources.

FIGURE 9.34
Tips on writing effective copy. Courtesy Broadcasting Unlimited.

FIGURE 9.35
The production person remains the station's true artist whether the studio be cutting-edge digital or old-world analog. Courtesy WIZN.

23. Microphones are designed with different pickup patterns to accommodate different functions: omnidirectional (all directions), bidirectional (two directions), and unidirectional (one direction).

24. Audio editing ranges from simple repairs to complicated rearrangements of sound elements. Today the once conventional razor cut approach to tape editing has been replaced by nondestructive digital and multitrack methods.

25. Digital audio workstations, which rely on computer technology and software (Pro-Tools is very popular), are currently used in a growing number of radio production studios.

26. The station copywriter, who writes the commercials, promos, and PSAs, must be familiar with the intended audience and the product being sold. The station's format and programming approach influence the style of writing. Copy should be typed in upper-case, be double-spaced, and have one-inch margins. Sound effects are noted in parentheses, and phonetic spellings are provided for difficult words.

27. Aspiring announcers must be able to read copy aloud with proper inflection and enunciation. A naturally resonant and pleasant-sounding voice without a regional accent is an advantage.

28. The practice of voice-tracking is reducing the number of announcing jobs. More and more, local station announcing originates elsewhere.

29. Every station maintains a sound library for use in spot mixdowns. Commercially produced sound effects, bed music collections, and unfamiliar cuts from CDs and even LPs are common source materials. Digital equipment and workstations allow producers to create their own in-house effects.

FIGURE 9.36
At many stations, Pro Tools is the new sound and effects library. Courtesy Digidesign.

SUGGESTED FURTHER READING

Adams, Michael H., and Massey, Kimberly. *Introduction to Radio: Production and Programming*. Madison, Wisc.: Brown and Benchmark, 1995.

Alburger, James R. and Hall, Mel. *The Art of Voice Acting*. Boston: Focal Press, 2002.

Alten, Stanley R. *Audio in Media*, 6th ed. Belmont, Calif.: Wadsworth Publishing, 2002.

Bartlett, Bruce. *Stereo Microphone Techniques*. Boston: Focal Press, 1991.

Ford, Ty. *Advanced Audio Production Techniques*. Boston: Focal Press, 1993.

Gross, Lynne, and Reese, David E. *Radio Production Worktext: Studio and Equipment*, 3rd ed. Boston: Focal Press, 1999.

Hausman, Carl, et al. *Modern Radio Production*. Belmont, Calif.: Wadsworth Publishing, 1999.

Hilliard, Robert L. *Writing for Television and Radio*, 8th ed. Belmont, Calif.: Wadsworth Publishing, 2003.

Hoffer, Jay. *Radio Production Techniques*. Blue Ridge Summit, Pa.: Tab Books, 1974.

Hyde, Stuart W. *Television and Radio Announcing*, 7th ed. Boston: Houghton Mifflin, 1995.

Keith, Michael C. *Broadcast Voice Performance*. Boston: Focal Press, 1989.

—. *Radio Production: Art and Science.* Boston: Focal Press, 1990.

McLeish, Robert. *Radio Production,* 4th ed. Boston: Focal Press, 1999.

Mott, Robert L. *Sound Effects: Radio, TV, and Film.* Boston: Focal Press, 1990.

National Association of Broadcasters. *Guidelines for Radio Continuity.* Washington, D.C.: NAB Publishing, 1982.

—. *Guidelines for Radio Copywriting.* Washington, D.C.: NAB Publications, 1993.

Nisbet, Alec. *The Technique of the Sound Studio,* 4th ed. Boston: Focal Press, 1979.

—. *The Use of Microphones,* 3rd ed. Boston: Focal Press, 1989.

O'Donnell, Lewis B., Hauseman, Carl, and Benoit, Philip. *Announcing: Broadcast Communication Today,* 4th ed. Belmont, Calif: Wadsworth Publishing, 2000.

—. *Modern Radio Production,* 5th ed. Belmont, Calif.: Wadsworth Publishing, 2000.

Oringel, Robert S. *Audio Control Handbook,* 6th ed. Boston: Focal Press, 1989.

Orlik, Peter B. *Broadcast Copywriting,* 4th ed. Boston: Allyn & Bacon, 1990.

Pohlmann, Ken C. *Advanced Digital Audio.* Indianapolis, Ind.: SAMS, 1991.

Priestman, Chris. *Web Radio: Radio Production for Internet Streaming.* Boston: Focal Press, 2001.

Reese, David E., et al. *Broadcast Announcing Worktext.* Boston: Focal Press, 2000.

Rumsey, Francis. *Tapeless Sound Recording.* Boston: Focal Press, 1990.

—. *Digital Audio Operation.* Boston: Focal Press, 1991.

Runstein, Robert E. *Modern Recording Techniques,* 2nd ed. Indianapolis: Howard Sams, 1986.

Watkinson, John. *Digital Audio and Compact Disc Technology,* 3rd ed. Boston: Focal Press, 1995.

Engineering | 10

Pioneer Engineers

Anyone who has ever spoken into a microphone or sat before a radio receiver owes an immense debt of gratitude to the many technical innovators who made it possible. Guglielmo Marconi, a diminutive Italian with enormous genius, first used electromagnetic (radio) waves to send a message. Marconi made his historical transmission, plus several others, in the last decade of the nineteenth century. Relying, at least in part, on the findings of two earlier scientists, James Clerk Maxwell and Heinrich Hertz, Marconi developed his wireless telegraph, thus revolutionizing the field of electronic communications.

Other wireless innovators made significant contributions to the refinement of Marconi's device. J. Ambrose Fleming developed the diode tube in 1904, and two years later Lee de Forest created the three-element triode tube called the Audion. Both innovations, along with many others, expanded the capability of the wireless.

On Christmas Eve of 1906, Reginald Fessenden demonstrated the transmission of voice over the wireless from his experimental station at Brant Rock, Massachusetts. Until that time, Marconi's invention had been used to send Morse code or coded messages. An earlier experiment in the transmission of voice via the electromagnetic spectrum also had been conducted. In 1892, on a small farm in Murray, Kentucky, Nathan B. Stubblefield managed to send voice across a field using the induction

method of transmission, yet Fessenden's method of mounting sound impulses atop electrical oscillations and transmitting them from an antenna proved far more effective. Fessenden's wireless voice message was received hundreds of miles away.

Few pioneer broadcast technologists contributed as much as Edwin Armstrong. His development of the regenerative and super-heterodyne circuits vastly improved receiver efficiency. In the 1920s Armstrong worked at developing a static-free mode of broadcasting, and in 1933 he demonstrated the results of his labor—FM. Armstrong was a man ahead of his time. It would be decades before his innovation would fully be appreciated, and he would not live to witness the tremendous strides it would take.

Had it not been for these men, and many others like them, there would be no radio medium. Today's broadcast engineers and technologists continue in the tradition of their forebears. Without their knowledge and expertise, there would be no broadcast industry because there would be no medium. Radio is first an engineer's medium. It is engineers who put the stations on the air and keep them there.

Radio Technology

Radio broadcasters utilize part of the electromagnetic spectrum to transmit their signals, and they are obliged to pay spectrum fees of up to $1,200 annually (depending on their size) for this privilege. A natural

FIGURE 10.1
Wireless transmitter in
1918. Courtesy
Westinghouse Electric.

wave portion of the spectrum for their purposes.

Electromagnetic waves carry broadcast transmissions (radio frequency) from station to receiver. It is the function of the transmitter to generate and shape the radio wave to conform to the frequency the station has been assigned by the FCC. Audio current is sent by a line from the control room to the transmitter. The current then modulates the carrier wave so that it may achieve its authorized frequency. A carrier wave that is undisturbed by audio current is called an unmodulated carrier.

The antenna radiates the radio frequency. Receivers are designed to pick up transmissions, convert the carrier into sound waves, and distribute them to the frequency tuned. Thus, in order for a station assigned a frequency of 950 kHz (a kilohertz equals 1,000 hertz [Hz]) to reach a radio tuned to that position on the dial, it must alter its carrier wave 950,000 cycles (Hz) per second. The tuner counts the incoming radio frequency.

resource, the electromagnetic spectrum is composed of radio waves at the low-frequency end and cosmic rays at the high-frequency end. In the spectrum between are infrared rays, light rays, x-rays, and gamma rays. Broadcasters, of course, use the radio

FIGURE 10.2
Station engineering
operations in the
digital age. Courtesy
Clear Channel.

AM/FM

AM and FM stations are located at different points in the spectrum: AM stations are assigned frequencies between 535 and 1,705 kHz on the Standard Broadcast band, and FM stations are located between 88.1 and 107.9 MHz (megahertz equals 1 million hertz) on the FM band.

Ten kilocycles (kc) separate frequencies in AM, and there are 200 kc between FM frequencies. FM broadcasters utilize 30 kc for over-the-air transmissions and are permitted to provide subcarrier transmission (SCA) to subscribers on the remaining frequency. The larger channel width provides FM listeners a better opportunity to fine-tune their favorite stations as well as to receive broadcasts in stereo. To achieve parity, AM broadcasters developed a way to transmit in stereo, and by 1990 hundreds were doing so. The fine-tuning edge still belongs to FM, since its sidebands (15 kc) are three times wider than AM's (5 kc).

FM broadcasts at a much higher frequency (millions of cycles per second) compared to AM (thousands of cycles per second). At such a high frequency, FM is immune to low-frequency emissions, which plague AM. Whereas a car motor or an electric storm generally will interfere with AM reception, FM is static free. Broadcast engineers have attempted to improve the quality of the AM band, but the basic nature of the lower frequency makes AM simply more prone to interference than FM. FM broadcasters see this as a key competitive advantage and refer to AM's move to stereo as "stereo with static."

Signal Propagation

The paths of AM and FM signals differ from one another. Ground waves create AM's primary service area as they travel across the earth's surface. High-power AM stations are able to reach listeners hundreds of miles away during the day. At night AM's signal is reflected by the atmosphere (ionosphere), thus creating a skywave that carries considerably further, sometimes thousands of miles. Skywaves constitute AM's secondary service area.

In contrast to AM signal radiation, FM propagates its radio waves in a direct or line-of-sight pattern. FM stations are not affected by evening changes in the atmosphere and generally do not carry as far as AM stations. A high-power FM station may reach listeners within an 80- to 100-mile radius since its signal weakens as it approaches the horizon. Since FM outlets radiate direct waves, antenna height becomes nearly as important as power. Generally speaking, the higher an FM antenna the further the signal travels.

Skywave Interference

The fact that AM station signals travel greater distances at night is a mixed blessing. Although some stations benefit from the expanded coverage area created by the skywave phenomenon, many do not. In fact, over 2,000 radio stations around the country must cease operation near sunset, and thousands more must make substantial transmission adjustments to prevent interference. For example, many stations must decrease power after sunset to ensure noninterference with others on the same frequency: WXXX-AM is 5,000 watts (5 kW) during the day, but at night it must drop to 1,000 watts (1 kW). Another measure designed to prevent interference requires that certain stations direct their signals away from stations on the same frequency. Directional stations require two or more antennas to shape the pattern of their radiation, whereas a nondirectional station that distributes its signal evenly in all directions needs only a single antenna. Because of its limited direct wave signal, FM is not subject to the post-sunset operating constraints that affect most AM outlets.

FIGURE 10.3
1940s "Air King" table model AM/FM receiver.

stations. Under this system the nation's 10,000 radio outlets operate free of the debilitating interference that plagued broadcasters prior to the Radio Act of 1927.

AM classifications are as follows:

- **Class A**: Clear channel stations with power not exceeding 50 kW. Their frequencies are protected from interference up to 750 miles. Among the pioneer, or oldest, stations in the country are KDKA, WBZ, WSM, and WJR.
- **Class B**: Stations with power ranging from a minimum of 250 watts to a maximum of 50 kW. They must protect Class I outlets by altering their signals around sunset. As a Class B station, WINZ-AM in Miami is required to reduce power from 50 kW to 250 watts so as not to intrude on other stations at 940 kHz. These stations also operate on regional channels. If a station is authorized to operate in the expanded band (1610–1700), the maximum power is 10 kW.
- **Class C**: Stations that operate on local and regional channels with power between 250 and 1,000 watts. They may operate without time restrictions.
- **Class D**: Stations that operate either daytime, limited time, or unlimited time with a nighttime power less than 250 watts. Daytime-only stations are Class D.

Station Classifications

To guarantee the efficient use of the broadcast spectrum, the FCC established a classification system for both AM and FM

Section 73.21 of the *Code of Federal Regulations*, Part 73, provides more details on AM station classifications.

New AM band space (1,605 to 1,705 kHz) is currently being allocated, and the FCC is encouraging existing AM license holders to shift to the new space as a means of reducing interference on the clogged band.

FM classifications include the following:

- **Class C**: The most powerful FM outlets with the greatest service parameters, these stations may be assigned a maximum

ERP of 100 kW and a tower height of up to 2,000 feet. Class C radio waves carry, on average, 70 miles from their point of transmission.

- **Class B**: These stations operate with less power—up to 50 kW—than Class Cs and are intended to serve smaller areas. The maximum antenna height for stations in this class is 500 feet, and signals generally do not reach beyond 40 to 50 miles.
- **Class A**: The least powerful of commercial FM stations; they seldom exceed 3 kW ERP (except in select cases where a ceiling of 6 kW is imposed) and 328 feet in antenna height. The average service contour for stations in this category is 10 to 20 miles.
- **Class D**: Set aside for noncommercial stations with 10 watts ERP, this type of station is most apt to be licensed to a school or college.

In the 1980s the FCC introduced three new classes of FM stations under Docket 80-90 in an attempt to provide several hundred additional frequencies, and more subclasses were added later. They are as follows:

- **Class C1**: Stations granted licenses to operate within this classification may be authorized to transmit up to 100 kW ERP with antennas not exceeding 984 feet. The maximum reach of stations in this class is about 50 miles.
- **Class C2**: The operating parameters of stations in Class C2 are close to Class Bs. The maximum power granted Class C2 outlets is 50 kW, and antennas may not exceed 492 feet. Class C2 stations reach approximately 35 miles.
- **Class C3**: These stations operate with shorter antennas and with power that typically exceeds 6 kW ERP.
- **Class B1**: The maximum antenna height permitted for Class B1 stations (328 feet) is identical to Class As; however, Class

FIGURE 10.6
Lines leading from station transmitter to antenna base. FCC rules require fencing for safety purposes.

FIGURE 10.7
Stations receive their power from conventional utility companies. From *FCC Broadcast Operator's Handbook*, Figure 3-1.

FIGURE 10.8
Unmodulated (undisturbed) carrier. From *FCC Broadcast Operator's Handbook*, Figure 5-1.

FIGURE 10.9
Amplitude modulated (AM) carrier. From *FCC Broadcast Operator's Handbook*, Figure 5-2.

FIGURE 10.10
Frequency modulated (FM) carrier. From *FCC Broadcast Operator's Handbook*, Figure 5-4.

FIGURE 10.11
Standard AM and FM band. From *FCC Broadcast Operator's Handbook*, Figures 4-7 and 4-8.

B1s are assigned at least 25 kW ERP. Class B1 signals carry 25 to 30 miles.

Due to the ongoing revisions made to FM classifications, we suggest you consult section 73.210 of the current *Code of Federal Regulations*, Part 73.

Digital Audio Broadcasting (DAB)

Radio is undergoing a true metamorphosis as analog signal processing is being supplanted by digital processing. The reason for the transformation is simple: The demand for better and more evolved sound is at an all-time high. Stations must convert to digital, or they will not be competitive with audio products such as CD and DAT players or digital satellite radio.

The conversion to digital broadcasting is being planned and is likely to be fully implemented within a few years. At the 1992 World Administrative Radio Conference (WARC), conducted by the International Telecommunications Union (ITU) in Spain, the FCC proposed use of the S-band (2,310 to 2,360 MHz) for the propagation of DAB signals.

Although some things remain to be resolved, in-band on-channel (IBOC) digital radio, as created by iBiquity, has been given the go ahead (At this writing, iBiquity digital radio was forced back to the lab to improve its receiver reception quality.) This is something the NAB has long supported as a means for maintaining a station's brand identity as established by its frequency numbers.

Whereas the present system of analog broadcasting essentially replicates sound waves (with inherent shortcomings), digital converts sound waves into a bitstream of 1's and 0's for processing into a low bandwidth. In digital, sound waves are assigned numeric values and become coded pulses.

Simply put, in digital, sounds are quantified. This allows for a more accurate representation of audio signals. Unlike analog, which is limited in what it can reproduce,

FIGURE 10.12
Radio spectrum table.

VLF (Very Low Frequency) 30 kHz and below	—*Maritime use*
LF (Low Frequency) 30 kHz to 300 kHz	—*Aeronautical/maritime*
MF (Medium Frequency) 300 kHz to 3000 kHz	—*AM, amateur, distress, etc.*
HF (High Frequency) 3 MHz to 30 MHz	—*CB, fax, international, etc.*
VHF (Very High Frequency) 30 MHz to 300 MHz	—*FM, TV, satellite, etc.*
UHF (Ultra High Frequency) 300 MHz to 3000 MHz	—*TV, satellite, CB, DAB (proposed), etc.*
SHF (Super High Frequency) 3 GHz to 30 GHz	—*Satellite, radar, space, etc.*
EHF (Extreme High Frequency) 30 GHz to 300 GHz	—*Space, amateur, experimental, etc.*

digital provides greater frequency response and dynamic range. Thus, more audio information is conveyed to the listener, who hears more. Another positive feature from the broadcast operator's perspective is the fact that digital signals do not require as much power as do analog signals.

Obviously when DAB is implemented, new receivers will be introduced to the consumer public. Part of their appeal, according to telecommunications professor Ernest Hakanen, is the fact that they "will allow for much more faithfulness of signal reproduction. DAB receivers will be designed to use reflected signals as alternative sources of information when the primary signal deteriorates. Using receivers that correct the fading and interference problems associated with AM and FM broadcasts, DAB signals that include specific information that can 'tell' the receiver how to compensate for information lost between transmitter and receiver can be received."

Eventually the existing analog system of AM and FM broadcasting will be passé. It is not likely, however, that the conversion to DAB will occur overnight. Some predict that analog broadcasting will be around for a few more years and that, even when digital is the preeminent broadcasting system, analog AM and FM stations will still be out there—that is, until the FCC no longer perceives them as providing a viable service. In any event, the switch to digital is mandated, and so is inevitable. Analog broadcasting will go the way of the turntable.

Radio engineer Aaron Reed expresses his views on the issues that will confront the full implementation of digital radio. "Dealing with the political boondoggle and the necessary paradigm shift in how 'radio' will be done after its implementation (from the technical changes necessary to augment the programming delivery to the altering of the way people think of radio as a mostly one way medium) will prove a major challenge to any engineer. Couple that with station managers demanding they be digital because 'the other guy is' but then balking at the hefty price and you can see the problems. It won't be easy, and inevitably many stations will try to do it on the cheap and fail because DAB is not something that can be done incrementally. Just saying your station is digital is not going to get the listeners. Something far more radical in the programming services that stations offer will be required. The potential is there. Whether engineers and their moneymen are willing to do it is the big question."

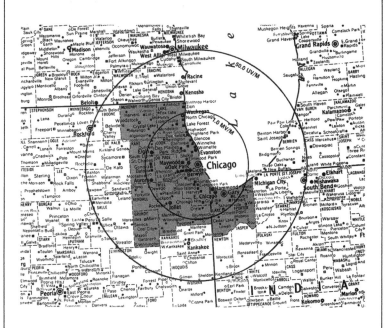

WLS FM COVERAGE

The map below indicates the area "covered" by the WLS FM signal. The inner circle represents 1 millivolt per meter. The outer circle represents the total reception range—50 microvolts per meter. Our transmitter move to the Sears Tower in June of 1983 provided a 22% increase in square mile coverage—the maximum allowable under present FCC rules.

Eleven County Metro Area (effective Fall '84) includes: Cook, IL, DuPage, IL, McHenry, IL, Kane, IL, Lake, IL, Grundy, IL, Will, IL, Kendall, IL, Lake, IN Porter, IN and Kenosha, WI (AREA SHADED ON MAP).

FIGURE 10.13
Coverage maps show where a station's signal reaches. Courtesy WLS.

FIGURE 10.14
WNBC's (now
WFAN) coverage
maps illustrate the
difference between
daytime and nighttime
reach. Courtesy
WNBC-AM.

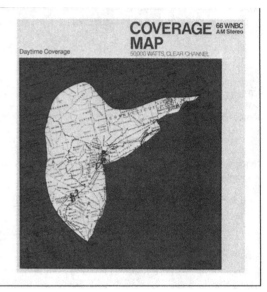

FIGURE 10.15
AM signal radiation.
From *FCC Broadcast
Operator's Handbook,*
Figure 3-2.

FIGURE 10.16
Nondirectional and
directional antenna
radiation. From *FCC
Broadcast Operator's
Handbook,* Figure 7-2.

Smart Receivers

It will soon be possible to get more than just audio from a radio receiver. In fact, consumers will be able to format scan without actually having to listen to stations. These so-called smart receivers may also feature emergency alerting capabilities, traffic announcements, advertisements and promos, and other informational services via a built-in LCD display panel. This was proposed in the early 1990s by Radio Broadcast Data Systems but never realized. Now with the onset of digital radio it is nearer to fruition.

Some programmers oppose the idea because they feel that it is difficult to categorize a format given the existing options, especially with a limited number of letters. The thought of a quasiteletext component to radio inspires mixed emotions in many broadcasters. Will people be *watching* radio, and what exactly will that mean? In the main, however, "screen" radio is perceived as an important value-added feature for the medium.

Although it is difficult at this time to predict the impact and role of these innovations, it is certain that eventually receivers will do more than simply tune frequencies. The conversion to digital will insure this.

One other plus offered by smart-receiver technology is that it will allow car radios to retune automatically a different station offering the same format when a vehicle leaves the coverage area of the first station.

Becoming an Engineer

Most station managers or chief engineers look for experience when hiring technical people. Formal training such as college ranks high but not as high as actual hands-on technical experience. "A good electronics background is preferred, of course. This doesn't necessarily mean ten years of experience or an advanced degree in electronic engineering, but rather a person with a solid foundation in the fundamentals of radio electronics, perhaps derived from an interest in amateur radio, computers, or another hobby of a technical nature. This is a good starting point. Actually, it has been my experience that people with this kind of a background are more attuned to the nature of this business. You don't need a person with a physics degree from MIT, but what you do want is someone with a natural inclination for the technical side. Ideally speaking, you want to hire a person with a tech history as well as some formal in-class training," contends Kevin McNamara, director of engineering, Beasley Broadcasting Group.

Chief engineer Jim Puriez concurs. "A formal education in electronics is good, but not essential. In this business if you have the desire and natural interest, you can learn from the inside out. You don't find that many broadcast engineers with actual electronics degrees. Of course, most have taken basic electronics courses. The majority are long on experience and have acquired their skills on the job. While a college degree is a nice credential, I think most managers hire tech people on the basis of experience more than anything else."

Station engineer Sid Schweiger also cites experience as the key criterion for gaining a broadcast engineer's position. "When I'm in the market for a tech person, I'll check smaller market stations for someone interested in making the move to a larger station. This way, I've got someone with experience right from the start. The little station is a good place for the newcomer to gain experience."

In his column in *Radio World* (June 9, 1999), editor Paul J. McLane lamented the dearth of young people entering the field and the need for specialists with various technical and computer skills. Wrote McLane, "Fluency never stops. People I respect say radio engineers should learn to think large, and that goes for digital audio and data training."

Numerous schools and colleges offer formal training in electronics. The number shrinks somewhat when it comes to those institutions actually providing curricula in broadcast engineering. However, a number of technical schools do offer basic electronics courses applicable to broadcast operations.

Before August 1981 the FCC required that broadcast engineers hold a First Class Radiotelephone license. To receive the license, applicants were expected to pass an examination. An understanding of basic broadcast electronics and a knowledge of the FCC rules and regulations pertaining to station technical operations were necessary to pass the lengthy examination. Today a station's chief engineer (also called chief operator) need possess only a Restricted

FIGURE 10.17
In digital processing of sound, an analog waveform is quantified, that is, given a numeric/binary value.

FIGURE 10.18
Certain features of a smart receiver turn the radio medium into a visual data system. Courtesy RDS.

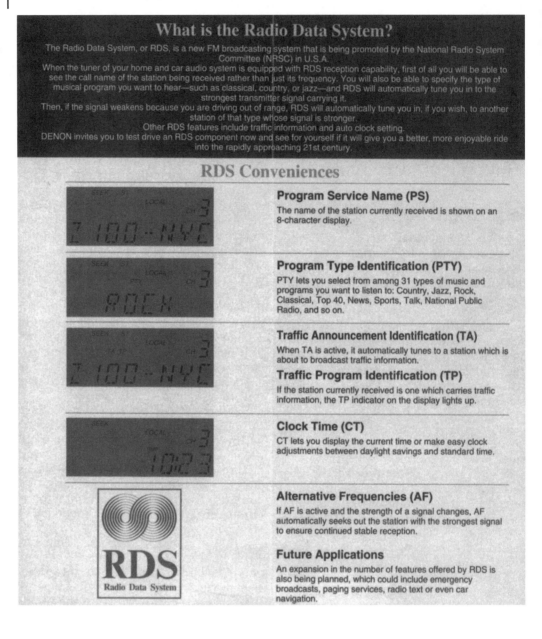

Operator Permit. Those who held First Class licenses prior to their elimination now receive either a Restricted Operator Permit or a General Radiotelephone license at renewal time.

It is left to the discretion of the individual radio station to establish criteria regarding engineer credentials. Many do require a General Radiotelephone license or certifi-

cation from associations, such as the Society of Broadcast Engineers (SBE) or the National Association of Radio and Telecommunications Engineers (NARTE), as a preliminary means of establishing a prospective engineer's qualifications. Appendices at the end of this chapter contain reproductions of SBE and NARTE membership application forms.

Communication skills rank highest on the list of personal qualities for station engineers, according to McNamara. "The old stereotype of the station 'tech-head' in white socks, chinos, and shirt-pocket pen holder weighed down by its inky contents is losing its validity. Today, more than ever, I think, the radio engineer must be able to communicate with members of the staff from the manager to the deejay. Good interpersonal skills are necessary. Things have become very sophisticated, and engineers play an integral role in the operation of a facility, perhaps more now than in the past. The field of broadcast engineering has become more competitive, too, with the elimination of many operating requirements."

Due to a number of regulation changes in the 1980s, most notably the elimination of upper-grade license requirements, the prospective engineer now comes under even closer scrutiny by station management. The day when a "1st phone" was enough to get an engineering job is gone. There is no direct "ticket" in anymore. As in most other areas of radio, skill, experience, and training open the doors the widest.

The Engineer's Duties

The FCC requires that all stations designate someone as chief operator. This individual is responsible for a station's technical operations. Equipment repairs and adjustments, as well as weekly inspections and calibrations of the station transmitter, remote control equipment, and monitoring and metering systems, fall within the chief operator's area of responsibility.

Depending on the makeup and size of a station, either a full-time or part-time engineer will be contracted. Many small outlets find they can get by with a weekly visit by a qualified engineer who also is available should a technical problem arise. Larger stations with more studios and operating equipment often employ an engineer on a full-time basis. It is a question of econom-

ics. The small station can less afford a day-to-day engineer, whereas the larger station usually finds that it can ill afford to do without one.

Beasley Broadcast Group's McNamara considers protecting the station's license his number one priority. "A station is only as good as its license to operate. If it loses it, the show is over. No other area of a station is under such scrutiny by the FCC as is the technical. The dereg movement in recent years has affected programming much more than engineering. My job is to first keep the station honest, that is, in compliance with the commission's rules. This means, keep the station operating within the assigned operating parameters, i.e., power, antenna phase, modulation, and so on, and to take corrective action if needed."

Chief engineer, Steve Church, says that maintenance and equipment repairs consume a large portion of an engineer's time. "General repairs keep you busy. One moment you may be adjusting a pot on a studio console and the next replacing a part on some remote equipment. A broadcast facility is an amalgam of equipment that requires care and attention. Problems must be detected early or they can snowball. The proper installation of new equipment eliminates the chance of certain problems later

FIGURE 10.19
Station engineer at the workbench. Courtesy WMJX-FM.

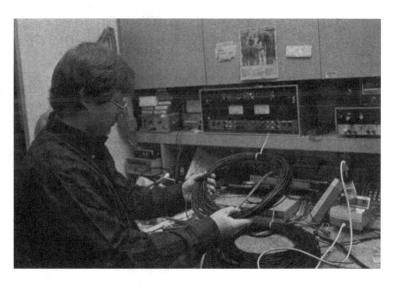

FIGURE 10.20
A station engineer
must be
knowledgeable about
the sophisticated state-
of-the-art audio
processing equipment
(such as the limiter
and processor shown
here) used by many
stations, especially in
metro markets where
great sound gives a
station an important
competitive edge.
Courtesy CRL Audio
and Broadcast
Electronics.

on. The station's chief must be adept at a whole lot."

Other duties of the chief engineer include training techs, monitoring radiation levels, planning maintenance schedules, and handling a budget. Many stations hire outside engineering firms to conduct performance proofs, but it is ultimately the responsibility of the chief operator to ensure that the outlet meets its technical performance level. Proofs ascertain whether a station's audio equipment performance measurements fall within the prescribed parameters. A station's frequency response, harmonic distortion, FM noise level, AM

noise level, stereo separation, crosstalk, and subcarrier suppression are gauged. If found adequate, the proof is passed. If not, the chief sees to it that necessary adjustments are made. Although the FCC no longer requires that Proof of Performance checks be undertaken, many stations continue to observe the practice as a fail-safe measure.

The duties of a station engineer are wide ranging and demanding. It is a position that requires a thorough grasp of electronics relative to the broadcast environment, knowledge of FCC rules and regulations pertaining to station technical operations, and, especially in the case of the chief engi-

FIGURE 10.21
Station engineers must
possess a high level of
proficiency with
computer technology.
Courtesy BE.

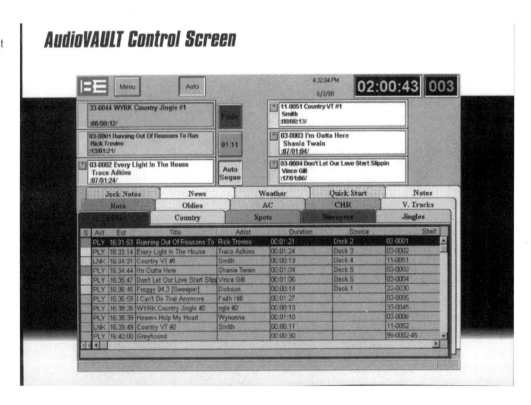

neer, the ability to manage finances and people.

Station Log

In 1983 the FCC dispensed with its requirement that radio stations keep maintenance and operating logs. In their place the commission created a new and considerably modified document called the Station Log, which stations must maintain. The new log requires that information pertaining to tower light malfunctions, Emergency Alert System (EAS) tests, and AM directional antenna systems be entered. Station Logs are kept on file for a period of two years.

Despite the fact that the FCC has eliminated the more involved logging procedures, some stations continue to employ the old system. "I like the accountability that maintenance and operating logs provide. We still use them here, and they are inspected daily. Despite the elimination of certain requirements, namely, the tech logs, a station is still required to meet the operating stipulations of their license. Actually, enforcement action has been on the rise at the FCC, perhaps in reaction to the deregs. The commission is really interested in station technical operations. Keeping daily logs ensures compliance," says McNamara.

73.1820 Station log.

(a) Entries must be made in the station log either manually by a properly licensed operator in actual charge of the transmitting apparatus, or by automatic devices meeting the requirements of paragraph (b) of this section. Indications of operating parameters that are required to be logged must be logged prior to any adjustment of the equipment. Where adjustments are made to restore parameters to their proper operating values, the corrected indications must be logged and accompanied, if any parameter deviation was beyond a prescribed tolerance, by a notation describing the nature of

FIGURE 10.22
The luxury of solid-state electronics—pull out the bad, put in the good. Courtesy IGM.

the corrective action. Indications of all parameters whose values are affected by the modulation of the carrier must be read without modulation. The actual time of observation must be included in each log entry. The following information must be entered:

(1) *All* stations: (i) Entries required by § 17.49 of this chapter concerning any observed or otherwise known extinguishment or improper functioning of a tower light:

(A) The nature of such extinguishment or improper functioning.

FIGURE 10.23
Maintaining prescribed technical parameters is one of many engineering responsibilities.

(B) The date and time the extinguishment or improper operation was observed or otherwise noted.

(C) The date, time and nature of adjustments, repairs or replacements made.

(ii) Any entries not specifically required in this section, but required by the instrument of authorization or elsewhere in this part.

(iii) An entry of each test of the Emergency Broadcast system procedures pursuant to the requirement of Subpart G of this part and the appropriate EBS checklist. All stations may keep EBS test data in a special EBS log which shall be maintained at any convenient location; however, such log should be considered a part of the station log.

(2) Directional AM stations without an FCC-approved antenna sampling system (See § 73.68): (i) An entry at the beginning of operations in each mode of operation, and thereafter at intervals not exceeding 3 hours, of the following (actual readings observed prior to making any adjustments to the equipment and an indication of any corrections to restore parameters to normal operating values):

(A) Common point current.

(B) When the operating power is determined by the indirect method, the efficiency factor F and either the product of the final amplifier input voltage and current or the calculated antenna input power. See § 73.51(e).

(C) Antenna monitor phase or phase deviation indications.

(D) Antenna monitor sample currents, current ratios, or ratio deviation indications.

(ii) Entries required by § 73.61 performed in accordance with the schedule specified therein.

(iii) Entries of the results of calibration of automatic logging devices (see paragraph (b) of this section), extension meters (see § 73.1550) or indicating instruments (see § 73.67) whenever performed.

(b) Automatic devices accurately calibrated and with appropriate time, date and circuit functions may be utilized to record entries in the station log provided:

(1) The recording devices do not affect the operation of circuits or accuracy of indicating instruments of the equipment being recorded;

(2) The recording devices have an accuracy equivalent to the accuracy of the indicating instruments;

(3) The calibration is checked against the original indicators as often as necessary to ensure recording accuracy:

(4) Provision is made to actuate automatically an aural alarm circuit located near the operator on duty if any of the automatic log readings are not within the tolerances or other requirements specified in the rules or station license;

(5) The alarm circuit operates continuously or the devices which record each parameter in sequence must read each parameter at least once during each 30 minute period;

(6) The automatic logging equipment is located at the remote control point if the transmitter is remotely controlled, or at the transmitter location if the transmitter is manually controlled:

(7) The automatic logging equipment is located in the near vicinity of the operator on duty and is inspected periodically during the broadcast day. In the event of failure or malfunctioning of the automatic equipment, the employee responsible for the log shall make the required entries in the log manually at that time;

(8) The indicating equipment conforms to the requirements of § 73.1215 (Indicating instruments– specifications) except that the scales need not exceed 2 inches in length. Arbitrary scales may not be used.

(c) In preparing the station log, original data may be recorded in rough form and later transcribed into the log. (43 FR 45854, Oct. 4, 1978, as amended at 44 FR 5873 Oct. 11, 1979; 47 FR 24580, June 7, 1982; 48 FR 38481. Aug. 24, 1983; 48 FR 4480 Sept. 30, 1983; 49 FR 33603, Aug. 23, 1984)

§ 73.1835 Special technical records.

The FCC may require a broadcast station licensee to keep operating and maintenance records as necessary to resolve conditions of actual or potential interference, rule violations, or deficient technical operation. (48 FR 38482, Aug. 24, 1983)

§ 73.1840 Retention of logs.

(a) Any log required to be kept by station licensees shall be retained by them for a period of 2 years. However, logs involving communications incident to a disaster or which include communications incident to or involved in an investigation by the FCC and about which the licensee has been notified, shall be retained by the licensee until specifically authorized in writing by the FCC to destroy them. Logs incident to or involved in any claim or complaint of which the licensee has notice shall be retained by the licensee until such claim or complaint has been fully satisfied or until the same has been barred by statute limiting the time for filing of suits upon such claims.

(b) Logs may be retained on microfilm, microfiche or other data-storage systems subject to the following conditions:

(1) Suitable viewing-reading devices shall be available to permit FCC inspection of logs pursuant to § 73.1226, availability to FCC of station logs and records.

(2) Reproduction of logs, stored on data-storage systems, to full-size copies, is required of licensees if requested by the FCC or the public as authorized by FCC rules. Such reproductions must be completed within 2 full work days of the time of the request.

(3) Corrections to logs shall be made:

(i) Prior to converting to a datastorage system pursuant to the requirements of § 73.1800 (c) and (d) (§ 73.1800, General requirements relating to logs).

(ii) After converting to a data-storage system by separately making such corrections and then associating with the related data-stored logs. Such corrections shall contain sufficient information to allow those reviewing the logs to identify where corrections have been made, and when and by whom the corrections were made.

(4) Copies of any log required to be filed with any application; or placed in the station's local public inspection file as part of an application; or filed with reports to the FCC must be reproduced in full-size form when complying with these requirements. (45 FR 41151, June 18, 1980, as amended at 46 FR 13907, Feb. 24, 1981; 46 FR 18557, Mar. 25, 1981; 49 FR 33663, Aug. 24, 1984)

The Emergency Alert System (Formerly the Emergency Broadcast System)

In 1994, the FCC established the Emergency Alert System (EAS), which replaced the old Emergency Broadcast System (EBS). The latter came into existence following World War II as the nation and the world entered the nuclear age. The system was designed to provide the president and heads of state and local government with a way to communicate with the public in the event of a major emergency.

In the 1990s, EBS was viewed as outmoded due to the revolution in technology, and it was significantly revamped. EAS is intended to upgrade the effectiveness of broadcast warnings by employing digital equipment and sophisticated automation. Its speed and timeliness are greatly enhanced under the new protocol. Stations were expected to have the new EAS system fully installed by mid-1997. At present, stations take the following steps should the president and/or heads of state and local government agencies deem it necessary to alert the public of a potential or imminent disaster:

Allen Myers

The FCC and Radio

FIGURE 10.24
Allen Myers.

In evaluating the service to the radio medium provided by the Federal Communications Commission, it is necessary to understand that the Commission was created by Congress in the Communications Act of 1934 and that the agency, therefore, carries out the wishes of that body. If the Commission wants to implement regulations for which it lacks the statutory authority, it must first obtain the approval of Congress.

The Commission's service to the radio medium is twofold. First, it sets the technical standards under which the medium operates. Second, it ensures an adequate and equitable distribution of radio services throughout the United States. The Commission was established by Congress with these specific objectives in mind.

Prior to the existence of the Commission and its predecessor, the Federal Radio Commission, radio broadcasting in this country was in a state of chaos. There was no spectrum planning. Operators put the stations on the air wherever they wanted. If a new station caused interference to a station already on the air, the operator of the older station often would just increase power—sort of an electronic shouting match. There were also no standards for radio receivers to prevent them from causing radio-frequency interference. So when Congress created the FCC, it charged it with making the radio medium "serve the public interest need and necessity."

The Commission's principal missions are accomplished with this objective in mind. Some of the agency's rules set minimum and maximum power requirements for radio stations; others set interference and distance standards—all with the objective of making sure that when a listener tunes to a radio station, he or she will be able to hear it clearly. The Commission's role in setting technical standards also extends to the equipment used in the transmission and reception of radio signals. Manufacturers of transmitters and receivers are required to receive FCC "type acceptance" approval before putting their products on the market. This insures that a clean signal is transmitted and received and that the equipment does not cause interference to other stations or electronic services. Other Commission rules deal with spectrum planning and are intended

to ensure an equitable distribution of radio stations throughout the country so that as many communities as possible will have a local radio station and possibly access to several different stations to provide a multitude of voices.

The Commission recognizes the different types of services that radio stations provide to listeners. To this end, it will often establish rules to foster the growth of a group of stations providing a unique service. For example, in 1945 the Commission reserved the first 20 channels in the FM band (88.1 to 91.9 MHz) for radio stations licensed to nonprofit, educational institutions and organizations to be operated as noncommercial, educational radio stations. The Commission then established a set of rules for this type of station, including both technical standards and spectrum planning.

Finally, in looking at the Commission's service to the radio medium, one must realize that the Communications Act is a living document. It has been amended many times to allow for new technologies in the radio medium, and the Commission has implemented regulations to carry out these changes. There is no doubt that the Communications Act will continue to be amended to take into consideration future changes in radio service and the Commission will proscribe regulations implementing these changes.

The views expressed by the author are not necessarily those of the Federal Communications Commission.

FIGURE 10.25
Operating log currently in use at WFBQ-FM. Courtesy WFBQ-FM.

1. Receive Emergency Action Notification (EAN) via AP/UPI feeds, network feed, or EAS decoder display. Continue to monitor for further instructions.
2. Discontinue normal programming.
3. Transmit EAN announcement.
4. Transmit EAN header codes followed by the attention signal.
5. Monitor Local Primary Source (LP), State Relay Source (SR), any other broadcast station for further instructions.
6. Transmit emergency messages as soon as they are available.
7. Announce termination of EAN.

Stations not designated to remain in operation in the event of an EAN then remove their carriers from the air after advising listeners where to tune for further information. Those participating stations continue to broadcast information as it is received from the nation's base of operations. Every radio station is required to install and operate an EAS monitor. Failure to do so can result in a substantial penalty imposed by the FCC.

Stations are also required to test the Emergency Alert System by airing both an announcement and an attention signal. EAS tests are documented in the Station Log when they are broadcast. The entry must include the time and the date of the test.

The Federal Emergency Management Agency (FEMA) makes funds available to stations designated to remain on the air during an authentic emergency through the Broadcast Station Protection Plan. Under this provision the government provides financial assistance to EAS stations for the purpose of constructing and equipping a shelter designed to operate for at least 14 days under emergency conditions.

In the 1990s, the FCC began an inquiry into whether the system needed updating or replacement. Critics of the old EBS claimed that the system had become obsolete. In late 1992, proposed EBS revisions included the following:

- Replacement of the existing emergency alerting system
- Updating of EBS equipment
- Cable media involvement in emergency alerting
- Self-testing of the system
- Mandated equipment standards
- Rules to prohibit false and deceptive use of the system
- Revised EBS test script

The new EAS embraces many of these revisions, as well as additional innovations and procedures.

Automation

The FCC's decision in the mid-1960s requiring that AM/FM operations in markets with populations of more than 100,000 originate separate programming 50 percent of the time provided significant impetus to radio automation. Before then combo stations, as they were called, simulcast their AM programming on FM primarily as a way of curtailing expenses. FM was still the poor second cousin of AM. (In the late 1980s the FCC dropped most of its simulcast requirements. Since then many stations have resorted to simulcasting as a means of dealing with the realities of fierce competition and a declining AM market.)

Responding to the rule changes, many stations resorted to automation systems as a way to keep expenses down. Interestingly enough, however, automation for programming, with its emphasis on music and de-emphasis on chatter, actually helped FM secure a larger following, resulting in increased revenue and stature.

Today, over a third of all commercial stations are automated. Some are fully automated (computer driven); others rely on automation for part of their broadcast day. Automation is far more prevalent on FM, but in the late 1970s and 1980s many AM outlets were employing automation systems to present Nostalgia and Easy Listening programming. The advent of AM stereo also has generated more use of automation on the Standard Broadcast band.

Although a substantial initial investment usually is necessary, the basic purpose of automation is to save a station money, and this it does by cutting staffing costs. Automation may also reduce the number of personnel problems. However, despite early predictions that automation eventually would replace the bulk of the radio workforce, very few jobs have actually been lost. In fact, new positions have been created.

Automated stations employ operators as well as announcers and production people (unless satellite-fed by syndicators). The extent to which a station uses automation often bears directly on staffing needs. Obviously, a fully automated station will employ fewer programming people than a partially automated outlet.

An automation system consists of a computer that also produces logs, music sheets, invoices, affidavits, and so on. Automated operations typically consist of a fully loaded computer system containing all of a station's music and announcement inventory. Indeed, the day of in-house loading of format elements is all but gone. Satellite syndicators using computers control local station ingredients (news, weather, promos, spots) remotely from the uplinks.

Today, due to the prevalence of computers, larger stations may employ a manager of information systems (MIS), who serves the computer tech needs of an outlet or entire cluster operation. This is another example of the so-called "station in a box" trend.

Posting Licenses and Permits

The FCC requires that a station's license and the permits of its operators be posted.

What follows are the rules pertaining to this requirement as outlined in Subpart H, Section 73.1230, of the FCC's regulations.

§ 73.1230 Posting of station and operator licenses.

(a) The station license and any other instrument of station authorization shall be posted in a conspicuous place and in such a manner that all terms are visible at the place the licensee considers to be the principal control point of the transmitter. At all other control or ATS monitoring and alarm points a photocopy of the station license and other authorizations shall be posted.

(b) The operator license of each station operator employed full-time or part-time or via contract, shall be permanently posted and shall remain posted so long as the operator is employed by the licensee. Operators employed at two or more stations, which are not colocated, shall post their operator license or permit at one of the stations, and a photocopy of the license or permit at each other station. The operator license shall be posted where the operator is on duty, either:

   (1) At the transmitter; or
   (2) At the extension meter location; or
   (3) At the remote control point, if the station is operated by remote control; or
   (4) At the monitoring and alarm point, if the station is using an automatic transmission system.

(c) Posting of the operator licenses and the station license and any other instruments of authorization shall be done by affixing the licenses to the wall at the posting location, or by enclosing them in a binder or folder which is retained at the posting location so that the documents will be readily available and easily accessible. [43 FR 45847, Oct. 4, 1978, as amended at 49 FR 29069, July 18, 1984]

FIGURE 10.26
FM station classification table. Courtesy FCC.

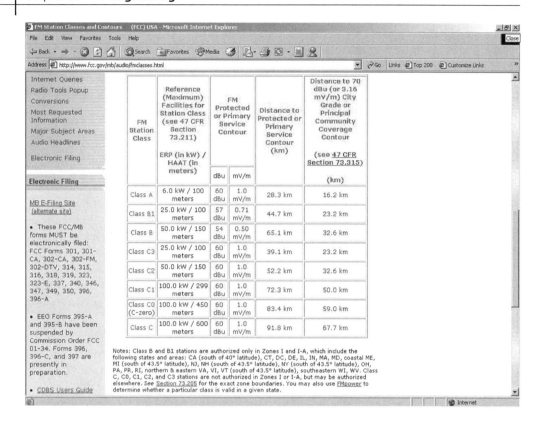

FM Station Class	Reference (Maximum) Facilities for Station Class (see 47 CFR Section 73.211) ERP (in kW) / HAAT (in meters)	FM Protected or Primary Service Contour		Distance to Protected or Primary Service Contour (km)	Distance to 70 dBu (or 3.16 mV/m) City Grade or Principal Community Coverage Contour (see 47 CFR Section 73.315) (km)
		dBu	mV/m		
Class A	6.0 kW / 100 meters	60 dBu	1.0 mV/m	28.3 km	16.2 km
Class B1	25.0 kW / 100 meters	57 dBu	0.71 mV/m	44.7 km	23.2 km
Class B	50.0 kW / 150 meters	54 dBu	0.50 mV/m	65.1 km	32.6 km
Class C3	25.0 kW / 100 meters	60 dBu	1.0 mV/m	39.1 km	23.2 km
Class C2	50.0 kW / 150 meters	60 dBu	1.0 mV/m	52.2 km	32.6 km
Class C1	100.0 kW / 299 meters	60 dBu	1.0 mV/m	72.3 km	50.0 km
Class C0 (C-zero)	100.0 kW / 450 meters	60 dBu	1.0 mV/m	83.4 km	59.0 km
Class C	100.0 kW / 600 meters	60 dBu	1.0 mV/m	91.8 km	67.7 km

Notes: Class B and B1 stations are authorized only in Zones I and I-A, which include the following states and areas: CA (south of 40° latitude), CT, DC, DE, IL, IN, MA, MD, coastal ME, MI (south of 43.5° latitude), NJ, NH (south of 43.5° latitude), NY (south of 43.5° latitude), OH, PA, PR, RI, northern & eastern VA, VI, VT (south of 43.5° latitude), southeastern WI, WV. Class C, C0, C1, C2, and C3 stations are not authorized in Zones I or I-A, but may be authorized elsewhere. See Section 73.205 for the exact zone boundaries. You may also use FMpower to determine whether a particular class is valid in a given state.

FIGURE 10.27
Satellite networks may interface with station automation systems. Courtesy SMN.

SET UP SUGGESTIONS FOR BROADCAST OF SMN FORMATS

Examples of how some SMN affiliates have set up simple broadcast systems that are effective in delivering a high quality sound.

#1   AUTOMATION SYSTEMS

In the 60's and 70's many stations purchased automation systems that gave the station operator hours of walk-away time. The good news is that with Satellite Music Network (SMN) you can put that system back to work for you.

Treat the SMN format as another source. If you have a network source input use us there or as you would any tape machine or cartridge machine. You can use the conact closures for the spot breaks as an end of message (EOM) pulse for that particular source. Your contact closures for the liners, sweepers and I.D.'s should be hooked up to separate cartridge machines to fire them individually. We call these dedicated carts.

All dedicated carts should be connected with their audio outputs paralleled to the audio going out over the air at all times. A good place to insert the dedicated cart audio is at the audio processor input by using a combining pad or some other audio combining device. The dedicated cart audio can also be combined at the output of the automation system.

#2   REEL AND AUDIO SWITCHER

Another set up utilizes a reel to reel machine and a switcher.

Basically all an audio switcher needs to do is turn off or isolate the network audio while you take a local spot break. You can build a latching relay using the contact closure going into the spot break to latch the audio off the air signal line. When the break is done they use the contact closure for the liner cart machine, but release the latch and return the network audio to the on-air buss (connection).

The reel to reel machine can be loaded with commercial spots that are timed for each break. Some stations can have as much as 12 hours walk away time with this system depending on their spot load. It is necessary to provide a function to stop your reel after each spot break so you do not get out of sequence. The liners, I.D.'s and sweepers need to be on dedicated carts with the cart audio paralleled with the on-air audio buss. This is called the old sound on sound concept.

#3   CART MACHINES AND AUDIO SWITCHER

Basically the same as example #2 except the reel to reel is replaced with sequenced cart machines that can handle the spot breaks. The only difference in this system is that the carts need to be changed out after each spot break. All other functions remain the same.

A

B

FIGURE 10.28
Rack rooms in cluster operation. Courtesy Clear Channel.

CHAPTER HIGHLIGHTS

1. Guglielmo Marconi first used electromagnetic (radio) waves to send a message at the end of the 19th century. Marconi used earlier findings by James C. Maxwell and Heinrich Hertz.

2. J. Ambrose Fleming developed the diode tube (1904), and Reginald Fessenden transmitted voice over the wireless (1906).

3. Edwin Armstrong developed the regenerative and superheterodyne circuits, and first demonstrated the static-free FM broadcast signal (1933).

4. Broadcast transmissions are carried on electromagnetic waves. The transmitter creates and shapes the wave to correspond to the "frequency" assigned by the FCC.

5. Receivers pick up the transmissions, converting the incoming radio frequency (RF) into sound waves.

6. AM stations are assigned frequencies between 535 and 1,705 kHz, with 10-kc separations between frequencies. AM is disrupted by low-frequency emissions, can be blocked by irregular topography, and can travel hundreds (along surface-level ground waves) or thousands (along nighttime skywaves) of miles.

7. Because AM station signals travel greater distances at night, in order to avoid skywave interference, over 2,000 stations around the country must cease operation near sunset. Thousands more must make substantial nighttime transmission adjustments (decrease power), and others (directional stations) must use two or more antennas to shape the pattern of their radiation.

8. FM stations are assigned frequencies between 88.1 and 107.9 MHz, with 200-kc separations between frequencies. FM is static free, with direct waves (line-of-sight) carrying up to 80 to 100 miles. Both AM and FM stations are licensed for eight years as of this writing.

9. To guarantee efficient use of the broadcast spectrum and to minimize station-to-station interferences, the FCC established four classifications for AM stations and seven classifications for FM. Lower classification stations are obligated to avoid interference with higher classification stations. Recent FCC actions have created more subclassifications.

10. Analog is being replaced by digital audio (DAB) because the latter provides superior frequency response and greater dynamic range. New spectrum space may be allocated to accommodate the digital service.

11. A station's chief engineer (chief operator) needs experience with basic broadcast electronics, as well as a knowledge of the FCC regulations affecting the station's technical operation. The chief must repair and adjust equipment, and perform weekly inspections and calibrations. Other duties may include installing new equipment, training techs, planning maintenance schedules, and handling a budget.

12. A Proof of Performance involves checking the station's frequency response, harmonic distortion, FM noise level, AM noise level, stereo separation, crosstalk, and subcarrier suppression.

13. Although the FCC dispensed with the maintenance and operating log requirements (1983), a Station Log must be maintained. The log lists information about tower light malfunctions, EAS tests, and AM directional antenna systems.

14. The Emergency Alert System (formerly the Emergency Broadcast System) implemented after World War II, provides the government with a means of communicating with the public in an emergency. Stations must follow rigid instructions both during periodic tests of the system and during an actual emergency.

15. Over one-quarter of today's commercial stations are fully or partially automated. More prevalent in FM stations, automation reduces staffing costs but requires a significant equipment investment. Automated programming elements are aired when a trip mechanism is activated by a cue tone, which is impressed on all program material. Either an operator or a computer can maintain the programming chain. At many stations, satellite programming services use computers (at both uplink and downlink sites) to control station automation systems.

16. A manager of information systems (MIS) maintains a station's computer systems.

17. Direct satellite-fed stations need little equipment since programming originates at the syndicator's studios.

18. The FCC requires that a station's license and the permits of its operators be accessible in the station area.

1,000 COUNTIES — 40 STATES

It was July 18, 1922. On this day, John Glenn celebrated his first birthday in neighboring Ohio and WHAS pioneered Kentucky broadcasting as a 500-watter in Louisville.

The years flew by and WHAS helped transform a sprawling, backwoods Kentuckiana area into a rich, diversified market. WHAS has continued to pioneer with specialized departments for News, Sports, Farm, Home and Public Affairs programming.

Today, WHAS programs are airborne by a 50,000 watt, clear channel thrust and have boosters who respond from nearly 1,000 American counties in more than 40 states.

Pioneering is a good life. And in Kentuckiana, the good life for listeners and advertisers begins at eight-forty . . . WHAS 840 Radio.

840 RADIO LOUISVILLE, KY. 50,000 WATTS, 1-A CLEAR CHANNEL

Measure of a Great Radio Station

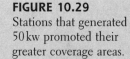

Represented Nationally by Henry I. Christal Co., Inc.

FIGURE 10.29
Stations that generated 50 kw promoted their greater coverage areas.

FIGURE 10.30
A 1970s PC-based
program controller
running an
automation system.
Courtesy IGM
Communications.

FIGURE 10.31
Satellite-linked
automation systems
are available in certain
formats. Diagram
shows how the system
works. Courtesy
Broadcast Electronics.

APPENDIX: Federal Communications Commission

Fact Sheet: Hints on Filing Comments with the FCC

The FCC is interested in any experiences, knowledge, or insights that outside parties may have to shed light on issues and questions raised in the rule-making process. The public and industry have the opportunity to comment upon Petitions for Rule Makings, NOIs, NPRMs, Further NPRMs, Reports and Orders, and others' comments on the aforementioned documents. It is a common misconception that only a lawyer can file comments with the FCC, but all that is necessary is an interest in an issue and the ability to read and follow directions.

Prior to drafting comments it is crucial to read and understand fully the item on which you wish to comment. Usually, the NPRM, NOI, or other item will specify and invite comment upon the issue(s) that the Commission is interested in studying further. Examination of the issue(s) and relevant documents is the most important part of the comment process. Comments may take any form, but the following hints may assist you in writing them.

Format. There is no required format for informal comments, although if you plan to file formally, it is required that they be typed, double-spaced, and on 8.5" × 11" paper. Additional requirements for formal filings are set forth in Sections 1.49 and 1.419 of the FCC Rules. The Docket Number or Rule Making Number of the item at hand should be included on your comments, and can be found on the front page of the Commission document or public notice. You should also include your name and complete mailing address.

Content. Your comments should state who you are and what your specific interest is. (You do not need to represent yourself in an official capacity. You may, for example, express your opinion as a concerned consumer, concerned parent, etc., and sign your name.) State your position and the facts directly, as thoroughly but as briefly as possible. Explain your position as it relates to your experience and be explicit. Make clear if the details of a proposed rule or only one of several provisions of the rule are objectionable. If the rule would be acceptable with certain safeguards, explain them and why they are necessary.

Support. Statements of agreement or dissent in comments should be supported to the best extent possible by factual (studies, statistics, etc.), logical, and/or legal information. Support should illustrate why your position is in the public interest. The more support made, the more persuasive the comments will be.

Length. Comments may be any length, although it is preferred that they be succinct and direct. If formal comments are longer than ten pages, a summary sheet is required.

Time frame. Your comments should be submitted well within the time frame designated on the original document or public notice. It is almost always included on the first page of an NPRM or NOI. However, if the deadline has passed, you can still submit your views informally in a permissible ex parte presentation.

Filing. Send your written comments to Secretary, Federal Communications Commission, 1919 M Street, N.W., Washington. D.C. 20554. If you wish your comments to be received as an informal filing, submit the original and one copy. If you want your comments to be received as a formal filing, you should submit an original and four copies. For more specific filing information, please refer to the FCC Public Notice "Guidelines for Uniform Filings" available from the same address.

Reply comments. As the name implies, reply comments are used to respond to comments filed by other parties. You may file reply comments even if you did not submit comments initially. When drafting reply comment, use the same guidelines expressed earlier regarding content and be careful not to raise additional or irrelevant issues.

Tracking your comments. After you have properly filed your comments with the FCC, they will be part of the official Commission record. To track the progress of proceedings in which you have filed comments, you may check the Daily Digest or Federal Register for releases and notices. The Daily Digest can be obtained from the Office of Public Affairs, 1919 M Street, N.W., Washington, D.C. 20554 or from a daily recorded listing of texts and releases at 202-418-2222.

For further information. For further information, you may contact the Secretary's office at the FCC directly, at 202-418-0300. Explicit information about filings in rule-making proceedings can be found in Sections 1.49 and 1.419 of the FCC Rules. Copies of any FCC documents can be obtained through the FCC's duplicating contractor, ITS, 1919 M Street N.W., Room 246, Washington, D.C. 20554, 202-857-3800, or from one of the private distributors of FCC releases. A list of distributors is available from the Public Service Division, 1919 M Street, N.W., Room 254, Washington, D.C. 20554, 202-418-0190.

FIGURE 10.32
SBE Application.

An invitation to join SBE

Who are we?

The Society of Broadcast Engineers, formed in 1963 as the Institute of Broadcast Engineers, is a non-profit organization serving the interests of broadcast engineers. We are the only society devoted to all levels of broadcast engineering.

Our membership, which is international in scope, is made up of studio and transmitter operators and technicians, supervisors, announcer-technicians, chief engineers of large and small stations, engineering vice presidents, consultants, field service and sales engineers, broadcast engineers from recording studios, schools, CCTV and CATV systems, production houses, advertising agencies, corporations, audio-visual departments, and all other facilities that utilize broadcast engineers.

What can we do for you?

Help you keep pace with our rapidly changing industry through educational seminars, and a look at new technology through industry tours and exhibits at monthly chapter meetings, regional conventions, and our national meeting held in conjunction with the National Association of Broadcasters (NAB).

Give you national representation. To serve as a voice for you in the industry; a liaison for you with governmental agencies as well as other industry groups.

To provide a forum for the exchange of ideas and sharing of information with other broadcast engineers and industry people.

To promote the profession of broadcast engineering.

To establish standards of professional education and training for broadcast engineering, and to recognize achievement of these standards.

In addition to the intangible benefits of membership in the SBE, the tangible benefits of an insurance program, communications through **The SBE Signal**, certification and re-certification opportunities, and a readily available network of specialized professionals.

All this adds up to an increase in your worth as a broadcast engineer to your employer.

Where does your money go?

A small office staff handling membership, certification, and the day-to-day business of the Society. Many duties of the SBE are handled by officers and board members who volunteer their time with no remuneration.

A library of videotape training material for loan from the national headquarters.

The production of our bi-monthly newsletter, **The SBE Signal**.

Allows SBE representation—through a professionally designed informational booth at state and regional meetings as well as NAB and NRBA.

A portion of your annual dues returns to subsidize the local chapter.

Supplements expenses for special events such as NAB, Chapter Chairman and Certification Chairman Meetings, and invitational opportunities to represent the SBE.

How to be one of us

Membership categories include Student, Associate Member, Member, Senior Member, Honorary Member, and Fellow.

Qualification for Member grade requires that the individual be actively engaged in broadcast engineering or have an academic degree in electrical engineering or its equivalent in scientific or professional experience in broadcast engineering or a closely related field or art.

The cost of membership is $20 annually for member and associate member grades, and $10 for student memberships.

What do we want from you?

First, we'd like to have your name on the SBE roster.

Strength in numbers gives us additional clout. And we want and need your participation and input at the regional and national levels as well as at the local level.

Certification Program

The program issued its first certificates on January 1, 1977, and now conducts tests at various times and places for those people, either members or non-members, who wish to have a certificate attesting to their competence as broadcast engineers. The certificates are issued for two different levels of achievement in either radio or TV and are valid for five years from date of issue. Recertification may be accomplished by earning professional credits for activities which maintain competence in the state-of-the-art or by re-examination.

Emphasis in the tests is on practical working knowledge rather than general theory. The tests are as valid for people in related industries as they are for broadcasters.

An entry-level certificate was added to the certification program in January 1982 to attract new technical talent to the broadcast industry and provide incentive for them to grow with technology.

The certification program is conducted by the SBE to benefit everyone in the industry. The program recognizes professional competence as judged by one's peers, and encourages participation in seminars, conventions, and meetings to help keep abreast of the constantly changing technology in broadcast engineering.

If you ever wanted to meet the people who design the equipment you use,

■ to talk with your fellow engineers and technicians,

■ to tour the many facilities that employ engineers and technicians,

■ to keep abreast of the state-of-the-art equipment,

■ to upgrade your skills for certification,

■ here is the opportunity to become a member of the most prestigious society in its field.

SOCIETY OF BROADCAST ENGINEERS, INC.
P.O. Box 50844, Indianapolis, Indiana 46250

Group Insurance Program

When you join the SBE, you have the opportunity to participate in the Group Insurance Program for SBE members and their dependents, which offers a wide range of coverage to suit your individual needs. The low rates are made possible through the economics of group administration and by the fact that SBE does not profit from the insurance program. Please note that requests for coverage under some of the plans are subject to insurance company approval.

■ Term Life Insurance Plan offers options of up to $195,000 for eligible members, with lesser amounts for dependents.

■ High-Limit Accident Insurance provides protection wherever you go, 24 hours a day, and eliminates the need for special accident insurance every time you travel.

■ Disability Income Plan protects your income by providing monthly benefit payments when you are unable to work due to a disabling illness or accident.

■ Excess Major Medical Plan supplements your regular hospital/medical coverage in the event of a catastrophic illness or accident, paying up to $1,000,000 after you satisfy your deductible.

■ In-Hospital Plan pays up to $100 per day for every day you spend in the hospital—up to 365 days—directly to you, to spend as you wish.

■ Major Medical Expense Insurance is designed for members who have little or no basic medical coverage.

For further information concerning membership, certification, application, regional meetings and conventions, contact the Society of Broadcast Engineers, Inc., P.O. Box 50844, Indianapolis, IN 46250, (317) 842-0836.

FIGURE 10.32
continued

SUGGESTED FURTHER READING

Abel, John D., and Ducey, Richard V. *Gazing into the Crystal Ball: A Radio Station Manager's Technological Guide to the Future.* Washington, D.C.: NAB, 1987.

Antebi, Elizabeth. *The Electronic Epoch.* New York: Van Nostrand Reinhold, 1982.

Butler, Andy. *Practical Tips for Choosing and Using Consulting and Contract Engineers.* Washington, D.C.: NAB Publications, 1994.

Cheney, Margaret. *Tesla: Man out of Time.* Englewood Cliffs, N.J.: Prentice Hall, 1983.

Considine, Douglas M., ed. *Van Nostrand's Scientific Encyclopedia.* New York: Van Nostrand Reinhold, 1983.

Davidson, Frank P. *Macro: A Clear Vision of How Science and Technology Will Shape Our Future.* New York: William Morrow, 1983.

Ebersole, Samuel. *Broadcast Technology Worktext.* Boston: Focal Press, 1992.

Finnegan, Patrick S. *Broadcast Engineering and Maintenance Handbook.* Blue Ridge Summit, Pa.: Tab, 1976.

Grant, August E. *Communication Technology Update.* Boston: Focal Press, 1995.

Hilliard, Robert L. *FCC Primer.* Boston: Focal Press, 1991.

Mirabito, Michael, and Morgenstern, Barbara. *The New Communication Technologies,* 2nd ed. Boston: Focal Press, 1994.

National Association of Broadcasters. *Understanding DAB,* 2nd ed. Washington, D.C.: NAB Publications, 1994.

Noll, Edward M. *Broadcast Radio and Television Handbook,* 6th ed. Indianapolis, Ind.: Howard Sams, 1983.

Reitz, John R. *Foundations of Electromagnetic Theory.* Reading, Mass.: Addison-Wesley, 1960.

Roberts, Robert S. *Dictionary of Audio, Radio, and Video.* Boston: Butterworths, 1981.

Starr, William. *Electrical Wiring and Design: A Practical Approach.* New York: John Wiley & Sons, 1983.

Watkinson, John. *The Art of Digital Audio.* Boston: Focal Press, 1992.

Wilson, David. *A Broadcast Engineering Tutorial for Non-Engineers.* Washington: NAB, 1999.

Consultants and Syndicators

Radio Aid

Two things directly contributed to the rise of radio consultants: more stations—from 2,000 in the 1950s to 12,000 in 2000—and more formats—from a half dozen to several dozen during the same period. Broadcast consultants have been around almost from the start, but it was not until the medium set a new course following the advent of television that the field grew to real prominence. By the 1960s consultants were directing the programming efforts of hundreds of stations. In the 1970s over a third of the nation's stations enlisted the services of consultants. Today, the field of radio consultancy has shrunk drastically due to the corporatization of the radio industry. The ranks have dwindled to the point where only a handful of independent radio consultants remain. Whether the radio consultancy function will be completely absorbed by corporations remains to be seen. However, consultants continue to play an important role in the shaping and management of the medium today.

Observes prominent radio consultant George Burns, "The principal role of radio consultants has evolved considerably since Mike Joseph started the whole thing in the 1950s. We began by being very specifically task oriented. A consultant was assumed to have greater expertise at the job than anyone that the station could afford fulltime. Currently consultants serve primarily as outside (and, it is hoped, impartial) monitors of station progress. The job is to assure man-agement that everything possible is being done to maximize the station's potential. If something is not functioning properly or needs to be changed, consultants are expected to give voice to these concerns. Over the years, the job has become infinitely more complex. Musical and nonmusical aspects of programming have spread widely apart. Research has become a separate discipline. And lately, the marketing side of radio has achieved a 'life of its own.' Different consultants approach each station's progress from varying points of view. Specialization was inevitable."

Stations use consultants for various reasons, says Fred Jacobs, president of Jacob's Media: "Stations realize that they need an experienced, objective ear to make intelligent evaluations. Consultants are also exposed to ideas and innovations from around the country that they can bring to their client stations. As radio has become more competitive, stations understand that their need for up-to-date information about current trends in programming and marketing has increased."

Dave Scott, president of Century 21 Programming, Dallas, Texas, adds that a lack of research expertise on the local station level prompts many stations to use consultants. "We're well into the information age, the age of highly sophisticated research techniques and computerized data. It takes a lot of resources to assess a market and prescribe a course of action. Most stations do not have the wherewithal. At Century 21 Programming, each of our consultants goes through

FIGURE 11.1
There are an
abundance of radio
consulting services
from which stations
can choose. Courtesy
Shane Media and
Lund Consultants.

HOT STUFF!

MARKET AUDIT

Does your station need a check-up?

Shane Media can give your station a customized evaluation that provides full examination of your programming and positioning.

We come into your market and analyze your station and other key stations for vulnerabilities. We get out in the market each day and speak with members of your community about their radio listening to gain a full understanding of the dynamics of your market. Together we review our evaluation and establish a working outline. We will then send a comprehensive written report that includes all market findings and an action plan.

SHANE MEDIA START-UP PACKAGE

This is for the station that's ready to take on the Country battle.

Starts with a Market Audit designed to position your station against the Country leader. Includes Logo/Branding Strategy, Marketing Evaluation, Formatic Development, Production, necessary Staffing, check-ups plus the Hot List Library and Weekly Update Package.

HOT LIST LIBRARY

Today's Country music compiled into a ready-to-use rotation system customized to reflect the tastes of your region.

Rotations are balanced in Power, Secondary and Tertiary categories that keep your station in step with the hot sounds of today's contemporary Country tastes -- Garth Brooks, Alan Jackson, Clint Black, Reba McEntire.

The Hot List Library has the capability of defining what's HOT in your region of the United States. It includes coding for tempo, texture, etc. Shane Media will assist with the implementation of the system.

WEEKLY UPDATE PACKAGE

Are you looking for a second opinion when adjusting your music library?

Shane Media has developed the "Music Update" - a weekly fax featuring information on new Country music along with recommended rotations. Includes information on how new music is playing all over the country. Great way to keep your Hot List Library current.

You also receive TACTICS -- a bi-monthly trend report that provides cutting edge information on management, programming, research and sales.

How Do You Put Us To Work?

Normally it goes like this:

Call us.

We'll ask questions. We'll answer questions. We'll get a picture of your position and your needs.

We may be able to tell you exactly what we recommend, how we will do it, and what it will cost.

Or, we may feel that one of us should sit down with you, see and hear the market firsthand, and then recommend.

It all starts with your phone call. And that's all it costs you if you don't think you need one of the revenue and audience building services we provide.

Find out how we can improve your

Ratings

Sales

Profits

Call John Lund:
415/692-7777

Or FAX us:
415/692-7329

THE LUND CONSULTANTS
to Broadcast Management, Inc.

We're in business to help your ratings, sales, and profits grow

1330 Millbrae Avenue
Millbrae, CA 94030-2829

6242 Hampton Drive North
St. Petersburg, FL 33710-4834

415/692-7777

There really is a firm that helps radio stations improve programming, sales, and profit.

For over a decade, The Lund Consultants have provided more listeners for stations like yours...

THE LUND CONSULTANTS
to Broadcast Management, Inc.

more ratings surveys and research data than most station owners, managers, or program directors will in a lifetime. The way the marketplace is today, using a consultant generally is a wise move. Radio stations that attempt to find their niche by trial and error make costly mistakes. A veteran consultant can accelerate a station's move on the road to success."

Boston-based radio consultant Donna Halper agrees with Scott and adds, "Consultants give their client stations an objective viewpoint and another experienced person's input. Consultants are support people, resource people, who bring to a situation a broader vision rather than the purely local perspective. Consultants, and not just out-of-work PDs who call themselves consultants but in reality aren't, have a lot of research, information, and expertise they can make available to a client with an ailing station."

Mikel Hunter of Mikel Hunter Broadcast Services, Las Vegas, says consultants help stations develop a distinctiveness that they need in order to succeed. "Unfortunately most station PDs are bandwagon riders. Many watch what other stations do around the country and clone them in their markets. Sometimes this works. Often it doesn't. It likely was a consultant who helped design the programming of that successful station being copied, and the consultant did so based on what was germane to that particular market, not one a thousand miles away. Therein lies the problem. Simply because a station in Denver is doing great book by programming a certain way does not guarantee that a station in Maryland can duplicate that success. A good consultant brings originality and creativity to each new situation, in addition to the knowledge and experience he possesses. The follow-the-leader method so prevalent among programmers actually creates a lot of the problems that consultants are called on to remedy."

Fewer than 100 broadcast consultants are listed in the various media directories around the country. More than half of this number specialize in radio. Says Ed Shane, "I remember a time when there were 250 programming consultants listed in the *R&R* directory. The number has tumbled since consolidation. One-man shops that couldn't make it as clients were swallowed by competing companies. Some consulting firms merged (Holland Cooke and McVay Media, for example). Others folded to go in-house at major companies (Jack Taddeo to Capstar, for instance)."

Generally, consultancy companies range in size from 20 to 50 employees, but may be composed of as few as two or three. Many successful program directors also provide consultancy to stations in other markets in addition to their regular programming duties. A growing number of station rep companies provide their client stations consultancy services for an additional fee.

Consultant Services

Stations hire program consultants to improve or strengthen their standings in the ratings surveys. An outside consultant may share general program decisions with the station's PD or may be endowed with full control over all decisions affecting the station's sound, contends Donna Halper. "I have as little or as much involvement as the client desires. Depending on the case, I can hire and train staff (or fire staff), design or fine-tune a format, or simply motivate and direct deejays, which is actually anything but simple. Whatever a station wants, as a professional consultant I can provide. Usually, I make recommendations and then the owner or GM decides whether or not I will carry them out. At some of my stations, I've functioned as the acting PD, for all intents and purposes. At other client stations, I've been sort of the unofficial mother figure, providing support, encouragement, and sometimes a much-needed kick in the behind."

Among other services, Fred Jacobs says his company offers "in-market visits for monitoring and strategizing; ongoing monitors of client competition from airchecks or station 'listen lines'; critiques of on-air talent, assistance/design of music scheduling and selection; computer programs that assist with promo scheduling, database marketing, and morning show preparation; design of off-air advertising and coordination with production; and design/implementation of market research for programming, image, and music."

Most consultant firms are equipped to provide either comprehensive or limited support to stations. "In some cases, consultants offer a packaged 'system for success' in the same way a McDonald's hamburger franchise delivers a 'system for success' to an investor. The consultant gets control. In other instances, consultants deliver objective advice or research input to a station more on a one-to-one basis. This parallels the role of most accountants or attorneys in that the decisions are still made by the station management, not the consultant," notes Century 21's Dave Scott.

In the mid-1990s, niche consultants came into vogue. For example, a consulting service called Air Support focuses on improving the ratings of station morning shows by working on "talent development, preparation, creativity, and performance," reports *Radio Ink*.

Program consultants diagnose the problems that impair a station's growth and then prescribe a plan of action designed to remedy the ills. For example, station WXXX, located in a 20-station market, is one of three that programs current hits, yet it lags behind both of its competitors in the ratings. A consultant is hired to assess the situation and suggest a solution. The consultant's preliminary report cites several weaknesses in WXXX's overall programming. The consultant's critique submitted to the station's general manager may be written like this:

Dear GM:

Following a month-long analysis of WXXX's on-air product, here are some initial impressions. A more extensive report on each of the areas cited herein will follow our scheduled conference next week.

1. Personnel: Morning man Jay Allen lacks the energy and appeal necessary to attract and sustain an audience in this daypart. Although Allen possesses a smoothness and warmth that would work well in other time slots, namely midday or evenings, he does not have the "wake-up and roll" sound, nor the type of humor listeners have come to expect at this time of day. The other "hot hit" stations in the market offer bright and lively morning teams. Allen does not stand up against the competition. His contrasting style is ill-suited for AM drive, whereas midday man Mike Curtis would be more at home during this period. His upbeat, witty, and casual style when teamed with newspeople Chuck Tuttle and Mark Fournier would strengthen the morning slot.

Tracy Jessick and Michelle Jones perform well in their respective time periods. Overnight man Johnny Christensen is very adequate—potential as midday man should Curtis be moved into morning slot. Weekend personnel uneven. Better balance needed. Carol Mirando, 2 to 7 p.m. Sunday, is the strongest of the part-timers. Serious pacing problems with Larry Coty in 7 to midnight slot on Saturday. Can't read copy.

2. Music: Rotation problems in all dayparts. Playlist narrowing and updating necessary. Better definition needed. As stands, station verges on Adult Contemporary at certain times of the day, especially during a.m. drive. On Monday the 14th, during evening daypart, station abandoned currents and assumed Oldies sound. More stability and consistency within format essential. Computerized music scheduling possible solution. Separate report to follow.

3. News programming: General revamping necessary. Too heavy an emphasis during both drive periods. Cut back by 20 to 30 percent in these two dayparts. Fifteen-minute "Noon News" needs to be eliminated. Tune-out factor in targeted demos. Same holds true for half-hour, 5 to 5:30 p.m., "News Roundup." Hourly five-minute casts reduced to minute headlines after 7 p.m. Both content and style of newscasts presently inappropriate for demos sought. Air presentations need adjusting to better, more compatibly suit format. Tuttle and Fournier of morning show are strong, whereas p.m. drive news would benefit from a comparable team. Ovitt, Hart, and Lexis do not complement each other. Van Sanders is effective in

evening slot. More sounders and actualities in hourly newscasts. Greater local slant needed, especially on sports events.

4. General programming: Too much clutter! A log-jam in drive dayparts. Spots clustered four deep in spot sets, sometimes at quarter hour. So much for maintenance. Rescheduling needed for flow purposes as well. "Consumer Call" at 8 a.m., noon, and 5 p.m. not suitable for demos. "Band News" good, but too long. One-minute capsule versions scheduled through day would be more effective. Friday evening "Oldies Party" too geriatric—breaks format objective. Sends target demos off to competition by appealing to older listeners with songs dating back to 1960s. Public affairs programs scheduled between 9 a.m. and noon on Sundays delivers teens to competition that airs music during same time period. Jingles and promos dated. Smacks of decade ago. New package would add contemporary luster needed to sell format to target demo.

5. Promotions: "Bermuda Triangle" contest aimed at older demos. Contest prizes geared for 25- to 39-year-old listener. Ages station. Concert tie-in good. Album giveaway could be embellished with other prizes. Too thin as is. Response would indicate lack of motivation. True also of "Cash Call." Larger sums need to be awarded. Curtis's "Rock Trivia" on target. Hits demos on the money. Expand into other dayparts. Bumper stickers and "X-100" calendar do not project appropriate image. New billboards and bus-boards also need adjusting. Paper ads focus on weak logo. Waiting to view TV promo. Competition promos are very weak. A good "X-100" TV promo would create advantage in this area. Opportunity.

6. Technical: Signal strong. Reaches areas that competition does not. Significant null in Centerville area. Competition's signals unaffected. Occasional disparity in levels. Spots sometimes very hot. Promos and PSAs, especially UNICEF and American Cancer Society, slightly muddy. In general, fidelity acceptable on music. Extraneous noise, possibly caused by scratches or dirt, on some power rotation cuts. Stereo separation good. Recommend compressor and new limiter. Further plant evaluation in progress. A more detailed report to follow.

Following an extensive assessment of a station's programming, a consultant may suggest a major change. "After an in-depth evaluation and analysis, we may conclude that a station is improperly positioned in its particular market and recommend a format switch. Sometimes station management disagrees. Changing formats can be pretty traumatic, so there often is resistance to the idea. A critique more often recommends that adjustments be made in an existing format than a changeover to a different one. There are times when a consultant is simply called upon to assist in the hiring of a new jock or newsperson. Major surgery is not always necessary or desired," says Donna Halper.

Today the majority of stations in major and medium markets switching formats do so with the aid of a consultant. According to the NAB, 3 to 5 percent of the nation's stations change formats each year. Consultant fees range from $500 to more than $1,200 a

K-ONE
AM 1450

The #1 Combo

KOZZ 105.7
CLASSIC ROCK & ROLL

August 13, 1991

Burkhart, Douglas and Associates
6500 River Chase Circle, East
Atlanta, Georgia 30328

I wanted to take a few minutes to thank your staff for the hours you've put in to help make KOZZ a winner!

Greg Gillespie gives us a great deal of his time, makes himself available and always gets back to me even when he's on the road. Greg works from the time he gets up till the time he turns in when he's visiting KOZZ -- it's nice to know he's never too busy to answer our questions or offer input. Greg played a very significant part in our success. We came in #1 Adults 25-54 in both the Birch and the other survey that we don't subscribe to. When you consider that we did it with $9,000.00 and 10 billboards it's down right astounding!

Looking forward to bigger and better numbers in the Fall and continuing our relationship for years to come.

Yours truly,

Harry Reynolds
Program Director

HR/ca

FIGURE 11.2
Consultants make a dramatic difference at many stations.
Courtesy Burkhart/Douglas & Associates.

day, depending on the complexity of the services rendered and the size of the station.

Consultant Qualifications

Many consultants begin as broadcasters. Some successfully programmed stations before embarking on their own or joining consultancy firms. According to Rick Sklar,

FIGURE 11.3
Consultants offer various services to stations. Courtesy Shane Media.

They're the consultants for companies that "don't use consultants."

They're our station's secret weapon.

- Today's # 1 stations choose Shane Media for programming.

- Now, a full menu of research services, too.

- Our 20th Year of thinking ahead!

SHANE MEDIA
(713) 952-9221
Radio Programming and Research
www.shanemedia.com

deceased president of Sklar Communications, consultants who have a background in the medium have a considerable edge over those who do not. "The best way to fully understand and appreciate radio is to work in it. As you might imagine, radio experience is very helpful in this business." Jacobs agrees with Sklar. "Ideally a consultant should have a successful background in programming, with expertise in a number of areas, including research, sales, marketing, and promotion. The key word is *success*—a solid track record in a number of different market situations is invaluable. Consultants also need to have strong communication and tracking skills to best work with a variety of clients in markets around the country." Not all consultants have extensive backgrounds in the medium. Most do possess a thorough knowledge of how radio operates on all its different levels, from having worked closely with stations and having acquired formal training in colleges offering research methodology, audience measurement, and broadcast management courses. "A solid education is particularly important for those planning to become broadcast consultants. It is a very complex and demanding field today, and it is becoming more so with each passing day. My advice is to load up. Get the training and experience up front. It is very competitive out there. You make your own opportunities in this profession," says Century 21's Dave Scott.

Both Halper and Scott rate people skills and objectivity highly. "Consulting requires an ability to deal with people. Decisions—for example, changing formats—sometimes result in drastic personnel changes. A consultant must be adept at diplomacy but must act with conviction when the diagnosis has been made. Major surgery invariably is traumatic, but the idea is to make the patient, the station, healthy again. You can't let your own personal biases or tastes get in the way of what will work in a given market," observes Halper. Dave Scott shares Halper's sentiments. "A consultant, like a doctor, must be compassionate and at the same time maintain his objectivity. It is our intention and goal as a program consultant service to make our client stations thrive. As consultants, we're successful because we do what we have to do. It's not a question of being mercenary. It's a question of doing what you have to do to make a station prosper and realize its potential."

Consultant company executives also consider wit, patience, curiosity, sincerity, eagerness, competitiveness, and drive—not necessarily in that order—among the other virtues that the aspiring consultant should possess.

Consultants: Pros and Cons

There are as many opponents of program consultants within the radio industry as there are advocates. Broadcasters who do not use consultants argue that local flavor is lost when an outsider comes into a market to direct a station's programming. Donna Halper contends that this may be true to some degree but believes that most professional consultants are sensitive to a station's local identity. "Some consultants do clone their stations. Others of us do not. In fact, I'd say most do not. For those of us who recognize local differences, there need not be any loss whatsoever as a consequence of consultant-recommended changes. But the hits are pretty much the hits, and good radio is something that Tulsa deserves as well as Rochester. So I do try to localize my music research and acquire a good feel for the market I'm working in. But as far as basic rules of good radio are concerned, those don't vary much no matter what the market is. It's important for a station to reflect the market it serves, and I support my clients in that. Because I work out of Boston doesn't mean that my AOR client in Duluth should sound like a Boston album rocker. It should sound like a solid AOR station that could be respected in any city but fits the needs of Duluth."

Consultant Dwight Douglas says that localization is essential for any radio station and that consultants are amply aware of this fact. "It is an industry axiom that a station must be a part of its environment. An excellent station will be uniquely local in relating to its audience. That tends to take the form of news, weather, sports, public service, general information, and jock talk. A good consultant will free a station from music worries and allow it to concentrate on

FIGURE 11.4
Consultant's response to commonly asked questions. Courtesy Donna Halper and Associates.

Donna Halper & Associates
Radio Programming Consultants
304 Newbury St., #506
Boston, MA 02115
(617) 786-0666

QUESTIONS I AM OFTEN ASKED ABOUT HIRING A CONSULTANT

1. What kind of station would hire a consultant?

All kinds! From major market #1 stations that want to stay that way to new stations that need help choosing a format or hiring staff.

2. Aren't most consultants just out-of-work Program Directors?

Not today. Competition is too intense. Most of us who have stayed in the consulting field have years of experience in one thing: CONSULTING.

3. Should I hire a 'big name' consultant?

Since the majority of consultants today are experienced, you should choose one based on what his/her areas of expertise are. Interview a few consultants and you will see that each has some specialty-- whether it's a certain format (some consultants prefer to do only one format) or a certain market size. Choosing the right consultant for your station is an important decision, and you shouldn't do it on name alone.

4. What can a consultant offer my station that my own people can't provide?

First, consultants aren't there to replace your people, nor do they want them to look bad. While staff changes may result from the recommendations of a consultant, our first purpose is to offer you an UNBIASED, outside overview of how your station sounds, both its strengths and its weaknesses. We work WITH your people, providing research, guidance, training, market studies, etc. Often, because we are not caught up in the day-to-day circumstances, we can offer a fresh, objective point of view.

5. What are the benefits of HALPER & ASSOCIATES?

I'm glad you asked. We've been in business since 1980. (Before that, Donna Halper spent 13 years in major markets as an announcer, Music Director, PD, news reporter, and writer/producer of special programming.) Our specialties include critiques/positioning studies, staff training and motivation, and talent development. We work in markets of all sizes, but we are best-known for our ability to turn around failing small and medium market stations. We also do motivational seminars, and are expert at handling morale problems. Unlike some consultants who only do one format, Halper & Associates can show success stories in AC, Gold, CHR, Urban, Classic Rock, Full-Service/M-O-R, and Country. SINCE 1980, OVER 90% OF OUR CLIENTS HAVE SHOWN RATINGS GROWTH. And, our critiques and market studies have been used by some of the biggest and best companies. Also, Halper and Associates has experience with Canadian radio, and we have consulted in Puerto Rico.

6. Can you promise results for every client?

No consultant wins 'em all, although we'd like to. But, our slogan has always been "NO PROMISES...JUST RESULTS." We are proud of our many satisfied clients and our renewal rate is quite high. Many of our clients say they would never use another consultant. So, when it's time to think about a consultant, choose DONNA HALPER & ASSOCIATES. We can get results for you. To find out more, call us at 617-786-0666. We'll give you the attention you might not get from the "big names," affordable rates, and, most important, you can count on us to make a positive impact on your station and its staff! DONNA HALPER GETS RESULTS!!!

A Good Consultant Can Make A Difference...

With so many good consultants out there, it can be a difficult task to choose the one who is right for your station. To help you make such an important decision, **HALPER & ASSOCIATES** offers a few facts about what we can do for you:

1. **HALPER & ASSOCIATES** has gotten results for our clients since 1980. Our staff and our reputation are solid.

2. **HALPER & ASSOCIATES** has success stories in nearly every format, from CHR to Urban, Gold to Classic Rock, Country to AC, News and MOR. We've helped turn around many stations — both AM's and FM's. Recently, for example, we took a declining Urban/CHR from a 5.3 to an 8.4 in one year. An AC client of ours has grown from a 13.0 to a 17.1 in two years. Since 1980, over 90% of our clients have shown ratings increases. Many are now #1 or #2.

3. **HALPER & ASSOCIATES** gets results in markets of all sizes, from the East Coast to the West Coast, Canada and Puerto Rico. We have clients in major and large markets, but we have become known for our work in small and medium markets. We understand the special challenges of these markets and can make an impact even if you don't have a huge promotion budget or a legendary air staff.

4. **HALPER & ASSOCIATES** offers more than just better ratings. Our specialty is motivation and talent development. We can help to bring out the best in your staff, handle morale problems, or give your department heads the training and input they need to do their jobs more effectively. We are also known for our thorough market analyses, critiques and positioning studies. We can help you find the right format, or fine tune the one you now have.

5. **HALPER & ASSOCIATES** never clones stations or deals in fad formats. Each of our clients is unique. We are there whenever you need us.

No promises. Just results.

Donna Halper and Associates
Radio Programming Consultants
304 Newbury Street #506
Boston, Mass. 02115
(617) 786-0666

FIGURE 11.5
Consultant promotional piece. Courtesy Donna Halper and Associates.

resource, but both the station and the consultant must pool their wisdom to make the plan work."

Jacobs strikes a similar note of caution regarding the importance of local connection. "With a consultant, a station can conceivably lose some of its localness if there isn't adequate effort to give it a hometown flavor. But the loss of local presence is far more likely with satellite-delivered formats. Consultants need to work closely with station management (and vice versa) to find local ties and signposts, because listeners care most about what's happening in their town. It's always important to understand that there are regional differences in taste, personalities, and music. Many high-powered on-air personalities would be hard-pressed to duplicate their success in another market."

The cost factor is another reason why some stations do not use consultants. "Consultants can be expensive, although most consultants scale their fees to suit the occasion, that is, the size of the market. A few hundred dollars a day can be exorbitant for many smaller stations. But the cost of the research, analysis, and strategy usually is worth the money. I believe that a station, in most cases, gets everything it pays for when it uses a consultant. It's worth investing a few thousand to make back a million," contends Dwight Douglas.

Dave Scott believes that certain stations can become too dependent on consultants. "A consultant is there to provide support and direction when needed. If a station is infirm, it needs attention, perhaps extensive care. However, when a station regains its health, an annual or semi-annual checkup is usually sufficient. A checkup generally can prevent problems from recurring."

Mikel Hunter agrees with Scott, adding, "A radio doctor needs the cooperation of his client. On the other hand, a station must insist that a consultant do more than diagnose or critique. Positive input, that is, a remedying prescription, is what a consultant should provide. Conversely, a station should

developing local identity. We work hard at customizing formats to suit the geodemographics or lifestyles of the audiences of our client stations."

A station has an obligation to retain its sense of locality regardless of what a consultant may suggest, contends Mikel Hunter. "No station should simply turn itself over body and soul to a consultant. Local flavor does not have to be sacrificed if a station has a strong PD and a general manager who doesn't insist that the PD merely follow the consultant's suggestions. A station should not let itself become a local franchise. Consultants are a valuable be willing to use the aid that the consultant provides."

Statistically, those stations that use programming consultants more often than not experience improved ratings. In case after case consultants have taken their client stations from bottom to top in many of the country's largest markets. Of course, not all succeed quite so dramatically. However, a move from eleventh place to sixth in a metro market is considered a noteworthy achievement and has a very invigorating effect on station revenue. "The vast majority of consultants benefit their clients by increasing their position in the book. This means better profits," notes Halper, who has improved the ratings of 90 percent of her client stations.

About the future of radio consultancy, George Burns says, "I see the role of consultants undergoing considerable change in the next few years. The rules of ownership and the very principles under which our industry is organized are altering radically. Consultants will probably take even more of an advisory role and have less involvement in the day-to-day operations of a station. The new and larger broadcasting companies, in all size markets, will keep expertise in-house and rely less on outside input in these areas. I see consultants operating at 'higher levels' in the future. They will be working on organization, continuing education, motivation, compensation, human resources, and other 'top management' concerns. Consultants, I believe, will become more policy oriented and less concerned with groundlevel activities."

Program Suppliers

The widespread use of automation equipment commencing in the 1960s sparked significant growth in the field of programming syndication. Initially the installation of automation systems motivated station management to seek out syndicator services. Today the highly successful and sophisti-

cated program formats offered by myriad syndicators often inspires stations to invest in automation equipment. Of course, many of the large radio corporations create programming for distribution to their own stations, and this has had an impact on the number of program suppliers still in operation. However, it is estimated that nearly half of the country's radio outlets purchase syndicated programming, which may consist of as little as a series of one- or two-minute features or as much as a 24-hour, year-round station format.

Program specialist Dick Ellis cites economics as the primary reason why stations resort to syndicators. "When I programmed for Peters Productions they supplied high-quality programming and engineering at a relatively low cost. For instance, for a few hundred dollars a month a small market operator gets a successful program director, a highly skilled mastering engineer, all the music he'll ever need (no service problems with record companies) recorded on the highest quality tapes available. It takes a programmer eight hours to program one twenty-four-hour cut reel. It takes a mastering engineer eight hours to remove all the pops and clicks found on even brand new records, plus place the automation tones. All of this frees the local operator to concentrate his efforts on promotion and, of course, sales."

William Stockman, who led Schulke Radio Productions (SRP was purchased by

FIGURE 11.6
Courtesy Jacobs Media.

```
Pro's and con's of using a consultant:

    +'s                                    -'s

* Objective, experienced view      * Overreliance on consultant
* Exposure to new ideas              and not enough local input
* Ongoing evaluation of the        * Program director gets too
  station                            much advice from too many
* Input about stations from          sources
  around the country
* National research and information
* Experience/assistance in a wide
  range of areas including music,
  promotion, marketing, talent
  management, etc.
```

Bonneville Broadcasting System in the mid-1980s), says that stations are attracted to syndicators because of the highly professional, major market sound they are able to provide. "By using SRP's unique programming service, a smaller station with limited resources can sound as polished and sophisticated as any metro station."

Both economics and service motivate radio stations to contract syndicators, contends former Satellite Music Network (now part of ABC Radio) programmer Lee Abrams (now heading the programming effort of XM Satellite). "Stations are attracted to our affordable, high-quality programming. It's just that simple. Syndies provided an excellent product within a cost-effective context. Their expertise in delivering niche concepts was very appealing to radio operators."

The late and great Rick Sklar observed, "In today's cost-conscious economic climate, more and more radio station operators are turning to suppliers of twenty-four-hour formats for their programming. Whether delivered via satellite, conventional tape, CD or DAT, these increasingly sophisticated products are not only penetrating new markets but larger markets as well, where until now, traditional thinking has held that locally originated programming was the only way to go."

The demand for syndicator product has paralleled, if not exceeded, the increase in the number of radio outlets since the 1960s. Again, the new millennium has brought a change in the field of program syndication with the large radio corporations often assuming the chore of program generation in-house.

Every part of the broadcast day is served by syndicators, and morning drive in particular, observes Ed Shane. "Syndicated morning shows are widespread and proliferating. There are almost too many to keep track of. At a quick glance, you've got Bob and Sheri, John Boy and Billy, Bob and Tom, Mark and Brian, Steve and DC, Big D and Bubba, Mancow, Stern, and on and on."

Syndicator Services

The major program syndicators usually market several distinctive, fully packaged radio formats. "In its heyday, Peters Productions made available a complete format service with each of their format blends. They were not merely a music service. Their programming goal was the emotional gratification of the type of person attracted to a particular format," says Dick Ellis, whose former company offered a dozen different formats, including Beautiful Music, Easy Listening, Standard Country, Modern Country, Adult Contemporary, Standard MOR, Super Hits, Easy Contemporary, and a country and contemporary hybrid called Natural Sound.

Century 21 Programming also was a leader in format diversity, explains Dave Scott. "Our inventory included everything from the most contemporary super hits sound to several Christian formats. We even offered a full-time Jazz format. We had programming to fit any need in any market."

Drake-Chenault Enterprises (now owned by Jones Satellite Networks) was among the oldest and largest of syndicators and specialized in Beautiful Music. Today Classical Music Network, TM Century, Jones Satellite Network, Westwood One, United Station Radio Network, and NBG Radio Networks also are among the most successful of those syndicators marketing several program formats. Some syndicators prefer to specialize in one or two programming areas. For example, Bonneville Broadcasting and Churchill Productions primarily specialize in the adult Easy Listening format.

Syndicator formats are fully tested before they are marketed, explains Stockman. "At Schulke our strategy was to reorient the music from essentially a producer-oriented to a consumer-oriented product. Music was tested on a cut-by-cut basis in several markets coast-to-coast. Using patented and proven methodology, music was carefully added or selectively deleted. By determining what songs the listeners like to hear and which songs they dislike, SRP assembled a totally researched library that has been on the air via our subscriber stations since March 1983. Every song played on our stations has been rated by the listeners as a 'winner' and all the 'stiffs' that have a high dislike factor have been eliminated altogether."

Customized sound hours are designed for each format to ensure consistency and compatibility on the local station level. "An exact clock is tailored for our client station after our market study. The format we provide will perfectly match the station in tempo, style, music mix, announcing, promos, news, weather, and commercial load," says program syndicator Dave Scott. Observes Ed Shane, "The key to using syndicator or network programming is to make it sound like it belongs to the station. Even big personality shows like Rush and Dr. Laura can make use of local avails and bumpers for personalized call letters and promos."

Audience and market research and analysis are conducted by syndicators before implementing a particular format. "Our clients receive comprehensive consulting services from our seasoned staff. We begin with a detailed study of our client station's market. We probe demographics, psychographics, and population growth trends of a station's available audience. We analyze a client's competition quantitatively through available ratings and qualitatively from airchecks. Then the programming our service provides is professionally positioned to maximize our client's sales, ratings, and profits. All of our programming is solidly backed by systematic studies of the listening tastes of each format's target audience. Our research includes call-out and focus group studies, in-depth market analysis, attitudinal audience feedback, psychographic patterns and tests, and several in-house computers with ratings data online," says Dave Scott.

Format programming packages include hundreds of hours of music, as well as

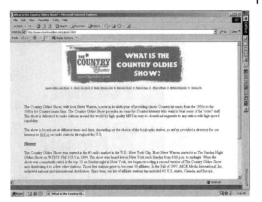

FIGURE 11.7
Short form programs offered by syndicators flesh out a station's clock. Courtesy WFMT.

breaks, promos, and IDs, by seasoned metro market announcers. Customized identity elements, such as jingles and other special formatic features (taped time checks), are made available by the majority of syndicators. "We try to cover all bases to ensure the success of our clients. We back each of our formats a dozen different ways. For example, image builders in the form of promotions, contests, and graphics also are an element of our programming service at Radio Arts," says programmer Larry Vanderveen.

To stay in step with the ever-changing marketplace, syndicators routinely update the programming they provide their subscribers. "When you want people to listen to a station a lot, you've got to keep them interested in it. To do so you have to air a sound that's always fresh and current. Tape updates are plentiful. We give stations the most extensive initial collection of music tapes available. Then we follow them up with hundreds more throughout the year. For instance, our CHR, AOR, and Country subscribers receive over 100 updates annually. All categories have frequent updates, so our client's sound stays fresh and vital," says Dave Scott, who adds that the lines of communication are kept open between the client and syndicator long after the agreement has been signed. "Since the success of our clients is very important to us, continuing consultation and assistance via a toll-free hotline is always available twenty-four hours a day. Automation-experienced broadcasters are in our production studios around

FIGURE 11.8
Century 21's catalog of
syndicated formats in
the 1990s. Courtesy
Century 21.

Eighteen Successful Sounds: One's Right For You

The Z Format.
Since 1973, Century 21's contemporary hit Z Format has delivered the best track record in the business!

The Hot Z Format.
Today's hottest hits give you the most popular music, so your station will be the most popular in your market!

Album Oriented Z.
Century 21's album rock format is available either unannounced or uniquely custom-voiced.

The A-C Format.
Adult contemporary music goes hand-in-hand with a big, responsive audience.

Good Ol' Rock & Roll.
Here are the top hit oldies of the 50's, 60's & 70's that still sound good today.

SUPER·COUNTRY.
You can choose from our *three* different formats: modern, traditional, or pop/crossover country.

The C-C Format.
This Country-Crossover Format blends country with adult contemporary music.

The E-Z Format.
Century 21's E-Z Format moves "middle-of-the-road" music into *your* lane.

MORE BEAUTIFUL.
MORe Beautiful blends middle-of-the-road vocals with the finest instrumentals.

Simply Beautiful.
Beautiful music is the favorite format of broadcasters seeking trouble-free, stable operations.

MEMORY MUSIC.
Here's the ideal mixture of M-O-R and nostalgia. Music vintages are tailored to your station.

SACRED SOUNDS.
Century 21 delivers four Christian formats: beautiful, adult contemporary, traditional & country gospel.

The Jazz-Z Format.
As either a full- or part-time format, Century 21's Jazz-Z sound gives your station unique popularity.

the clock, and consultants can be reached at work or home any time. Help is as close as the phone."

Syndicators assist stations during the installation and implementation stage of a format and provide training for operators and other station personnel. Comprehensive operations manuals are left with subscribers as a source of further assistance.

Syndicators offer programs on a barter basis, for a fee without presold spots, or for a fee containing spots. Leasing agreements generally stipulate a minimum two-year term and assure the subscriber that the syndicator will not lease a similar format to another station in the same market. Should a station choose not to renew its agreement with the syndicator, all material must be returned unless otherwise stipulated.

The majority of format syndicators also market production libraries, jingles, and special features for general market consumption.

What is the difference between a network and a syndicator? Ed Shane explains, "Networks and syndicators are essentially or almost the same. Premiere calls Rush Limbaugh a 'network' and Dr. Laura a 'syndicated show.' United Stations Radio Network works the same way. (It has more to do with the way spots are sold than the realities of programming.) Westwood One is more of a network, combining CBS News, CNN Radio, long form music programs, Metro Traffic and News with syndicated programming like country music specials. ESPN is networked for all talk shows and live sports (NFL football play-by-play, for example) by ABC."

Hardware Requirements and Quality

Syndicated programming typically was designed for automation systems (which have all but been replaced by satellite-fed programming). "All Century 21 program-

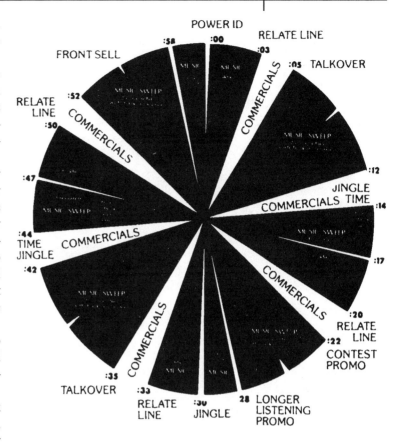

FIGURE 11.9
Sample customized sound hour. Courtesy Century 21.

ming was aired smoothly with a minimum of equipment. Of course, sophisticated systems can be fully utilized by our formats, but you can run our material with the most basic automation setup," notes Dave Scott, whose company, as well as most other format syndicators, required that stations possess the following automation equipment:

- Four reel-to-reel tape decks capable of holding 10 1/2-inch NAB reels; some formats will work with only two or three reel-to-reel decks (or CD or DAT players when the station has upgraded to this new technology)
- End-of-music sensors, to alert operators of necessary tape changes
- Sufficient multiple cart playback systems for spot load, news, PSAs, weather, promos, IDs, and so forth

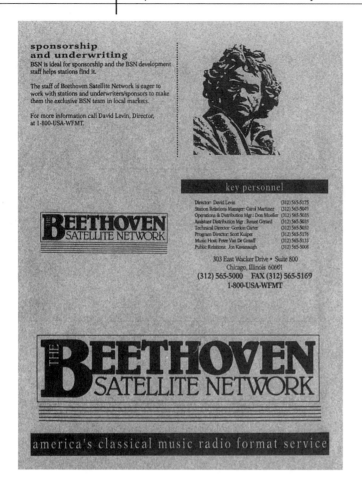

FIGURE 11.10
Satellite program
services. Courtesy
WFMT.

- Two single-cartridge playback units or use of extra trays in spot players
- One time-announce unit with two size-C cartridge players and controller.

Scott also notes that his company now provides clients with the newest in sound reproduction technology. "Century 21 offered 160 hours of full-form programming on CD and DAT. Right now we have hundreds of clients on CD product as compared to 350 on reel-to-reel. We also provide subscribers with high-quality DAT players when they choose to go in that direction."

Technical and engineering assistance is made available to subscribers. "We provide periodic on-site station technical reviews together with ongoing technical consultation, continuing new technology develop-

ment, and new equipment evaluation," explains Bonneville's Marlin Taylor.

The use of satellites by syndicators has grown enormously since 1980. An NAB survey concluded that over three-quarters of the nation's stations receive some form of satellite programming. The majority of stations with satellite dishes use them to draw network feeds. However, the percentage of stations receiving product from syndicators and other programming services has more than doubled during the past couple of decades, and the use of station hardware (other than computers) for syndicator programming is nearly extinct. It is more cost effective and efficient to catch the digital satellite signals than it is to handle actual product on the local station level. In fact, the majority of program syndicators have ceased to mail material to stations, opting to beam it to them instead.

Satellite-fed syndicator programs are often archived for later replay. Drew Carey of Clear Channel Communications discusses the procedure for doing so for one of his company's shows: "The Bob & Tom Show is designed to air in its entirety for the full four hours as sent with no editing. Stations in the Central, Mountain, and Pacific time zones run the show either at 5 to 9 a.m. or 6 to 10 a.m. depending upon their competitive situation. Stations use one of three methods to delay broadcast of the show: 1. Station automation systems (record to system, such as Audio Vault, then replay automatically), 2. Record to DAT then replay (requires the station be staffed overnight and during playback), and 3. Record to mini-disc the replay (requires the station be staffed overnight and during playback)."

Concerning audio quality, syndicators are very particular about sound quality and make every effort to ensure that their programming meets or exceeds fidelity standards. "Our company uses the finest quality recording studio equipment. Actually, it's far superior to any broadcast-grade gear. Therefore, it is quite important that subscribers

FIGURE 11.10
continued

FIGURE 11.11
SMN offers an explanation of their system, which requires little equipment on the client-subscriber level. This is one of the many cost advantages of satellite programming. Courtesy SMN.

have adequate hardware, too. We utilize a number of highly regarded audio experts to make our sound and our client's the very best possible. In fact, we use special audiophile 'super disks,' master tapes from record companies, noise reduction, click editing, and precise level control or slight equalization, if needed," says Scott.

Periodic airchecks of subscriber stations are analyzed from a technical perspective to detect any deficiencies in sound quality.

CHAPTER HIGHLIGHTS

1. The significant increase in stations and formats created a market for consultants. Today the ranks of radio consultants has been reduced due to consolidation.

2. Consultants provide various services, including market research, programming and format design, hiring and training of staff, staff motivation, advertising and public relations campaigns, news and public affairs restructuring, and technical evaluation (periodic airchecks of sound quality).

3. Aspiring consultants should acquire background experience in the medium, solid educational preparation, and strong interpersonal skills.

4. Station executives opposed to using consultants fear losing the station's local flavor, becoming a clone of other stations, and the substantial cost.

5. Statistically, stations using programming consultants more often than not experience improved ratings.

6. Increased use of programming syndication is related to the increased use of computers and satellites. Most of the nation's stations purchase some form of syndicated programming.

7. Syndicated programs are generally cost effective, of high quality, and reliable, thus allowing smaller stations to achieve a metro station sound.

8. Program syndicators provide a variety of test-marketed, packaged radio formats—from Country to Top 40 to Religious. Packages may include music, breaks, promos, customized IDs, and even promotions. Package updates are frequent.

9. Networks and syndicators are essentially one and the same.

10. The number of syndicators using satellites to deliver programming is at an all-time high. Many deliver programming only via satellite.

APPENDIX: Station Critique

To: GM/BRadio Fr: Donna L. Halper, Halper & Associates Re: Critique of tapes of B

Thanks for sending along the latest batch of tapes for me to critique. I do hear some improvements since I last visited the station. On the other hand, I am still hearing some areas that we need to work on. Most of what I noticed are problems with formatics, although a few little things stood out. In no particular order:

1. Bet is back to being too close to the mike, causing her to pop her Ps again. The good news is that on this tape, her voice is now VERY

midrange—and not high-end or "cutesy," and she sounds more natural. The bad news is that she seems determined to use verbal clichés (however, she is not the only one with this habit). For example, when she reads the liner about "playing the music that made FM great," she repeatedly says "and here's another great example" when she introduces the next song. She is also trying too hard to make simple format elements sound enthusiastic: the school lunch menu basically just needs to be read, rather than embellished upon for two minutes. I know she is *trying*, but it just sounds artificial to get *that* excited about school lunches. The entire staff seems stuck on the phrases *keep it locked* and *music from . . .* ("that was music from the Beatles; now here's music from Steely Dan"). In real life, do we really talk that way, or do we talk about great SONGS, or use phrases like "a classic from. . . ." We need to VARY what we say, or else we sound like robots. Thus, if I just said "Now, here's a classic from Bob Dylan," I don't want to use that phrase for every front-sell. Ditto for "keep it locked"—it's a rather overused AOR phrase as it is, but boy, do our jocks say it a lot . . . can't we find some other ways to invite people to listen?

2.   Virtually everyone seems to have acute liner-itis. It's a disease where you want to read a lot of liners all at once. I heard "the all-new B-, the station that plays the classic hits and the music that made FM great!!!" ONE LINER PER BREAK IS JUST FINE, THANKS. If we just used "the all-new B-" or "your station for Classic Hits," we don't need to add in two more liners. A good front-sell might be as simple as "on the home of classic hits, B-, here's Cat Stevens." Or "playing the music that made FM great, we're B-, with Fleetwood Mac." Simple is better, in other words.

3.   How much weather do we need in middays? During morning drive, the announcer should give time, temp, and say good morning to the audience each break; that isn't necessary the rest of the day. Unless there are major storms coming, I wouldn't have so many weather forecasts during the workday—folks already got there, the kids are in school, etc. But we should still be friendly: I seldom heard Dave say his name (I assume it was Dave?), and I like a liner that thanks people for listening or invites them to tell a friend about the All-New B-.

4.   Although I agree that call letters are crucial, I heard them used way too much at some times: It is not conversational to say "on the all-new B-, here's Bob Seger on the all-new B-." That just sounds repetitious. My training has been to use call letters going into a song, and use them when coming out of a long music set ("That was Traffic on the All-New B-, and we also heard Joan Baez and Dan Fogelberg.") But to use them two or three times within the same front-sell strikes me as too much of a good thing. Also, I'm hearing B- a lot more than I'm hearing Classic Hits. And a final grammatical note—you CAN'T say "the classic hits of all time"—you can play the greatest hits, but *classic hits* is a format description and a positioning statement. I'd suggest "playing ALL the classic hits" or "playing nothing but classic hits" or "playing the classic hits of the past and the classic hits of today"—you get the idea.

5.   More clichés–why is Wednesday called *hump day?* Again, do we really talk that way? And in several of the forecasts I heard various people do, I heard about *scattered rain*—I knew that showers could be scattered, but rain? I remind everyone to keep being CONVERSATIONAL— how would you talk to a FRIEND? Would you really say "It's 52 minutes past the hour of 6 o'clock"? I also like consistency—some jocks, as mentioned earlier, said their name often, some said it repeatedly, some seldom said it at all. Some used one liner over and over, some used a variety. These elements must be formatted in so that all the liners are rotated evenly. Also, I'm not sure if it was the skimmer, but I heard some problems with levels when a song ended. The jock's voice sounded much louder or much softer than the song at certain times. A request—could you tape an hour of each jock and NOT scope it down—in other words, just put a tape in a boombox and let it run, so that I can hear an uninterrupted hour, commercials and all? I'd like to hear what the audience heard.

More critique later—I'll go over the music in more detail in my next memo. What I heard sounded basically hit-oriented, which is good, but let's stress CLASSIC HITS too, because we are getting to a point where the variety of the music is right on target! I'll be in touch.

P.S. I meant to mention that the PSA or Street-Sheet outro may be too long, although it may also be the jock ad-libbing. The ending of a PSA should be brief and to the point. What I heard was over a MINUTE of numbers and advice—"If your church, social club, or nonprofit organization has a message you want to be publicized, just send the who-what-when-where-how-and-why, etc."—boy, that's wordy!!! It's better to be simple,

FIGURE 11.12
Many syndicators use satellites to feed programming to client stations. This greatly simplifies the distribution process. Handling of tapes and mailing is eliminated. Satellite syndication also keeps station equipment costs down. Courtesy IDB.

FIGURE 11.13
Satellite Music
Network program
clock. Courtesy SMN.

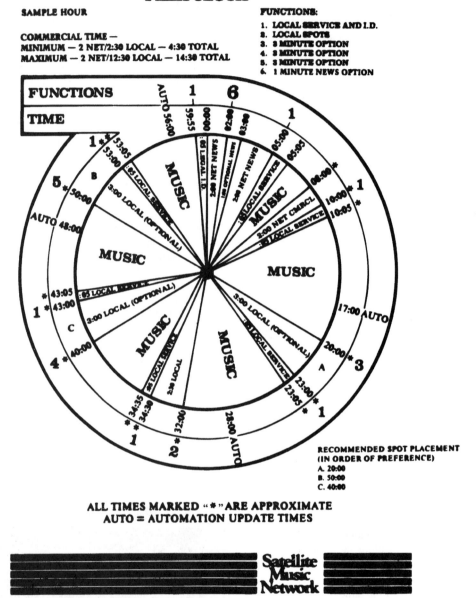

without tons of addresses and phone numbers. You are wiser to advise those with something to send to call B- for our fax number, rather than taking up so much time telling them they can phone it or fax it or mail it, then giving the address on top of everything. This slows the station down too much. It also goes without saying that the way something is sent to us on a press release may not sound good read verbatim on the air. What *I* heard B- reading sounded as if we had just put the press release right into the studio with no rewrite. Local news and local PSAs should be rewritten for clarity, and it helps that they be conversational. (I would also like to hear our local news, by the way, plus how Chris sounds.) Perhaps the announcers were nervous because they were doing an aircheck, but they do need to become accustomed to taping themselves regularly so that they can eliminate the verbal crutches they use and make their show sound smoother.

Waveform of commercial CD with clicks and tape hiss.

FIGURE 11.14
Syndicator features provide stations with the seasoning to keep programming interesting. Courtesy Shane Media.

FIGURE 11.15
Syndicators are especially sensitive to quality control. Here a commercial CD is enhanced by a syndicator's computer prior to shipment to a client. Courtesy Century 21.

FIGURE 11.16
This interview with
Ron Hartenbaum was
conducted by Jay
Williams, Jr. Courtesy
same.

NETWORK RADIO/SYNDICATION

Interview with: Ron Hartenbaum, CEO, Jones Radio Networks (New York)

Difference between network and syndication? "You can't separate them, there is no difference. It's a fallacy to think there is; the same thing is happening" with network and syndication. In the old model, the FCC used to separate networks as they distributed programming regularly using dedicated telephone lines (and that distribution method was how a network was described). That was done throughout the 30's, 40's and 50's. "That's an ancient way of distribution, with bad fidelity, and no longer applies. Now network-syndication programming is distributed in a variety of ways . . . CD, the Internet, wired and wireless, satellite . . . it's based on which method is the most 'cost effective' for them."

"There is no difference between syndication and network—it's all national programming. A Matchbox 20 Concert or a Tony Bennett special for the Thanksgiving Weekend might be distributed by CD, as there is not an urgent time constraint. Breaking news, though, wouldn't go out on CD. You would use the distribution method that is best and most cost efficient for the product you're sending out. If it's live, immediate, and interactive (with phone calls) such as Rush Limbaugh, it's delivered via satellite; if it's not time sensitive, it may be mailed out on CD. But it's all national radio."

"It's all audio. It's how do we deliver a signal to as many ears as we can. How do we deliver an audience to an advertiser." And the trend is to deliver increasingly specific audiences that can appeal to specific types of advertisers. "National radio and network radio are the same."

Even the old radio networks have changed, although they retain part of their names. CBS/Viacom Radio is now handled by Westwood One, itself a division of Viacom. The GE/NBC Network is also distributed by Viacom. ABC/Disney is still the ABC Radio Network.

Current Example. Jones Radio works with the CNN Radio Network "en Espanol." CNN creates the news, but Jones Radio Network handles all the advertising and all the affiliate sales. Programming is delivered on the Internet. And using the special client feature, in a special password protected part of the web site—called Ala Carta—stations can pick the items and information that best suits their specific mix of Hispanics in their individual communities. For example, New York might want programming for Puerto Rican and Cuban Hispanics that would not be needed in Los Angeles where most of the population consists of Mexican and Central American Hispanics. This distribution flexibility and choice are both the present and future of syndication.

National radio revenues are over $1 billion annually. There are only four major companies: Westwood One (the largest with almost half that revenue), ABC, Premier and Jones; there once were over a dozen.

"But how to you look at Sirius and XM? These are national radio stations just using a different model." In other words, people looking to buy national radio would include these two satellite radio systems in their plans.

Ron also believes that "streaming media" could have been part of national radio but was killed by the "greed of music publishing and actor's union's rights fees. Internet radio was economically squashed before it could get started—everybody ended up losing."

FIGURE 11.16
continued

The future: There probably won't be much more consolidation and there could even be more producers and distributors of content in the future.

The distribution model is always changing. Ron used the example of mail . . . moving from horseback to rail, truck, airplanes and the Internet. But it's still mail.

He suggests that a triangle is the best way to show the business model. At the top is product/program/content. At the lower left corner is the audience/circulation/distribution. At the lower right side is generation of ad sales revenue. If you make a good product (program) than "people will want it"; they'll want to listen to it or watch it. If they watch, you can generate ad sales revenue (and then, "if you're smart, you'll put some of that revenue back into the product"). Jones is in all three parts of this model—programming, distribution and sales. Ron adds: "You learn in business school that if you're standing still, you're losing. You have to constantly evolve your product and your product lines" and that means you have to invest in them.

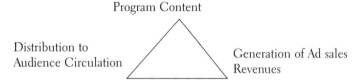

Ron also believes that there are only three ways that programming/content is being distributed: Pay/subscription, Ad supported, or a blend of the two. "Someone has to make money. There are costs to generate news and to develop music programming."

[He has this analogy for college students who think music is free and should remain that way—"what if you went to college, went to all the classes, took all the tests, wrote all the papers, and handed in the work and didn't get a grade? 'Where's my grade?,' you'd say; we'd say that we've downloaded all your information on the Internet and we don't need to give you a grade."]

[We also discussed news programming and Ron gave some thoughts you may want to use in a separate section. There is increasing pressure on these big companies to eliminate money-losing divisions. Either you amortize your costs over a variety of channels and outlets (as NBC) or you look to mergers to be able to reduce those costs (ABC's talks with CNN). Rupert Murdoch was one of the first to work with a "global platform" and "by having papers and networks all over the world, he doesn't have to open a foreign bureau, he's already there. A Fox News anchor can get information from a New York *Post* reporter in New York or a co-owned newspaper in Sydney in seconds. You must either get more customers for your programming or reduce your costs."]

SYNDICATION

Interview with Tom Griswold, of the Bob & Tom Show, Indianaplis "quotations" are from Tom Griswold

Show is delivered to 125 stations nationwide via satellite.

It's distributed by Premier Radio Network (owned by Clear Channel).

Interesting note . . . Premier used to have separate salespeople for certain shows and they are now moving to a model where all the sales people will sell all the shows.

Shows are fed live from 6–10 a.m. Eastern time . . . with three six minute breaks per hour for local programming (commercials, news updates, etc). Some stations, mostly in the Mountain States or on the West Coast, will tape delay the broadcast to fit their morning time slots.

Bob and Tom try to entertain . . . and don't focus on their local area at all. "If you listen to the show, you wouldn't know where we were here" (Indianapolis). Tom doesn't think syndicated shows like Bob and Tom will replace local shows but believes "there will be a mix of local and syndicated shows. There is still a big demand for a lot of local content."

"We tip-toed into it (syndication) starting out with three affiliates. But the show took off quickly. One magazine had voted us as one of the 'most stolen-from radio shows in America,' and it was great to be able to get our show out there."

Preparing for a show. "There's at least one aspect that's easier. If you make a comment about a local institution, it could cost your station billings from some advertiser who gets upset. But when you're getting material from all over the nation, rarely do you get negative feedback. And there's a lot more ammo to choose from nationally—you don't have to rely on what happened at the local school board."

Live is very important. "I could listen to tapes or CD's, but I listen to radio just to keep in touch."

XM and Sirius—"both of them will make it" . . . maybe not with the same stockholders, but they will be able to produce great shows and have great talent. These national satellite radio networks "are delivering variety with low commercial loads; local radio stations have lots of commercials and all sound the same. XM even went after Howard Stern—they know the next step is to get great talent on the air." John considers satellite radio national radio or syndicated radio, just in a slightly different form.

SYNDICATION

Interview with John H. Garabedian

Radio and TV entrepreneur, former president of Superadio Networks, and current host of "Open House Party." John also started V66 in Boston, probably the first music video television station.
"Quotation marks" are from John Garabedian

Much of the live programming is done using C-Band satellite distribution (vs. the less reliable KU satellite systems). The costs of satellite distribution keeps coming down and a satellite uplink only costs about $ 150,000, so programming can come from almost anywhere.

Hundreds of successful programs are distributed nationally . . . including Delilah, Paul Harvey news, Rush Limbaugh and Howard Stern. It's over a $ 1 billion business.

John says there's not much difference between network radio and syndication but suggests the difference is that Network programs are rated by RADAR, a national service (now owned by Arbitron) that produces ratings for radio network programming. He says that other than that, there is really no difference.

He says that Superadio, now owned by Access One Communications (also owners of American Urban Radio Network and individual radio stations), sends out over 5000 CD's a week!

John believes that "live and local shows" are overrated in radio.

"Everyone in radio thinks you have to have a local morning show to win. That radio is local. That's wrong. Don't waste your time with the 'Bob and Debbie' show. The people who control radio in the future will be the people who have the talent . . ." "Howard Stern died for our (syndicators') sins. He said, 'Don't put on local shows—just put on the Howard Stern Show and you'll be # 1,' and he was right."

The goal of the big radio groups is "to control all their own programming. There will be more centrally programmed live shows." If they don't do it nationally, they'll probably start doing it regionally. "They can take the best talent from all of their classic rock stations and make one really great radio station" that people will really want to listen to and save a fortune in costs in the process. "And local PD's won't screw up making bad music decisions." All programming, he believes, will become more national.

FIGURE 11.18
This interview with John H. Garabedian was conducted by Jay Williams, Jr. Courtesy same.

SUGGESTED FURTHER READING

Broadcasting Yearbook. Washington, D.C.: Broadcast Publishing, 1935 to date, annually.

Deweese, Scott B. *Radio Syndication: How to Create, Produce, and Distribute Yom Own Show.* Bellevve, WA: Elfin Cove Press, 2001.

Fornatale, Peter, and Mills, Joshua. *Radio in the Television Age.* Woodstock, N.Y.: Overlook Press, 1980.

Hall, Claude, and Hall, Barbara. *This Business of Radio Programming.* New York: Billboard Publishing, 1977.

Howard, Herbert H., and Kievman, Michael S. *Radio and Television Programming.* Columbus, Ohio: Grid Publishing, 1983.

Inglis, Andrew F. *Satellite Technology.* Boston: Focal Press, 1991.

Keith, Michael C. *Radio Programming: Consultancy and Formatics.* Boston: Focal Press, 1987.

Kempner, Marvin A. *Can't Wait Til Monday Morning: Syndication in Broadcasting.* Orlando, FL: Rivercross Publishing, 1998.

Mirabito, Michael M., and Morgenstern, Barbara L. *The New Communication Technologies,* 2nd ed. Boston: Focal Press, 1994.

The Radio Programs Sourcebook, 2nd ed. Syosset, N.Y.: Broadcast Information Bureau, 1983.

Series, Serials, and Packages. Syosset, N.Y.: Broadcast Information Bureau, annually.

Shane, Ed. *Selling Electronic Media.* Boston: Focal Press, 1999.

Vane, Edwin T., and Gross, Lynne S. *Programming for TV, Radio, and Cable.* Boston: Focal Press, 1994.

Wasserman, Paul. *Consultants and Consulting Organization Directory,* 3rd ed. Detroit: Gale Research, 1976.

Glossary

ABC American Broadcasting Company; network.

Account executive Station or agency salesperson.

Actives Listeners who call radio stations to make requests and comments or in response to contests and promotions.

Actuality Actual recording of news event or person(s) involved.

ADI Area of Dominant Influence; Arbitron measurement area.

Adjacencies Commercials strategically placed next to a feature.

Ad lib Improvisation; unrehearsed and spontaneous comments.

Affidavit Statement attesting to the airing of a spot schedule.

AFTRA American Federation of Television and Radio Artists; union composed of broadcast performers: announcers, deejays, newscasters.

Aircheck Tape of live broadcast.

AM Amplitude modulation; method of signal transmission using Standard Broadcast band with frequencies between 535 and 1,605 (1,705) kHz.

AMAX Enhanced AM receiver developed by the NAB.

Announcement Commercial (spot) or public service message of varying length.

AOR Album-Oriented Rock radio format.

AP Associated Press; wire and audio news service.

Arbitron Audience measurement service employing a seven-day diary to determine the number of listeners tuned to area stations.

ASCAP American Society of Composers, Authors, and Publishers; music licensing service.

Audio Sound; modulation.

Audition tape Telescoped recording showcasing talents of air person.

Automation Equipment system designed to play prepackaged programming.

Average quarter-hour (AQH) persons See the research glossaries in Chapter 6.

AWRT American Women in Radio and Television.

Back announce Recap of preceding music selections.

Barter Exchange of airtime for programming or goods.

BEA Broadcast Education Association.

Bed Music behind voice in commercial.

Blasting Excessive volume resulting in distortion.

Blend Merging of complementary sound elements.

Book Term used to describe rating survey document; "bible."

BM Beautiful Music radio format.

BMI Broadcast Music Incorporated; music licensing service.

Branding Establishing station identity and value.

Bridge Sound used between program elements.

BTA Best-time-available, also run-of-station (ROS); commercials logged at available times.

Bulk eraser Tool for removing magnetic impressions from recording tape.

Bumper Music played to intro segments on talk programs and features.

Call letters Assigned station identification beginning with "W" east of the Mississippi and "K" west.

Capstan Shaft in recorder that drives tape.

Cart Plastic cartridge containing a continuous loop of recording tape.

CFR *Code of Federal Regulations.*

Chain broadcasting Forerunner of network broadcasting.

CHR Contemporary Hit Radio format.

Clock Wheel indicating sequence or order of programming ingredients aired during one hour.

Cluster Combining the operations of several stations.

Cold Background fade on last line of copy.

Combo Announcer with engineering duties; AM/FM operation.

Commercial Paid advertising announcement; spot.

Compact disc (CD) Digital recording using laser beam to decode surface.

Console Audio mixer consisting of inputs, outputs, toggles, meters, and pots; board.

Consolidation See *Clustering.*

Consultant Station advisor or counselor; "radio doctor."

Control room Center of broadcast operations from which programming originates; air studio.

Cool out Gradual fade of bed music at conclusion of spot.

Co-op Arrangement between retailer and manufacturer for the purpose of sharing radio advertising expenses.

Copy Advertising message; continuity; commercial script.

Cost per point (CPP) See the research glossaries in Chapter 6.

Cost per thousand (CPM) See the research glossaries in Chapter 6.

CPB Corporation for Public Broadcasting.

CRMC Certified Radio Marketing Consultant.

Crossfade Fade out of one element while introducing another.

Cue Signal for the start of action; prepare element for airing.

Cue burn Distortion at the beginning of a record cut resulting from heavy cueing.

Cume See the research glossaries in Chapter 6.

DAB Digital audio broadcasting.

DARS Digital Audio Radio Service.

DAT Digital audio tape.

Dayparts Periods or segments of broadcast day: for example, 6 to 10 a.m., 10 a.m. to 3 p.m., 3 to 7 p.m.

Daytimer AM station required to leave the air at or near sunset.

Dead air Silence where sound usually should be; absence of programming.

Deejay Host of radio music program; announcer; disk jockey.

Demagnetize See *Erase.*

Demographics Audience statistical data pertaining to age, sex, race, income, and so forth.

Direct Broadcast Satellite (DBS) Powerful communications satellite that beams programming to receiving dishes at earth stations.

Directional Station transmitting signal in a preordained pattern so as to protect other stations on similar frequency.

DMX Digital music satellite service.

Donut spot Commercial in which copy is inserted between segments of music.

DOS Director of Sales.

Double billing Illegal station billing practice in which client is charged twice.

Downsizing Reducing staff by combining functions and departments.

Drivetime Radio's prime time: 6 to 10 a.m. and 3 to 7 p.m.

Dub Copy of recording; duplicate (dupe).

EBS/EAS Emergency Broadcast System/ Emergency Alert System.

Edit To alter composition of recorded material; splice.

ENG Electronic news gathering.

Erase Wipe clean magnetic impressions; degauss, bulk, deflux, demagnetize.

ERP Effective radiated power; tape head configuration: erase, record, playback.

ET Electrical transcription.

Ethnic Programming for minority group audiences.

Fact sheet List of pertinent information on a sponsor.

Fade To slowly lower or raise volume level.

FCC Federal Communications Commission; government regulatory body with authority over radio operations.

Fidelity Trueness of sound dissemination or reproduction.

Fixed position Spot routinely logged at a specified time.

Flight Advertising air schedule.

FM Frequency modulation; method of signal transmission using 88- to 108-MHz band.

FMX System used to improve FM reception.

Format Type of programming a station offers; arrangement of material, formula.

Frequency Number of cycles-per-second of a sine wave.

Fulltrack Recording utilizing entire width of tape.

Gain Volume; amplification.

Generation Dub; dupe.

Grease pencil Soft-tip marker used to inscribe recording tape for editing purposes.

Grid Rate card structure based on supply and demand.

Gross rating points (GRP) See the research glossaries in Chapter 6.

Ground wave AM signal traveling the earth's surface; primary signal.

HD High definition radio.

Headphones Speakers mounted on ears; headsets, cans.

Hertz (Hz) Cycles per second; unit of electromagnetic frequency.

HLT Highly leveraged transaction.

Hot Overmodulated.

Hot clock Wheel indicating when particular music selections are to be aired.

Hype Exaggerated presentation; high intensity, punched.

IBEW International Brotherhood of Electrical Workers; union.

IBOC In Band On Channel.

ID Station identification required by law to be broadcast as close to the top of the hour as possible; station break.

Input Terminal receiving incoming current.

Institutional Message promoting general image.

IPS Inches per second; tape speed: 1, 3, 15, 30 IPS.

ISDN Integrated Services Digital Network.

ITU International Telecommunications Union; world broadcasting regulatory agency.

Jack Plug for patching sound sources; patch-cord, socket, input.

Jingle Musical commercial or promo; signature, logo.

Jock See *Deejay.*

KDKA Radio station first to offer regularly scheduled broadcasts (1920).

Kilohertz (kHz) One thousand cycles per second; AM frequency measurement, kilocycles.

Leader tape Plastic, metallic, or paper tape used in conjunction with magnetic tape for marking and spacing purposes.

Level Amount of volume units; audio measurement.

Licensee Individual or company holding license issued by the FCC for broadcast purposes.

Line Connection used for transmission of audio; phone line.

Line-of-sight Path of FM signal; FM propagation.

Liner cards Written on-air promos used to ensure adherence to station image; prepared ad-libs.

Live copy Material read over air; not prerecorded.

Live tag Postscript to taped message.

LMA Local marketing (or management) agreement.

Local channels Class D AM stations found at high end of band: 1,200 to 1,600 kHz.

LPFM Low power FM.

Make-good Replacement spot for one missed.

Market Area served by a broadcast facility; ADI.

Master Original recording.

Master control See *Control room.*

MBS Mutual Broadcasting System; radio network.

Megahertz (MHz) Million cycles per second; FM frequency measurement, megacycles.

Mergers Consolidation or combining of assets and resources.

Mini-disc machines Digital cart decks employing floppy disc technology for audio reproduction and archiving.

MIS Manager of Information Systems.

Mixdown Integration of sound elements to create desired effect; production.

Monitor Studio speaker; aircheck.

Mono Single or full-track sound; monaural, monophonic.

MOR Middle-of-the-Road radio format.

Morning Drive radio's primetime daypart: 6 to 10 a.m.

MSA Metro Survey Area; geographic area in radio survey.

Multitasking Performing several duties.

Multitracking Recording sound-on-sound; overdubbing, stacking tracks.

Music sweep Several selections played back-to-back without interruption; music segue.

NAB National Association of Broadcasters.

NAEB National Association of Educational Broadcasters.

Narrowcasting Directed programming; targeting specific audience demographic.

NBC National Broadcasting Company; network.

Network Broadcast combine providing programming to affiliates: NBC, CBS, ABC, MBS.

Network feed Programs sent via telephone lines or satellites to affiliate stations.

News block Extended news broadcast.

NPR National Public Radio.

NRSC National Radio Systems Committee.

NTR Nontraditional revenue.

O and Os Network or group owned and operated stations.

OES Optimum effective scheduling.

Off-mike Speech outside normal range of microphone.

Out-cue Last words in a line of carted copy.

Output Transmission of audio or power from one location to another; transfer terminal.

Overdubbing See *Multitracking.*

Overmodulate Exceed standard or prescribed audio levels: pinning VU needle.

Packaged Canned programming; syndicated, prerecorded, taped.

Passives Listeners who do not call stations in response to contests or promotions or to make requests or comments.

Patch Circuit connector; cord, cable.

Patch panel Jack board for connecting audio sources: remotes, studios, equipment; patch bay.

PBS Public Broadcasting System.

Pinch roller Rubber wheel that presses recording tape against capstan.

Playback Reproduction of recorded sound.

Playlist Roster of music for airing.

Plug Promo; connector.

Popping Break-up of audio due to gusting or blowing into mike; blasting.

Positioner Brief statement used on-air to define a station's position in a market.

Pot Potentiometer; volume control knob, gain control, fader, attenuator, rheostat.

Production See *Mixdown.*

Promax Broadcast promotion and marketing executives association.

PSA Public Service Announcement; noncommercial message.

Psychographics Research term dealing with listener personality, such as attitude, behavior, values, opinions, and beliefs.

Punch Emphasis; stress.

Quadraphonic Four-speaker/channel sound reproduction.

RAB Radio Advertising Bureau.

Rack Prepare or set up for play or record: "rack it up"; equipment container.

RADAR Nationwide measurement service by Statistical Research, Inc.

Rate card Statement of advertising fees and terms.

Rating Estimated audience tuned to a station; size of listenership, ranking.

RCA Radio Corporation of America; NBC parent company.

RDS/RBDS Technology that enables AM and FM stations to send data to "smart" receivers, allowing them to perform several automatic functions.

Recut Retake; rerecord, remix.

Reel-to-reel Recording machine with feed and take-up reels.

Remote Broadcast originating away from station control room.

Reverb Echo; redundancy of sound.

Rewind Speeded return of recording tape from take-up reel.

Ride gain Monitor level; watch VU needle.

Rip 'n' read Airing copy unaltered from wire.

rpm Revolutions per minute: 33 1/3, 45, and 78 rpm.

RTNDA Radio and Television News Directors Association.

Run-of-station (ROS) See *BTA*.

Satellite Orbiting device for relaying audio from one earth station to another; DBS, Comsat, Satcom.

SBE Society of Broadcast Engineers.

SCA Subsidiary Communication Authority; subcarrier FM.

Secondary service area AM skywave listening area.

Segue Uninterrupted flow of recorded material; continuous.

SESAC Society of European Stage Authors and Composers; music licensing service.

SFX Abbreviation for sound effect.

Share Percentage of station's listenership compared to competition; piece of audience pie.

Signal Sound transmission; RF.

Signature Theme; logo, jingle, ID.

Simulcast Simultaneous broadcast over two or more frequencies.

Spec spot Speciall tailored commercial used as a sales tool to help sell an account.

Splice To join ends of recording tape with adhesive; edit.

Splicing bar Grooved platform for cutting and joining recording tape; edit bar.

Sponsor Advertiser; client, account, underwriter.

Spot set Group or cluster of announcements; stop set.

Spots Commercials; paid announcements.

Station Broadcast facility given specific frequency by FCC.

Station identification See *ID*.

Station log Document containing specific operating information as outlined in Section 73.1820 of the FCC *Rules and Regulations*.

Station rep Company acting in behalf of local stations to national agencies.

Stereo Multichannel sound; two program channels.

Stinger Music or sound effect finale preceded by last line of copy; button, punctuation.

Straight copy Announcement employing unaffected, nongimmicky approach; institutional.

Stringer Field or on-scene reporter.

Subliminal Advertising or programming not consciously perceived; below normal range of awareness, background.

Sweep link Transitional jingle between sound elements.

Syndicator Producer of purchasable program material.

Tag See *Live tag*.

Talent Radio performer; announcer, deejay, newscaster.

Talk Conversation and interview radio format.

TAP Total audience plan; spot package divided between specific dayparts: AAA, AA, A.

Tape speed Movement measured in inches per second: 3, 7, 15 IPS.

Telescoping Compressing of sound to fit a desired length; technique used in audition tapes and concert promos, editing.

TFN Till further notice; without specific kill date.

Trade-out Exchange of station airtime for goods or services.

Traffic Station department responsible for scheduling sponsor announcements.

Transmit To broadcast; propagate signal; air.

TSA Total survey area; geographic area in radio survey.

Underwriter See *Sponsor*.

Unidirectional mike Microphone designed to pick up sound in one direction; cardioid, studio mike.

UPI United Press International; wire and audio news service.

VOA Voice of America.

Voiceover Talk over sound.

Voice-tracking Prerecorded announcer.

Volume Quantity of sound; audio level.

Volume control See *Pot*.

VU Meter gauge measuring units of sound.

WARC World Administrative Radio Conference; international meeting charged with assigning spectrum space.

Wheel See *Clock*.

Windscreen Microphone filter used to prevent popping and distortion.

Wireless telegraphy Early radio used to transmit Morse code.

Wow Distortion of sound created by inappropriate speed; miscue.

Index